THE NORFOLK
REGIMENT

THE NORFOLK REGIMENT

ON THE WESTERN FRONT
1914–1918

STEVE SMITH

FONTHILL

Though far away, forever in our thoughts

From a Norfolk Regiment epitaph in Hooge Crater Cemetery

For my Great Grandfather Private G/5203 Frank Smith 7th Buffs (The East Kent Regiment) who went to war in August 1915 but was lost from sight and sound on 21 March 1918.

Fonthill Media Limited
Fonthill Media LLC
www.fonthill.media
books@fonthill.media

First published in the United Kingdom and the United States of America 2021

British Library Cataloguing in Publication Data:
A catalogue record for this book is available from the British Library

Copyright © Steve Smith 2021

ISBN 978-1-78155-827-0

Typeset in 10pt on 13pt Sabon
Printed and bound in England

Foreword

In my experience, Norfolk people are not easily excited and even less easily impressed. We are, by and large, unassuming and undemonstrative and somewhat wary of those who display more ostentatious or flamboyant traits. By nature, reticent and reserved, we are, I suspect, hard for outsiders to fathom.

Cecil Upcher, a young architect *cum* citizen soldier from Hingham, was certainly of that opinion. As a Norfolk man, he instinctively understood the quiet qualities of his fellow countrymen, which were invisible to others. In a diary he kept while serving as a subaltern in one of the so-called 'Kitchener battalions' of his county regiment, he recalled, by way of example, the mystification felt by their divisional commander.

Noted Upcher:

> Apparently, he came round the camp one day when most of the men were out on working parties and spoke to some of those left and they, in their usual Norfolk way, would hardly say a word to him. So, he formed a bad impression of us, and fairly strafed the Col[onel] for having a rotten batt[alio]n and said they all looked very gloomy. Poor man, of course no one understands a Norfolk man unless they've lived all their life in Norfolk!

Exaggeration or not, the sentiment was clear and borne out by a fellow officer in the aftermath of the trials and tribulations of an arduous and costly autumn campaign on the Somme. Terence 'TAK' Cubitt observed:

> To see these men out here makes one proud to be a native of Norfolk—they are the finest chaps God ever made. They may not be so smart as the London Regiments but

when it comes to the push—and that's the real test—they are beyond all praise. I can only thank God that it's fallen to my lot ... to command such men as they.

What Cecil Upcher and 'TAK' Cubitt recognised as the stolid, if sometimes underappreciated virtues of stoicism and staunchness, would serve many generals well during four unparalleled years of remorseless conflict that demanded of its combatants every last bit of stamina and every last ounce of resolution.

From the gruelling retreats of 1914 to the spectacular advances of the last 100 days, the men of the Norfolk Regiment would share in the myriad tragedies and triumphs experienced by an army, which, contrary to popular mythology, achieved a victory on the Western Front that is unsurpassed in British military history.

All told, five of its battalions played their part in the British Army's greatest feat of arms at a cost of more than 4,000 lives, and it is in honour of their sacrifice that this book has been written, not just as an act of remembrance but as a means of encouraging a deeper understanding of the men who served and the struggles they endured.

It is history on an epic scale, chronicled with an eye for the human detail that the author is eminently well-qualified to undertake.

A man of Kent who settled in Norfolk almost two decades ago, following an eighteen-year career in the Royal Air Force that ended at RAF Coltishall, Steve Smith is a long-time member of the International Guild of Battlefield Guides whose passion for researching the services of his adopted county's regiment is matched only by his compassion for the men who proudly wore the Britannia cap badge.

His has been a remarkable odyssey, combining painstaking trawls through countless private and public archives with an expert knowledge of the ground over which they fought, culminating in a uniquely accessible and insightful study of a single regiment's war effort.

Part authoritative narrative history and part exhaustive battlefield guide, this is a history that evokes both the courage and the carnage of war, not to mention the camaraderie of men *in extremis* while also providing the reader with the essential information required to follow in their footsteps.

In so doing, he has not only achieved his purpose of ensuring that their deeds live on, but he has provided us with a valuable corrective that redresses the balance of history in favour of a regiment whose hard-won honours and harrowing sacrifices have for too long been overshadowed by more celebrated triumphs and more notorious traumas experienced by other units.

Here, at last, the spotlight is focused not on Mons, but on the delaying action at Élouges where the 1st Norfolks helped save a large portion of the British Expeditionary Force from disaster; not just on the missed opportunities of the opening assault at Loos, but on the forlorn attack carried out by the 7th

Norfolks that marked the battle's grim nadir; not on the disastrous assaults that have become synonymous with the first day of the Somme offensive, but on the outstanding success achieved by the 8th Norfolks in front of Montauban; and not on the massed tank attack at Cambrai, but on the magnificent, if little-remembered victory won by the 9th Norfolks.

Each of these actions, and many more besides, are illuminated by a treasure trove of eyewitness testimony, which go to prove that, in Steve Smith, poet John McCrae's 'torch' of remembrance is in safe hands and, as a result of his Herculean efforts, continues to burn bright in glowing tribute to the men who confounded many a first impression to gain the lasting admiration of those officers who found in their quiet determination and modest courage a distinctively Norfolk brand of *esprit de corps*.

Steve Snelling

Acknowledgements

A book like this cannot be written without the help and support of loved ones. With that in mind, primarily I need to thank my wife, Claire, and my daughters, Lauren, Lily, and Eden. All of them have accompanied me to the battlefields of France and Belgium and understand and support my passion for this type of history.

There are others, who through their help, guidance, and friendship, I have felt fully supported in this venture. They are Steve Snelling and Ian Castle. Ian has supported me through the process of getting the book published with invaluable advice and help and Steve very kindly agreed to write the foreword for the book.

Kate Thaxton has been extremely supportive in this venture. Kate is the curator of the Royal Norfolk Regiment Museum and provided me with free access to their records, which allowed me to gather a better understanding of the battalions I have written about.

Thanks also go to people like Sarah Salmon who have supported me in the past through things like allowing me to give talks on this subject in the Norwich Library that has, in turn, allowed me to meet people who have connections and information to share, which has made this book unique.

Nic Blythe, Christopher Reeve, Chris Durrant, Elaine Polton, Margaret Sowter, Peter Thatcher, Brian Thaxter, Jenny Howard, Wendy Salmon, Barbara Thomas, Nigel Cooper, Ady Church, and Kitty Lynn—without your support and the sharing of the information on your relatives and people, which has included allowing me to hold and record history in my hands, I cannot thank you enough for that. This has made the book all the more special where I have told this story. If I have missed anyone, then I apologise.

To Taff Gillingham, my thanks go out to him for becoming my Christmas Truce mythbuster partner each year when the football myth comes around. Taff has done so much more to debunk that myth, but I hope this book helps to back that up with the chapter on that subject.

A special thanks also goes to the past and present staff and students at Aldenham School. I have had the honour of guiding them to the battlefields of France and Flanders for eight years and have always enjoyed their friendship and company. It was absolutely amazing to find within their school archives that one of their Old Aldenhamians served in the Norfolk Regiment, but more on him within the book.

Finally, I would like to thank Alan Sutton and everyone at Fonthill Media for allowing me to publish the book.

Contents

Glossary of Terms

ADS:	Advanced Dressing Station: The most advanced medical post behind the Regimental Aid Post.
Advd:	Abbreviation of Advanced.
AEF:	American Expeditionary Force; the US declared war in April 1917 and President Woodrow Wilson sent the AEF to the Western Front under the command of General John Pershing. By July 1918, there were over a million US soldiers in France. The AEF suffered 264,000 casualties (including 50,500 killed in battle and 25,000 killed by disease).
AIR:	American Infantry Regiment.
ANZAC:	Australian and New Zealand Army Corps.
A&SH:	Argyll & Sutherland Highlanders.
Army:	This comprised two or more corps under a general; between 120,000 and 200,000 soldiers.
Barracks:	Buildings specifically designed for occupation by military personnel.
Barrage:	A barrier of excessive, continuous artillery or machine-gun fire in 'lines' on a specific area designed to destroy the enemy or make them keep their heads down.
Battalion:	The basic infantry unit under a lieutenant-colonel and comprising about thirty-five officers and 750 soldiers; this varied widely from army to army and from period to period.

Battery:	An artillery section consisting of about 150 soldiers under a major and armed with four to eight guns of a particular type (e.g., howitzers).
Battle Order:	A British term for reduced infantry equipment; the pack was removed and the haversack put in its place, to reduce weight and facilitate movement in action.
Bde:	Abbrivation for Brigade
BEF:	British Expeditionary Force.
Berm:	An area at the back of a trench; ledge used to keep grenades from rolling into trench.
BHQ:	Battalion Headquarters
Big-Bertha:	A German 42-cm howitzer with a 15-km range built by Gustav Krupp's factories in 1914 and nicknamed after his wife. Four Big Berthas were built and all were used during the assault upon Verdun from February 1916. *See* 'Paris Gun'.
Blighty:	A wound ensuring a return to England ('Blighty'); from Hindi '*bilayati*' (foreign country) and taken up by British troops in India.
Boche:	A German (derogatory); from the French, an alteration of '*Alboche*', which comes from '*caboche*' (blockhead).
Bombardier:	A Royal Artillery corporal; pronounced 'bombadeer'.
Bombardment:	A heavy assault or attack by artillery.
Box Barrage:	A box barrage is an artillery bombardment focused on a small target area, such as a key position or section of trench, with the aim of destroying it utterly.
Bridgehead:	A way of holding a sufficient amount of territory on the enemy side of a river in order for other troops to then move forward to capture other positions.
Brigade:	This is made up of four battalions, totalling about 120 officers and between 4,000 and 5,000 NCOs and enlisted men, commanded by a brigadier.
Bullring:	British training camp behind the lines, which prepared recruits for service at the front by inculcating an 'offensive spirit'. The British training ground at Étaples, infamous for its severe discipline, was called the Bullring.

Bully Beef:	Tinned, boiled, or pickled beef, the principal protein ration of the British Army.
CCS:	Casualty Clearing Station: Main medical establishment immediately behind the front line.
CEF:	Canadian Expeditionary Force; over 600,000 Canadians enlisted in the CEF.
Chinese Attack:	A faked attack. When a preliminary bombardment ceased, the defending troops would return to their trenches to meet the presumed attack, whereupon the artillery would start firing again and catch the defenders out of their shelters.
Chlorine Gas:	Was one of several chemical weapons used during the First World War. It appeared as a grey-green cloud, smelling of bleach. Much deadlier than mustard gas, it caused death by asphyxiation and burning of the lungs and airways.
Coal Box:	A German high-explosive artillery shell similar to a Jack Johnson.
Communication Trench:	This was a narrow trench used to go to and from frontline trenches and support trenches, for messengers to relay messages to the front line and back, and for telephone wire to be strung up to the frontline system.
Company:	A unit made up of four platoons totalling 240 men under a major or captain; four companies make up a battalion.
Corps:	A unit made up of two or more divisions, under a lieutenant-general, totalling about 1,200 officers and between 30,000 and 60,000 NCOs and enlisted men.
Court-Martial:	A judicial court of military officers who try infractions of military law; it has the right to pass the death sentence.
Creeping Barrage:	A barrage intended to suppress the enemy long enough to enable troops to occupy his position. The trick was to act in the brief interval between the lifting of the barrage and the return of the enemy. Troops were trained to walk literally into the barrage as it lifted or moved.
CT:	Communication Trench
Daisy Cutter:	A shell with impact fuse to explode immediately on touching ground.

DCLI:	Duke of Cornwall's Light Infantry
Demobilisation:	In the transition from war to peace, the disbanding or discharging of troops depot base of regiment or departmental corps, where servicemen are trained and kitted out before joining units (e.g., battalions, batteries) or held, for example, after being in hospital. Also, a place for stores, ammunition or fuel.
Derby Scheme:	A voluntary recruitment instituted by Lord Derby just prior to 1916 conscription.
Digger:	An Australian soldier (slang).
DLI:	Durham Light Infantry
Division:	A unit of three brigades and supporting artillery, supply, and medical units totalling 600 officers and about 18,000 NCOs and enlisted men; commanded by a major-general.
DORA:	Defence of the Realm Act (8 August 1914). Under DORA, one could not discuss military matters in public, buy binoculars, trespass on railway lines or bridges, light fireworks or bonfires, or ring church bells. The British government could take over any factory or land, censor newspapers, and try any civilian breaking these laws.
Doughboy:	An American soldier (slang); at first disparaging, later positive; from the buttons on the Union Army uniforms of the Civil War that resembled doughnuts. The English called US soldiers 'Yanks' (Yankee Doodle) or 'Sammies' (Uncle Sam).
Drum Fire:	An artillery barrage fired not in salvo but by each gun in succession.
DCM:	Distinguished Conduct Medal. An award given to British soldiers for acts of gallantry in the field. Another award, the Military Medal, was introduced in 1916 due to the overwhelming number of DCMs being awarded in the war. Both the DCM and the MM were discontinued in 1993. Over 80 per cent of all DCMs were awarded during the First World War.
DSO:	Distinguished Service Order, instituted under Queen Victoria on 9 November 1886 to reward meritorious or distinguished service in war; it was given to officers only. Although the DSO was

	awarded for acts not directly involving actual combat with the enemy during the first two and a half years of the Great War, from 1 January 1917officers were issued guidance stating that the award was reserved for distinguished conduct under enemy fire.
Duckboard:	A narrow path of wooden slats in a trench or over field mud.
Dud:	A shell that has landed but failed to explode.
Dugout:	A rough shelter in the side of a hill or the wall of a trench, varying from a small one-man area to a deep dugout ten or more feet underground. *See* 'fox hole'.
Enfilade:	(French) To fire down a trench or at a row of men length-ways, rather than cross-ways.
Estaminet:	(French) An impromptu, shabby café selling food and wine to soldiers behind the lines.
FA:	Field Artillery.
Fascine:	A long, firmly bound bundle of brushwood used in filling up trenches and ditches, constructing batteries, or reinforcing a defensive line.
Field Dressing:	Each soldier's small bag of bandages and pins for application to minor wounds.
Field Punishment Number 1:	A punishment of soldiers that involved being tied to a gun-wheel and being put on a bread and water diet.
Fire Bay:	A trench from where soldiers fired, protected on each side by earth and sandbags.
Fire Step:	A step upon the forward face of a trench upon which men stood to fire or observe. The floor of the trench was lower so that the soldiers could walk upright without exposing their heads above the top.
Five-Nines:	Artillery shells
FO:	Field Order: orders issued in the field.
FOO:	(Artillery) Forward Observation Officer
General Staff:	A group of military officers acting in a staff or administrative role under the command of a general officer.
GHQ:	General Headquarters of the American Expeditionary Forces (Pershing's HQ).
GOC:	General Officer Commanding

Hindenburg Line: This was a defensive section of the Western Front, constructed by the Germans in 1916–17. It ran through northern France and was intended to block an anticipated Allied offensive. Named after the German commander in chief, the Hindenburg Line comprised concrete fortifications, machine-gun posts, trenches, and barbed wire.

Hun: A German (derogatory); Kaiser Wilhelm originally associated Germany with the ancient nomadic tribe that plundered Europe.

Infantry: This refers to divisions or regiments of foot-soldiers, sections of an army that move about, advance and fight on foot. The vast majority of soldiers who fought on the Western Front belonged to the infantry.

Inf.:   Abbreviation of Infantry

Jack Johnson: German howitzer shell with a calibre of 150 mm (5.9 inches). Named for the world heavyweight boxing champion from 1908–15, an American called Jack Johnson (1878–1946) who was the first black world heavyweight champion, in reference to the black smoke the shells threw up upon impact. Also called a 5.9 or Five-Nine in reference to its size in inches.

Jumping-Off Line: The line or position from which an attack is launched; also called 'take-off line'.

KOSB: King's Own Scottish Borderers

KSLI: King's Shropshire Light Infantry

Lewis Gun: Designed in the United States in 1911 by US Army Col. Isaac Newton Lewis (and based upon an earlier overly-complex design by Samuel McLean), the Lewis gun comprised an early light machine gun and was widely adopted by British and Empire forces from 1915 onwards.

Listening Post: A forward position usually set beyond barbed wire (in no-man's-land) for closer enemy observation, overhearing enemy conversation, or tapping phone lines

Lyddite: Was the high explosive widely used during the Great War.

Maconochie Stew: A British ration of turnips, carrots, and potatoes, in a thin soup. Named for the Aberdeen Maconochie Company that produced it.

Maxim:	A single-barrelled quick-firing machine gun.
MC:	Military Cross, this was awarded for an act or acts of exemplary gallantry during active operations against the enemy on land, to captains or officers of lower rank up to warrant officers. (NCOs or other ranks instead received the Military Medal.) It was first established by King George V on 28 December 1914
MGC:	Machine Gun Corps.
MM:	Military Medal. This was awarded to personnel of the British Army, and formerly also to personnel of other Commonwealth countries, below commissioned rank, for bravery in battle on land. It was first established by King George V on 25 March 1916.
Mills-Bomb:	A British hand grenade developed in 1915; it remained in service until the 1960s.
Mine:	An underground passage extending under an enemy's works to secure access or deposit explosives for blowing up a military position.
Minenwerfer:	('Mine Thrower') German short-range mortar on wheels; nicknamed 'Minnie'.
Mobilisation:	To make ready or muster forces for military service.
Mortar:	A muzzle-loading canon firing low-velocity shells at short range and at a high angle; it is essentially a short tube designed to fire a projectile at a steep angle so that it falls straight down on the enemy. *See* 'howitzer'.
Mustard Gas:	A volatile, corrosive poison gas (dichloroethylene sulphide) first used by the Germans at Ypres in 1917; it attacked mucous membranes, lung tissue, and eyes, causing severe skin wounds, lung burns, and conjunctivitis.
NCO:	Non-Commissioned Officer; with a rank from ·corporal to staff sergeant.
Neurasthenia:	A psychological disorder resulting from explosion of shells or bombs at close quarters; characterised by chronic fatigue and weakness, memory loss, hallucinations, flashbacks, insomnia, nightmares, and depression. Also called 'battle fatigue', 'shell shock', and (from mid-1970s) Post-Traumatic Stress Disorder (PTSD).

No-Man's-Land: The territory between both trenches on the Western Front; a desolate, barren wasteland of barbed wire, shell craters, mud, debris, and corpses; it varied from yards to miles in width, but averaged about 100 to 500 yards. Dates from the 1300s, when it meant the waste ground between two kingdoms.

Objective: The successive lines which troops are to take or advance to according to schedule.

OC: Officer Commanding.

Officer (or commissioned officer): A commissioned officer is a higher-ranking member of the military. Officers are responsible for leadership and tactical and strategic decision making. In the Army, lower officer ranks include subalterns, lieutenants, and captains, while higher officer ranks include majors, colonels, and generals.

Old Contemptible: A nickname adopted by the original BEF of 1914 because the Kaiser supposedly referred to it as a 'contemptible little army'. There is evidence to suggest that the Kaiser never said this and that this was made up and used as propaganda.

OP: Observation Post, from which enemy movements or actions are observed.

Other Ranks: Are the enlisted soldiers of the army. They do not have a commission and they do not hold positions of high command.

Over the Top: Troops emerging from a trench at the start of an attack (often facing certain death); in civilian use, it meant taking the final plunge to do something dangerous.

Pals: Men from the same town or trade who were encouraged to enlist together in Kitchener's army in 1914. *See* 'Kitchener's Army'.

Parados: The side of a trench farthest from the enemy; raised earth behind the rear trench wall used to help diffuse the shock of high explosives going off behind the line.

Parapet: The side of a trench facing the enemy; raised soil of rocks in front of a trench line used to protect troops from enemy observation and fire.

PBI: Poor Bloody Infantry.

Pillbox:	A low, reinforced concrete machine-gun post.
Pipsqueak:	Any second-lieutenant; also, a small German trench gun.
Platoon:	A small infantry detachment of sixty men commanded by a lieutenant; there are four platoons in a company.
Potato Masher:	A nickname for German hand grenade or the club used in trench raids.
Quartermaster:	An army officer in charge of supplies, rations, ammunition, fuel, and the administration of all quarters and barracks in his regiment or battalion.
RAP:	Regimental Aid Post.
RE:	Royal Engineers
Red Cap:	a term to describe a British military policeman.
Redoubt:	A small, temporary, self-contained refuge for soldiers outside the main defences; a usually square or polygonal fortification
Red Tabs:	A British staff officers (slang); from the lapel tabs on General Staff officers' uniforms.
Register:	A term used by gunners, meaning to locate a target by means of each gun in a battery firing rounds; a forward observation officer would inform the battery of what adjustments were required in order to hit the target.
Respirator:	A gas mask in which air was inhaled through a metal box of chemicals.
Regt:	Abbreviation for Regiment.
Revetment:	A retaining wall (lumber planks, tin sheets, etc.) supporting the sides of a trench.
RFA:	Royal Field Artillery; responsible for using all types of available artillery.
RFC:	Royal Flying Corps; it later became the Royal Air Force on 1 April 1918.
RGA:	Royal Garrison Artillery, which used medium-sized artillery pieces.
RH:	Railhead: railway station where replacements and supplies of a camp or division are received from warehouses in the rear.
RLO:	Regimental Liaison Officer.
RND:	Royal Naval Division was effectively part of the British Army but manned by sailors of the Royal

	Navy; they fought as soldiers on the Western Front and Gallipoli.
RSM:	Regimental sergeant-major of the British Army, the highest NCO of the regiment.
Runner:	A messenger; a soldier who carried messages by hand.
Sap:	A tunnel used to approach the enemy positions to plant high explosives unobserved; narrow trench dug an angle from an existing trench.
Sapper:	A rank and term used to describe the Royal Engineers and their mining companies
Sausage:	A type of very large, high-explosive German shell. The force of the explosion is so great that anyone caught in its radius will likely die instantly even if no shrapnel hits them. Also called a Flying Pig, a Rum Jar, or a Minnie.
SB:	Stretcher Bearer.
Sector:	An area allotted to and occupied by an army, army corps, division, brigade, regiment.
Shellshock:	A medical condition caused by prolonged exposure to trench warfare. *See* 'neurasthenia'.
Shrapnel:	Small metal balls exploded from a shell in flight (not pieces of the shell itself, which are called fragments); named *c.* 1793 after its inventor, Col. Henry Shrapnel.
Sniper:	A hidden enemy sharpshooter.
Stand-To:	The highest state of military alert where all troops must be ready for immediate action with weapons at the ready; frontline soldiers were required to man the fire step of their trench. Routinely done at dawn and nightfall when attacks were most likely.
Stick Grenade:	A German hand grenade attached to a stick for easier throwing.
Stokes Mortar:	A British light trench mortar that fired a 10-pound projectile up to 1,200 metres. Its bombs were often called Toffee Apples and Plum Puddings.
Subaltern:	A British commissioned officer below the rank of captain; first and second-lieutenants.
Support Trench:	A secondary line of defence behind the frontline system also used to house the supply areas, command elements, and artillery areas.

Tank:	An armoured vehicle first used in the Battle of the Somme in 1916, where it failed badly (but fared better at the Battle of Flers). As a deception, the original shipping crates of these vehicles were labelled 'Tanks' as in water tanks.
Tommy:	A British private soldier. Used as early as 1743 and popularised by Rudyard Kipling's poem 'Tommy' (1892) and the music hall song 'Private Tommy Atkins' (1893).
Traverse:	These were built into a trench and were usually a protrusion of earth or sandbags to reduce the effect of shells when they landed and prevent the enemy from easily overrunning a trench line.
Trench:	A long, narrow excavations (at times fortified) used to shelter troops from enemy fire; they have been called 'trenches' since the 1500s.
Trench Block:	An obstacle placed in a trench to hinder the movement of enemy raiding parties; commonly found in communications trenches.
Trench Coat:	A short, waterproof overcoat, belted and double-breasted, with straps on shoulders and arms; originally worn only by officers.
Trench Fever:	An influenza-like disease spread by lice; characterised by fever, weakness, dizziness, headaches, severe back and leg pains, and a rash.
Trench Foot:	A fungal infection and swelling caused by exposure to damp and cold; if the foot became gangrenous it was often amputated.
Unit:	An army term for a body of troops.
VAD:	Voluntary Aid Detachment.
VC:	Victoria Cross, this was first established by Queen Victoria on 29 January 1856, to recognise valour in the Crimean War and is the highest military decoration, awarded for valour and devotion to duty in the face of the enemy to members of the armed forces, regardless of rank. The VC was awarded to just 633 individuals between 1914 and 1918.
Very Light:	Aerial flares used to watch enemy activity at night or to illuminate no-man's-land during night attacks to maximise defensive actions.
Vickers:	A British machine gun: heavy machine gun used by the British Army from 1912.

Western Front:	The 400-mile-long zone in France and Flanders where British, French, Belgian, and later Americans fought against the Germans.
Whiz-Bang:	A high-speed shell whose sound as it flies through the air arrives almost at the same instant as its explosion; later synonymous with excellent or top notch.
Wire Break:	The passage system through the wire tangles used for offensive operations so that the army wouldn't be hindered by its own wire tangles on the attack.
Xrds:	Crossroads
Ypres:	The small Belgium town in the medieval region of Flanders that was the focus of some of the most violent combat of the Great War; British soldiers called it 'Wipers'.
Zeppelin:	A large, hydrogen-filled airship named after Count Alfred von Zeppelin; used for strategic bombing by the German Army and Navy.

How to Get There and Map Advice

To get you to the sites I write about in this book, I am going to recommend you have the following items to hand. First of all, a good up-to-date satnav. This will get you to the locations I ask you to start at and will also allow you to get to the central points I recommend you stay at.

Secondly, I recommend you use the French 'Série Bleue' 1:25,000 Topographic Survey Maps or, if following a route in Belgium, the Belgian 'NGI/IGN Series' 1:10,000 maps. These will help you if you are walking the ground. I would also recommend that you use trench maps to replicate their modern-day counterparts by looking at the trench systems as they were at the time of these actions.

You can also opt to use the Linesman, which are trench maps that you can use on your PC and on handheld devices.

Also, trying to move ahead with the times, I have also used the reference for the 'what3words' app that can now be used on Android and Apple IOS phones. I used this system on my final recce of sites in France and Flanders in January 2020. If you have it on your smartphone, you can use my what3words reference to see if you are in the right place. This app gets you down to a 3-metre-square grid anywhere in the world.

I have used this app to get you to a spot where you can use my guide to look at sites. This is not necessarily the exact point; in certain instances, you will have to walk to the places I have plotted.

I have included my own homemade maps in this book. I use a mixture of overlaid Belgian, French IGN, and Michelin maps. They do not cover everything I write about, but I have tried to draw the areas that I think will be the most visited or I feel are some of the lesser places that are visited but involved certain battalions in important events in the First World War timeline. The first two maps I use for this purpose are detailed because, to my mind, they incorporate two actions that then had the knock-on effect of bring us to the point where the Western Front began to form.

My advice for these maps is use their keys to get you to a site.

Blue arrows and red stars show you locations on my maps. Red arrows and red rectangles will show you positions of British units and green arrows will show you the directions where the Germans came from or faced when in action.

Where I have not included actions or sites into my maps, I am asking you to default back to the local maps and trench maps to get you to the places you want to go to as well as using satnav and apps such as what3words.

One of the things you will see in this book is grid references to trench maps. So, in order for you to have an idea of how you can read those on a First World War map, here is an overview on how you do that.

Trench maps came into being after the original maps of 1914 became static. The original maps were on a scale between 1:40,000 to 1:120,000, and these proved inadequate when you needed to show things like a German trench or a wood. It was also a requirement that artillery had more accurate maps so they could bring fire onto a specific point.

So, Royal Engineer specialists such as observers and topographers were directed to make maps of the new frontline, which would also need to be corrected when things changed. This came into being in January 1915.

Maps were set to this format:

1. The whole area shown on each map was first divided into a series of large rectangles, each identified by a capital letter of the alphabet. These rectangles were in turn subdivided into smaller squares numbered 1 to up to 36 on larger maps. These squares covered a ground area of 1,000 by 1,000 yards. So, for example, one of these 1,000 by 1,000 squares would be identified as T2, which you will read about in the chapter on the assault on La Coulotte in 1917.
2. Each of these numbered squares was then subdivided into a two by two matrix of four squares, each measuring 500 by 500 yards. These were lettered in lower case 'a', 'b', 'c', and 'd'. 'a' is top-left, 'b' is top-right, 'c' lower-left, and 'd' lower-right. So, the reference for one of these 500-yard squares would be for example T2d.
3. To achieve better accuracy with artillery, each of the 500-yard squares was then subdivided into a ten by ten matrix of 50 by 50-yard squares. A specific point could then be identified by counting along the x-axis (west to east) in 50-yard segments, and then up the y-axis (south to north).
4. To make this even more accurate, this 50-yard square was divided not into a ten by ten grid, but a 100 by 100 one. Each square in this grid would measure 5 yards square—about the size of a machine-gun pit or a small blockhouse. An example of this is a German strongpoint at T1d.8.8, which was a machine gun that enfiladed the 1st Battalion Norfolk Regiment at La Coulotte.

5. My advice in this is when beginning to look for a position, look for the capital letter of the larger squares to which they belong.

So, an example for you look at is Oppy Wood, which was assaulted by the 5th Division on 28 June 1917. They list the assault line as being between B18d.75.15 to B12d.45.10. This comes from a trench map listed as Sheet 51B. NW Scale: 1:20000, Edition: 7A, published June 1917. Trenches corrected to 25 May 1917.

That can be deciphered as the following:

1. Sheet 51B.NW, this puts the map in the Map 51B area, which was the Arras–Cantin area. This was also divided into four sections, NW, NE, SW, and SE (e.g. north-west, north-east, south-west, and south-east).
2. Scale: 1:20000, Edition: 7A, published June 1917. Trenches corrected to 25 May 1917. This basically refers to the map scale, what edition of map, and when it was published. The final aspect lists the date that it is most current to. As you might imagine, it was necessary to keep the maps up to date using intelligence and aerial observation to provide the attacking troops with the most accurate information about the enemy positions.
3. B18d.75.15 to B12d.45.10. This is the line that the 15th Brigade, which included the 1st Battalion Norfolk Regiment, who assaulted this position along with the 16th Warwickshire Regiment, 1st Cheshire Regiment, and the 1st Bedfordshire Regiment.

As you might imagine, this was a long line of troops. This goes from south to north and west of Oppy Wood; we will look at place names in a little while. It starts in square 'd' of Grid 18 and moves up to square 'd' in Grid 12. You will also note that this trench has the name of Oppy Trench. The trench line within is in red. Red was always used for the enemy positions and blue for our positions. So, hopefully from this you can make out the area that the 15th Brigade assaulted.

The last thing we need to look at regarding trench maps is place names.

These came about from the fact we began to name positions for ourselves, for instance nicknames or links to their regiments. Positions can be identified from them and examples you will read about are strongpoints, such as the Schwaben Reboubt; a building, such as Falfemont Farm; and a trench, such as Bayonet Trench. All of these positions will be looked at in the book.

My preferred route has always been to either take the Dover–Calais ferry or EuroTunnel, you can also take the Calais–Dunkirk ferry. From the locations of either Calais or Dunkirk, you will normally take one of two routes to get you to central points from where to set up a base to travel to and from.

From Calais to Arras, you will take Junction 47 to get onto the A26. This dual carriageway will take you directly to that town.

From Calais to Ypres, take Junction 47 for the A16 and head towards Dunkirk and then Junction 20 for the A25, which has a signpost for Ieper/Ypres. At Junction 13 of the A25, you will come off and take the N38 to Poperinge and then from Poperinge the N38 will take you to Ypres.

From Calais to Bapaume, you will take Junction 47 to get onto the A26. This toll road will take you directly to Arras, from there you will then take Junction 15 for the A1. At Junction 14, you will turn off for Bapaume.

From Calais to Cambrai, you will take you will take Junction 47 to get onto the A26. This toll road will take you directly to Arras, which you will pass by, and remaining on the A26, you will take the exit onto A2/E19 towards Valenciennes/Bruxelles to get onto the A2 and then take Junction 14 for Cambrai.

Using one or a couple of these four places, you can then tour the sites I will write about, and in the next chapter I will explain why.

My advice to you about this is to plan this out as much as you can before you go over. Make sure you have this book, your maps, and your own research with you so that it makes it easier for you when out on the ground.

Believe me when I say that even the most experienced battlefield expert gets lost and confused.

Where to Stay

I have recommended one of four places to stay. And you might want to know why, so here is why.

Bapaume

Bapaume was of strategic importance for both sides in First World War. It was captured by the Germans in 1914 and remained in their hands until early 1917 when they withdrew to the Hindenburg Line. On 17 March 1917, the Australians occupied the town after the German withdrawal. Everything had been destroyed, except the town hall, which the Australians used as a place for visitors to come and view the damage locally. Tragically, a week later, thirty people were killed when a time bomb, left by the Germans, exploded.

Bapaume changed hands a number of times and fell back into German hands on 24 March 1918, but was eventually recaptured by New Zealand troops on 29 August 1918. At the end of the war, the town was in ruins and the whole area around it was declared 'Zone-Rouge' (Red-Zone) due to the amount of unexploded ordnance left, and it took five years for this to be cleared; it was a further decade before any farming could be done around the area.

Reconstruction of the town of Bapaume was not complete until 1935, just four years before the next war.

Today, Bapaume is a beautiful market town on the heart of the Somme battlefield. If you prefer a quieter place from which to tour the area, then I recommend this town. It is perfect for exploring the Somme, Cambrai, or the 1918 battlefields for the Norfolk Regiment who pushed east and north-east of here.

Arras

Arras is the capital of the Pas-de-Calais region of northern France and sits on the River Scarpe. The town can be traced back to the Iron Age and Roman times.

During the First World War, Arras was evacuated by the French Army on 29 September 1914 and German forces entered the city. They were driven out by the French Army a day later. The frontlines remained close to the town for most of the war.

Underneath the town, there are ancient cellars dug out of the soft stone called 'Boves'. These cellars were used by Allied forces for the duration of the war as shelter, living space, and medical stations. Tunnelling companies also excavated tunnels for the launch of the Battle of Arras on 9 April 1917. British troops were hidden and assembled in the chalk tunnels before the attack, leaving the relative safety of the underground tunnels on the day to attack the German line.

By the end of the war, Arras was very badly damaged from the German artillery shelling and aerial bombing. The ancient buildings, the belfry, and medieval gabled house fronts were rebuilt after the war.

Arras was only 6 miles from the frontline, and after the hostilities ended, three-quarters of the city had to be rebuilt.

In the Second World War, it also saw fighting, including an ill-fated counterattack on 20 May 1940 when Viscount Gort attacked the Germans with a battle group called Frankforce. A severely depleted force hit the Germans, which had an initial success, but then superior German forces, including Erwin Rommel's 7th Panzer Division, eventually pushed the British and French back. The city has two squares that are filled with shops, hotels, and restaurants.

Arras is perfect to tour the battlefields of April 1917 and the 1915 battlefields to the north around Loos. It can also be used to go further afield and look at Cambrai, the fighting around Armentières, and the Somme.

Cambrai

Cambrai is labelled the City of Art and History and is a commune of the Hauts-de-France located in the department of Nord and is about 25 miles from Arras. The town's origins can be traced back to the Gallo-Roman period. Cambrai becomes the capital of the Nerviens instead of Bavay in the fourth century, but it is in the sixth century that the town really soared thanks to the establishment of episcopal activity.

In the Middle Ages, the town occupied a strategic position, being the frontier between the Kingdom of France and the German Holy Empire.

In the First World War, the area around Cambrai was chosen by the British as the scene for an offensive in 1917. The town, one of the principal railway intersections, and German garrisons of the Western Front lay on a vast chalky plain, which was ideal terrain for the tanks. The town was indeed protected on its western side by the powerful defences of the Hindenburg Line; however, British intelligence knew that the point of attack was held by troops who had been weakened by great losses at Ypres and subsequently transferred to a portion of the front, which the Germans considered to be of minor importance.

Today, it is a perfect central point to look at the battlefield of Cambrai or to look at the fighting after August 1918. It also allows you to visit further afield and is only an hour and a half away from 1914 sites of interest I will write about in this book.

Ypres

Ypres saw war from October 1914 and was fought over and around its environs throughout the conflict. The British arrived there on 14 October and put up a defence and to block the route for the German Army through Ypres to the ports on the French and Belgian coast. Soldiers in the British Army quickly turned the name of Ypres into a much easier word to pronounce. They called it 'Wipers'.

The defence of Ypres was key to the British hold on this sector of the Western Front. The town was an important strategic landmark blocking the route for the Germans, and if Ypres fell, there would be nothing stopping the Germans from getting to the Channel ports.

Many thousands of Allied troops died to maintain the Allies' possession of this place. From October 1914 to October 1918, five major offensives occurred at Ypres (now Ieper) in Belgium. By the time the last shells fell in Ypres in October 1918, nearly 200,000 Commonwealth servicemen had been killed. On the German side of the wire, many thousands of German lives were also lost in the landscape around Ypres.

By the end of the war, the entire town lay in ruins with its medieval and renaissance buildings completely flattened. At the end of the war, Winston Churchill wanted Ypres to remain like that as a memorial to the sacrifice that was made by British and Commonwealth troops between 1914 and 1918.

However, the inhabitants of Ypres returned and had other ideas, and the whole of the town was reconstructed from scratch during the 1920s and 1930s. The Cloth Hall, which sits centrally in the town and which also became a ruin, was also rebuilt and was not fully restored until 1967.

Today, Ypres is a place where thousands of battlefield tourists go to pay their respects to the men of the BEF who served there, and the town will provide you with a focal point with which to tour the Ypres Salient and the battles fought by the Norfolk Regiment to the south of this famous town.

An Overview of Cemeteries and Memorials

It is quite possible that you are visiting the Western Front to find a relative who was killed serving with the Norfolk Regiment. This chapter looks at the Commonwealth War Graves Commission. Most people know this wonderful organisation, but just in case you do not, then I think it is best to quote from their website.

The Commonwealth War Graves Commission (CWGC) honours the 1.7 million men and women of the Commonwealth forces who died in the First and Second World Wars, and ensures they will never be forgotten.

Our work commemorates the war dead, from building and maintaining our cemeteries and memorials at 23,000 locations in more than 150 countries and territories to preservation of our extensive records and archives. Our values and aims, laid out in 1917, are as relevant now as they were 100 years ago.

The Commission's principles are:
- Each of the dead should be commemorated by name on the headstone or memorial
- Headstones and memorials should be permanent
- Headstones should be uniform
- There should be no distinction made on account of military rank, race or creed

Since our establishment by Royal Charter we have constructed 2,500 war cemeteries and plots, erected headstones over graves and where the remains are missing, inscribed the names of the dead-on permanent memorials. More than a million burials are now commemorated at military and civil sites in more than 150 countries and territories.

In total, 4,203 men from the Norfolk Regiment are either buried in one of their cemeteries or commemorated on a memorial in France and Flanders. That can be broken down to 741 men in Belgium and 3,462 men in France.

A total 1,986 have no known grave and are commemorated on a number of memorials in Belgium and France. That equates to 1,806 men on memorials in France and 411 men on memorials in Belgium. Although Belgium has more cemeteries for the Norfolks, there is a larger concentration of men in France.

The best way to search for CWGC fallen is via their website at www.cwgc.org/, and you can email them via this address enquiries@cwgc.org.

However, if you do not have access to the internet, you can write to them at this address,

Commonwealth War Graves Commission
2 Marlow Road
Maidenhead
Berkshire
SL6 7DX
United Kingdom

Or by telephone via this number +44 (0)1628 507200.

They are always a very helpful bunch of people and if you are social media savvy, they are always happy to talk to you via their Facebook or Twitter page.

Memorials in Belgium and France

I think it is important to list the memorials in Belgium and France because many of them cover significant battles for the Western Front campaign. They are listed by country in which they now stand.

Belgium

The Menin Gate

The Menin Gate can be found in the famous town of Ypres. This commemorates casualties from the Commonwealth and the United Kingdom casualties lost in this sector up to 16 August 1917. It was unveiled by Field Marshal Lord Plumer on 24 July 1927, with veterans and relatives of those commemorated and local people attending the ceremony.

Every evening since 1928, at 8 p.m., buglers from the Belgian Fire Service have sounded the Last Post. The ceremony has become part of the daily life of Ypres and traffic is stopped from passing through the memorial. Only during the German occupation of the Second World War was the ceremony interrupted. At that time, it was held at Brookwood Military Cemetery in Surrey, England.

In total, 138 men are commemorated on the Menin Gate who served with the Norfolk Regiment.

What3words: vines.flagged.tested.

Tyne Cot Memorial

It is believed that Tyne Cot or Tyne Cottage was a barn named by the Northumberland Fusiliers, which stood near the level crossing on the road from Passchendaele to Broodseinde. Around this were a number of blockhouses or 'pillboxes'. These resembled the local cottages seen by men back home in Northumberland, and they were eventually captured by the 3rd Australian Division on 4 October 1917 in the advance on Passchendaele.

The Tyne Cot Memorial now bears the names of almost 35,000 officers and men who have no known graves who died in this sector from 18 August 1917, including 1,200 men from New Zealand who are not listed on the Menin Gate.

The memorial was unveiled by Sir Gilbert Dyett, the Australian soldier and veterans' rights activist, on 20 June 1927.

In total, 257 men are commemorated on the Tyne Cot Memorial who served with the Norfolk Regiment and it is the largest concentration of men for the regiment in this area.

What3words: recoding.shunt.tragically.

Ploegsteert Memorial

This commemorates more than 11,000 servicemen of the United Kingdom and South African forces who died in this sector during the First World War and have no known grave.

The CWGC notes:

> Most of those commemorated by the memorial did not die in major offensives and most were killed in the course of the day-to-day trench warfare which characterised this part of the line, or in small scale set engagements, usually carried out in support of the major attacks taking place elsewhere.

And certainly, as you will see, this is clarified by the casualties listed from the Norfolk Regiment and how they died.

The memorial was designed by Harold Chalton Bradshaw and was unveiled by the duke of Brabant on 7 June 1931.

In total, sixteen men are commemorated on the memorial who served with the Norfolk Regiment.

What3words: healthier.twirls.reshape.

France

La Ferté-sous-Jouarre Memorial

The La Ferté-sous-Jouarre Memorial commemorates 3,740 officers and men of the BEF who fell at the Battles of Mons, Le Cateau, the Marne, and the Aisne between the end of August and early October 1914 and have no known graves.

The memorial was designed by George H. Goldsmith, a decorated veteran of the Western Front, and unveiled by Sir William Pulteney, who had commanded the III Corps of the BEF in 1914, on 4 November 1928.

In total, seventy-two men are commemorated on the memorial who served with the Norfolk Regiment.

What3words: waffled.corrupted.knocks.

Le Touret Memorial

The Le Touret Memorial commemorates over 13,400 British soldiers who were killed in this sector of the Western Front from the beginning of October 1914 to the eve of the Battle of Loos in late September 1915 and who have no known grave. The memorial was designed by John Reginald Truelove, who had served as an officer with the London Regiment during the war, and unveiled by the British ambassador to France, Lord Tyrrell, on 22 March 1930.

In total, fifty-three men are commemorated on the memorial who served with the Norfolk Regiment.

What3words: brands.rentals.jabs.

Loos Memorial

The Loos Memorial commemorates over 20,000 officers and men who have no known grave, who fell in the area from the River Lys to the old southern boundary of the First Army, east and west of Grenay, from the first day of the Battle of Loos to the end of the war. The memorial was designed by Sir Herbert Baker with sculpture by Charles Wheeler. It was unveiled by Sir Nevil Macready on 4 August 1930.

In total, 278 men are commemorated on the memorial who served with the Norfolk Regiment.

What3words: crinkles.sticky.reunion.

The Thiepval Memorial

The Thiepval Memorial, the Memorial to the Missing of the Somme, bears the names of more than 72,000 officers and men of the United Kingdom and South African forces who died in the Somme sector before 20 March 1918 and have no known grave. Over 90 per cent of those commemorated died between July and November 1916.

The memorial also serves as an Anglo-French Battle Memorial in recognition of the joint nature of the 1916 offensive and a small cemetery containing equal numbers of Commonwealth and French graves lies at the foot of the memorial. This includes four unidentified men from the Norfolk Regiment.

On 1 August 1932, Prince Edward, prince of Wales, unveiled the memorial.

In total, 762 men are commemorated on the memorial who served with the Norfolk Regiment, and this is the largest concentration for the Regiment in France.

What3words: meddled.battled.reunion.

Arras Memorial

The memorial commemorates almost 35,000 servicemen from the United Kingdom, South Africa, and New Zealand who died in the Arras sector between the spring of 1916 and 7 August 1918.

The memorial was unveiled on 31 July 1932 by Lord Trenchard.

In total, 323 men are commemorated on the memorial who served with the Norfolk Regiment.

What3words: journey.mentions.shuts.

Cambrai Memorial

The Cambrai Memorial commemorates more than 7,000 servicemen from Britain and South Africa who died in the Battle of Cambrai whose graves are not known.

The chateau at Louverval was taken by the 56th Australian Infantry Battalion at dawn on 2 April 1917. The hamlet stayed in Allied hands until the 51st (Highland) Division was driven from it on 21 March 1918 during the great German advance, and it was retaken in the following September.

It was unveiled by Lieutenant-General Sir Louis Vaughan on 4 August 1930. It was unveiled at the same hour on the same day as the memorials at Le Touret, Vis-en-Artois, and Pozières in France.

In total, 110 men are commemorated on the memorial who served with the Norfolk Regiment.

What3words: bending.distancing.suffuse.

Vis-en-Artois Memorial

This memorial bears the names of over 9,000 men who fell in the period from 8 August 1918 to the date of the Armistice in the Advance to Victory in Picardy and Artois, between the Somme and Loos, and who have no known grave.

The memorial was designed by J. R. Truelove, with sculpture by Ernest Gillick. It was unveiled by the Rt Hon. Thomas Shaw on 4 August 1930.

In total, 111 men are commemorated on the memorial who served with the Norfolk Regiment.

What3words: imagination.rosebuds.hydration.

Pozières Memorial

The Pozières Memorial relates to the period of crisis in March and April 1918 when the Allied Fifth Army was driven back by overwhelming numbers across the former Somme battlefields, and the months that followed before the Advance to Victory, which began on 8 August 1918.

The memorial commemorates over 14,000 casualties of the United Kingdom and 300 of the South African Forces who have no known grave and who died on the Somme from 21 March to 7 August 1918.

The cemetery and memorial were designed by W. H. Cowlishaw, with sculpture by Laurence A. Turner. The memorial was unveiled by Sir Horace Smith-Dorrien on 4 August 1930.

In total, forty-seven men are commemorated on the memorial who served with the Norfolk Regiment.

What3words: resells.ditty.warthogs.

I will cover the battles that most of these men fell in a timeline through the book. In the postscript, I will also challenge some of the myths about the Great War, which will include casualty numbers. But it is important to note that when I mention casualties at the end of a chapter, this will cover killed in action, died of wounds, wounded, missing, and, if relevant, captured.

Introduction

This book came about due to my experiences of walking the ground the Norfolk Regiment fought over on the Somme and Ypres as a battlefield guide.

I have lived in Norfolk since 1998 and qualified as a battlefield guide in 2004, after leaving the RAF—my last tour being at RAF Coltishall. Every year, I am lucky enough to guide groups around the battlefields of the First World War, and this often connects me to the men of the Norfolk Regiment who now lie in foreign fields. So, I am also often either on the ground or close to the ground where they served or went over the top, many of these sites are off the beaten track.

So, unlike others who write books on local First World War history, I can say I have actually walked all of the ground I write about in this book. Also, based on this experience, it has meant much of what I have researched for the book comes from three specific visits to the battles mentioned in the chapters. They were in October 2017, November 2018, and January 2020. On each occasion, I looked at areas and went to them. For instance, in 2017, I spent all of my time around the Ypres Salient.

Not only have I walked the ground, but I have catalogued and photographed these battlesites and have visited their nearby war dead in the Commonwealth War Grave Commission (CWGC) 'Silent-Cities' in France and Belgium.

For me, this has been the most important thing to do. You cannot undertake a project like this without going to where these sacred sites are, and based on that and my research, I am proud to say I did this in their honour. I did this knowing they fought in every major engagement from Mons in 1914 to the final advance in 1918.

While I have written this book something has always resonated in me and it is something I tell my school groups when I stand at a specific site where a poem was written. That place is Essex Farm near Ypres. Here there is a cemetery that holds the remains of 1,200 men who were either killed in action or died of wounds near to an Advanced Dressing Station (ADS) where in 1915 John McCrae wrote his famous poem that has become an anthem for the Great War; it is called 'In Flanders Fields'.

Why do I mention this poem? Well, for starters, two men from the Norfolk Regiment are buried in Essex Farm Cemetery and I often tell their story while I take groups around, but it is also because I ask just one thing from my students when we look at the site and recite the poem.

In the third verse, it states:

> *The torch; be yours to hold it high.*
> *If ye break faith with us who die*

I ask my students, who are generally aged between thirteen and fifteen, that their generation must take the torch from my generation and keep it burning so the memory of the men who fell fighting in the First World War is not forgotten.

This book is my torch for the five battalions of the Norfolk Regiment who served on the Western Front.

My book uses their war diaries, histories, and official histories and other written histories but has a lot of unseen accounts from men who served in the battalions that fought in France and Flanders. These men will tell their own story of the regiment on the Western Front. I have also had full access to the records held by the Royal Norfolk Regiment Museum. With this in mind, I have tried to ensure that, where possible, they complement and help to confirm what was happening in the timeline for their particular battalion.

Depending on the timeline, it has either sometimes been easy or difficult to locate accounts that marry up to the actions I write about in this book. You will see that predominantly these accounts come from 1st and 9th Battalion men and less so for the 8th and 12th Battalions. Sadly, the least mentioned in this way is the 7th Battalion.

So, in some chapters you will get a very detailed story and in others not so. I apologise for that, but I hope that any chapter you read will give you an idea of their time on the Western Front because this is their story to tell as well. I can assure you that each one looks at accounts from various stories to help build the picture.

With that in mind, you will also see that I have used other regiments in this history. I have done this because they mention the Norfolk Regiment in their histories or war diaries. This has helped me to link the Norfolk Regiment to a timeline.

What I can also guarantee in every chapter is you will be able to stand on the ground written about by the use of directions. This book can be used as a guide book to get you to the places where the five battalions were at given times between 1914 and 1918. So, before you delve into the chapters, if you are using the book for that purpose, please read the chapters on how you should approach that. I would hope you do not get lost or bogged down on a muddy track because you did not follow my instructions.

I must warn you that some of the sites are not as well trodden as others. You will need strong boots or walking shoes and accept that you and your car might get muddy. Be prepared for the fact that it can get quite inclement in France and Flanders, and some of the sites can be tough going to get to. But I promise that if you allow for these things, you will be able to get down to ground level at the sites where they served.

I will end on this. I have accrued hundreds of images and used numerous resources to research this book. As you might imagine, not all of the images or maps that I have used have gone into this book. If you feel I can help you with anything prior to going over there with this book in your hand, then please feel free to email me via the address I have listed below.

Steve Smith
July 2020
stevesmith1944@hotmail.com

1

The Road to War:
June to August 1914

On 28 June 1914, Archduke Franz Ferdinand of Austria, heir to the Austro-Hungarian throne, and his wife, Sophie, duchess of Hohenberg, were assassinated in Sarajevo by Gavrilo Princip, one of a group of six Bosnian Serb activists.

This one act, on one man, although it could not have been perceived at the time, would plunge the world into its first global war, and the events that would set its outbreak would fall like dominos. The assignation prompted the various countries of Europe to take sides as they tried to settle old scores, and various talks were held in a bid to stop a new European war. Britain had taken an active role very early on in trying to avert this growing crisis, with the then-Foreign Secretary Sir Edward Grey chairing a conference between Britain, France, Italy, and Germany in London in July 1914.

Here the lines had been drawn, and it had effectively put Britain siding with France and Italy, while the Germans kept their cards very firmly to the table. Britain, along with France, stated that it would side with neutral Belgium should Germany invade this small country. On top of all of this, Russia was sabre rattling as well as she supported Serbia, who in turn was being threatened by the Austria-Hungarian Empire, who had just lost its heir to the throne to Serbian activists. And so, all during the summer of 1914, there was a very stark countdown to war, which had prompted Edward Grey to remark to a friend, 'The lights are going out all over Europe and I doubt we will see them go on again in our lifetime.'

To my mind, never a truer word was ever said to how the politics of Europe would be played out all through the twentieth century and into the twenty-first century, bringing war after war, whether civil or global, which, in essence, still affects the countries who took part in it even today.

On 28 July 1914, Austria-Hungary declared war on Serbia. On 30 July 1914, Russia mobilised her troops, which in turn led the Germans to give an ultimatum that if the Russians did not cease this within twelve hours, then they would begin their own mobilisation, which they did. Austria began to shell Belgrade on this date and began a full mobilisation of her troops. France and Germany mobilised their troops on 1 August 1914. On the same day, Germany's ultimatum to Russia ended and Germany declared war on them at 7 p.m., prompting the Russian foreign minister to state to the German ambassador: 'You could have prevented war by a word; you would not do so. In all my efforts to preserve peace, I received not the slightest help from you'.

On 1 August 1914, Belgium mobilised and Germany sent them a note stating that it had received intelligence that France intended to send troops to the Meuse via Givet and Namur and requested that Belgium allow Germen troops 'free and un-resisted ingress'; this was refused and Germany was told that any entry into Belgian soil would be repelled.

The Belgians looked to Britain and France to honour their promise of assistance and they were promised that '[we] would be true to our engagements to uphold the integrity of Belgium.'

This prompted the British government to take immediate measures whereby the Territorial Force was embodied (e.g. called up), and the Naval Reserves were likewise mobilised. The British government of the time felt that a full war footing would almost certainly be inevitable. By this time, on 2 August 1914, Germany launched her long-awaited Schlieffen Plan. This plan had first come to light in 1905 when it had been mentioned that the best way to win a future war was to defeat France quickly, thereby stopping Britain and Russia coming to its aid. It planned for a rapid advance, with German troops sweeping through neutral Belgium and Luxembourg and would then swing along the French coast eventually turning west towards Paris.

Germany declared war on France at 6.45 p.m. on 3 August 1914 and in turn did the same to Belgium on 4 August 1914. Her troops began to pour into Luxembourg and Belgium.

However, the Germans were surprised when their advance was held up by the Belgian Army, which could only muster 117,000 men in total, with six infantry divisions, totalling 43,000 men. They were further set back when Russia pre-empted a strike on her borders by advancing into East Prussia. However, the German Army started to quickly overwhelm Belgium's defence system and continued to move onwards.

Britain eventually fully mobilised on 4 August 1914 when Germany had ignored an ultimatum to withdraw her forces out of Belgium. This ultimatum had been sent by the foreign minister which stated:

Owing to the summary rejection by the German Government of the request made by His Majesty's Government for assurances that the neutrality of Belgium will be respected, His Majesty's Ambassador at Berlin has received his passports and His

Majesty's Government have declared to the German Government that a state of war exists between Great Britain and Germany as from 11 p.m. on 4th August.

The British Expeditionary Force (BEF) of six infantry and one cavalry division, under the command of Field Marshal Sir John French, landed in France between 12 and 17 August 1914, although elements had been landing since 7 August. One of those divisions included the 1st Battalion Norfolk Regiment.

2

1st Battalion, Élouges to La Bassée: 4 August to 30 October 1914

The 1st Battalion Norfolk Regiment, under the command of Lieutenant-Colonel Colin Robert Ballard, which was based in Palace Barracks at Holywood in County Down, when war was declared, were part of 15th Brigade of the 5th Division, a regular unit, one of two regular battalions of the Norfolk Regiment to be present at the start of the war.

I have been lucky to get access to memoirs written by Private Herbert Reeve (8658). He had been with the 1st Battalion since November 1911 and put down his experiences of the war in a letter to his friend who we only know as George, he noted his recollections of war being declared:

> So, came 1914. We were out camping in the Dublin area when we were confined to Barracks, but nothing happened until August 1914 when war was declared. Many Boer War soldiers were called up under Section D—they were the finest chaps I knew. I was then given a Lance Corporal stripe with a section of these men under my command. They were wonderful pals but the biggest scroungers on earth!

Mobilisation was quick, with the 15th Infantry Brigade's history noting:

> In accordance with the order received at Belfast at 5.30 P.M. on the 4th, the 15th Brigade started mobilizing on the 5th August 1914, and by the 10th was complete in all respects. We were practically ready by the 9th, but a machine-gun or two and some harnesses were a bit late arriving from Dublin, not our fault. Everything had already been rehearsed at mobilization inspections, held as usual in the early summer, and all went like clock-work. On the 8th we got our final orders to embark on the 14th, and on the 11th the embarkation orders arrived in detail.

As noted, the brigade, with a complement of 127 officers, 3,958 men, 258 horses, and seventy-four vehicles, embarked on 14 August 1914, their history noting that they left with 'Great waving of handkerchiefs and cheering as we warped slowly out of Belfast docks at 3 P.M. and moved slowly down the channel.'

They landed at Le Havre on 16 August 1914. As the BEF embarked, the king sent a message to his troops; it said:

> You are leaving home to fight for the safety and honour of my Empire. Belgium, whose country we are pledged to defend, has been attacked, and France is about to be invaded by the same powerful foe. I have implicit confidence in you, my soldiers. Duty is your watchword, and I know your duty will be nobly done.
>
> I shall follow your every movement with deepest interest and mark with eager satisfaction your daily progress; indeed, your welfare will never be absent from my thoughts. I pray God will bless you and guard you, and bring you back victorious.

The BEF moved rapidly towards the Germans, and this swift advance was one of the things that ultimately thwarted the Schlieffen Plan. The BEF was not a large body of men—only totalling 80,000 men—and, as a result, the French commander in-chief, Joseph Joffre, had placed this small but highly trained army on his left flank, where he believed there would not be much fighting. The plan called for the French to take the brunt to stop the German Army, but in the event, they were bloodily repulsed.

The advance of the BEF, meanwhile, was stopped on 23 August at the Battle of Mons, and it was here that the British 1st and 2nd Corps met the German 1st Army commanded by General von Kluck.

This saw the British fielding around 70,000 men and 300 artillery pieces, making their defensive line along the Mons–Conde Canal, fighting against 160,000 men and 600 artillery pieces on the German side. The Germans vied to cross the canal in order to capture the main bridges there. Although the BEF was a professional body of men who were well-trained, they had no hope of holding Mons, and by 1 p.m. they were retreating before the Germans, who had managed to cross the canal and gain footholds. The French Army was also capitulating in other sectors, and the BEF ran the risk of being outflanked on both sides as the Germans gained ground. Retreat was the only option and the order to do so was given by Field Marshal French in the early evening. At this point, the 1st Norfolks had not seen any offensive action and would not do so until 24 August, when they were ordered to Dour with the 1st Cheshires and the 119th Battery Royal Field Artillery to act as the reserve.

On 18 August, the 15th Brigade arrived at Le Cateau, and by 22 August, they moved through Dour and then onto the Bois de Bossu, where they went into the reserve with the 13th and 14th Brigades positioned along the canal. It was on this day that the 1st Norfolks lost their first man. Private William Porter (6271) was born in Shouldham and first enlisted on 9 September 1902 at the age of nineteen years and eleven months. He left the Regular Army in 1905, but in 1914, he was asked to extend his time in the army reserve and was called to action as a member of the 1st Battalion. Following the Battle of Mons, he was listed as missing and later an official statement was issued confirming that William Porter had 'died on or since 22-8-14'. He was married to Florence Porter and had two children, Leslie and William. He has no known grave and is commemorated on the La Ferte-sous-Jouarre Memorial.

The 13th and 14th Brigades were now withdrawing and, through an error made by other units, it was found that the left flank of the 5th Division was threatened. As a result, the 1st Norfolks and the 1st Cheshires, under the command of Lieutenant-Colonel Ballard, were ordered to advance north in a counterattack. They ended up along the Élouges–Audregnies–Angre road supported by the 2nd and 3rd Cavalry Brigades, who were in the vicinity of Audregnies.

For this aspect of the fighting, we have the excellent personal account, held in the Royal Norfolk Regiment Museum archives, of Private Robert Sheldrake (6324) from North Elmham, who served with 'B' Company:

> During the afternoon of 24th August, we were manoeuvring round getting into position. My company took up a position in the hollow of a railroad and as we were marching up, the first dead soldier I saw, a cavalryman, was being carted down on a stretcher, his horse lying dead nearby, they had rode into some barbed wire.
>
> About midday the terrible battle began, all I can describe it by is a terrible roaring of cannon, with innumerable shells and bullets singing through the air, mingled with the terrible rat tat tat of the machine guns brigaded together, mowing down troops like corn before the scythe. I lay between the two fires, we being sheltered in the hollow of the railroad both from view and fire. We crawled up the bank occasionally. I fired 20 to 30 rounds where I thought there appeared to be some men moving amongst some corn sheaves 700 to 800 yards away. I cannot say I hit anyone; it is more likely the opposite.

The position described by Sheldrake was in a sunken road next to a single-track railway that fed the industrial aspect of this area.

At 12.30 p.m., with Ballard's force obtaining contact with the cavalry, the Germans struck from the direction of Quievrain, the Bois de Deduit, and Baisieux. The 2nd Cavalry Brigade were ordered to attack and did so; they sustained heavy casualties, but this gave Ballard's force time to position itself as flank guard.

Herbert Reeve witnessed this attack: 'We were ordered to dump everything except rifle and ammunition. It was during this afternoon that I saw the cavalry charge and the advancing Germans coming across the fields towards us'.

The Germans, advancing from the direction of Quievrain, were met with fire from 'L' Battery, while 119th Battery fired upon the German artillery. Meanwhile, the Norfolks fired upon German infantry who were streaming out of Quievrain and the Cheshires turned their attention to enemy forces coming from the direction of Bois de Deduit.

Sadly, this was not enough; Ballard was given reports that an entire German army corps was moving to the south and he ordered a retreat at 2.30 p.m. The Norfolks fell back in two parties and had to leave 100 of their wounded at Élouges.

Herbert Reeve was present when the retreat began, noting:

> We were then ordered to retire, with cavalrymen with us on foot, as they had lost their horses in the charge. We never collected our equipment which we had dumped so we had no overcoat, no cigarettes, or any of the other possessions we treasured. A Platoon of our Company was ordered to cover our retreat, they were trapped and had to surrender on the first day of Battle.

Robert Sheldrake witnessed part of this withdrawal:

> After laying in this terrible death trap for two or three hours in the blazing sun we got the order to retire as the enemy were much stronger than us, and were drawing close. Our gallant Captain with about eight men covered our retreat, and according to their accounts later on, they had an exciting time, shooting the enemy over at close range, one of their party got severely wounded, but they said they put the first field bandage on before leaving him....
>
> We left them in a cottage, this being the last we saw of our medical officer. Then we continued our hasty retreat through the town, receiving a drink from frightened looking inhabitants on the way. When I caught up to a large party in the centre of the town a kind gentleman gave us some new laid eggs, I sucked one and felt greatly revived.
>
> When we halted a few hours later to water the horses and men, and called the rolls my battalion missed nearly 400 officers and men. The Cheshires in our Brigade missed nearly 800. We recalled what some of them said to us in the morning, as we were marching through to the front. They said, 'You are in for it' but it turned out the opposite, we got the advantage being nearer the enemy, the shells passed over us and caught them.

Ballard's troops managed to withdraw towards Audregnies, where they dislodged the Germans from their vantage point before being surrounded and overwhelmed around Athis. It was the gunners of the 5th Division who succeeded in stopping the German advance, allowing the survivors of Ballard's force to reach their muster point at St Waast.

The history of the 15th Brigade recorded:

> Just beyond Athis we found the Norfolks, who had been fighting at Élouges all the morning, and then we came across the sad little remainder of the Cheshires, only

about 200 left out of 891 who had gone into action that morning near Élouges.... The Norfolks had lost poor Cresswell, their Adjutant, such a good fellow, and one or two other officers. But although their losses had been serious they were nothing like so bad as the Cheshires.

In this action, the Norfolks had lost over 250 men, of which fifty-four officers and men were killed in action.

Guidebook

To find the 1st Norfolk's positions for Élouges, go into the village and take the N553, Rue de la Chapelle, and head toward Audregnies. As you head out of Élouges, you will see a housing estate on your right and the road bears round to the left. From this point onward, 'B' Company, who were in reserve, would have been positioned facing west as you continue onward to Audregnies. If you continue onward, they were spread out along the verge for about half a mile. At their farthest point, the sketch made by a 1st Battalion officer can be seen. In 1914, a railway line ran over the Audregnies road, now long gone. The old railway bridge can still be made out by the foundations seen on the right as you head toward Audregnies as can be the sunken road that Sheldrake describes as the 'hollow of a railroad'. This position became a coloured sketch that was made by a 1st Battalion officer after the war.

What3words: hello.unhappily.petitioning.

Return back toward Élouges town and you will pass houses and then see a very small car park on your left. Park here and then walk up the footpath you will see in front of you, this used to be part of the old Élouges–Quievrain railway. Carry on for another half a mile and you will come to crossroads. To your right is an old railway halt building and a wind farm. To your left, you will see a dirt track; take this track. On your left is the field where the remainder of the Norfolks were positioned. The German attacks came from the west and the north.

What3words: fundraiser.manned.puncture.

Return back to your car. Now head into the town and keep on the N553. The road will eventually bear round to the left and you will see the church on your left and a large area for parking. If possible, park by the church and then take the small road to the right of it. You will come to Élouges Communal Cemetery and within it is a small CWGC plot. This plot holds the remains of twenty-five 1st Battalion men.

As the CWGC website notes: 'The 1914 burials, in rows A and C, were mainly from the 5th Division; they are in trench graves, and the actual position of each body in the row is not known'.

What3words: amused.snips.pity.

* * * * *

On the morning of 25 August 1914, the 15th Brigade was on the move before daylight, and the 14th Brigade formed the rearguard as the Retreat from Mons started.

The brigades were told to requisition what they could from the country and the brigade CO, Major-General Lord Albert Edward Wilfred Gleichen, rode on ahead, stopping at farmhouses on the way; he bought chickens and cheese and oats wherever possible, but it was noted there was very little to be had.

They witnessed refugees on the road fleeing south-westwards, noting:

> ... pitiful crowds of women and old men and children, carrying bundles on their backs, or wheeling babies and more bundles in wheelbarrows, or perambulators, or broken-down carts. Some of the peasant women were wearing their best Sunday gowns of black bombazine and looked very hot and uncomfortable; children with their dolls or pet dogs, old women and men hobbling along, already very tired though the sun had not been up more than an hour or two, and sturdy young mothers carrying an extraordinary quantity of household stuff, trooped along, all of them anxiously asking how far off the Germans were, and whether we could hold them off, or whether they would all be killed by them,—it was a piteous sight.

The route saw the brigade skirting the forest of Mormal and then heading for Le Cateau. Here, the brigade received orders on the road to occupy part of an entrenched position to the west of the town. Gleichen only put a few men into the trenches as an observing line, and sent his commanding officers round to study them, in case they had to be held in force and bivouacked the rest of the brigade half a mile behind them.

Orders came in overnight were that they were to continue the retirement first thing in the morning; but when morning came, the Germans were so close that it was decided that it would be impossible to do so, and fresh orders were issued to hold the position they were in. The defensive line would put the village of Troisvilles on their left. Gleichen noted:

> The Dorsets were to hold this village and several hundred yards of trenches to the east of it. On their right came the Bedfords in trenches, with of course a proportion in support, and the Cheshires were put in a dip of the ground in rear of them. The 13th Brigade was on the right of the Bedfords, with the K.O.S.B.'s touching them. The Norfolks I put in a second line, in rear of the right of the Bedfords and the left of the K.O.S.B.'s, mostly along a sunken road where they dug themselves well into the banks.
>
> The 27th Brigade of Artillery, under Onslow, was put under my orders; two batteries of it were in our right rear, and the third was taken away by Sir C. F., to strengthen the right I believe.
>
> 'A' battery of the 15th Artillery Brigade was also put in close behind the Bedfords, in the dip of ground afore-mentioned, whence they did excellent execution without

being seen by the enemy. Divisional Headquarters were at Reumont, a mile behind us, with a wood in between; but we were, of course, connected up by telephone with them, as well as with our battalions and our artillery. We, i.e., the Brigade Headquarters, sat in the continuation of the hollow sandy road, in rear of the Bedfords and on the left of the Norfolks.

By 7 a.m., the 15th Brigade was in position with the 9th Brigade (3rd Division) on their left. The 4th Division, which had only arrived only that morning by train, was guarding the left flank of the line, assisted by elements of the Cavalry.

As the day wore on, the Bedfords were engaged with infantry in their front, but neither they nor the Dorsets saw much action and it fell to the 13th, 14th, and 19th Brigades who began to be heavily shelled.

I do not buy the phrase 'Lions Led by Donkeys' and the Black Adder idea that the generals were all safely behind the lines pushing their drink trolleys closer to and from Germany, and this next account shows that senior officers often put themselves in danger when Gleichen noted:

> At one moment, it must have been about 12 o'clock or later, I saw to my horror the best part of a company of Bedfords leave their trenches in our front and retire slowly and in excellent order across the open. So, I got on my horse and galloped out to see what they were doing and to send them back, as it seemed to me that some of the K.O.S.B.'s were falling back too, in sympathy. I'm afraid that my language was strong; but I made the Bedfords turnabout again, although their officer explained that he was only withdrawing, by superior battalion orders, in order to take up an advanced position further on the right; and with some of the Cheshires, whom I picked up on the way, they advanced again in extended order.

The 1st Norfolks were positioned to the right in a sunken road that ran from Troisvilles to Le Cateau and initially spent several hours trying to cut down a very big tree. In the 15th Brigade history, it was noted:

> [This was a] conspicuous feature in the whole of our position, and formed an excellent object on which the enemy could range. It was all very well; but as soon as they had cut it half through, so as to fall to the south, the south wind, which was blowing pretty strongly, not only kept it upright but threatened to throw it over to the north. This would have been a real disaster, as it would have blocked completely the sunken road along which the ammunition carts, to say nothing of artillery and other waggons, would have had to come. So, it had to be guyed up with ropes, with much difficulty; and even when teams hung on and hauled on the ropes, they could make little impression—the wind was so strong. Eventually they did manage to get it down, but even so it formed a fairly conspicuous mark.

Herbert Reeve had survived Mons and was present for Le Cateau:

> The Adjutant of the Battalion, Captain Cresswell, was killed at Mons, and a Captain Megaw was then promoted Adjutant. He told us to scrounge our rations from the roadside as no transport was available as it had all been lost at Mons, including cookers for serving meals or making tea. Our Company Commander, Major Luard D.S.O., was a wonderful fellow. He then handed over to me a mule which carried four cases of 303 to be distributed along any line of resistance we occupied during the Battle of Le Cateau....
>
> We were in a reserve line that morning when the Artillery retired. Gun carriages carried wounded and at last we had to retire too, as we were being outflanked by the Germans on our left. This was a shambles of a retreat. I was leading my mule across a field to retire, when German guns no more than 200 yards away opened fire on us, wounding my mule severely, although I managed not to get hit. Following the road of retreat towards St Quentin, I received a chit from a Staff Officer ordering me to abandon my mule which could hardly walk, and this chit I handed to Captain Luard about four days later when I caught up with the retiring Company.

This is confirmed by Robert Sheldrake, who had also managed to get out of Élouges:

> We marched about twenty miles that day. We halted in the middle of the afternoon and some companies dug outpost trenches and my company done outpost duty in them at night. There was a thunder storm that night and it was very difficult to distinguish the thunder from the roar of cannon. The next morning another company took over the advanced trenches and we dug some more in the bank alongside a road.
>
> The pioneers were busy cutting down a lone tree, that would sure be good object for range finding, but before it was down the enemy got the range and hit one of the men. Then we retired to go to another flank where a Scottish Borderer Regiment was being slaughtered. On the way I saw our commander had found a novel position for viewing the battle, he had scaffold erected behind a house and he was peeping over the top with his telescope.
>
> In the middle of the afternoon we got the order to retire, and we were glad of it too, as the shells were dropping too close and thick for us to be very comfortable. Our Captain said he was damned sorry he had to retire, he being so used to fighting the black tribes in Africa, of course he could not see the need to retire from the larger numbers of the most powerful army in Europe.

The village of Inchy came under a terrible bombardment and German infantry got into it, which resulted in both sides shelling the village, causing fires; the 3rd Division was heavily attacked by the enemy's infantry, but this was beaten off.

However, repeated German attacks and shelling eventually saw the line beginning to break, and it was reported that the 28th Royal Field Artillery lost nearly all their guns and nearly all the detachments and horses were killed.

An attack on the 19th Brigade penetrated the British line, and this forced the retirement of the 14th and 13th Brigades. As this happened, the Norfolks held their nerve and covered the retirement, but then had to retire themselves and ended up at Reumont. The 15th Brigade were very lucky at Le Cateau and managed to leave without very many casualties. But as the brigade retired, they came under sustained shrapnel fire and casualties began to mount, which included the wounding of a number of commanders. The order came that they were to fall back south-westwards along the road to Estrées. The chaos of this withdrawal was witnessed by Private Sheldrake:

> I came to a field where a Regiment had left in a hurry during the night (said to have been surprised by the enemy) covered with food and kit of all descriptions, bread, boiled beef, slices of bacon. I took my breakfast here, and enough for dinner, also a pair or two of socks, knife, fork, razor and toothbrush and one of two small articles I required to make up for mine I left at Mons. There was also rifles, whole sets of equipment and a great number of rounds of ammunition laying about too, I am sorry to say. The road was strewn with broken wagons, dead horses, sacks of sugar flour, and anything to lighten the load. It looked a terrible sight to see roads covered with army materials.

The 1st Norfolks, minus one and a half companies, sheltered in a quarry with the 2nd Royal Welsh Fusiliers and the 1st Scottish Rifles; as the Germans advanced from the north-east, they fired on them before retiring, where they ended up to the right of Honnechy where they positioned themselves to the right to give them a better field of fire against German troops advancing up the valley of the Selle from Le Cateau. Reports here thought that the Norfolks lost a lot of men in this action, but this was not so:

> Ballard and his Norfolks joined us in bits, and we heard that they had had a hard time falling back through Reumont and done very well as rear-guard. There were stories at first of their having suffered terribly and lost a lot of men; but it was not in the least true,—they had had comparatively few casualties.

The retreat continued toward Estrées and the brigade began to break up, but the Germans did not pursue giving the BEF a breather as they retired.

Guidebook

From Cambrai, take the D643 to Le Cateau–Cambresis. Having passed through Inchy, keeping on the D643, on your right you will come to the D98, signposted Troisvilles. Take this turning and continue into the village. Just prior to the war memorial, there is a turning on the left. Take that turning. The other option for you is to continue on the Cambrai–Le Cateau road and turn right at the roundabout onto the D932. Roughly 600 metres from here, there is a track on your right; take that track. On a French IGN map, this is given the name L'Abre Rond. This is the same track. Be careful: this is just a farmer's track that is uneven in places and prone to flooding. Personally, having driven down this track, I would advise that you take great care if you take your car down it. Continue on for about half a mile; pretty much central to this road is where the Norfolks were positioned for the battle.

What3words: origins.remedy.delimit.

Now return back to the D932 and head toward Reumont. Once in the village you will come to a turning on the left signposted Mairie. Take this turn and continue on and take the left turn onto Rue de Boheries. Turn at the next left, Rue Grand Mere, and start to travel out of the village. As you pass the large red-bricked farm building on your left, you will come to a natural break between that and the next house. This is where most of the Norfolks were after they retired from a sunken lane.

What3words: parts.raked.trampolines.

Return back to the D932 and turn left and head toward Maurois. Once in the village, you will see a turning on the left, which has a CWGC sign for Honnechy British Cemetery. Take this turning and continue on the D115 until you come to the Rue du Calvaire on your left, this is the same road you would take for the CWGC Cemetery.

Prior to reaching the cemetery, the houses thin out on your right. This is where the Norfolks positioned themselves to give themselves for a better field of fire against the enemy advancing from the valley of the River Selle from Le Cateau.

What3words: chamber.champions.dowries.

*****

The BEF withdrew to Saint-Quentin with the British having sustained 8,000 casualties at Le Cateau; the infantry especially paid a heavy price. This battle was to be fought in some respects as though Wellington and Napoleon were facing one another again. This is because trench warfare was still a thing of the future, although as you have read, trenches were used by the 15th Brigade, but it had predominantly been fought by two standing armies with very little cover.

Herbert Reeve was witness to this withdrawal:

Then came St Quentin. In the square stood C.S.M. Joe Haggar directing units of any Brigade or Division as to which route to take on the continued retirement. So, we slept rough with no overcoat and after about four days from leaving St Quentin, Units of the Battalion got together. We marched so long, our feet were so swollen that we dare not take our boots off as we should never get them on again. We retired through a large Forest, and then one morning Captain Luard addressed us with the words 'The retirement is suspended, we are now on the attack and we are Flank Guard to the Division that is on the extreme left of our Army'. History tells us that we had to control the left of our flank so as to defend the Channel Ports. On the second day, we were fired on by German Artillery whilst we were marching in column. We scattered, and Captain Luard shouted 'Advance, we do not retire, push forward'. This we did and captured a village where the German dinners were being cooked. So, the Battalion now had German cookers to supply us with cooked meals, the first we had had since losing our cookers at Mons.

The CSM mentioned in Reeve's account was Joseph Haggar who would be mentioned in despatches for his participation in the retreat and would later on go from the 1st Battalion to the 9th Battalion. Haggar would also be be wounded and also suffer from trench fever, but he would survive the war. The whole of the BEF continued to retreat and the 1st Norfolks acted as the brigade rearguard for most of the time, continually moving, and often coming under fire, they continued to move south. With the Allies in a certain amount of disarray, the Germans began to set their sights on Paris. Relations between the French and the British at this time had reached an all-time low, and Sir John French was of the opinion that he must withdraw the BEF to reorganise. The French military saw this as a disastrous move, and it was only after the direct intervention of the minister for war, Lord Kitchener, that John French relented and agreed to keep the BEF at the front so long as their flanks were not threatened.

As the Germans tried to surround Paris, their 1st and 2nd Armies went southeast of the capital and exposed their right flank, something that had worried the original planner of the Schlieffen Plan. The French commander, Joseph Joffre, noticed their error and managed to get John French to agree to commit the BEF to assisting the French Army in attacking the Germans all along the frontline.

Robert Sheldrake certainly approved of this change in the tide of the battle: 'The next day we started advancing and glad of it we were too, as we had quite enough of retiring, it is not very pleasant, either mentally or physically I can assure you'. But this did not come without a price and he also noted the sacrifice made by others and their fate:

I also passed a British Cavalryman lying dead in the gutter with nobody in charge of him. It did not look to me to be the proper course to adopt. I considered one man could have been left to see the proper thing was done by him, not left in the gutter like a lump of dirt. Some mother in England, some sweetheart or perhaps little children, treasured that dead body. The next day I was to see some more of this kind of neglect, there was a man of my regiment killed by shells and left, nobody even taking his identity ticket, this an artillery sergeant told me he had taken the next morning [This was a Pte Waters]. There were also about a dozen men left on the field of battle the next day no notice being taken of it as far as I could see.

Only one man with that surname was serving in the 1st Battalion when this incident was recounted. Private Thomas Waters (3/6790) had been with the battalion since it had landed in France. He survived his time with the 1st Battalion and, at some point, ended up in the 579th Home Service Company of the Labour Corps. So, it looks to me that he actually survived this incident and was evacuated out. Certainly nobody with that surname died in 1914 and that also takes into account surname changes such as Walters.

On 5 September, a desperate struggle ensued when the Battle of the Marne began. The BEF was now in an advance in what the Official History of the war termed the 'Advance to the Aisne' and this had begun on 9 September when the BEF began to pursue the German 1st Army.

Robert Sheldrake went into action on this date:

During the afternoon my company by marching under cover in ditches and through a wood managed to reinforce some Dorsets in a firing line under some apple trees, with a little bank just sufficient to cover the head from fire when laying down flat. We were ordered to fire at a ridge about 800 yards away occupied by the enemy. Thousands upon thousands of rounds of ammunition were fired and the result appeared to have been about a dozen on each side killed and a score or two wounded. There was a very (brave/foolish) officer here with the Dorsets, when we arrived he had his arm bandaged up, but he continued running along the line giving orders and showing himself and our position up to the enemy he was quite worthy of a D.C.M. but I heard he was carried in during the evening shot through the body so he may have also won a cross.

The bullets from the enemy's machine guns were clipping the leaves off the trees just above our heads beautifully.

I have no idea who the Dorset officer is, he can certainly be one of four who were wounded that day, but the action is confirmed in the Official History, which occurred at Pisseloup Ridge (also known as Hill 189), which stated:

The Germans at 2 p.m. even launched a counter attack against the left of its line, but the effort was at once smothered by British shrapnel. After more than an hour deadlock, the Norfolk and Dorsetshire of the 15th Brigade between 3 and 4 p.m. came up to the western edge of Bois des Essertis, on the flank of Hill 189, where they were abruptly checked by a violent fire from rifles and machine guns and from the battery at La Sablonniere. Unable to make progress, they stood fast and engaged in a short-range fight with the German infantry, which was entrenched within a hundred and twenty yards of them. Forty-seven dead Germans were found the next day in trenches opposite to the Dorsetshire...

The situation on the Marne had been decided when the French 6th Army had managed to stop the Germans. Their plight had initially been quite desperate, but reinforcements arrived and German units were now in retreat.

From the Official History:

The German Armies were falling back, mostly in a north-easterly direction, along the whole front as far as the Argonne, with exhausted horses, deficient supplies, and signs of failing ammunition. It remained to be seen how much further the Allies could push their success. There was no sign yet of any movement of enemy reinforcements from the north, but there were some indications that the enemy might hold the line of the Aisne: it was impossible, however, to forecast in what strength, and whether as a mere rear-guard or as a battle position.

And so, with the Marne ending and the First Battle of the Aisne about to begin, it was here that the 1st Norfolks went back into action at Missy on the Chemin des Dames. Here it was decided that the 15th Brigade would clear the Chivres Spur, which led to the Conde Fort situated north of that position. On 14 September 1914, at 4.30 p.m. a mixed group of twelve companies were sent to carry this out.

Brigadier-General Gleichen noted:

I had got together three companies of the Norfolks, three of the Bedfords, two Cheshires (in reserve), two East Surreys (14th Brigade), and two Cornwalls (13th Brigade, who had arrived via the broken bridge at Missy and some rafts hastily constructed there)—twelve companies altogether.

This force got through the opening into the wood where they found a few Germans and drove them back, killing some. Then they came to horse-shoe-shaped road further on in the wood, and some men lost their direction and began firing in front of them at what they thought were the enemy. Sadly, this was not the case and friends ended up firing on friends and a number of men turned about and retired down the hill into Missy.

This action resulted in a group of Norfolks getting well forward into the wood, where Major Charles Luard and Captain Thomas Bowlby, along with around twenty-five men, were killed or captured. Gleichen wrote of this action in the brigade history:

Luard (Norfolks) and a party of twenty-five men were well ahead in the wood, and received the order to retire, for Luard was heard shouting it to his men. But nothing has since been heard of him, and I much regret to say that he was either taken prisoner with most of his men, or, more probably, killed.

Gleichen was right with his last point and both Major Luard and Captain Bowlby were killed. Another witness to this and who also became a casualty this day was Private Sheldrake:

Then we marched into a village and were under shot and shell all day, passing some time in cellars of the houses. It was a very rainy morning again. In the afternoon we moved out under a wall. Then about 5 p.m. in the evening we climbed up a hill, passing through a company of another regiment with several wounded, and who told us there was danger ahead. But my gallant Captain dashed ahead with neither sword nor revolver in hand shouting for men to follow him, (his long looked for time had come at last).

We had not only to face the enemies fire, but our comrades below were keeping up the fire from down below on the ridge he was on.

We passed through some trees and about a score of us got into an open space about 20 or 30 yards from a German trench. I turned round and saw a German in amongst our men in the edge of the wood we had just left, so whether they had cut my comrades off or not I cannot say, for I got a bullet in my left arm that appeared to have been a ricochet from behind, no doubt one of my own men's bullets.

We got the order to lay down, and I told my comrade (Cpl W Brunning) that I was wounded, he said lay still, and I crouched down behind a little lump for cover as best I could, but after a while I thought I heard my men advancing, so I popped up my head to get a look, but got two more bullets into my back for my pains. So, I laid and thought no other thing but that my time had come. It was a funny position to lay in between two fires and could not move and expected a bullet or perhaps a bayonet to come and finish me off the little spark of life left at any moment. I thought of my wife and dear little children. I also thought my arm was smashed to pieces and it would be as well for me to be killed, so I was not a burden for the remainder of my life, but it was not to be so I am thankful to say now.

Herbert Reeve was not present for this action, but did witness other aspects of this fight:

This was the beginning of the Marne battle. We crossed blown-up bridges by barges erected by the Engineers. I was then provided with another mule for carrying 303 ammo. And so, came the Battle of the Aisne. This we crossed by bridges erected by the Engineers at a place called Missy. It was here that I criticised our leaders in Command. My Company Commander, Captain Luard and Captain Bowlby were ordered to capture the village on a hill.

I took my mule behind a church wall to distribute 303 ammo, the mule was killed and I delivered the ammo on foot. Alas, both Captain Luard and Captain Bowlby lost their lives, together with many Other Ranks.

Major Luard was aged thirty-eight and the son of the late Major-General R. E. Luard and the husband of Dorothy Frances Luard. Captain Bowlby was aged thirty-two and the son of Charles Cotsford Bowlby and Rosalie Bowlby of 17 Fairfax Road in Hampstead. Neither have known graves and are commemorated on the La Ferte-Sous-Jouarre Memorial.

Private Sheldrake's comrade can be identified as Corporal James Henry Brunning (6289). Sadly, he did not survive this action either. Aged twenty-nine, he had served in 'C' Company and was the son of Mr and Mrs Brunning of 108 Nelson Street Dereham Road in Norwich. He is now buried in II. G. 4. in Buzancy Military Cemetery. I had the honour of visiting his grave in January 2020.

Robert Sheldrake survived this action, but went into captivity:

When it was getting dark the Germans came round and searched my haversack for food, one slipped his hand in my trouser pocket and took my purse with about 6/- in it. But I had no food for them I had just eaten the last before I climbed the hill, I had a few apples, I daresay they took them. I was laying quite still pretending I was dead, till another party came later on and threw me over to get at my jack knife in my breast pocket (they had the idea that we carry these knives to slay their wounded with, just the same as I had heard our men say the German medical men carry a revolver to shoot their badly wounded, these fables are bound to circulate).

Then I shouted out in pain and told them not to shoot me. One man could speak English, he told me I should be alright, and they searched for letters or anything I had. I asked him to cut off my straps and he gave me my water bottle and lifted me up and told me there was some more men a little way down the hill, I could make my way down to them and get back to my camp.

There was several dead laying about. I had not gone far when two more Germans prowling round looking for loot from the dead spied me and carted me off to their officer, grabbing hold of my wounded arm. So, you see I had a narrow escape getting back again to the English lines.

One man marched me through a wood about a mile and a half until we arrived at Fort Clermont, an old open fort. I arrived here just before the greater part of their wounded, so I soon got my arm dressed. They cut off my coat and jacket and kept them, so I lost my watch and chain worth about £2 and everything was gone now, except my trousers, putties, braces and boots, the shirt and socks being cut off when I got to Chaumy, they had done their duty.

The order was given to retire and an early reconnaissance and attack was planned for the next morning, 15 September, to be led by the Norfolks. The attack would see the 1st Bedfords positioned on the railway to the west, the 1st Cheshires on the right, the Norfolks right front of village, with the 1st DCLI on the left.

The attack did not go well:

A careful reconnaissance was made by Done and some other Norfolk officers as soon as it was light; but the result was not promising. Fresh German trenches had been dug commanding the open space, and more wire had been put up during the night. The Norfolks were told off to lead the assault, with the Bedfords in support and the Cheshires in reserve. The Dorsets were still above Sainte Marguerite, helping the 12th Brigade, and were not available. We began by shelling that horrible Chivres Spur, but it produced little effect, as the Germans were in the wood and invisible. The Norfolks pushed on, but gradually came to a standstill in the wood, and the day wore on with little result, for the wood was desperately blind, and we were being heavily shelled at all points.

The Norfolks retired to Missy, and at 7.40 p.m. the 15th Brigade were ordered to evacuate the north bank over a new bridge.

By 16 September, the brigade was in Jury, situated to the south-west of Missy, where they stayed for a week while the 14th Brigade held the line at Missy:

It was a pretty little valley with wooded hills, running northwards to the Aisne, and on our right was a big plateau with huge haystacks dotted about the corn-fields, which served as excellent observing stations for our artillery, of which by this time we had a vast mass. The other (north) bank of the Aisne was clearly visible from here—in fact from the top of the biggest haystack there was a regular panorama to be seen, from the twin towers of Soissons Cathedral on the left to the enemy's trenches above Vailly and beyond—a beautiful landscape typical of La Belle France, even to the rows of poplars in the distance, marking the Routes Nationales from Soissons to other places of distinction.

Here the 15th Brigade held the line and dug in—a shape of things to come—and joined the line with the 4th Division who held the line from St Marguerite westwards.

At this point, the Norfolks had been sent off to support the 3rd Division, and by 27 September, they were at Chassemy where they stayed until 7 November 1914.

In total, between 14 and 17 September 1914, the 1st Norfolks lost fifty-two men killed (most have no known grave).

Guidebook

Come into Missy-sur-Aisne from the D925 and at the T-Junction turn left. Take the next right, signposted Chivres-Val, to get onto the D53. Take the next right turn and at the T-junction turn left. This road will take you up to the Bois de

Missy. Park up at the village cemetery and when you face the cemetery gates you will see a track next to it.

This is the wood that Major Luard and Captain Bowlby fought with a handful of Norfolks. The track is steep and you need to be fit to climb up here. Walk along this track until the bricked wall on you right ends. You will see a path on your right, which leads to a small ravine with thick walls on either side. On your right, you will see the remains of shelters. This takes you to the position that was described as the horse-shoe-shaped road.

This is where the 15th Brigade fired on each other and is the rough position where Luard and Bowlby went into the wood to be lost. It is also the area where Robert Sheldrake was wounded and then captured.

What3words: conductors.battle.sandpit.

*****

At the end of this, both sides vied to outflank the other in what became known as the 'Race to the Sea'. The German 6th Army had reached Bapaume on 26 September and advanced to Thiepval on the 27th, in the middle of what was to become the Somme battlefield of 1916. The German aim was to drive westward to the English Channel, seizing the industrial and agricultural regions of Northern France, cutting off the supply route of the BEF and isolating it. However, between 1 and 6 October, the German 6th Army's offensive north of the Somme was halted by the French 10th Army under the direction of General Ferdinand Foch.

German cavalry encountered the French 21st Corps near Lille and were stopped there. The only gap remaining was in Flanders, with the Belgians on the Yser to the north and the French in Picardy to the south. The Germans now turned their attentions to the Artois Region in France and Flanders where the BEF had redeployed in order to shorten their supply route through Boulogne and Calais.

The Belgian Army's escape south-west down the Flanders coast was covered by a British force; this included the 7th Division and was under the command of General Sir Henry Rawlinson, which had originally been sent to relieve them but arrived too late.

The Belgians, later reinforced by the British Royal Naval Division, fought the Germans at Antwerp, but this finally fell to the Germans on 10 October. The Belgian and British forces then withdrew to a line on the River Yser. All the Belgian and British troops managed to leave, with the exception of one of the naval brigades, which were interned in Holland.

Although the loss of Antwerp was a severe blow to the Allies, the delay in their capitulation slowed down the German advance to the coast. The British had time to move up from the Aisne and the Belgians were able to establish themselves on the extreme left of the line between Dixmunde and the sea. The Germans reached Lille on 13 October and the British reached Balleuil the next day.

The line formed in Artois was established by the Battle of La Bassée fought between 12 and 27 October with the British holding Arras, but the Germans managed to capture Lens.

On 7 October 1914, the 1st Norfolks entrained, having rejoined the 15th Brigade, and were sent to the trenches situated to the east of Béthune at La Bassée.

Lieutenant-General Gleichen explained why:

> The idea was that we were to push forward to Festubert and act as a pivot, with our right near the canal at Rue de l'Épinette, to the 3rd Division and the remainder of the Corps, which were swinging slowly round to their right so as eventually to face south-east and take La Bassée.
>
> At first my orders directed me to leave a gap between myself and the canal, the gap being filled by French troops; but shortly afterwards I was told that the Brigade was to hold from Festubert to the canal, relieving the French cavalry here, who were to hold on till we got there; and I paid a visit to the French cavalry General at Gorre to make sure that this would be done. The line was a horribly extended one—about two miles; and the prospect was not entrancing.

The battle opened here when the Germans attacked along the canal; but they were checked by the Dorsets. On 13 October, it was learnt that a company of the 1st Cheshires had been captured or killed by the Germans about Rue d'Ouvert. Gleichen noted that this day was 'terrible' and the Germans shelled Givenchy heavily with the 1st Bedford holding onto one part of the village while the Germans held the other. Sadly, the artillery was too much for them, and after losing about sixty casualties, many of them killed by falling houses, they gradually fell back to trenches in rear of the village.

The Dorsets on the left of the Bedfords and the 1st KOSB on their left were on the south side of the canal where they dug in and drove the Germans back but were attacked from the left rear, and a heavy fire poured upon their men as they retired on their supports. They were also shot down from the embankment on the south of the canal—from just where they had expected the 1st KOSBs to be. It is also said that the Germans carried out a ruse here where they made out they were surrendering and when the Dorsets came out they were cut down.

I cannot confirm the truth in that and whether that is true or not, but it ended up with the Dorsets moving back to Pont Fixe after losing thirteen officers killed or wounded and 396 other ranks suffering a similar fate.

The Brigade HQ had to withdraw in the evening from Festubert to what was described as a 'foul big farm about half a mile back'. This stink came from a cesspool in the middle of the yard. It was labelled 'Stink Farm'.

On 14 October, there was a general order given to push forward with the canal to their right, but the 15th Brigade could not get forward and the 13th Brigade, on the other side of the Canal, were also held up.

On 15 October, the French attacked Vermelles, and the 15th Brigade were ordered to support them but the French made no progress so the attack was called off.

On 16th October, under the cover of thick mist, the 15th Brigade moved the Bedfords into Givenchy and the Norfolks went into Rue d'Ouvert and St Roch. Then the Devons were ordered to make the footbridge to Canteleux, but in the darkness came under a heavy fire and fell back.

On 17 October, figures were seen strolling about Canteleux, with the Norfolks reporting that they had about sixty men in it who had penetrated the position during the night. In the afternoon, the 15th Brigade was ordered to advance to the line straddling the Canteleux Bridge to Violaines. The Devons pushed on with the French, but were again obliged to retire from the vicinity of the bridge by heavy fire, and took up their position in the advanced position that the Dorsets had occupied on the 13th.

The Cheshires were able to work their way well forward and reported their arrival at Violaines at 4 p.m., having reached the position via Rue du Marais; by the evening, the 14th Brigade was in touch with the Cheshires and continued to move forward very slowly.

From the Official History of the Great War:

> Nevertheless, Givenchy was retaken on the 16th by the 15th Brigade and, on the following day, though his right was held up by enfilade fire from across the canal, Br Gen Count Gleichen made a substantial advance, the Norfolks reaching Canteleux, half way between Givenchy and La Bassée, and the Cheshire at 4 p.m. securing Violaines, still further to the east and only a mile north west of La Bassée.

On 18 October, a general advance was ordered for 6 a.m. But any attack was doomed to failure if the French did not advance on the right and the Germans held the south bank of the Canal, which exposed the brigade's right flank to a terrible enfilade fire.

On 19 October, another attack was ordered for 7 a.m. in conjunction with the French. But in the event, the attack did not occur until noon and the French 295th Regiment attacked the canal and footbridge obliquely, and lost heavily.

Eventually, after conferring with Generals Morland and Franklin, after it was pointed out that any attack would expose the right flank to a deadly enfilade fire from across the canal, Gleichen was ordered not to advance in force. On the 20th and 21st, the Germans kept the 15th Brigade fairly busy, but there were no major attacks.

It was on 22 October that the 1st Norfolks were called into the battle, and at 6 a.m., the 1st Cheshires were invaded in front and flank by a surprise attack of the enemy in great force and had to fall back towards Rue du Marais, losing heavily, and eventually ended up at Violaines. At 8.30 a.m., three companies of

Bedfords were sent from Givenchy to St Roch to support the 13th Brigade, who were hanging at Rue du Marais, and it was ascertained the combined 13th and 14th Brigades were to make a counterattack on Rue du Marais in the afternoon. This did not happen, but sporadic fighting here was enough to stop the Germans for the time being.

Here the Norfolks were positioned between Violaines and Canteleux and along with the rest of the 15th Brigade had to fall back on a line roughly between Festubert and Givenchy. On 23 October, Gleichen noted a very telling overview of what was left here of regiments that had been fighting since Mons:

My Brigade now consisted of the Devons (14th Brigade), West Ridings (13th Brigade), and the Norfolks (15th Brigade). The remains of the Cheshires and Dorsets were withdrawn and put into the Rue de Béthune hamlet in rear of Festubert, under orders of the 13th Brigade as their reserve, whilst the Bedfords were attached to, I think, the 14th Brigade, somewhere Quinque Rue way. It was a glorious jumble, and what happened to the rest of the 13th Brigade I do not know. I believe they combined in some way with the 14th, but I know that two days afterwards the Brigadier was left with only one fighting battalion, the West Kents, I think.

An expected night attack did not happen this day, and on 24 October, another report came in that they were to be attacked. This attack did not materialise and it was not until 25 October that another determined attack took place.

Herbert Reeve had a lucky escape at Festubert:

October had arrived and the 5th Division were then relieved for a spell. We then found ourselves being transferred to the left of our line and we arrived at La Bassée Canal and Festubert. Of course, no real defence line had been established. We occupied ditches and banks, and it was here that I again had one of those awful experiences. Eight of us were in a ditch in front of Festubert, when we were enfiladed by a large German patrol—it was a foggy morning. Reinforcements arrived, but I was the only one who escaped alive from that ditch. When we were relieved at night, we had lost two officers, but coloured troops had cut trenches for our relief. We spent three weeks in Festubert. We had boiled chicken for dinner (pinched, of course!) and roast chicken to take with us to the trenches. Some old soldiers ransacked empty shops and so changed their under-clothing. I had no change of underclothing until November, so you see it was three months since leaving Belfast the previous August before I had a change of underclothing. No mules for me now, with the front lines being consolidated.

The Norfolks lost one officer and fifty men killed or wounded in this attack, but by now, the emergency was over as the 15th Brigade had now been reinforced by the Indian (Lahore) Division. But another telling account notes that for every four men from the Indian infantry there was just one Norfolk man left.

The officer who fell here was Lieutenant Thomas Algernon Fitzgerald Foley, who died aged twenty-four and was the son of Mrs Frances Jane Foley, of 'Rudhall' of Ross-on-Wye, Herefordshire, and the late Vice-Admiral Francis John Foley:

> He had just made a most gallant advance to the trenches with his men under heavy fire, and had reached there safely. He was in the very foremost of the British lines when he fell, and he died at the head of his men, driving back a most desperate attack by overwhelming numbers of the enemy. He was buried, like a soldier, where he fell. The actual place where he was laid to rest is close to the most advanced trenches, as our line in that part of the battlefield has not advanced a yard since the day when he fell gallantly defending it.

Lieutenant Foley has no known grave and is commemorated on the Le Touret Memorial.

Nothing occurred until 29 October, when the Germans again attacked in force:

> But the ball began full early by a violent attack on the Devons at dawn, and another at 7 on the 2nd Manchesters, both hard pressed, but both repulsed—the Manchesters, who were short of ammunition, getting well in with the bayonet. I sent one company of the Norfolks to support the Devons, but I could barely afford even that. The enemy was entrenching within 200 to 400 yards of all my battalions, pushing out saps from their trenches along the ditches and folds of the ground, and connecting up their heads in a most ingenious and hidden manner. The French were not attacked, so they sent a couple of companies at my request to Les Plantins, behind the Norfolks. However, after another attack between 9 and 10 a.m. the Germans dried up for the present.

Luckily for the 15th Brigade, they were relieved fully by the Lahore Division on 30 October 1914. There was very little left of the brigade:

> Our prayers were destined to be answered, for on this morning we were ordered, in spite of the desultory fighting going on, to hand over to Macbean's Brigade and go north. This only meant the Brigade Staff, two companies Bedfords, and about 300 Cheshires and 300 Dorsets who had been in reserve to the 14th Brigade; but they were not in a very happy condition, for they had hardly any officers left and had been extremely uncomfortable for the last week, being hauled out of their barns on most nights and made to sleep in the wet open as supports in case of attack.

However, to assist the newcomers, the Norfolks and half of the Bedfords remained in the trenches around Givenchy until 13 November when they moved northward to Ypres.

Guidebook

From Violaines, take the D167, Rue de Wandhofen, heading towards Givenchy-les-la-Bassée. As you come out village, stop on the verge with a small road turning right opposite you. If you now look back towards Violaines and then pan from left to right, you are looking at the direction the 15th Brigade took as they retreated, being followed by the German 13th Division. The 15th Brigade would have crossed this road before their line ended in the fields on your left between Givenchy-les-la-Bassée and the small hamlet of Rue d'Ouvert.

What3words: amble.contrasting.populate.

3

1st Battalion, Messines–Wulverghem Road: Christmas Truce 1914

It is now time to look at something that has been contested for many years. Before we look at that, it is time to just take stock of where we are in the First World War timeline.

A furious battle ensued around the Belgian town of Ypres; in fact, it became known as the First Battle of Ypres. It was here that the hard-pressed BEF took the brunt of the German attacks, and virtually every British infantry unit that had been in France since August saw action there; many would lose up to 70 per cent of their fighting strength at the end of Ypres and this famous town would become known as 'Wipers' to every British soldier who would serve there from then onwards. The battle for it would commence on 18 October with the Germans pushing the British from the direction of Becelaere.

The Germans renewed their attacks on 30 October on a smaller scale on the front from Gheluvelt, 5 miles to the east of Ypres, to the Messines Ridge. To the north of this line, where I Corps was positioned, the situation was very uncertain for a time and at Gheluvelt itself the Germans broke through, although they were soon driven out again. The regular waves of enemy attacks proved very costly to both sides, the Germans themselves referring to it as 'The murder of the children of Ypres'. This is based on the story that many of the German infantry were young men who had only just finished their education prior to joining up. To the south the British Cavalry Corps was driven from Messines Ridge. Allied reinforcements were moved to the front around Ypres to stabilise the Allied position and to prepare for the next attack.

The third major assault, which began on 11 November, covered an even narrower area with the centre of the attack set astride the famous Menin Road, with Ypres itself being the principle objective. South of the road the British successfully withstood the continuous German attacks, but to the north they broke through. Fortunately, the Germans hesitated at this critical point even though there was nothing in front of them apart from a line of British guns. A counterattack by an improvised force, which included cooks and batmen, was a success and because of this battle, Ypres would remain symbol of Allied resistance and would forever be set in stone within the history of the BEF in the First World War. It became such a significant place that it would be fought over another four times in the conflict.

Although the crisis was over, fighting continued until 24 November. Casualties were severe on both sides, with the loss of irreplaceable professional manpower. The British alone suffered losses of 50,000 men killed or wounded; the French and Germans casualties were much higher. The line then settled and neither side succeeded in gaining the upper hand. The war of movement stopped and a new type of warfare ensued.

The exhausted armies on both sides began to dig in and trench warfare was born with a continuous line of trenches stretching from the Belgian coast to the Swiss border. By the end of 1914, the BEF had incurred 86,000 casualties.

What is perhaps fitting for this part of the First World War is that the men of the BEF did not fail their king:

> Though their dearest friends, comrades of many years, fell beside them, they fought with the majesty of their ancestors, without anger or malice, trusting always in the good cause of their country. Their good health in quagmire of trenches under constant rain of itself testified to their discipline. Sober, temperate and self-respecting they were not to be discouraged by wounds or sickness. There could be no fear as to the final victory, if only more armies of such soldiers could be brought into being in sufficient numbers and without delay, and conveyed in security across the Channel to France.

From the Official History of the Great War:

> At the beginning of December 1914, the 1st Battalion Norfolk Regiment was serving in and out of the trenches around Neuve-Église and then eventually Wulverghem situated to the south of Ypres. By now this area had become a quieter sector now that the 1st Battle of Ypres came to an end and the Norfolks were getting to know their craft as they learnt about trench warfare and many men died through sniping and artillery.

Herbert Reeve had a nasty shock here:

> I was then promoted Corporal, and we found ourselves transferred to a place called Neuve-Église about twelve miles to the right of Ypres. We had been relieved by the

Cavalry, they looked so clean and smart and they smiled and said that they had left their long-faced friends [meaning their horses] to take a quiet rest. We relieved the French at this place and it must have been December by then. The French dead hung on the barbed wire and there were the dead in the trenches. A pal of mine saw a heap of something covered with straw, he reported this to Serjeant Ambrose and said that it must be a heap of potatoes. So, we were on the scrounge that night and went to investigate, and what do you think we found?—just a heap of dead Frenchmen covered with straw.

On 3 December, they relieved the 1st Battalion Dorsetshire Regiment in trenches on the Wulverghem–Messines road. The war diary for the battalion is very basic and there is no mention of casualties within it.

The history of the Norfolk Regiment in the Great War had this to say about this period:

Wherever they were, the men were working hard. If they had not to supply working parties for the improvement of trenches, they were busy at training, either general or in special subjects, attacks, machine gun or Lewis gun instruction, or one of the innumerable special branches which characterize warfare in the twentieth century. In the front and support trenches it was always the same, utter discomfort, constant shelling by the German artillery in varying quantities, and with varying results in the shape of casualties. One day there would be no casualties, the next perhaps fourteen or fifteen, the next two or three.

However, with records that we can access, we know that eight men were killed between 4 and 23 December 1914. The first man to be killed was Private William Fuller (8640), aged nineteen, who was the son of Fred and Maria Fuller of 120 Ber Street in Norwich who was killed in action on 4 December. Next came Private Walter George Hardiment (7271), also aged nineteen, the son of Ann Sophia Hardiment of 15 Morley Street in Norwich.

Private Arthur Coggles (7068) and Private Edgar Shearman (7021) were killed in action on 6 December 1914. I visited Arthurs' grave in Poelcappelle British Cemetery in December 2015, just over 100 years after he died, and it is sad that Edgar, who was aged thirty-two, has no known grave and is now commemorated on the Menin Gate.

Edgar was the son of Mrs E. Shearman of Sugar Alms Houses in King's Lynn and the husband of Jane E. Shearman of 4 Wanford's Cottages Wood Street in King's Lynn. Again, there is no mention in the war as to what happened to them.

This area was considered to be a quiet sector, but in 1914, it was far from being that way and there were still actions being fought in that sector right up to Christmas.

On 14 December an attack was launched by the 8th Brigade at Wytschaete; this failed with heavy casualties. On 18 December 1914, another attack was launched by the 22nd Brigade at La Boutillerie; this also failed with heavy casualties. On 19 December, one man from the Norfolks was killed; this was Lance Corporal Sydney Bacon (7310) from Shouldham. On 20 December, two men were lost. These were Private Jack Grigglestone (6361) from Thorpe Hamlet and Private Sydney Samuel Cork (7090) who died of wounds. Jack has no known grave and is commemorated on the Menin Gate and Sydney was buried in Nieuwkerke (Neuve-Église) Churchyard. Finally, Private Albert Edward Woodbine (7188) was killed on 22 December, aged twenty-six, and was the son of Mr and Mrs John Woodbine of 117 Goldwell Road in Lakenham.

Famous wartime cartoonist Bruce Bairnsfather recounted an episode that has been leapt on by others and it became one of the focal points for many of the centenary events in held in 2014. This included the abomination that is now the football memorial that stands close to St Yvon and on the edge of Ploegsteert Wood, known as Plugstreet Wood to the British soldiers who served there. He stated: 'Around noon, a football match was suggested. Someone had evidently received a deflated football as a Christmas present'.

This mention of football came forty years after the event when he was interviewed in 1954 for a television piece. And, according to Lieutenant Kurt Zehmisch, two English soldiers brought a football to the German trenches. The first account is false and the writings of Lt Zehmisch have been misinterpreted. I will come onto those later.

Also, in an online article in *The Telegraph*, dated 11 December 2014, the title stated: 'Belgian monument unveiled to mark "humanity" of British and German soldiers who put down their arms and left their trenches to play football during an unofficial truce on Christmas Day 1914'.

These headlines and articles were printed all over the world and there is that romanitised notion that men got out of their trenches and all played a jolly old game of football in no-man's-land when the guns fell silent. Except that football between the British and Germans never took place at St Yvon and so the memorial to it is citing a piece of history that did not happen there.

The Christmas Truce that occurred on 25 December 1914 is fact and there are numerous accounts from the time that confirm this. But what is not as easy to confirm is the notion that both sides played football against each other. Certainly, many of the veterans who were there that day refute this and there are few primary sources that mention this occurring.

Secondly, this has not been helped because we also have accounts from veterans recorded later on, such as that made by Ernie Williams in 1983, who had served with the 1/6th Cheshire Regiment, where he states:

> The ball appeared from somewhere, I don't know where, but it came from their side—it wasn't from our side that the ball came. They made up some goals and one fellow went in goal and then it was just a general kick about. I should think there

were about a couple of hundred taking part. I had a go at the ball. I was pretty good then, at 19. Everybody seemed to be enjoying themselves. There was no sort of ill-will between us. There was no referee, and no score, no tally at all. It was simply a melee—nothing like the soccer you see on television. The boots we wore were a menace—those great big boots we had on—and in those days the balls were made of leather and they soon got very soggy.

This is now widely considered by experts to be a fabrication of the truth where Ernie Williams was almost prompted into saying what he felt the interviewer, Malcolm Brown, wanted to hear. It is reputed that Malcolm Brown himself did not believe Ernie's tale. And certainly, when he is trying to intimate that football was played by hundreds of soldiers on both sides, surely if that were so, there would have been accounts from the time? So sadly, there is the misconception that all over the line this occurred.

The accounts and reports about football have to be carefully studied because virtually all of them are false mainly because they came out a good while after the event (e.g. in 1916 or even later on as with the case of Ernie Williams).

Another example of how things get misinterpreted is this account, again in the same sector as where Bairnsfather served. Henry Williamson wrote about the Christmas Truce several times. He mentions football once in a fictional novel, *A Fox Under My Cloak*, published in 1955: '... a football was kicked into the air, and several men ran after it. The upshot was a match proposed between the two armies, to be held in a field between the German lines'. The watchword here is 'proposed'. And yet the account by Henry Williams is also taken to be an accurate account of football being played.

The other way that accounts come is from men serving in regiments that if you actually looked at where they were, they were not in the same place or can be discounted because of what others said at the time.

This is what Malcolm Brown and Shirley Seaton had to say about it in their excellent book *Christmas Truce*, which was first published in 1984 when we still had veterans who had witnessed the truce to speak to. I would urge anyone who is interested in reading more about the truth behind the Christmas Truce to read this book:

To many people it has come to be accepted that the central feature of the Christmas Truce was a game, or possibly games, of football in which British and Germans took part. Indeed, to some, the whole event is not so much 'the truce' as 'the football match'. It is, of course, an attractive idea, carrying as it does not only the heart-warming thought of enemies at friendly play, but also the appealing if politically niave implication that nations would be far better employed in settling their differences in the fields of sport rather than on the field of war. Yet there are those, including some veterans of 1914, who doubt if any football match took place at all.

And this is why we have to state that Bairnsfather's mentioning of football in the TV interview is not true. This came way after the event took place. There is no doubt Bairnsfather and Zehmisch were serving at St Yvon when the Christmas Truce happened. In *Bullets & Billets*, Bairnsfather gives a very clear account of what happened at St Yvon on Christmas Day 1914 and all it does is help to corroborate what others said who were serving with the 1st Regiment Warwicks at the time.

Captain Robert Hamilton noted that 'A' Company of the 1st Regiment Warwicks would have played the Saxons but were relieved. CSM George Beck (6229) wrote in his diary that the Germans shouted across a challenge to play football on Christmas Eve, but then there is no mention of a game being played. What we can also confirm is that 'C' Company of 1st Regiment Warwicks played a game among themselves. This is now generally agreed that this is the game mentioned by Lt Zehmisch of IR134, whose account from his diary actually says: 'The English brought a soccer ball from the trenches, and pretty soon a lively game ensued'.

That statement even now could be interpreted as confirming football was played between both sides. However, the reality is that Taff Gillingham of Khaki Chums fame met the son of Rudolf Zehmisch and Barbara Littlejohn, the daughter of Bruce Bairnsfather, in March 2002. This is what he had to say about what they said about this incident:

> … both Rudolf and Barbie were very clear on one thing—that there was no football between 1st R. Warwicks and IR134 at Plugstreet. Rudolf made it very clear that his Father's diary refers to British soldiers playing a game amongst themselves. At no point does he refer to a game between the Warwicks and his own men. The German military historian Rob Shaefer agrees with Rudolf.

In relation to Bruce Bairnsfather, Taff goes on to say:

> Barbie was equally adamant. As she pointed out, had there been any football there her Father would have mentioned it in his book and almost certainly drawn a cartoon of it as, in her words, 'My Father loved the absurd things in life'.

And this is my final argument with regards to Bruce Bairnsfather. He details everything about the day in *Bullets and Billets*, and the main theme he concentrates on when he sees the Germans in no-man's-land is this meeting:

> I spotted a German officer, some sort of lieutenant I should think, and being a bit of a collector, I intimated to him that I had taken a fancy to some of his buttons. We both then said things to each other which neither understood, and agreed to do a swap. I brought out my wire clippers and, with a few deft snips, removed a couple of his buttons and put them in my pocket. I then gave him two of mine in exchange.

The reality is that, of the thousands of men who may have taken part in the truce, only around twenty to thirty men may have played football with the Germans. We do have accounts from German soldiers, written soon after the truce, to state that they played against their British opponents, but it is one specific incident that only occurred in one specific part of the Western Front.

Two German soldiers, one called Johannes Niemann, both served in IR133 and Niemann recounts his experiences while serving in trenches on a frozen meadow at Frelinghien:

> Then a Scot produced a football ... a regular game of football began, with caps laid on the ground as goalposts. The frozen meadow was ideal [to play on]. One of us had a camera with us. Quickly the two sides gathered together in a group, all neatly lined up with the football in the middle.... The game ended 3:2 to Fritz.

The second account comes from a letter discovered more recently where the second soldier from IR133 wrote to his mother and mentioned, 'playing ball with the English' so this helps to confirm the account by Johannes Niemann and the position mentioned by Niemann correlates to his regiment playing against the 2nd Battalion Argyll and Sutherland Highlanders. However, we do not have anything concrete from the 2nd A&SH to confirm they played against the Germans.

Now that is perhaps enough to confirm football being played on Christmas Day, but there is one more story that can be corroborated from the thousands of them out there, which we will now look at, and it involves the 1st Battalion, Norfolk Regiment.

On Christmas Eve, the weather changed to a hard frost. In the evening, the Germans were seen to place Christmas trees with candles on their parapets and they are heard to be singing carols. It was here that something amazing would happen on Christmas Day.

Herbert Reeve was in the line for the truce but does not make mention of what others would witness during this time: 'And so, came Christmas 1914. We received Princess Mary's Christmas gift of pipe, tobacco and cigarettes, and I still have this in my possession, as issued. Then the fraternisation took place on Christmas Eve. My Company were in reserve line at the time'. The party line laid down by the Norfolk Regimental history has this to say about the Christmas Truce of 1914:

> On Christmas Day occurred the famous meeting with the Germans in 'No-Man's Land' which drew down the wrath of G.H.Q. and a demand for names of officers, who, it was held, should have prevented it. The matter was eventually dropped, and no harm was, as a matter of fact, done, seeing that our men managed to have a good look at the German defences, and took good care that the fraternization did not spread over to their own trenches.

It is little wonder when you look at that narrative that the reports of the Germans meeting the Norfolks was reported in a very official way by officers who reported back to GHQ. Of these reports, there are three in the war diary. The first comes from Lieutenant George Philip Burlton:

> On December 25th I was in command of the right-hand fire trench of the Noroflk Regiment's position. During the morning I noticed groups of the enemy and British Troops belonging to units if the 4th Division meeting half way between their trenches. At about 1 p.m., one of the enemy left the trench opposite our own and came unarmed toward us. I sent a Corporal to meet him half way. After a time more Germans crossed towards us and I allowed an equal number of my men to meet them. Seeing a German officer also out in the open I went to meet him myself. At about 2.30 p.m. all our men under my command were back in the trench.

Captain John Percival Longfield noted:

> On the afternoon of Christmas Day about 2.15 p.m. when I was in the fire trenches, the men near me, were sniping at the enemy who appeared to be exposing himself in a very unnessary manner. Shortly afterwards a report came from the right that both sides were talking together, our men were immediately ordered to cease fire and I went over to the right to see what was happening and found out that the situation was as reported.
>
> The Germans were then seen appearing in all directions and we permitted our men to meet them half way between the trenches, this being the only apparent way of keeping them from coming right on to our trenches. Both sides were of course completely unarmed.

OC 'A' Company, Captain John Bagwell, observed:

> At about 2.15 p.m. one of my Corporals came running along the back of the trench, in what I thought was a most reckless manner, and said that on my right our troops and the Germans were talking to each other. I ordered my men to cease fire, but told them not to leave the trenches, as I feared a trap. I went along to where our other company was, on my right opposite La Petite Douve Farm, with Captain Longfield, and found that it was quite true, and that both sides, as far as I couldsee to my right, were collected, unarmed, between the trenches, and were singing together. By this time the Germans opposite my Comapny, had all left their trenches, unarmed, and I permitted my men to go and meet them half way. Where the first start of the affair was, I do not know, but on both sides of me, as far as I could see, the same thing was taking place.

Of these reports, you can see that the officers were reluctant to place the blame on their shoulders, and the reports are very much a way of trying to lessen the blow on them.

It is also sad to note that two of the three were killed later on in the war. Lt Burlton was captured on 4 June and died on 5 June 1916 during a local German attack on the Bailleul–Arras road where mines were exploded under the British lines; the 1st Battalion lost sixty-five men killed, wounded, or missing, and he has no known grave and is commemorated on the Arras Memorial. Captain Longfield was killed in a bombardment on 30 September 1915 while the battalion was in trenches opposite Maricourt. He was aged twenty-nine and is now buried in Bray-sur-Somme Communal Cemetery.

But these reports aside, which make no mention of football, over a Twitter discussion about the 1st Battalion Norfolk Regiment and their involvement in the truce, it became very apparent that this battalion did play football in no-man's-land between the lines just to the north of the Wulverghem–Messines road.

In a newspaper cutting detailing the experiences of a soldier called Albert Wyatt, who came from Thetford, and who was in the trenches with the 1st Norfolks on 25 December.

Football in the Firing Lines

Thetford Corporal Among the Players

The strange Christmas scenes which occurred in the British and German firing lines are described in a letter written by Corporal A. Wyatt to his parents a short while ago. He regards it as the most historic day ever spent on the battlefield. He says that when 'A' Company, 1st Norfolks to which he belongs arrived in the trenches on the 24th December they found everything quiet. There was no rifle firing.

They had been in the trenches a short time when they heard someone singing Christmas hymns. Then all at once there were shouts of 'Three cheers for the English'. To their surprise the voice came from the German trenches. 'Then our men and the Germans,' Corporal Wyatt proceeds, 'started singing hymns together. The same thing carried on nearly all night and there was a sharp frost to make things look better. On Christmas morning it was very thick and we could not see far in front of us till about midday.

'Then we heard the Germans shouting, "Come over here, we will not fire!" They got out of their trenches and started walking about on the top. Our chaps, seeing them did the same. Then all at once came the surprise. The Germans started walking towards our trenches, and two or three of our chaps went out to meet them. When they met, the Germans speaking in English wished them a Merry Christmas.

'Then came the fun. Everybody on each side walked out to the middle of the two firing lines and shaking hands wish each other Merry Christmas. To our surprise we found we were fighting men old enough to be our fathers, and they told us they had had enough of the war, as they were nearly all married men.

'We finished up in the same old way, kicking footballs about between the firing lines. So, football in the firing line between the British and Germans is the truth as I was one that played.'

And we also have an account in an interview at the end of December 1914 with Company-Sergeant Major Frank Naden of the 1/6th Cheshire Regiment, which was printed in the *Evening Mail* in Newcastle on 31 December 1914; he states:

On Christmas Day one of the Germans came out of the trenches and held his hands up. Our fellows immediately got out of theirs, and we met in the middle, and for the rest of the day we fraternised, exchanging food, cigarettes and souvenirs. The Germans gave us some of their sausages, and we gave them some of our stuff.

The Scotsmen started the bagpipes and we had a rare old jollification, which included football in which the Germans took part. The Germans expressed themselves as being tired of the war and wished it was over. They greatly admired our equipment and wanted to exchange jack knives and other articles. Next day we got an order that all communication and friendly intercourse with the enemy must cease but we did not fire at all that day, and the Germans did not fire at us.

What is significant about this is that Wyatt and Naden would have been serving with each other in the same place because the 1/6th Cheshires were attached to the 1st Norfolks to be trained in trench warfare. Naden's accounts also backs up a lot of what Albert Wyatt stated and to me confirms this aspect of what occurred as being accurate.

This incident has become something that was put into film in 2014 when the Sainsbury's advert about the Christmas Truce came out. If you look at the British soldiers in the advert, you will see that they are men of the Cheshire and Norfolk Regiment.

Sadly, the truce did not last, as Herbert Reeve noted: 'We went to the front line the following night and were met with a hail of bullets—an end to any such fraternisation. The High Command took a poor view of this and we were immediately posted further left towards Ypres, at a place called Dranouter'.

The argument about football and the truce is something that comes around each Christmas, and people often brag that they have proof that football was played elsewhere, including the area where the UEFA memorial now stands. I have yet to see any evidence of those boasts.

Guidebook

To get to the site, take the N314 from Messines heading towards Wulverghem. If you are coming from Ypres, you would turn right; if coming from Ploegesteert, you would turn left. Approximately 1.5 km on you, can turn right onto Kortestraat and you are now positioned in no-man's-land between the British and German lines of December 1914. To your front is Mittel Ferme, to your right is Back Ferme. In the distance, you will see Mount Kemmel. No-man's-land was in the fields either side of this road with the British trenches running north to south and cutting across the Messines road and the German positions clustered around the two farms you can see.

What3words: irritated.rebellion.bravery.

4

The Service Battalions of the Norfolk Regiment: The Kitchener Men

At the start of hostilities, as we have already seen, the county had two regular battalions of the Norfolk Regiment serving in other parts of the world. But the Norfolk Regiment also had the 3rd (Reserve) Battalion, who were based at Britannia Barracks in Norwich, as well as the Territorial Force (TF) units, which were volunteer battalions. Part of this force was the East Anglian Division, the units of which were on their annual summer camp when war was declared, so emergency orders were sent to recall them. By 5 August 1914, they were fully mobilised for full-time war service, and by 20 August, the entire division was positioned around Chelmsford, Bury St Edmunds, and Norwich.

The TF was designed to be a home force but could be used for overseas service should crisis erupt in the Empire. It officially came to be on 1 April 1908 and Norfolk raised three infantry battalions—the 1/4th, 1/5th, and 1/6th (Cyclists)—as well as one cavalry battalion (the King's Own Royal Regiment of Norfolk Yeomanry) and various units that would support the main battalions such as the reserve battalions, field ambulance, artillery, and service corps.

Although the 4th and 5th TF battalions went to other theatres of war, with the 6th Battalion remaining at home, many of these men did end up in the regular battalions later on in the war and we will meet a different version of the 1/1st Yeomanry Battalion in 1918.

So, before long, the Regular Army needed to be expanded, and a further three regular Norfolk battalions were raised. The 7th (Service) Battalion Norfolk Regiment, under the command of Lieutenant-Colonel John W. V. Carroll, was formed at Shorncliffe on 22 August 1914 as part of K1.

K1 came under the 'Kitchener Battalions'. This was based on, as part of a national decision made by Field Marshal Earl Kitchener of Khartoum, who had taken on the role of minister of war on 5 August 1914. He had wasted no time in looking at expanding the army with volunteers. These volunteers would sign up for general service for the duration of the war, and on 6 August 1914, parliament sanctioned an increase of 500,000 men of all ranks.

On 11 August 1914, the famous call to arms 'Your King and Country need you: a call to arms' was published. It called for the first 100,000 men to enlist. This figure was achieved within two weeks. On top of that, Army Order 324, dated 21 August 1914, created six new divisions for these volunteers. This first recruitment drive became known as 'K1'. The initial divisions raised became the 9th (Scottish) Division, 10th (Irish) Division, 11th (Northern) Division, 12th (Eastern) Division, 13th (Western) Division, and the 14th (Light) Division.

Being the first Kitchener Battalion, the 7th Battalion came under orders of 35th Brigade in the 12th (Eastern) Division. You often hear the term 'Pals' battalions for this aspect of First World War recruitment. This was the idea that these battalions were raised from local towns and villages made up of those that knew each other or were related. This is not so for the 7th Battalion, which initially took on 1,000 men. However, looking at each company, 'D' Company and half of 'C' Company was made up from men from London. It is also noted in the Norfolk Regiment history that there were men who came from Lancashire. In fact, only half of this battalion was made up from men from Norfolk.

K2 came soon after when, on 28 August 1914, another 100,000 men were requested by Kitchener. As a result of this, Army Order 382 was issued on 11 September 1914. This created another six divisions. These came to be the 15th (Scottish) Division, 16th (Irish) Division, 17th (Northern) Division, 18th (Eastern) Division, 19th (Western) Division, and 20th (Light) Division. Within K2 came the 8th (Service) Battalion Norfolk Regiment, under the command of Colonel Frederick Clinton Briggs, formed on 4 September 1914 at Shorncliffe as part of K2 and came under the orders of the 53rd Brigade in 18th (Eastern) Division.

Soon after, another 100,000 men were called and placed into another six divisions, called K3. These became the 21st Division, 22nd Division, 23rd Division, 24th Division, 25th Division, and 26th Division.

Therefore the 9th (Service) Battalion Norfolk Regiment was formed at Norwich on 9 September 1914 as part of K3 and came under orders of 71st Brigade in the 24th Division. It then moved to Shoreham, initially under the command of Major Edward Orams. However, by 1 October 1914, the battalion came under the command of Colonel Mansel Travers Shewen.

An example of a K3 man can be seen with Frederick Henry Howson. He was born in Easton on 27 January 1890 and was the youngest of seven brothers, Herbert, Horace, Howard, Charles, George, and William. By 2 April 1911, he was residing at Bexwell Road in Downham Market and was listed as school teacher. He enlisted on 9 September 1914 in Norwich and would disembark with the 9th

Battalion when they landed in France; we will look into that in more detail later on in the book.

Men joined up either by enlisting or by receiving a commission. Enlistment often followed recruitment meetings, such as the one held at St Andrew's Hall, Norwich, in August 1914. These kind of recruitment drives took place all over the county and soldiers' records show that they also enlisted in towns such as Great Yarmouth, Dereham, and King's Lynn. In order to be accepted, men had to be physically fit and a stringent medical examination was held, which could bar men who fell outside of the height requirements or had bad teeth.

The *EDP* made a point of describing to their readers how this process happened when they were allowed to witness a group of men who had decided to enlist:

> The chief incident of interest in recruiting operations at the Barracks yesterday was the swearing in of fifty young men from business houses in Norwich ad district. They met at the bottom of Kett's Hill just before three o'clock, and marched to the barracks. Though comparatively small numerically their neat well set up appearance and athletic bearing made their march up the approaches a gratifying sight. They will furnish good material for the drill sergeant. Some little time was occupied with the detailed filing in of their papers and other formalities.
>
> Later they were sworn in before Major Besant, and then marched off to receive their first day's pay. After this an uncertain feeling as to the next move was making itself unpleasantly felt. Most of the party had not come prepared to part with their civilian life all in a flash. They had anticipated release until the following day. But the whisper went around that they were to be quartered in the barracks that night. The case for release was put to an officer. It needed no pressing. There is a lot of downright humanity in the Army. The men were told they could all return to their homes for the night, but must turn up on parade at eight o'clock on the following morning. Some helpful hints as to what articles of clothing to bring until their uniforms arrive were given, and then the new recruits were taken to see what will be their new temporary quarters at the Barracks. With this they bade a cheery good-night to the non-commissioned officer in charge, and turned to talk buoyantly of the prospects of the morrow.

Those men who did not join up straight away often found themselves being forced to do so by other means, including public shaming. Clifford De Boltz was given a white feather in the street (the white feather became a symbol of cowardice given to those who seemed eligible to participate in the war effort but had yet to join up) and recalled: 'I felt quite embarrassed and threw the feather away in great disgust'. But it did the trick because he joined the 2/6th Norfolks, a cyclist battalion, and eventually went on to serve as an officer with the 1st Battalion.

For those who were suitable to be commissioned, which at the start of the war often depended on your education or standing in life, the path to joining the army was quite different. At the start of the war, the position of officer was oversubscribed and a number of men were unable to register in this role as a result or else because they did not fit in with the regiment's requirements.

There were many problems with this initial rush to join the colours and the influx of men meant that regiments were often unable to obtain the quantities of equipment and weapons necessary for the force to be sent overseas. Major H. P. Berney-Ficklin, who served with the 8th Norfolks, noted the preliminary issues faced as the battalion formed: 'The conditions in England at this time were practically indescribable. Men appeared in thousands ... all in civilian clothes and had to be found accommodation, food, cooking utensils and boots; and had at the time to be taught the first principles in soldiering'.

By 4 September, around 250 recruits for the 8th Battalion had arrived at St Martin's Plain. Within eleven days, this number had increased to 1,200, and by 20 September, the battalion had a complement of 1,320 officers and men. The battalion was sent to Shorncliffe in Kent and initially men had to share cutlery and plates and were put in accommodation of sixteen men per tent. A number of men had to wear a blue uniform rather than khaki, some had no boots these remained in short supply, even when the battalion moved to Colchester, and it was not until June 1915 that the battalion could be considered fully operational. There were also shortages of places for men to wash, which meant that the entire battalion was regularly marched down to the sea.

A letter printed in the *EDP* on 3 September 1914 revealed another issue in the form of the distances that Norfolk men had to travel in order to enlist. As a result, Lord Kitchener appointed Lord Suffield of Hardbord House, Cromer; Colonel C. B. Custance, of Weston Hall, Norwich; and the Hon. William Cozens Hardy of Letheringsett Hall, Holt as special recruiting agents for the Army, announcing:

> Any village agent for recruiting who may have men who wish to enlist should communicate with the nearest recruiting officer or special recruiting agents at once, so that arrangements can be immediately made for examination and attestation of recruits as near their [home-town] as possible.

Reservists were also called up, and on 18 November 1914, the *Eastern Daily Press* reported the first of them being sent off to the 1st Battalion:

> There was a stirring scene at Thorpe Station yesterday when Sections A and B of the Reservists entrained for war service, their first duty being to join the 1st Battalion of the Norfolk Regiment. These are men with about nine years' service, all of them seemingly in the prime of life and pink of soldierly condition. There were about 500 of them, many drawn from Norfolk, but by no means all, for one came from as far away as Newcastle. The train was timed to leave at a quarter to three, long before that hour a crowd, mostly consisting of poor and sorrowful-looking women, many

of them carrying children or pushing a perambulator, gathered on the platform. Hundreds of other people joined them, attracted from the throngs of spectacle-hunters who now daily beset Thorpe Station. The men without any sort of musical embellishment for their march, stepped briskly from the Britannia Barracks and along the Riverside Road.

Inside the station they passed between two crowded lines with difficulty preserved by the police, and many an affecting incident was witnessed, the women having forced themselves front for the sake of a last farewell. The train started out of the dock at about three, the men returning lustily a cheer sent crowd behind the barriers.

Issues were also met with the standards the Army were setting, and this was also noted by the press, the *EDP* noting:

In order to avoid a fruitless journey to the Britannia Barracks it should be carefully borne in mind that for the present the increased standard of measurement is being rapidly enforced. This is working a little hard in some cases. For instance, where men were medically passed before the new regulation, but were not sworn in, they are now liable when they are summoned for their swearing in to find themselves rejected on the ground that they are too far below the new standard to justify enlistment. A few instances of this kind, which brought to the victims, were observed at the Britannia Barracks yesterday.

This unfortunately led to some men having signed up earlier being turned away and this embarrassing issue was noted by the *EDP* who managed to speak to a man who fell foul to this type of change:

'The part about it I don't like', remarked one young fellow from the country, 'is that it makes you look so silly among your friends. I've been up to Norwich twice already on this business, not knowing each time whether I should return home. The result was all my friends bade me goodbye at each parting, and now here I am on my way home again.' One inquired into this particular case as well as into three others where young men had come from a distance. The replies, courteously furnished showed that it was impossible for the authorities to have acted otherwise in view of the new regulation, as they understand it is to be applied. It was suggested that the men need not give up hope, as the probability is that the standard will soon be lowered again.

Age was also a barrier and only men aged between eighteen and thirty-five were accepted. This too changed as the war progressed, and by November 1914, the *EDP* stated: 'Age on enlistment to 19 to 38. Ex-Soldiers up to 45. Minimum height 5 ft 3 ins; chest 34 ins. Must be medically fit'.

In fact, the maximum age would rise to fifty if the applicant had already served as an NCO and at the opposite end to this, underage boys were joining the war effort was not widely known at the beginning of the war, but there is evidence that this did happen. John Norton, who joined the Norfolk Regiment underage, records how he managed to enlist with the help of a recruiting sergeant who was prepared to turn a blind eye: 'I was only sixteen, but I tried to join up too. The recruiting sergeant asked me my age and when I told him he said, "You better go out, come in again, and tell me different." I came back, told him I was nineteen and I was in'. Norton would go on to serve in the 8th Norfolks.

As the war progressed, as was noted by the *EDP* earlier in this chapter, as casualties mounted, the medical requirements for recruits were lowered.

5

1st Battalion, St Eloi and Hill 60: March to June 1915

The 1st Battalion continued to serve around Ypres in early 1915 and continued to learn their new trade of trench warfare, we will look at that in more depth in the next chapter, but it is right that I start this chapter with more observations from Herbert Reeve who was serving with them in trenches close to Messines:

> January 1915 came to an end. We buried one Officer, one Sergeant and three Other Ranks in the Churchyard of Dranouter Church. On 1st February 1915 I was wounded. They placed me in Dranouter Church for one night. The Red Cross train took me, and many others, to a Channel Port, and I arrived at the Norfolk and Norwich Hospital four days later. We were under canvas outside the hospital. I was operated upon the next day and, as a walking patient, I was sent to Cromer Hospital the following day. My arm healed quickly and I was directed to report to Headquarters in Felixstowe in the middle of March 1915.

Herbert's observations here are a little bit muddied, I would suggest, by time. I have visited Dranouter Churchyard and there are six men from the 1st Battalion buried here. One, Victor Watts, died on 30 January 1915 and the rest died between 14 and 26 February 1915. Herbert was back in Blighty by 6 January 1915, as records confirm he was sent to the Queen Alexandria Military Hospital on Millbank on this date prior to being sent back to Norfolk. The war diary records the loss of five men killed and fourteen wounded in January 1915. But I therefore wonder if he confused Dranouter with a cemetery very close to that Belgian town as the main body of 1st Battalion's dead were buried in Wulverghem-Lindhoek Cemetery situated very close to Dranouter. Here casualties lie from December 1914 through to the end of January 1915 as described by Herbert. I feel that sometimes it is best to point these types of observations out to show that sometimes men's accounts are not always accurate.

So, having initially spent their first experiences of trench warfare around Messines, on 3 March 1915, the 1st Battalion Norfolk Regiment moved north and occupied Trenches around St Eloi. This was and still is a small village between Messines and Ypres.

The village of Saint Eloi is principally remembered today for its wartime history of underground mine warfare. Within the small confines of the area, both British and German forces detonated some thirty mines. In 1915 alone, the British exploded thirteen mines and twenty-nine camouflets (counter-mining charges), and the Germans twenty mines and two camouflets.

I will digress a bit here and also look at the 1/1st Battalion Cambridgeshire Regiment. The 1/1st Battalion can be linked to the 1st and 7th Battalion Norfolk Regiment, and you will read about their exploits with the 7th Battalion later on. The Cambridgeshires had been on the Western Front since 14 February 1915 and were learning about trench warfare in this sector. Due to the water table, the trenches were effectively sandbagged walls of around 5 feet in height. The Cambridgeshires history describe these as 'Grouse Butts' that held thirty men in each at intervals of 80 yards, with no parodos and with the trench being open to the rear and sides. Behind this position, there were no support trenches all the way back to Voormezeele. The Norfolk's history is quite scant on what happened here, so that is why I have defaulted to the Cambridgeshire's history to give you an overview of what happened at St Eloi.

At 5.30 p.m. on 14 March 1915, the sector was attacked when the Germans exploded two mines under the British lines and a determined attack was launched. Although the line was defended tenaciously, the Germans managed to capture St Eloi, the British frontline, and a position known as the Mound, which was a literally a 30-foot-high mound of earth situated to the south of the village. The Germans also placed a barrage on the British rear lines and main supply routes to stop any re enforcements from bolstering the lines. Edward Riddell, author of the Cambridgeshires' history, was there to witness the attack:

At 5.30 p.m., whilst I was gazing towards the Mound, I suddenly saw the trench there lifted into the air; sandbags and debris seemed to rain around, and a moment later there came a dull 'boom' of the explosion. At the same instant the whole German line opened fire; away by the Mound I saw the enemy advancing. We immediately opened fire on our front. I remember firing my revolver at two men; whether I hit them I know not; in fact, I have no clear recollection of what did happen for several minutes.

The reason I came to know and also research the Cambridgeshire's war is because of one man who has relatives who live in Norfolk. Company Sergeant-Major

Harry Betts, MC, DCM & Bar, (325753) wrote a diary for this period; at this time, he was serving as a private.

Harry's diary was written between 14 February 1915 and 26 April 1916. It is entitled 'The Diary of the doings of the 1st Batt Cambs Regt France 1915–1916'. His entries are very brief, sometimes with only one or two words. But they are an amazing insight into his observations on the first year and a bit of the Cambridgeshire Regiment.

Harry joined up on 7 September 1914 and joined the battalion on 10 September 1914. He saw almost continuous service with the regiment. He moved quickly up the ranks, and by 1917 was one of the youngest company sergeant-majors in the British Army. His exploits and gallantry are documented in both the war diary and the regimental history, which is an amazing feat for an 'Other Rank'.

Harry makes mention of this action and his company, along with 'A' Coy, under the command of Major Goodwyn L. Archer, was ordered to the front.

March 14th. Spent Sunday under cover because enemy could see us from the trenches about 8.30 a.m. a chap named Symonds was hit with a bullet in the jaw. Was told off to bury him soon after was found to be talking. About 4.30 a.m. prepared to get ready for 24 hours in the trenches.

About 5 o clock the Germans broke through our first line at St Eloi, the nearest trenches to us. And started bombarding the village we were in, we were ordered to throw all packs off and advanced to the British line with fixed bayonets.

We advanced to the reserve lines where our troops were forced back to. The enemy were continuing bombarding our reinforcements for about 16 hours.

These two companies were now holding part of the sector to the south of St Eloi with the rest of the battalion now situated at the Convent at Voormezeele.

March 15th. About 3.0 a.m. Major Saint led about 25 of us into the village of St Eloi where the Germans were advancing on in close formation. We got the furniture of the houses and barricaded the road and had to retire. Our major getting recommended for.... At the same time there was a great call in England for more shells and recruiting was being done in the Shire. Arrived in Dickebusch about 7 a.m. was packed into a big house the whole battalion of the Cambridgeshires. Roll was called about 10 a.m. During this our first engagement we lost one of our most respected Capt of B Company, Capt Tebbutt son of our late Colonel of Cambridge. Went digging trenches just behind our original front line that we had returned. Some went to find our packs at Voormezeele but found most of them looted.

March 16th. Trench digging about half a mile behind the firing line. Was shelled by the enemy waited till dark and marched to Dickebusch.

The Cambridgeshires successfully, with one of their MG teams, countered a German attack, which they decimated. An insight into this defence at St Eloi can be found in a poem written by John Henry Gent. John had landed with the Cambridgeshires on the same day as Harry. His poem details what he witnessed at St Eloi:

> *Twas the 14th March,*
> *And a Sunday, too,*
> *When the message came to tell us*
> *The Germans had broken through!*
>
> *We fell in, in fighting order,*
> *Under officers good and true;*
> *And though our first time in action,*
> *We meant to see it through.*
>
> *We were only Cambs. Territorials;*
> *The Mound was at St Eloi;*
> *We had got to make a name that night-*
> *It was either do or die!*
>
> *Fritz had taken our first line trenches;*
> *He wanted our second line as well;*
> *But we rigged up some new defences,*
> *And let him have it like hell.*
>
> *Twas the Prussian Guards that made the attack*
> *They outnumbered us four to one;*
> *So, I am told, did their casualties*
> *After the battle was done.*
>
> *Twas early on Monday morning,*
> *When the British counter attacked; And just as day was dawning,*
> *They had taken those trenches back.*

John Gent remained with the Cambridgeshires before moving onto the Machine Gun Corps and was invalided out of the Army on 12 March 1918.

Between 14 and 23 March, the battalion lost two officers and seven other ranks killed or died of wounds during this engagement. This action threatened the 15th Brigade front due to the loss of St Eloi, and the 27th Division had the task of recapturing the village which they did less the Mound. The 1st Battalion moved up from Kruistraat, which was hit by artillery as they left. Their war diary is very brief for this period: 'Took over trenches from Cheshires. Heavy shelling owing to attack on St Eloi Lt McCurry killed, 6 killed, 19 wounded'.

In the Norfolk Regiment history, they incorrectly spell Walter McCurry's name as McCurdy. Lieutenant Walter Tennyson McCurry was aged twenty-two and had been in France and Flanders since 8 December 1914. He was serving with the Royal Army Medical Corps and Royal Belfast Academical Institution, commonly known as 'Inst' on their Great War website, which notes his passing thus:

Walter was the elder son of Joseph and Jessie Graham McCurry of Belfast Bank House, Shankill Road, Belfast. After Inst, he studied at Queen's University, Belfast, where he was a member of the Officer Training Corps, and secretary of the Belfast Medical Student Association. He got his primary fellowship at the Royal College of Surgeons in 1912 and was sent to France during the early stages of the war.

He took part in the retreat from Mons in 1914, and at the beginning of 1915, refused a post in a base hospital, considering it to be the duty of the younger men to go to the trenches. He was attached to the 1st Norfolk Regiment.

He was killed in action, aged 22, near Ypres, while attached to the 1st Norfolk Regiment. On that day, the battalion were in trenches south-east of Ypres, when they were heavily shelled. Walter was killed while attending to the wounded in a dressing station.

QCB, the Queen's University student magazine reported 'those of us who knew Walter feel sure that the manner of his death was such as he himself would have chosen, for he gave up his life while helping his countrymen and serving his Empire'.

After his death, the *School News* June 1915 edition contained two items relating to Walter, a tribute and a poem in his honour:

It seems so short a time since he was with us at school, and the memory of his fine character, with its bright frankness and candour, was still so fresh, that the pathos of his early death affected in a peculiar way all who had known him at Inst.

Passing from school to university, and finding his real work in medicine, he rapidly distinguished himself in a study for which he seemed to discover his special vocation. He had just finished his course when war broke out; immediately he offered his services, and at once was sent to the front. Through all that terrible autumn and pitiless winter, he worked at exhausting pressure with his fellow officers of the RAMC, struggling to deal with the never-ending procession of the wounded and doing good at every step. Then his own moment came, and took him as he might have wished to be taken, when he was actually tending a wounded man.

We think of him as one whom the beauty of his character and young life might seem almost to have marked him out as the costly sacrifice which patriotism demands.

To W T McC

Brave Youth, with sunshine in your smiling eyes, you gave your life to save another's
woe.
Whether to God or man the greater prize, the world can never know.
Willing to serve, you heard the nation call and, in the field, you eased the battle's
pain:
Willing to die, if need be, you gave all, and have not given in vain.

Walter also said this in a letter to his father,

Above all things don't worry. If you keep bright and smiling it will do mother a lot of good. Don't be downhearted. My risks are very small compared with those of the fighting men, but I want to prepare you for this - I may soon be sent as medical officer to a regiment. This may mean more exposure, but the danger is not much increased. One, however, should look at these things not through narrow personal spectacles, but take a broader, patriotic view. You cannot make omelettes without breaking eggs. You cannot have the prosperity and comfort that Britain now enjoys, and for which she has in the past shed blood, without losing, without losing lives.

And so, I come to my point—that instead of worrying about the whole skin of one's relatives at the front people at home should rather think of the ultimate result of this war, and be prepared, if necessary, to lose their friends.

After his death, Walter McCurry would be mentioned in despatches in June 1915, and he is now buried in Ramparts Cemetery, Lille Gate. In total, the 1st Battalion lost eight killed in the fighting around St Eloi.

Another Norfolk Regiment officer who became a casualty at St Eloi was 2Lt William J. H. Brown. William, a qualified doctor, had enlisted with the 9th Battalion London Regiment (Queen Victoria Rifles) as a private (2528) on 1 September 1914, but was given a commission in the Norfolk Regiment on 5 September 1914. During fighting at Trench 26a at St Eloi, he suffered a through and through wound from a rifle bullet that entered the left side of his front chest at the fifth rib cartilage near the sternum and exited through the back at the right side at the ninth intercostal space fracturing his seventh rib. William was evacuated to England at Lady Carnarvon's hospital near Newbury where he spent forty-five further days in hospital. On 27 April 1915, he was sent to convalescent leave at the Old Hall Snettisham, until declared fit for 'light duties' by the Eastern District Medical Board whereupon he reported to the Norfolk Regiment on 9 June 1915.

After St Eloi, the battalion spent time in and out of trenches around Verbranden-Molen and Hill 60 where another notable loss was Captain William Cecil Kennedy Megaw who was killed in action in an artillery strike on 31 March 1915. He had been with the 1st Battalion since they had landed in France and had been with the regiment since 16 August 1905. He had been acting adjutant since Mons and was mentioned in despatches by Sir John French twice and awarded the Military Cross for gallantry, which was published in the *London Gazette* on 16 February 1915. Aged twenty-nine, he was the son of Kennedy and Mamie Megaw of Chesham Road in Brighton and the Husband of Alice May Megaw of Farnborough.

One officer, Captain Hume Smith Cameron, wrote to a friend on 13 April 1915, describing his time here:

> The regiment is up here in the trenches for eight days, so ere the arrival of the last day, I hope to get square with my correspondence. We are doing two days in the firing line and two in support, and alternate this until the days are over, when we move back to a rest camp where we remain for five or six days.
>
> Contrary to expectations we are occupying a very favourable sector, for the firing line, which is from eighty to two hundred yards from the Germans, the ground slopes away to the rear. On this slope is a fine pine wood in which are located the support lines at a distance of about two hundred yards from the front line. Hence, we are able to move up to the fire trenches under excellent cover.
>
> My company is spending today and tomorrow in the wood and we are having a glorious time, for the weather is very good, a fine change from the stuff served up to us in January and February.

The pine wood Captain Cameron was talking about was called Ravine Wood and still exists today. Sadly, this sector became heavily contested soon after this.

On 17 April, they were about 150 yards away from three mines being exploded on Hill 60. Hill 60 was a man-made hill at 60 metres above sea level in the area of Zillebeke, south-east of Ypres. It was man-made as a result of spoil that was excavated for a railway cutting for the Ypres–Comines railway.

The high ground had been in German possession since 10 December 1914, and it was a dominant feature. The British took over this sector in February 1915 and a number of mines were built under the German lines with a mind to capture the position.

At 7.05 p.m. on 17 April, two pairs of mines and one single mine were exploded by the British under Hill 60, and following the explosions, both the Royal West Kents and the King's Own Scottish Borderers, both 13th Brigade of the 5th Division, attacked, supported by the fire of the 15th Brigade, and captured Hill 60. This included the 1st Battalion, and the war diary records the furious fighting that ensued between 18 and 20 April 1915:

> At 7 p.m. Hill 60, about 800 yards to the left front of our left trench, was blown up by three mines. These were blown up in quick succession. After the third explosion our artillery and our line of trenches opened a heavy fire simultaneously.
>
> Our fire was immediately answered by hostile artillery who opened a heavy fire dropping shells all round our front and support trenches.

We were opposed by practically no rifle fire. The enemy were caught leaving their trenches and fire was immediately directed on them by our firing line and machine gunners. About 11.30 p.m. the rifle fire became more noticed. The shelling continued till about 12.30 a.m. after which it was more or less quiet.

Furious counterattacks by the Germans took place during the next four days.

18th April 1915

At 3 a.m. the enemy counter attacked Hill 60. We kept up a very heavy fire on them and the troops on Hill 60 drove them off. At 6 p.m. our troops again attacked the Germans so as to get a firmer footing on Hill 60. We as yesterday kept up a heavy covering fire in support of the attacking Battalion. The attack was successful and we gained some more ground. We came in for some heavy shelling and a certain amount of rifle fire.

Our casualties for these two days were:

Lt A F Todd wounded, died of wounds 21 April, Lt W B Byrons wounded. Other Ranks 11 killed and 46 wounded.

In the fighting for Hill 60, four Victoria Crosses would be won over this period, one of which would be won the on the night of 20-21 April, when 2Lt Geoffrey H. Woolley of the 9th Londons and a handful of his men were the only defenders on the hill where they continually repelled attacks to hold the position. He encouraged the men to hold the line against heavy enemy machine-gun fire and shellfire. For a time, he was the only officer on the hill. When he and his men were relieved on the morning of 21 April, only fourteen out of a company of 150 had survived.

The British attack prompted the Germans to launch a terrible bombardment, which not only hit the trenches but also targeted Ypres. Many houses were destroyed and the Cloth Hall itself was severely damaged. On 20 April, a furious counterattack saw the remnants of the Hill 60 defenders retreat to their original start line.

It was the shape of things to come as the Germans launched the Second Battle of Ypres. One of the reasons that the Germans reacted in the way that they did was because they had positioned gas canisters all along the line and some were placed around Hill 60, so it was important to try and maintain and hold onto this famous piece of Flanders less the British found out what was about to happen.

The Second Battle of Ypres was launched for a number of reasons. The main reason was because the Germans were now fighting on two main fronts, Russia and the Western Front. The German high command believed that they could defeat Russia because of the internal political struggle and that the Russians were the weaker foe. On the Western Front, it was proving more difficult to dislodge the British and French and until an offensive could be launched then more localised attacks would be needed to keep them on their toes.

The Ypres Salient had held after the First Battle of Ypres had ended with the Germans being stopped by the 2nd Battalion Worcester Regiment at Gheluvelt and the battle had raged until 11 November when the German advance stopped. But virtually all the BEF infantry units had lost nearly 70 per cent of their men at First Ypres and they were still very weak now. If the Germans broke though at Ypres, then there would be a very real risk of them getting to the Channel ports.

Therefore, it was decided that Ypres would be chosen to launch the first major gas attacks of the First World War. Some 30,000 cylinders full of chlorine gas were moved to this sector in great secrecy and were placed along the front in batches of twenty so that they covered a 40-yard front with each batch. Although the British and French were told by German prisoners that gas was going to be used, these reports were not taken seriously.

Therefore, at around 5 p.m. on 22 April 1915, the Germans released 168 tons of chlorine gas over a 4-mile front on the part of the line held by 10,000 troops who were mainly French Moroccan and Algerian soldiers of the French 45th and 78th Divisions. Approximately 6,000 French and colonial troops died within ten minutes, primarily from asphyxiation subsequent to tissue damage in the lungs. Many more were blinded. Many also fled their positions in terror, stopping only when they reached Ypres. The chlorine gas, being denser than air, also quickly filled the trenches and forced the defenders to climb out of their defences, thus exposing them to enemy fire.

One man who witnessed this initial onslaught, Private W. Underwood of the 1st Canadian Division, stated:

It was a beautiful day. I was lying down in a field writing a letter to my mother, the sun was shining and I remember a lark singing high up in the sky. Then, suddenly, the bombardment started so we got orders to stand to. We went up the line in two columns, one either side of the road. But as we reached the outskirts of the village of St Julien the bullets opened up and when I looked around I counted just 32 men left on their feet out of a company of 227.

Then we saw coming towards us the French Zouaves. They were in blue coats and red pants and caps.... They were rushing towards us, half staggering and we wondered what was the matter. We were a little perturbed at first, then when they got to us we tried to rally them, but they wouldn't stay. They were running away from the Germans. Then we got orders to shoot them down, which we did.

Then, as we looked further away we saw this green cloud come slowly across the terrain. It was the first gas anybody had seen or heard of, and one of our boys, evidently a chemist, passed the word along that this was chlorine. And he said, 'If you urinate on your handkerchiefs it will save your lungs, anyway.' So most of us did that, and we tied these handkerchiefs, plus pieces of putty or anything else we could find around our faces, and it did save us from being gassed. There were masses of Germans behind the gas cloud, we could see their grey uniforms as plain as anything, and there we were, helpless, with Ross rifles that we couldn't fire because they were always jamming.

With the survivors abandoning their positions, an 8,000-yard gap was left in the front line between the Belgians who held the ground north of the 45th Division and the Canadian 3rd Brigade. However, the German High Command had not foreseen the effectiveness of their new weapon, and so had not put any reserves ready in the area. With the coming of darkness and the lack of follow up troops the German forces did not exploit the gap. It was only in the morning that the Germans, who now occupied Pilckem Ridge, realised just how successful their attack had been. But by then, it was too late.

The Canadian 3rd Brigade managed to plug the line and hold off strong attacks around Keerselare. Amazingly, it is the fact that the Canadians stood their ground that saved them:

Chlorine, the gas employed, has a powerful irritant action on the respiratory organs and all mucous membranes exposed to it, causing spasms of the glottis, a burning sensation in the eyes, nose and throat, followed by bronchitis and oedema of the lungs. Frequently there is evidence of corrosion of the mucous membranes of the air channels and of the cornea. Prolonged or exposure to a high concentration of the gas will cause death by asphyxia, or, if not fatal, produce cardiac dilatation and cyanosis (blueness of the skin) as a result of the injury to the lungs.

It early became evident that the men who stayed in their places suffered less than those who ran away, any movement making the worse the effects of the gas, and those who stood up on the fire step suffered less-indeed they often escaped any serious effects-than those who lay down or sat at the bottom of a trench. Men who stood on the parapet suffered least, as the gas was denser near the ground. The worst sufferers were the wounded lying on the ground, or on stretchers, and the men who moved back with the cloud.

With regards to the 1st Battalion, their war did not change much, with them going in and out of the line with most of the heavier fighting taking place further north. But on 5 May 1915, they came under gas attack for the first time:

At 8.30 a.m. our trenches were gassed for the 1st time and the gas came down from Hill 60 opposite 37 and opposite 36. The men in the latter suffering considerably owing to the very close distance at which the gas was … from the cylinders. Our casualties were 75. The Germans did not attack.

From this attack, the battalion lost fifteen men, a number of whom died from the effects of gas. The Official History of the Great War noted:

At 8.45 a.m. on the 5th May, when, after a wakeful night, most of the trench garrison except the usual guards, were asleep tired out, the enemy released gas from two points against the hill, held by the Duke of Wellington's.

With a favouring wind, it slowly drifted, not across but along the trenches. Only one sentry saw the gas coming, and he at once sounded the alarm.

Orders had been given that, in case of attack by gas, the men were to move to the flanks to avoid it, and let the supports charge; but the manner in which the gas was released from a flank rendered this plan of little avail, as it affected a great length of front. Further the gas hung about the trenches so thickly that even with a cotton respirator, that had constantly to be redamped, it was impossible to stay in them. Some men ran back to the support line and those who remained were overcome, thus when the Germans advanced after the gas had been flowing 15 minutes, they secured all but a small portion of the front line in the lower slopes of the hill.

Furious counterattacks led to the Germans having to retire, but they managed to keep hold of the crest of Hill 60. The Germans tried another gas attack, but this had little effect as it was released in small quantities. Further attempts to capture the crest failed due to the fact that large areas on either side of Hill 60 had to be captured and held, but this could not be achieved. One final effort by two companies of 2nd Battalion King's Own Yorkshire Light Infantry just led to them being either killed or captured.

The Official History noted: 'With this last desperate effort, fighting at Hill 60 came to an end, and this much disputed ground remained in German hands, continuing so until the Battle of Messines in June 1917'.

The pattern of going in and out of the line continued into June before the battalion was moved out of the sector. By the time that occurred, the war diary recorded that they had lost 205 men killed or wounded. In, total this can be narrowed down to fifty-six men who were either killed in action or died of wounds or as a result of gas.

Herbert Reeve had this to say about Hill 60:

The scene was awful, dead soldiers, their brass equipment tarnished and discoloured by gas. Gas alert sounded, but the wind changed and sent the gas back to the German trenches. Of course, I palled up with my old comrades who made many enquiries about Blighty. During April we received the first Trench Mortar Bombs from the German front line. These were as large as a 5-gallon drum. We heard a bang and saw this object twisting in the air. We could dodge them in daylight. They used to hit the trench or ground and then explode. We were now issued with an improved gas mask about every fortnight until a satisfactory one was produced. Our Company spent 35 days in the trenches at Hill 60 without being relieved.

In July 1915, they went to a new sector, one that had been taken over by the British from the French and which would become a name that would live in infamy; the battalion moved to the Somme.

Private Sidney Smith (9002) reflected on his time around Hill 60 in a letter to his mother on 1 August 1915:

> I couldn't tell you much last time but I will put a little in this time, we have made a move from Hill 60 and I can tell you I am not sorry as we did fifty six days in the trenches without a day's rest or having our boots off so I was properly knocked up, but we are round to Arras on the right of the line and we go to trenches tomorrow after only a few days' rest.
>
> I think our New Army must be on paper as I haven't seen much of it yet.
>
> Well, dear Mother I am glad we have left Ypres as the Germans blew three mines but as luck would have it we only lost one poor boy when we got to him he had about a ton of earth on him, several other men were bruised but not very serious. I expect if we had stopped there much longer it would have been up you go with the best of luck; I hope we shall have good luck in our new position.

Luckily for Sidney and the rest of the 1st Battalion, although they would not know it at the time, they were no longer the only battalion in France and Flanders and it was now that the New Army had either arrived on the Western Front or were about to land.

Guidebook

To get to Hill 60, take the n336 out of Ypres, known as Rijselsweg. Prior to the railway crossing, there is a turning on the left, this is Komenseweg, turn here. Continue on this road and eventually you will see a sign for Hill 60. Turn left when directed and you will cross over the railway bridge and Hill 60 will be on your right. There is a car park next to the site. Once parked up, walk back the way you came. The 1st Battalion were in trenches here in the area over the other side of the railway bridge, and they would be on your left from the railway cutting running towards where there is a row of houses.

What3words: phone.jabs.conversations.

Optional Visit

If you retrace your steps and head back the way you came, you will see a CWGC signed for Blauwepoort Farm Cemetery. This has the remains of fourteen Norfolk Regiment men, all from the 1st Battalion and all died fighting around Hill 60.

What3words: cones.snorers.suckle.

6

Trench Warfare and the Service Battalions Initial Moves: May to August 1915

Before we move onto the New Army battalions and their first actions, it is important to cover this aspect of the Western Front. There are many myths surrounding the trenches. Often people still believe that as soon as you went into them, you never came out again. That is not true. In most cases, you spent a period of time in them before being relieved by another regiment in your brigade. Periods of time generally went between four and eight days, although I have seen evidence where that was extended. For instance, the 1st Battalion spent twenty days in trenches facing Fricourt on the Somme in August 1915.

Even early on in the war, there were times when there was some sort of line and the enemy could be close, as noted by Herbert Reeve in his memoirs about the Aisne front in 1914:

> Eventually, we entered a line of some sort, away from the Aisne front. As you know, there were no real trenches. I remember one Sunday I was posted on outpost duty on a hill. I suddenly heard, in the distance, playing the tune of a hymn I knew so well. I reported this to C.S.M. Francklin, who told me that I had definitely heard the playing of the German National Anthem, so you see we were so close and yet so far.

Trench warfare was not one continuous push between two armies. Life in the trenches generally meant intense periods of boredom and toil mixed with short periods of action. Battalions would often only spend four days in a row in the frontline before being relieved by another battalion from their brigade. This would provide the battalion with a chance to rest up and to recuperate.

A typical day in the frontline would start at around dawn, with both sides standing to, as this was when the enemy was most likely to launch an attack.

The men would man the fire steps and often fired off thousands of rounds of ammunition, which became known as the 'Morning Hate'. This could also be mixed with artillery fire.

Once this was over, life would generally settle and then revolve around getting the men fed, with many using this time to try and relax or catch up on sleep. However, this quiet time could be rudely shattered by stray shells and snipers. Moreover, there were always chores to be done and many would find themselves on work details, ensuring that the trenches were well kept.

However, that could all change very quickly and Herbert Beales found himself wounded in a very swift artillery attack:

> I was in trenches when a shell burst right in front of me and buried five of us. Some comrades came to our assistance and extricated us from our perilous position. We were found completely soaked with much and water and nearly dead. Besides being in this critical state we were found almost overcome with poisonous fumes that emanate from the deadly shells.

As dusk fell, hot food could be brought up. The rum ration was also issued at this point. Once night fell, men could move more freely and parties were often put into no-man's-land to repair the wire or to gather intelligence about the German lines. This could also be a time when a relief of battalions took place, but this ran the risk of when attacks came. Lt-Col. Bernard Henry Leathes Prior of the 9th Norfolks noted one such experience in his memoirs for October 1916:

> … just before sunset the enemy put down a very heavy bombardment accompanied by very heavy and remarkably accurate machine gun fire and rifle fire. We expected an attack but it died down later on we had a comparatively calm night for the relief which was duly affected.

Occasionally, trench raids were sanctioned and parties would infiltrate the German lines. Trench raids were an integral part of trench warfare and were carried out all through the war by both sides. However, they could have dire consequences for the men who faced each other across no-man's-land. They evolved in 1915 and were popular with the high command that would send orders down the line to carry them out. Depending on the unit who was carrying them out hinged on how successful they could be, but where you were could also have a bearing on them. This was because many units, friend and foe, operated a 'live and let live' policy.

So, in those sectors that were considered quiet, it could be to the detriment of living a cushy life if you launched one. In a book written by historian Tony Ashworth, who has studied this type of warfare, one veteran put it like this: 'If the British shelled the Germans, the Germans replied, and the damage was equal; if the Germans bombed an advanced piece of trench and killed five Englishmen, an answering fusillade killed five Germans'.

For other units who wanted to be recognised as elite regiments, the trench raid was one way of showing their commanders that they were eager to engage the enemy and promotion could quickly follow for officers who led them; this type of officer is what Tony Ashworth has termed 'Thrusters'. Men who went on them were often trained and therefore spent time away from the line and were given extra rations so there were perks to going on them.

Captain Cameron of the 1st Battalion noted to a friend that his CO had gone out on his own raid around Hill 60 in April 1915, stating:

> The other night we had a little excitement for our skipper, who has a fair amount of the devil in him, went out in front of the firing line to see what the Germans were up to. In the pitch blackness, he succeeded in losing his way and eventually, thinking it to be the Norfolk line, he mounted the German parapet and promptly cursed the men for having such a bright fire. There were only four men at that particular point and when the Captain had discovered his mistake he beat a hasty retreat before the dazed Germans had time to realise what was happening and managed to reach home without getting any bullets into his body.

They were planned and implemented for a number of reasons, but the main ones were to capture prisoners or to gather intelligence. However, they were also used to keep the enemy on his toes and darkness would often be a time of fear for both sides as they tried to guard against them. For the attacker, it was a time of abject fear as they attempted to infiltrate the enemy's lines without being spotted, and many of the raids ended in failure before they even got within sight of a trench.

As already stated, they often incited the enemy to punish their attackers and it was not uncommon for both sides to launch a retaliatory raid to restore their honour or to exact revenge.

The importance of having the right man for this type of raid can be seen when Corporal William Drewey (15355) of 'B' Company of the 7th Norfolks attended a bombing course, and it was made very clear on what was required of a man who was to be considered as a bomber:

> The pupils for grenade training should be picked men and must be intelligent, active and alert. There is a great weakness in grenadiers owing to the former rule not being carried out. It is a general rule that their platoon officer, when he picks them out, get what we may term as slackers when on duty in the trenches and by making him a grenadier he thinks he will be out of his way.

One of the reasons for this type of 'hand-picking' was because trench raids or patrols were not without risk. One example of a loss of a man was on 1 January

1916 when Private Stanley Ernest Boyer Hazell (13544) was shot by a sniper while out on patrol. His CO stated in a letter to his parents:

> Your son was out on patrol duty to within a few feet of the enemy's trenches, and was nearly back when he fell, shot through the right side, and died in a few moments. Of all the 200 men under my command I could not find one being so near the ideal soldier your son Stanley. He never grumbled, and there are many here in the trenches who feel his loss for many a long day and night.

Stanley served in 'D' Company and was the son of Edith M. Harrison (formerly Hazell) of 95 St John's Park in Blackheath and the late Ernest Orton Hazell. He was aged twenty and is now buried in Grave I.B.4 in Albert Communal Cemetery.

Charles Milligan served with the 12th Battalion, who came to the Western Front in 1918. He also gave an insight into trench life:

> We took over positions in front of Nieppe Forest, not far from Hazebrouk, and each time we entered the line found us a little further forward, using hastily dug positions for shelter. On retiring for our rest periods, we set up makeshift bivouacs with our groundsheets and on one occasion of shelling scrambled the nearest ditch or pre-prepared slit trench.
>
> Our sector was quiet except for the morning and evening strafe by the gunners of both sides and in the daytime, we lay on our backs enjoying the sunshine and watching the birds descend to their nests in no-man's land between the trenches.
>
> Being attached to the company signal section we occupied a funk-hole in the forward side of the trench which we screened with a blanket in order to observe any glimpses of candlelight which we used to take down messages from our I/3 buzzer. Activity at night consisted of, improving our positions, bringing up the rations from the rear and mending the occasional break in our cable which ran along the ground. There were intermittent raiding parties by both sides to gain information and, if possible, collect a few prisoners for interrogation.

Others were less than complimentary of their sector of trench, Lt-Col. Prior from the 9th Battalion:

> The valley between Rainbow Trench and Gueudecourt was a dreadful place. It was under enemy observation and kept under almost continuous hostile shell fire, whilst from the left flank Bosche machine guns were able to enfilade the greater portion of the valley. There were no communication trenches and the passage of the valley was always a perilous undertaking.
>
> There was not a dug out in the sector allotted to the battalion and battalion headquarters was installed in a short shaft, probably the beginning of a dug-out, the opening of which faced towards the enemy and was altogether an undesirable place.

We will meet and discuss Lt-Col. Prior later on in the book.

Men were also prone to exploring captured positions as was noted by Captain Cyril Bassingthwaighte of the 9th Battalion when he was positioned around Loos in August 1917:

> Most of the cottages had been demolished by our shells during its occupation by the enemy, but the cellars gave excellent protection from the German guns when the position had been reversed. Here was to the found adventure, a dug out not yet explored, tempting souvenirs in the shape of German helmets, perhaps wired to an unseen bomb or mine, that would explode if touched. Stores of abandoned material were evidence of a hasty flight. Strawberries that had survived a direct hit were to be found in the gardens.
>
> Old German Headquarters, the scene of officer's habitation while in reserve, or support, billets for troops could be inspected and huge underground caverns, with iron and steel doors, that had in many cases resisted the terrific bombardment of the British guns.

James Cooper had come from the Norwich Volunteer Corps and landed in France at the end of 1916; we know this because his diary starts from 1 January 1917 when he reaches the 9th Battalion. He had the task of scouring areas for equipment while serving with the battalion:

> Found some of Fritz's bombs, took out the fuses and hope to get them home. While going up the line looking for machine gun belts, which we are short of, came across two Fritz. Evidently, they had been on sentry for they laid there in the trench (a side one) the flesh was turning black and covered with flies and maggots and the stench was awful. A little further along one laid across a dugout, evidently, he had made a dash to get in but was caught before he could get down. A little further on we trod on another body with his leg sticking out and a little further on saw a Jack boot with half a leg in. Then we came back, had quite enough for one day.

We will look further into James's war later on in the book.

The three service battalions landed in France in 1915 in fairly quick succession, the 7th Battalion landed on 30 May 1915, the 8th Battalion on 27 July 1915, and the 9th Battalion landed on 30 August 1915.

One man who would land in France at this time would be Edgar Gray, who arrived with the 7th Norfolks on 30 May 1915. Edgar would be one of the very few who would serve with the 7th Battalion all through the war.

The 7th Battalion initially served to the south of Ypres around Ploegsteert and the other two battalions found themselves on the Somme. The 8th Battalion would initially serve in trenches north of Aveluy and the 9th Battalion would serve at Montcarvel until they, along with the rest of their brigade, were ordered to move to Lonely Tree Hill situated to the south of the La Bassée Canal. We will look at that story later on.

It was the 7th Battalion who suffered their first casualties in trenches in July. Here they were again serving in Plugstreet Wood, when on 9 July 1915, the war diary notes: 'Two mines exploded by R. Canadians. Craters successfully occupied'.

On this day, although it is not recorded, the battalion lost Private Harry William Laxen Sharpin (12826). Harry was aged twenty-four when he died and the son of James and Elizabeth Mary Sharpin of The Orchard at Brinton near Melton Constable. He is also listed as being a 'Native of Sheringham'. In total, for their first stint in the trenches, they would lose five men killed and twenty-three men wounded.

It was not long until the 8th Battalion lost their first man; Private Herbert Arthur Pretty (17060), who was the son of Arthur James and Naomi Pretty of The Street in Pulham Market. He was wounded on 21 August 1915 while the battalion was in trenches at Aveluy and he died of his wounds on 31 August 1915. He was twenty years old and is now laid to rest in grave I. A. 2. in Mericourt-l'Abbe Communal Cemetery Extension.

An insight into the 8th Battalion's initial experiences can be found in a letter written by John Paul known as Jack, who was born on 10 April 1887. He was the only son of John and Caroline Paul of Roudham Junction, Bridgham. He was one of five offspring, the rest being girls. Jack joined up underage managing to enlist at the age of seventeen.

13090 Pte J Paul
B Coy 8th Battalion Norfolks
BEF France

10. 8. 15
Dear Nellie,
Many thanks for your letter received on the 3rd and trust you are quite well. I've taken no harm so far since being out here and the time seems to have gone fairly quickly.

The weather has generally been fine, but we have occasionally had good drenching showers and storms.

Of course, I'm not at liberty to say much on the subject, but we are now close behind the lines although we have not yet been in the firing line and have been within a few hundred yards in the reserve trenches, where a few rifle shots occasionally whiz past and our artillery shells go whizzing overhead.

We are in billets (farms etc) in a small village which we leave now soon for the trenches. Up to the present we have been quite alright, having had plenty of food and have obtained milk, fruit etc from the villagers.

Some of our fellows know French but most of us do not, but having been in touch with the people, we have been able to learn one or two phrases and are able to speak our requirements to them fairly well. We are near a town which has had a good shelling by the Germans all the people having evacuated.

The tower of a once beautiful church there, still partly remains and a statue of a golden virgin hangs over at about half angles.

Harold Groom has gone to Egypt (with your boss I expect).

Well must close now with best love,

From Your loving brother

Jack

What is of interest for me, as a battlefield guide, is that he mentions the church. Every soldier who served on the Somme would know this structure. It is known as the Basilica in Albert, and by the time Jack was in that sector, it had been heavily damaged in the fighting. The golden statue on top of the Virgin Mary and the Baby Jesus had been hit and was now hanging precariously on the side of the tower. There was a superstition that when the statue fell, the war would end. It eventually did in 1918 and the original statute disappeared. Since the war, the Basilica has been rebuilt and the statue replaced. It stands as a focal point in that sector and can be seen, certainly on a clear day, for miles around.

Another soldier managed to evade the censor and point out a rough position as to where he was. Lance Corporal Herbert Head (3/6477), serving in 'B' Company of the 1st Norfolks, wrote on one of two French postcards:

You will see I have put an X on the map where we are now but the name isn't on but if you find Amiens and then Bray you will see the X and I have marked where the trenches are. I put a cross where were in the last trenches near the village of La Boiselle the trenches run right through it, the Huns were one side of the street and our chaps the other at one point.

On the second postcard, which was a map of the Somme region, he duly placed his 'X'. At this time, between July and December 1915, the 1st Battalion were in trenches close to Fricourt so his 'X' was not that far out.

Later on, this book will look at some of the trench raids carried out by battalions of the Norfolks. But, for now, I want to cover another aspect of warfare used.

Mine warfare was a style of war that could be traced back to the middle ages and in the Great War an MP, John Norton-Griffiths, recruited miners from the collieries and tunnels of the London Underground. They became known as 'clay kickers' for the style of work they carried out to extract earth to make tunnels, and by February 1915, eight Tunnelling Companies had been formed.

The tunnellers worked at great risk in tight spaces, in constant silence with the grave risk of being discovered by the enemy who were listening out for this type of work. If found, counter-mining would take place. They worked in pairs by candlelight, one would dig out the earth with a grafting tool, and the other man would then pack it into sandbags that were hauled or trolleyed to the rear by others.

Both sides used to blow camouflets (caverns) that brought down each other's tunnels and often they broke through into each other's galleries and hand-to-hand fighting would ensue. Early on in the 8th Battalion's war in France and Flanders, they experienced this type of warfare.

On 22 November 1915, the 8th Battalion were in the line when an explosion occurred and recorded the events in their war diary:

> At 1.30 a.m. 22/23 Germans blew up a mine post at 120 where our trenches via E2 intersected at present occupied by Essex. The mine must have been a very large one as the force of the explosion was very great.
>
> Explosion was immediately followed by about 20 ... —heavy machine gun fire—a few rifle grenades and several whizz bangs. Luckily the fire had very much diminished by the time our men got to the spot afterwards.
>
> We were not much troubled by their fire, although a good many ... were fired, from this it would appear that the best thing to do when a mine is fired by us is to wait for a short time before opening 'rapid fire' on the spot as working parties will not be able to arrive immediately and fire in the first few minutes will therefore probably be wasted.
>
> The reason for the Germans opening this heavy fire however may have been to prevent us seizing the edge of the crater but this at the same time prevented them from seizing the opposite edge.
>
> The damage done by this mine was that all posts in 120 were levelled and the junction of Scone-Street—Guemart Street and the ILOT was all blown in. The mine must have been a very large one as the crater is 100 yards long and 50 yards broad and about 40 feet deep.
>
> Owing to damage done I had no channel of communication with the Essex excepting via Tummel Street but I succeeded in established the original front-line channel of communication by about 6.30 a.m. Posts were pushed forward on to the edges of the craters.
>
> The Germans appeared to have made no effort at all to hold their lip of the crater, but whilst we were working too, and it is therefore probable that their front-line trenches were also damaged. We were able to work our rebuilding line much later than would have ordinarily been the case owing to the mist.

What the war diary did not record is that five miners were killed 80 feet below when the German mine exploded, which in turn detonated a British charge of 5,900 lb. This is why the explosion appeared larger than it actually was.

Guidebook

Of the three battalions to land in 1915, I would recommend you visit the 7th Battalion site. From Messines, if you are coming from the direction of Ypres, take the N365 toward Ploegsteert. You will see five green and white signs to Commonwealth War Graves Cemeteries (CWGC) on your right, turn left here and park up at Prowse Point Cemetery. You will see the Christmas Truce memorial on your right. If you want to know about that memorial and the myths surrounding it, then please look at my chapter on the 1st Battalion in Christmas 1914. Walk up the road and then turn right where you see the four signs for CWGC cemeteries on the right. Take this track and it will take you into the wood. Walk all the way to the bottom of the wood where you will come to Rifle House Cemetery. Within this cemetery are eleven men who were killed serving with the 7th Battalion between July and September 1915.

What3words: inferior.cost.boost.

7

The 7th and 9th Battalions, The Battles of Loos, The Quarries: 26 September to 13 October 1915

On 21 September 1915, Colonel Shewen was promoted to command the 71st Brigade and the 9th Battalion was handed to Lt-Col. Ernest Stracey. As with my great-grandfather's battalion, the 8th Buffs, who were serving in the same division, the 9th Norfolks did not see a frontline trench during their initial time in France. They remained at Montcavrel and received training.

The battalion received orders to move on 21 September and reached Béthune that evening. From there, they marched onwards and eventually got to a position marked as Lonely Tree Hill in their war diary situated to the south of La Bassée. Here they formed up, but were not initially used; however, on 26 September, they were ordered to assist the 20th Brigade in attacking German positions at Vendin le Veil. The reason for this being that were going to be used in the ongoing battle at Loos.

The Loos battlefield lies immediately north of the mining town of Lens, in the heart of the industrial area of north-east France. The ground here is uniformly flat, dominated by slagheaps connected with the coalmining in the district.

In 1915, the various mining villages, collieries, and other industrial buildings presented a difficult challenge for any would-be attacker. The area is little changed today except that the mining activity has declined; some of the old slagheaps and pit-heads are no longer there, and some are much larger than they were in 1915 (especially so in the case of the Loos Double Crassier, which today is immense and visible from several miles in all directions).

The combined Franco-British offensive would attack eastwards against the German Sixth Army. The whole force, supervised by General Foch, would consist of the French Tenth Army and the British First Army. It would attack on a 20-mile front between Arras and La Bassée. Although artillery would bombard the whole front, no attack would be made on a central 4,000-yard strip facing the towns of Liévin and Lens. South of this gap, the French Tenth Army would throw seventeen infantry divisions against the enemy, supported by 420 heavy guns with two cavalry divisions ready to exploit the expected breakthrough. To the north, the British First Army would attack with the six divisions of I and IV Corps, having seventy heavy guns available, with two cavalry corps (Indian and III) to push the advance forward. The objectives were imprecise but optimistic; the cavalry was to reach the area of Ath and Mons, 50 miles away in Belgium.

Joffre's plan was brutally simple. The strong enemy positions would be crushed by four days' continuous artillery bombardment, with a four-hour final crescendo before the infantry attacked. The latter would be arrayed in great depth, each division placing no more than half of two brigades in the first line. A constant flow of men would follow, as would the reserves behind the assaulting divisions. All other armies from the coast to Switzerland would be ready to move forward once the enemy were destroyed in Artois.

Sir John French arranged for Second Army to carry out subsidiary attacks near Ypres, as would First Army north of the La Bassée canal in addition to their main assault role; a total 75,000 would make the initial attack.

Experience at Neuve Chapelle and Festubert had shown that troops attacking on a narrow front would suffer from concentrated fire. First Army therefore made their attack front as wide as possible, placing all six divisions of I and IV Corps in the line, but faced the dilemma that the numbers and weight of heavy artillery they had available was insufficient to support such a breadth of front. It was decided to use intense smoke barrages to conceal the front as far as possible, and also to employ chlorine gas for the first time as a means of compensating for the relatively lightweight artillery. Final detailed orders were issued by First Army on 19 September. Much secrecy was maintained about the use of gas; the word 'accessory' was substituted in all orders.

The key lesson from the Spring Offensive was that it was weight of shell, particularly of high explosive fired by the heaviest artillery, that destroyed enemy defences and gave the attacking infantry gaps through which they could break into the lines. The assaults were to be made across ground that was quite open, but observed from heights. It would be important for the infantry to be hidden by smoke from machine guns that would in some cases escape even the most violent bombardment. The preliminary bombardment gave away all elements of surprise regards location of the battle, but steps were to be taken to keep some surprise with regard to the timing of the attack.

The divisions of the General Reserve were to be held north and south of Lillers, under orders of the commander-in-chief. They were (Cavalry Corps) 1st, 2nd, and 3rd Cavalry Divisions and (XI Corps) the Guards, 21st, and 24th Divisions. The latter two formations had very recently arrived in France and had not yet seen the trenches. The infantry units began moving from St Omer on 20 September, with marches of over 20 miles throughout successive nights.

Sir John French instructed Sir Douglas Haig to prepare the attack plan on the basis that two divisions of the reserve would be placed at his disposal when required. Haig planned to use 21st and 24th Divisions as an immediately-available reserve, which enabled him to use all six of his existing divisions in the frontline assault. He assured his corps commanders that ample reserves would be available to reinforce or exploit successes. But, by 18 September, Haig had learned of French's intentions to keep the reserves at Lillers, some 16 miles from the battlefront. He protested, citing the experiences of Neuve Chapelle and Festubert, where it was clear that reinforcements were needed within perhaps three hours of start.

General Foch advised that 2,000 yards would be a more suitable distance. French, since Neuve Chapelle, acutely conscious of the threadbare supply of men, munitions, and equipment, would not agree. He did, however, give orders that by dawn on the day of assault, the heads of the 21st and 24th Divisions should be at Noeux-les-Mines and Beuvry respectively, with the Guards Division following up.

On 24 September, the reserve divisions were warned to carry extra rations as it may be some time before their cookers caught up with them. They also carried greatcoats on the march to the battle area, which began at 7 p.m. that night.

The British bombardment of German positions started on the morning of 21 September 1915 and carried on until the morning of the assault. Observation of the effect of the shooting was hampered by fine weather and wind throwing up clouds of chalk dust, and on the 23rd and 24th by a change to dull weather with mist. Various localised feint attacks were conducted, to persuade the enemy to man the forward trenches during the shelling. These ruses included the use of dummy troops, bayonets showing above the British parapets, bagpipes playing, men shouting hurrahs, etc.

At 5.50 a.m. on 25 September 1915, a heavy British bombardment hit the German frontline defences and gas was released. The gas formed a 30- to 50-foot-high blanket, moving forward slowly in places and virtually stood still in the British assault positions in other areas. The right-hand 7th Division found that the gas cloud generally moved well in this sector, but local wind variations meant that not all cylinders were turned on here. Many men struggled to breathe in their gas helmets as they advanced into the cloud and removed them, consequently suffering from gas themselves. Heavy losses were incurred by the lead units of 20th Brigade in no-man's-land from German shelling, which had been opened up to try to dispel the gas and smoke cloud. The 8th Devonshire suffered heavy machine-gun casualties, the wire in front of their sector having been only partially cleared. However, the 2nd Gordon Highlanders fared better and soon pushed past the German frontline towards Gun Trench and Hulluch.

By 9.30 a.m. on 25 September 1915, the 22nd Brigade of the 7th Division had captured the Hulluch Quarries and had sent patrols to the edge of Cité St Elie itself. However, further advance was found to be impossible without further support, and the positions captured thus far at the Quarries had to be consolidated. The 21st Brigade moved up from reserve in Vermelles, splitting into two sets of two battalions, and were ordered to advance through the positions gained so far. They were also halted in and around Gun Trench and the Quarries but were unable to penetrate uncut wire in front of Hulluch under fire from Cité St Elie.

The 21st and 24th Divisions had moved by a night march into the Loos valley. Progress was slow and exhausting and the men were carrying extra supplies, equipment, rations, and ammunition. At 1.20 a.m., the brigadiers of 24th Division met to consider their actions for the next morning.

The Official History of the Great War noted this about what happened next:

> The 71st Brigade, in rear of the 72nd, moved forward to the British original trenches, centre opposite Lone Tree, where it halted for the night. During the early hours of the 26th Br-General Shewen was ordered by the 7th Division, who furnished an officer as a guide, to detach one of his battalions 'to retake the Quarries'. The 9/ Norfolk was sent at 1 a.m., ... South of the Quarries, the Wiltshire and part of the Bedfordshire held the line along Stone Alley to Breslau Avenue. Here the Green Howards had rallied, thus linking up with the units in Quarry Trench.
>
> A counter attack was delivered on the Quarries from the old German front trenches at 6.45 a.m. on the 26th, by a battalion (9/Norfolk of the 71st Brigade) of the 24th Division, lent to the 7th Division by the XI. Corps for this purpose. Dead tired by its night march its attack immediately stopped by heavy fire and had to be abandoned after 13 officers and 409 other ranks had become casualties.

What is known from the battalion's war diary and from the First World War history of the Norfolk Regiment is that by 5.30 a.m., they were in the old German frontline, and at 6.45 a.m., as noted by the Official History, they went over the top advancing towards the Quarries. But the German fire was heavy from the start, especially from numerous snipers, and their advance faltered and they suffered heavy casualties. Major Kiesel of the 2nd Battalion Reserve Infantry Regiment 15 witnessed these attacks from Hulluch:

> The British artillery was apparently badly ranged in, because our casualties insignificant. At 1.00 pm the shelling ceased abruptly. Immediately after that, for a short while field artillery could be seen moving up. At 1.10 pm columns advancing on a broad front appeared from the same direction. I counted ten of them, alternately English and Scottish, each about 1,000 men to about 1,500 metres from the left flank of the battalion, two machine guns opened up, with the rifleman following suit a little later. Because the entire field of fire was covered with columns, the effect was excellent. Hundreds were seen to fall.
>
> However, undaunted, the columns continued their flanking march without ever turning to face the battalion. In order to halt any further advance, I ordered two

platoons of 6th Company and one platoon of 8th Company to move forward from Communication Trench 4. Despite British fire against the right flank, they advanced about 200 metres. At that point some of the British swung round towards them, which threw nearby columns into confusion. The remainder, ignoring everything, continued on their way to a point south of Hulluch.

At this time, the columns also came under flanking fire from Infantry Regiment strong. Some of the officers were mounted. As soon as the enemy approached casualties mounted into the thousands!

The columns were increasingly mixed up. Nevertheless, the enemy succeeded in closing right up to the wire obstacles. Here they suffered further significant casualties. Then the survivors turned tail and flooded in the opposite direction to the rear. The masses shrank until only about a tenth of them succeeded in getting back into safety.

Apparently large numbers had taken cover in the available trenches and dips in the ground, because the following day fifteen officers and 800 men were captured.

They had to seek cover and remained there, watching the 2nd Worcestershires going through their position in an effort to capture the quarries. At 7 p.m., the Germans fired flares and they then opened fire on the Norfolks. This fire was so heavy that the Norfolks had to retire to reserve trenches eventually being relieved by the Grenadier Guards.

Having marched back to Lone Tree, they then moved to Vermelles, reaching there at 6 a.m. on 27 September. A roll call identified five officers killed and nine wounded, with thirty-nine other ranks killed and 122 wounded. This totalled 209 men. It is noted in the Norfolk's history of the First World War that, in total, when they reached Ham on 29 September, they had sixteen officers and 555 other ranks from an original complement of thirty officers and 987 men. This totals a loss of fourteen officers and 432 other ranks killed, wounded, or missing in their initial baptism of fire on the killing field at Loos.

The Commonwealth War Graves Commission lists that between 26 and 27 September 1915, the 9th Norfolks lost sixty-nine men killed. One of these men can be identified as Private Samuel Percival Armfield (15895), a draper's assistant, who is pictured at the top of this article and records show he was just eighteen when he died.

One of the officers to die that day was 2Lt Cecil Wilson Morton White, aged twenty; he was the son of the Rev. Wilson Woodhouse White of Brockdish Rectory Diss and the late Edith Isabella White. A fellow officer wrote to his parents:

We were given an order to attack a German position six hundred yards away at 6.45 on Sunday last, and he and I and another officer jumped out of our trench with our platoons and crossed a small trench a little way ahead which was occupied by a

Scottish regiment. When we had got over that the enemy opened a tremendous rifle and machine gun fire upon us, and we lost heavily, as we were weighed down by packs and were hungry and tired after all we had gone through.

About eighty of us reached a trench, not the enemy's position, behind the parapet of which we halted for supports which did not come. The third officer had been knocked over, your son and I were the only officers with the men. He took a rifle and said to the man next him. 'Well I've got one German if I never get another.'

There was a man ten yards behind him wounded in the stomach, and your son turned around and shouted, 'For God's sake, man, don't drink that water!' and as he turned forward again he was shot in the middle of the forehead. He lived for eighteen hours and was never conscious again. There were a frightful number of casualties, and the qualified people could not get to him for twelve hours, especially under that fire; but I don't think he ever could have lived even if a doctor had been with him directly. He was a splendid fellow and a long way the best officer in the company. His men are terribly cut up about it.

Like most of the men who were lost that day, they have no known grave and are now commemorated on the Loos Memorial.

The battalion would now move with the rest of the 71st Brigade from the 24th Division to the 6th Division, where they remained until the end of the war. By October, they were in the Ypres Salient.

Guidebook

On the D947, at Hulluch, take the roundabout signposted for Vermelles, the D39. Park up at St Mary's ADS Cemetery, which you will come to on your left. Then walk back toward Hulluch. On your left, you will see a track. This can be very muddy and uneven, but you are now walking on the frontline for 25 September 1915. If you continue along this track, you will eventually see the Quarry on your right. This is where the 9th Battalion went over in an attempt to capture this position.

What3words: roommate.rubbing.backfired.

＊＊＊＊＊

At the end of September, the 7th Battalion was given orders to move and marched from Ploegsteert to Gonnehem and then to La Bourse. On 30 September, they took over trenches at the Chalk Pit from the Irish Guards. On their right, the line was held by the French, and on their left, the position was held by the 7th Battalion Suffolk Regiment. They went into the line with a complement of twenty-five officers and 926 other ranks.

By now, the Battle of Loos had been raging since 25 September 1915, when gains had been made by the British. But the battle had turned into a series of attacks that had failed after the Germans had managed to reorganise.

The Germans had counterattacked on 8 October 1915, which also ended in failure and they had lost heavily like their British counterparts on the killing fields of Loos. Further efforts were made by the British between 9 and 12 October, where local attacks were made with slight gains.

Between 1 and 4 October, by just occupying trenches in this sector, the battalion's casualty rate went up considerably and the war diary records that they lost eleven men killed and fifty-seven men wounded. Even when they were out of the line at Philosophe, they lost a further fourteen men wounded due to long-range shelling and an accident.

On 8 October, Maj. F. E. Walter took over command of the battalion from Lt-Col. John W. V. Carroll, who was moving on to command a brigade. But on 13 October 1915, the offensive was renewed at Loos where efforts were made to recover the Quarries and Fosse 8 and others were to consolidate the line of the Lens–La Bassée road between Chalk Pit Wood and the Vermelles–Hulluch road. Into this would come the 35th Brigade who would attack the Quarries.

So, on 12 October 1915, the battalion marched from Philosophe to trenches in front of the Quarries where they relieved the Coldstream Guards. The attack went in at 2 p.m., and this is what the Official History had this to say about it:

> The attack by the 35th Brigade against the Quarries also across open ground was made by the 7/Norfolk on the right and 7/Suffolk on the left leading, followed by the 5/Royal Berkshire and the 9/Essex. The volume of smoke proved inadequate to screen the operations from the Dump, as planned, and, in addition to receiving heavy frontal fire, the Brigade was enfiladed from Slag Alley and from a number of machine guns at the foot of the Dump, some of which took the 7/Suffolks in reverse.
>
> The Norfolk and R. Berkshire gained, mainly by bombing, many men being employed in passing bombs, about 300 yards of trench at the south-western end of the Quarries; and the Suffolk secured, partly by bombing and partly by an attack of one company over the open, about 200 and fifty yards of trenches, later known as 'The Hairpin', at right angles to the British line along the north-west side of the Quarries. The gap between the Norfolk and Suffolk was subsequently reduced by the Essex. But into the Quarries the attack failed to penetrate, and the Germans still maintained possession of them. Thus, by nightfall the 37th Brigade was holding Gun Trench and the southern part of Stone Alley, whilst the 35th Brigade had secured part of the south-western edge of the Quarries and the Hairpin.

More locally, using their war diary and the history of the Norfolk Regiment, we know the following:

Owing to the failure of the smoke screen, the Germans could be clearly seen manning their trenches when the attack was launched at 2 p.m. The Norfolk battalion soon began to suffer severely from a German machine gun opposite their right, enfilading their attack, which our trench mortars were unable to knock out. Its fire almost annihilated one squad as it tried to get through.

On the left fifty men succeeded in taking 200 yards of the enemy trench an held on there till the exhaustion of their supply of bombs forced them to retire till reinforced by 'A' Company and half of the Royal Berkshire.

Bombers under the command of 2Lt H. V. Franklin did manage to penetrate one of the main trenches along with a communication trench where they put in blocks. 'B' Company tried to follow the Berkshires but were held up with them, and it was impossible to reinforce the beleaguered defenders and those that attempted this were mown down by machine-gun fire in the first 20 yards.

There is an excellent account of the fighting around Hulluch from *Hauptmann Freiherr* Kurt von Forstner of the 1st Battalion Reserve Infantry Regiment 15:

Opposite Hulluch the British launched a series of five attacks. This was how the Supreme Army Headquarters communiqué described what happened. So what actually occurred? From the artillery observation post at 1.15 pm I witnessed a dreadful, yet deeply striking, scene. In the crater field north of the road [from Hulluch] to Vermelles, shells were crashing down, just like strong rain hitting a stony surface and splashing upwards. Huge fountains of earth and black smoke pillared up and, in between, were the greenish yellow clouds of heavy shrapnel rounds, interspersed with the white puffs signifying light shrapnel. The skies became ever more leaden, whilst the blanket of smoke which cloaked the earth thickened constantly. The company of the 233rd had the worst of it, huddled in a small section of the Artilleriegraben (Artillery Trench). The only hope was that the beaten zone of the shells would allow a few survivors to counter the attack with an intact machine gun and so retain the Artilleriegraben because, there was no doubt about it, this was all about a breakthrough to La Bassée via Haisnes!

They were about to make the attempt between Fosse 13 and Hulluch and we were extremely concerned about the two and a half companies which were manning the new trenches, which had hardly any protective wire and absolutely no mined dugouts. I toyed with withdrawing them immediately via the 8th Company positions and the central communications trench and placing them back in the old secure positions ... but that would have meant that those manning the Artilleriegraben would have been lost for certain.

A runner arrived to tell me that I was wanted urgently on the telephone by Hauptmann von Briesen, the Brigade Adjutant, but I stared on over the sea of smoke and studied the situation of my battalion. It seemed possible that our new trench had not yet been identified by the enemy artillery and, as a result, would be spared the drum fire. So that is how I decided to leave the company forward in the new trench.

Back! We raced as though the Devil was at our heels, for the shells and shrapnel rounds were pursuing us swiftly.... The telephone system was totally jammed as generals, general staff officers, adjutants, orderly officers, regimental and sector commanders made calls in all directions, at a time when the only conversations should have been between the artillery commander and the batteries, which had the best view of all with tripod binoculars in their observation posts.

Towards 3.00pm we smelled chlorine. li was a gas attack with a favourable wind. The overcast day almost like night. 2nd Company reported 'Gas attack!' We prepared to defend ourselves. It was the final report from the front. Thereafter all the telephone lines to the battalion command post were broken.

The battalion reported to the rear, 'Situation of Artilleriegraben and 2nd Company serious. They will never take the Hulluch position. If Hulluch is surrounded the battalion will assume that a relief force will be sent'. We had to mask up and we prepared to greet the Tommies if they suddenly appeared in our cellar. I climbed up into the rafters. Above the cloud of smoke, which hung like fog in the mountains, shone a pale, watery sun.

Down below Jakobsen opined, if this gas gets any thicker we shall have to pull out the air is totally poisoned, it is Impossible to breathe.' Our masks are unequal to the task. Within minutes our hearts were pounding and every breath was a struggle ... fire was coming down round our cellar ... ten direct hits on the house, now the enemy was attacking.... On orders from Brigade we had to send a patrol to establish contact with the Hohenzollernwerk. With a heavy heart, the battalion sent three trusted runners who had been carefully briefed. After three hours they returned with no positive information. They had not found the commander of the 233rd. However, three of our five lads who had been sent forward with essential supplies brought good news from the front one of the five had been hit by a shell and one collapsed, overcome by gas.

This man, written off as dead, regained consciousness after five hours, returned and was greeted with great jubilation). The three explained, 'The Tommies attacked 8th Company. They will not do so again. We should have gladly stayed forward. It would have been better than here.' One expanded further, 'As the gas became thicker behind us, we legged it forward rapidly!'

The telephone line to the old position was working. Leutnant Ducker reported a direct hit from a 380 mm shell in the trench. Two dugouts were crushed and six men were buried. After feverish work lasting for hours, only three men were rescued alive.

Leutnant Ducker also reported that the situation was serious on the right and that the Artilleriegraben and the Kiesgrube had been lost. *Unteroffizier* Heine and *Gefreiter* Niemann, the bravest of the brave, had to go out once more to clarify the situation. They were expected back at 9.30 pm. It became later and we gave them up as lost.

Then Heine arrived, carrying his groaning comrade on his back. He had been hit by a shell splinter in the small of his back....

However, already at 5.00 pm, the battalion could report back, 'Attack completely beaten off. A battle with hand grenades is continuing off to the right.' The gas clouds were dispersing and, with relief, we could unmask Encouraging reports arrived from the front. 2nd Company had only suffered two casualties as result of the bombardment so, the moment the bombardment had ceased and the gas cloud had lifted, they were ready and prepared, manning the parapet ... the enemy was hidden by smoke, but this swirled away in the wind just in time. Immediately, three strong waves of attackers could be seen.

Our close support guns and mortars ... destroyed section after section and the Tommies were soon attempting to deviate left and right.

Our troops were grateful for the accuracy of our artillery fire and the mortar bombs had a murderous effect. Our small arms then took over and did their duty to the full. Very few British soldiers escaped to run to the rear or north towards the lost Artilleriegraben.

One man caught up in all of this was Lance Corporal James Nourse from Heacham who told his story in the *Lynn News and Advertiser* after he was evacuated. During the advance, he was wounded and crawled into a shell hole. He laid out in no-man's-land that night, and the following day with very little water. Then he heard a shout:

Thus, he found his own platoon sergeant, who was badly wounded. Water was found in bottles belonging to men who had been killed, also biscuits and they made themselves as comfortable as possible while they waited for stretcher bearers. These failed to find them, however, and Nourse made an attempt to regain the British lines. Instead he got to the German lines and had a narrow escape, in fact, he had to sham being dead until darkness came over. Later he moved into a big shell hole, spent a day there, and not for some time did he find the British lines. Then parties were dispatched to bring the sergeant and others, while Nourse was sent to the base and on to England. He still keeps to his bed, but is going on well.

The 7th Battalion withdrew to the old British line on 14 October from Fosse Way to the Hulluch Road. There they remained suffering shelling and received a draft of 263 men between 15 and 17 October. On 19 October, the Germans counterattacked and the battalion stood-to, but were not used.

On 20 October, they marched back to Béthune where they were inspected by Major-General Scott on 22 October who congratulated them on their exploits on 13 October 1915. Between the 1 and 20 October 1915, the battalion lost 192 men killed and a large number of them have no known grave and are commemorated on the Loos Memorial. The history of the Norfolk Regiment notes that, in total, the battalion lost eleven officers killed or wounded and 422 men killed, wounded, or missing on the killing fields of Loos.

One of the sources shown to me in the Royal Norfolk Regiment Museum archives were letters written to Captain Hammond of the 7th Battalion enquiring about their loved ones who had been lost in the fighting. One letter resonated with me, which was dated 21 November 1915:

Captain J Hammond

Dear Sir,

We thank you for your letter of the 15th inst. In reference to our son Pte W. Scott 12452, and regret exceedingly that you are unable to find out what has become of him. We are not yet hopeless that he may yet turn up as first of all a parcel was returned to my parents in the North marked 'Hospital present location uncertain' it was initialled R.T.R. and this information was communicated to the British Red Cross Soc., who evidently advised the War Office as they wrote for the wrapper of the parcel which was sent to them.

Also, a sergeant friend of my son's wrote to France and had information that a 'Scott' of the 7th Norfolks was received into the 1st General Hospital at Etretat on the 16th October but this has not yet been confirmed. Again, a letter was sent from Liverpool which was returned marked 'wounded' initial R.T.R. and stamped, as before, present location uncertain. I now enclose this envelope in the hope it may assist you.

We first heard from Pte W. Joyce 12505 that my son had fallen and possible he may know more than Brown whom you mentioned in your letter however this is doubtful as we have had a letter from Joyce saying he feared that he was killed. There is one point I would like cleared up if it is possible and can you manage it, that is, was the ground cleared of dead and wounded after the German trench attacked was taken (I understand you did not retire) if so is it possible for Brown or Joyce who saw my son lying wounded to visit the place to see if there is any trace of his having been killed by shells whilst lying on the ground. Of course, I may be asking something ridiculous or very dangerous, not knowing the 'lay of the land' or the circumstances but as an officer you will know how to act and I am quite sure will equally well understand our feeling anxiety to know what has become of our boy. Again, thanking you or your letter and your offer to do anything if you could, and with best wishes for your personal welfare and of the Norfolk Regt. generally.

Yours faithfully,

H. Scott

The soldier in question was William Scott who had enlisted at St Paul's Churchyard, aged twenty; he had served in 'C' Company and was the son of Mr and Mrs H. Scott of 8 Edleston Road in Crewe. William was killed in action on 13 October and has no known grave and is now commemorated on the Loos Memorial.

This letter shows just how desperate families were for the truth as to what had happened to their loved ones and also just how much the families did not know about the realities of trench warfare. This letter is one of countless held in the regimental archives that tell a similar story. It is known that Captain Hammond replied to each letter.

Guidebook

On the D947, at Hulluch, take the roundabout signposted for Vermelles, the D39. Park up at St Mary's ADS Cemetery, which you will come to on your left. Then walk back toward Hulluch. On your left, you will see a track. This can be very muddy and uneven, but you are now walking on the frontline for 13 October 1915. If you continue along this track, you will eventually see the Quarry on your right. This is where the 7th Battalion went over in an attempt to capture this position.

What3words: roommate.rubbing.backfired.

8

On the Eve of the Somme, The Norfolk Regiment Battalions: 30 June 1916

On 26 May 1916, Lt Sidney Smith, who was serving in the 7th Norfolks, wrote to Edwin Winch, chief constable of Norwich City Police. Sidney had previously served in Norwich City Police but had joined the Army in 1914. In the letter, he noted: 'I am now about 28 miles from the firing line. I can hear the roars of cannon ... wherever you go you see camp after camp full of troops but I think they will be wanted and practically every man in England to end the war'. Certainly, Lieutenant Smith was correct when he noted that the troops in France in Flanders would be wanted.

The year 1916 started with great optimism for the Allies. They had hoped to launch simultaneous offensives from three sides in a bid for victory over Germany and her allies. The mistakes made in 1915 were not to be made in 1916. However, this was shattered when the Germans struck first when they launched an offensive at Verdun in the French sector.

French was replaced by Douglas Haig in December of 1915. He was a distinguished cavalry officer and had commanded an infantry corps in 1914 and then had become an army commander in 1915. He was also a devout churchgoer and believed he had God on his side. His first job was an instruction given by the British government that he must plan for an offensive. The plan called for the British Army to relieve the French at Verdun, to inflict heavy casualties on the Germans, and to put the British Army in a favourable position for victory in 1917. The Fourth Army, under the command of General Sir Henry Rawlinson, was given this task.

This would be achieved by attacking the German trenches along an 18-mile front and would involve 120,000 men. The main thrust would come between Montauban in the south, cutting through the old Roman road from Albert to Bapaume and then moving north through the River Ancre ending where the British lines faced the Germans at Serre. Haig also ordered the commanders of the 1st and 2nd Armies to mount threatening moves against the Germans. This would keep the Germans guessing as to where the main attack would come from. Finally, the Third Army's commander, General Sir Edmund Allenby, would attack Gommecourt to the north of the Fourth Army in a diversionary attack.

Once a breakthrough had been achieved, three cavalry divisions under the command of Lt-Gen. Sir Hubert Gough would break out with infantry divisions held at the rear and exploit the Fourth Army's success, taking the German second and third lines in one great push.

All this was to be aided by a massive artillery bombardment. This would last for five days and nights before the attack. Every available artillery piece would be used for this. It was believed that this bombardment would wipe out the Germans. The plan devised that the German barbed wire be destroyed and the German trenches caved in and their strongpoints smashed. With this achieved, the German defenders would be too stunned to fight leaving the infantry to mop up the survivors. They would then outnumber the defenders by seven to one. It would be easy to cross no-man's-land and take the German defences all the way to the French town of Bapaume. The bombardment would also continue after the initial attack. As the infantry advanced on the first German trench line, the bombardment would move onto the next one.

Unfortunately, it would not be as simple as all this.

By 1916, Haig was not satisfied with his predicament. He had preferred to have time to plan the British offensive with the French fighting alongside, which had been set for August 1916. Although the French would attack on the right of the British, it would only be along an 8-mile front with seven divisions and not the forty that had been promised before Verdun. He was also under enormous pressure to attack as soon as possible and he had confided in his commanders that he did not expect victory in 1916.

This region of France is named after the River Somme and the department the river is located in. The British sector lay in the extreme north-east corner and the river actually flowed through the French sector of the battlefield. Before the arrival of the British in July 1915, the Somme had always been considered a quiet sector of the front.

In 1916, that all changed. The British high command held the firm belief that there should be no cushy areas within their sector. They organised night patrols to attack the German defences and to take prisoners, thereby keeping the Germans on their toes. This filled the Germans with resolve and they strengthened their trench systems.

Using the 'defence in depth' method, this meant a series of frontline, second-line, and third-line trenches, all interspersed with machine-gun posts and barbed wire. In total, this meant that they built up to four reserve trenches behind their frontline. All the trenches were then tied into nine fortified villages and specially erected redoubts. Much of this had been learnt in 1915 when the French had attacked German positions at Serre. The whole sector had learnt from this and had bolstered their defences.

All these areas had woods linked to them and the whole area was laced with machine-gun posts, some 1,000 of them. These had the firepower to put out 500 rounds a minute and were the equivalent of forty soldiers firing in unison.

They also differed from their British counterparts in the way the trenches were constructed building their trenches in well-drained soil. In fact, the whole area is chalk down land, meaning that ditches did not have to be dug for drainage and the whole area is covered with rich soil. The area is very open and there are no hedgerows to speak of. The British trenches were poor in comparison. Some of the German dugouts went down as far as 40 feet in depth.

They had electricity, water, ventilation, and were well constructed. These dugouts often had two to three entrances and exits. The Germans also held the high ground all along the Somme allowing them the luxury of being able to look over their British counterparts. This would also have a deciding factor on what was to come.

On 24 June 1916, the largest bombardment of the war so far started. There were no shortages of shells as there had been in the battles fought in 1915. For every 50 feet of earth, there was one gun placed pointing towards the German line. The British gunners would fire more shells in the bombardment, in one week, than had been fired in the first year of the war.

The bombardment had a strict regime. Every morning would pour fire on the Germans for eighty minutes seeing every gun firing non-stop. The bombardment would then continue all day. At dusk, half the guns would fall silent and heavy machine guns would take their place to harass the German rear. The Germans were surprised by this immense bombardment. But, for the most part, they remained safe in their deep dugouts with only single sentries on duty to warn of attack.

More importantly and alarmingly, the shells designed to destroy their dugouts and wire had many failings. The ammunition designed to destroy the German wire was not doing its job. These shells were filled with shrapnel balls. They had to have the fuse set just right. If it were too short it would explode harmlessly over the wire, if it were set late the shell would hit the ground and the earth would take the impact.

The shells designed to destroy the German dugouts were equally inadequate. Alarmingly, the British did not possess enough big guns with which to do this and the ammunition stored for the attack had been rushed through the factories. This had resulted in up to one-third of the shells being duds. This enormous barrage could be heard as far away as England, and in one week, the British guns fired 1,508,652 shells.

The Germans, deep in their dugouts, knew that an attack was imminent, but when? A young German private kept a diary of the barrage in his sector. It shows that apart from the terrible noise most of the German soldiers were safe. Private Eversmann, 143rd Regiment of Infantry, wrote in his diary:

10 0'clock Veritable Trommelfeur (Drumfire). In twelve hours they estimate that 60,000 shells have fallen on our battalion sector. When will they attack? Tomorrow,

the day after? Who knows?' 'It is night. Shall I live till morning? Haven't we had enough of this frightful horror? Five days and five nights now this hell concert has lasted. One's head is like a madman's; the tongue sticks to the roof of the mouth. Almost nothing to eat and nothing to drink. No sleep. All contact with the outer world cut off. No sign of life from home nor can we send any news to our loved ones. What anxiety they must feel about us. How long is this going to last?

Many commanders were ordered to send out parties into no-man's-land to report on the progress of the bombardment. These reports varied and many led the high command into false optimism.

Evidence of the ferocity of this bombardment can be found in a letter written by Herbert Cooper from Worstead who was serving in the 8th Battalion Norfolk Regiment. He wrote to his sister on 26 June 1916:

Dear Sister,

I now write a few lines in answer to your letter. Hope they will find you and the boys quite well, me being the same just now. You must excuse paper and bad writing as we are in the midst of a terrific bombardment, no doubt it's heaven in Blighty.

By now what's taking place all along the line looks impossible for anything to live through this lot but no doubt some of us will see it to the end if we are lucky.

Well, I got the photo of the little boys all right, they are just taken so very grand, I don't think anymore. I hope you have heard something of George by this time, I haven't. Well I must finish this letter rather quick as nearly impossible to write at all with so much explosion going on all around you everywhere, it's enough to drive us all off our senses.

Now I will close with love to all.

From Brother John

XXXXXXXXXX

I've never seen anything of your husband although I know he's so very far from where we are.

This furious tirade of shells must have been quite heartening to the men who were there in the frontlines to witness it.

Norfolk Regiment who were serving on the Western Front was positioned prior to this battle. The 1st Norfolks were at Wailly near Arras and were about to go into the line there. The 7th Norfolks were at Franvillers prior to moving to Henencourt where they would be when the battle started. The 8th Norfolks were in frontline trenches facing the German strongpoint at Montauban. They were due to go over the top on 1 July 1916. The 9th Norfolks were supplying a working party of eight officers and 400 men for a working party around Camp K near Ypres. By the end of the campaign in November 1916, all of them would have fought there.

9

The 8th Battalion, The Battle of the Somme, Montauban to Delville Wood: 1–19 July 1916

On 1 July 1916, the 18th (Eastern) Division and the 30th Division had the task of taking the village of Montauban.

At 'Zero Hour', the first Norfolk regiment battalion to see action on the Somme, the 8th Norfolks, listed that they were positioned with the 7th Queen's on their right and the 6th Royal Berkshire Regiment on their left. This is incorrect. To their right were half of 'B' Company from the 7th Battalion the Buffs (East Kent Regiment) and then the 7th Queen's Royal West Surrey Regiment. These battalions faced the German line opposite trenches known as Breslau and Mine. To the right of the 7th Queen's was the 8th East Surrey Regiment. But a lot of things happened in this one small area of the Somme frontline and we need to cover the initial phase first.

The 8th Norfolks were positioned astride the Carnoy–Montauban Road situated to the north-west of Carnoy. To their right, this area, which can still be seen today, can be made out by using a tree line, which is now recorded as 'La Longue Haie' (The Long Hedge) on a modern-day French IGN map. On a trench map from 1916, this is registered as 'Talus Boise' (Timber Slope).

The first thing that happened in this area was that, at 7.28 a.m., a mine was fired under a German position known as Casino Point and two smaller explosive charges, known as 'Russian Saps' also at the western end of the 18th Division's area where it was known there were machine guns sited to fire on the flanks of the advancing troops.

Both the mines assisted the advancing troops, but they had not killed all the Germans in the garrison and this held up the advance of the 7th Buffs, 7th Queen's, and 7th Royal West Kents who lost many men as the Germans were able to pour fire into them. The Germans were also able to man their first support trench, which became their frontline and ensured that the trenches to the rear of this position were also manned.

This meant that as the British barrage lifted, there were around 300 Germans who were able to defend the area, but fortunately, the German's artillery was not able to pour heavy fire onto the area.

The explosion of the Casino Point mine had helped their advance where they along with the 6th Royal Berkshires had been able to advance and capture many German prisoners who had come out into no-man's-land. The war diary mentions that all resistance was 'cowed and at once surrendered. C Company on our right took around 30 prisoners from the west edge of the Mine craters'.

By 7.40 a.m., Mine Support had fallen; the battalion had been lucky in that it had suffered no casualties at this point. Bund support fell at 8 a.m. They only met resistance at a place called 'The Castle' and Breslau Support Trench, which held the advancing Norfolks to their right:

> The two assaulting companies on leaving Bund Support came under very heavy enfilade machine gun fire from the direction of Breslau Support and Back Trench and suffered heavily, Captain B.P. Ayre being killed and Captain J.H. Hall being seriously wounded.... There now remained no officer with the left leading company and two subalterns in the right leading company, which were reduced to about 90 and 100 respectively.

However, the lead troops, under CSM A. F. Raven, made good progress and found the wire cut and the Castle soon surrendered leaving Breslau Support and Back trench to resist. But the 8th Norfolks continued onward making for their next objective, which was called Pommiers Redoubt. Although they were checked by three German machine guns, these were soon silenced or seen to retreat when a bombing party managed to surprise and rush one of the crews:

> By 0750hrs the 8/Norfolks had captured part of Pommiers Trench. However, it was here that they could advance no further due to enemy fire from Breslau Support ... a platoon from the Support Company, under 2nd Lieut G.E. Miall-Smith, and the Battalion Bombers, under Sergeant H.H. West had also been sent up to this point, this strong point fell and the garrison of 150 Germans and 2 Officers of a Bavarian regiment surrendered, and right leading company was then able to push forward in to the East portion of Pommiers Trench which up to then had not been taken.

By now, the other brigades in the 18th Division had either captured, or were close to capturing all their first objectives and the battalion then consolidated their position. They could not assist the 6th Berkshires in the capture of a position called 'The Loop' and 'B' Company went assist 'C' Company. It was only until supporting elements of the 18th Division and the advance in Montauban by the

30th Division had cleared most of the German resistance that the 8th Norfolks could assist in the capture of the Loop, which happened at 3 p.m. when 'B' Company took this position allowing 'C' and 'D' to advance to Montauban Alley.

> Owing to machine guns firing from this line and from N.W. of Montauban 'D' Company on the left suffered heavy casualties, and 'C' Company, led by 2nd Lieut J.H. Attenborough made repeated attempts to get into Montauban Alley, but did not succeed until a bombing party, under 2nd Lieut L.A. Gundry-White, gained an entrance by way of Loop Trench on the left. Unfortunately, just before this had been affected, 2nd Lieut J.H. Attenborough with C.S.M. J. Coe had both been killed in an attempt to get into this trench.

John Haddon Attenborough was aged twenty-four and the son of the late George William and Elizabeth Sarah Attenborough, of South Ockendon, Essex and Jeremiah Coe came from West Lexham, both have no known grave and are commemorated on the Thiepval Memorial on the Somme.

But the advance of the 18th Division, along with the 7th and 30th Divisions to their left and right respectively cannot be underestimated. Their advances would pave the way for what was to come in the next few days and the Official History of the Great War makes particular note of the 18th and 30th Divisions:

> As a result of the successes of the 30th and 18th Divisions, XIII. Corps had driven the Germans from the entire sector of the Alley was captured and the 8/Norfolks managed to make contact with the 7/Queens on their right and the 6/Royal Berkshires on their left. By now 'C' and 'D' Companies were down to 70 and 80 other ranks with one officer in overall charge of them and 'B' company was sent up to support them. Montauban Ridge, allotted to it as the objective in the first phase of the battle. The corps attributed the success of its divisions to their training in open warfare; to thorough 'mopping up', so that no Germans sprang up behind the lines so shoot the attackers in the back; and to the preliminary ascertainment, by feints of where the German barrages would fall, and rapid movement of the troops over the belts of ground involved.

But this all came at a high price and both divisions lost over 6,000 men killed or wounded on the first day. What is even more tragic is that from 7.30 to 8.30 a.m., the British Army sustained over 30,000 casualties. A great majority of these lay in no-man's-land with no real hope of being rescued, or tended to by medics, and many died of their wounds. By the end of the first day, nearly 60,000 men had died or were wounded, a total of 20,000 were either killed outright, or died of their wounds. One of these men was John Roper from my village of Worstead.

John Henry Roper was born in 1894 and was the son of Edwin and Mary Roper of Briggate. He also had a brother, Edwin (Junior), and four sisters, Dorothy, Annie, Jane, and Evelyn. John is listed as a farm labourer in 1911.

I hold a record of part of his service history and that states that he died in the German trenches north of Carnoy. This further lists that he was originally buried in a position 2¼ miles north-east of Carnoy, 2¼ miles south of Fricourt and 5½ miles south-east of Albert. Tragically, his grave was never located after the war and he is now commemorated on the Thiepval Memorial.

Another casualty that day was Alfred Fox from Trowse. He had served over there with his brother, Percy since the 8th Battalion landed in France.

France

Sunday 4th 7/16

My dear Mother & Family

I want you all to be as brave as possible, for its sad news that I've got to inform you of this morning, Alfred being killed in our great battle on Sat.

It will come a great blow to you all I know but we must look at it as bright as possible, for mother he fell with nearly all the rest of our NCOs together with our Captain, the best in the world.

I've got to buck up & bear it bravely for our cause is hard enough, but I had fellows around me that morning who have lost two & three brothers in the fight, & I must thank God, to think that I am alive. He fell thinking of you. I went all through it all in the thickest & came out without a scratch.

Mother I/we have sympathy of the whole of D Company with us this morning, he was known & liked by the whole company. I can't help but feel proud to think I am his brother & you his mother, for he played a good part & put wonderful confidence in his men, he died the death of a fine Englishman.

You must tell Florence that Percy was wounded in the arm nothing serious, he's a lucky chap. Charlie Blake wasn't in it. Mason was wounded in the shoulder.

Now mother I can't write more this morning, do bear up & help me, for our case is only one of thousands, & you will hear how our company has suffered when they receive the official news.

Please to say we are now out of it & having a well-earned rest, have written to Alfred's wife this morning. God be with us till we meet again.

Your ever-loving son,

Percy

Will write again further…

Don't worry yourselves…

There is one thing to note in relation to an action that occurred with the 8th Battalion East Surrey Regiment. An officer in the regiment was so worried about how his untried and untested troops would act in the heat of battle that he came up with an idea. Capt. Wilfred Percy Nevill, known as Billie, decided to buy four footballs, one for each of his platoons and a prize was put up for the first platoon to get a ball into the German lines. At Zero Hour, they did just that. The spectacle was witnessed by many people and would become immortalised afterwards, Capt. Alfred Irwin of the 8th East Surrey Regiment witnessed what happened from the British lines.

Alongside Nevill would be Company Sgt-Maj. Charlie Wells (4797). Charlie came from Norfolk having been born and raised in Coltishall village. Sadly, Nevill was shot in the head as he rallied his men at the wire and CSM Wells died at his side, Maj. Irwin, Nevill's CO, recounted after the war: 'But so quickly Nevill and his second in command were both killed, plus his company sergeant major (Wells). I picked up all the chaps I could find and went over the parapet myself'.

Charlie Wells has no known grave and is now commemorated on the Thiepval Memorial. He was twenty-eight years old when he died and was the son of Charles and Nellie Wells of Chapel Lane in Coltishall. Billy Nevill is now laid to rest in Carnoy Military Cemetery close to where they went over the top on 1 July 1916.

The medical services were pushed to full stretch in a very short space of time. The medics could only cope with 9,500 wounded men at a time, but by nightfall, they had had to deal with 10,000 cases and another 22,000 were on the way.

The reason for this was that there were not enough ambulance trains to evacuate the wounded, and many men who might have been treated, had they been evacuated, simply died in the open at casualty clearing stations with no medical aid. Many others died as the Germans fired their counter barrages.

The 8th Norfolks remained in trenches to the west of Montauban and sent patrols from the along Caterpillar Trench and East Trench towards Caterpillar Wood. These patrols did not make contact with the enemy, and by now, the Germans were in full-blown retreat from this area. Although fire was received by German artillery it was noted as being at 'extreme range and inaccurate' by the Official History. This is not backed up by the war diary that states that a 5.9 Howitzer was firing from the north of Longueval and this wounded two officers and thirty-eight men over a two-day period.

On 2 July, the Germans attempted a counterattack around Montauban and the diary notes seeing SOS flares going up and the battalion stood-to, but their area remain quiet. What they had witnessed was the only serious German counterattack after the initial first day. Between 3 and 4 a.m., the German 12th Reserve and 16th Bavarian Regiments had attacked Montauban from the north and east. They were stopped by artillery from the 30th Division, although they were more successful in the French sector to the right. On the evening of 3 July, the 8th Norfolks were relieved by the 8th Suffolks and moved into bivouacs in Carnoy.

The action on 1 July 1916 is looked at as a defeat, where the cream of England was wiped out in one fell swoop. Certainly, this is so in many sectors of that terrible battle. But we must also remember the success and the gains made between Fricourt and Montauban, which would pave the way for the next phases of the battle, which other battalions of the Norfolk Regiment would take part in.

Guidebook

From Albert, take the D938 signposted Peronne & Fricourt. Continue on this road until you see a sign for Carnoy. Turn left here onto the D254. This road will take you to Montauban. Continue on this road until you see a hard standing on your right and two trees in front of you. This is the British frontline for 1 July 1916. This is also the 8th Battalion's jumping off point for that day, and they were either side of this road.

What3words: chalked.former.emerald.

Optional Visits

Return to Carnoy and visit Carnoy Military Cemetery, which contains the remains of thirteen men from the 1st, 8th, and 9th Battalions who died between December 1915 and October 1916.

What3words: daunt.bobbled.lightens.

Retrace your steps and head back toward Albert. Turn left when you see the sign for Bercordel-Becourt. At the next junction, turn right and you will see a sign for Norfolk Cemetery. Take this road and the cemetery will be on your right after about half a mile. There are seventeen Norfolk regiment men buried here—I say men, but one is a boy aged sixteen called Isaac Albert Laud who was shot by a sniper on 9 August 1915 while the 1st Battalion were in trenches near here. The soldiers buried here served in the 1st and 8th Battalions between August and December 1915 and the cemetery was begun by the 1st Norfolks in August 1915 and used by other units (including the 8th Norfolks) until August 1916.

*****

The Battle of the Somme did not end on 1 July 1916. It lasted a further 140 days.

Haig and Rawlinson had taken stock of their losses and gains from day one and began concentrate on the areas that had been taken, or had gained partial successes. This area can be pinpointed from an area starting at Ovillers La Boiselle to Montauban. Even though the British had suffered one of the greatest setbacks of the war, it is a testament to these men and to the commanders of 1916 that they were able to withdraw the beleaguered troops from the frontline and put in fresh divisions who were given the task of carrying on the offensive.

On 3 July, Bernafay and Caterpillar Woods fell to the 18th Division and the 27th Brigade of the 9th (Scottish) Division. The 19th (Western) Division were putting the pressure on the Germans defenders at La Boiselle and Ovillers, which had been held by the Germans on 1 July 1916, was looked at and the task of capturing the fortified village was given to the 12th (Eastern) Division.

After 1 July 1916, the 8th Battalion had spent the next few days clearing the battlefield and digging communication trenches before going to the rear lines and eventually ended up at Grovetown Camp close to Happy Valley. They were reinforced by a draft of 240 other ranks and ten officers, who came from the 1st, 7th, and 10th Norfolks and the battalion also trained for further attacks.

The 30th Division, which had seen action on 1 July, were given the task of taking the wood. It was a bitter battle, seeing much hand-to-hand fighting, with the same thing happening at Mametz Wood was eventually captured by the 38th (Welsh) Division on 12 July. It had taken the division from 7 July to do so and cost them 4,000 casualties, including 600 killed.

The British then turned their attention toward High Wood in a continuation of the push through German lines. The Battle of Bazentin Ridge opened at dawn on the 14th, in darkness, and was preceded by a short sharp five-minute artillery bombardment; this forced the exposed German defenders to their dugouts and the infantry moved forward. Bazentin-le-Grand and Bazentin-le-Petit were secured with a matter of hours. Having established a position at Bazentin-le-Petit, it became apparent to the British that High Wood itself was deserted; a large gap in the German lines was waiting to be exploited. Therefore, permission was sought from headquarters to dispatch infantry into the wood.

However, it was instead decided that here was an ideal scenario for the use of cavalry who could, it was stated, move far more quickly than infantry and may even break right through to Bapaume. During the delay between the request for an infantry advance into the wood being sent, between 9 a.m. and midday, by which time still no orders for a cavalry advance had been given, the Germans moved slowly back into the wood, effectively plugging the hole in their lines.

By the time the cavalry was finally sent forwards, at around 7 p.m., the Germans had established sufficient defences to be able to decimate the oncoming British with machine-gun fire. Despite the costly failure of the attack upon High Wood, the cavalry nevertheless secured a line from High Wood to Longueval. That night, the British, under heavy fire, attempted to establish a line inside the wood, in readiness for an attack upon the German forces situated in the north-western half of the wood on the following day.

The British commanders attempted to launch an attack upon Martinpuich in the north, missing the fact that the Germans had not yet been fully cleared from High Wood. Situated midway between Bazentin-le-Petit and Martinpuich, skirting the edge of High Wood, was sited a formidable trench system known as the Switch Line. This defensive line then continued onwards running to the north of Delville Wood. This meant that when the British attacked they were subjected to enfilading fire from the wood; therefore, a simultaneous attack from the western side of the wood failed with the 33rd Division attacking towards Martinpuich also being checked forcing the British to withdraw entirely from High Wood.

The battle on the 14th had also involved attacks on Longueval Ridge and the village of Longueval itself. This had been turned into a redoubt by the Germans and was littered with reinforced cellars, bunkers, and machine-gun posts linked by underground tunnels.

At 3.35 a.m., the 26th and 27th Brigades of the 9th (Scottish) Division attacked in darkness, seizing the southern part of the village, and patrols were sent into Delville Wood. But this whole area was heavily defended and the attack had incurred heavy losses, especially in the attack on Waterlot Farm, situated to the south of wood. The 1st South African Brigade, which had been the 9th Division's reserve, was sent in the village to assist in clearing the south of Longueval and was ordered to clear Delville Wood of Germans. But the advance was postponed to the next morning.

On 15 July, the South African Brigade, with a total of 3,150 officers and men, attacked Delville Wood. The South Africans managed to clear the southern edge of German forces but the remainder of the wood remained in German hands. The South Africans fought their action in poor weather with the enemy artillery dropping shells at a rate of 400 shells a minute. This transformed the wood into a shell of broken and shattered tree stumps, which would become pockmarked with massive shell holes. For five days, the South Africans remained in the wood repeatedly fighting off heavy German counter attacks and terrible hand-to-hand fighting ensued.

Casualties in the South African Brigade were horrendous, with the dead outnumbering the wounded by four to one. Attempts were made to reinforce the South Africans and the 76th Brigade from the 3rd Division managed to reach them on the morning of 17 July. However, the Germans launched two massive counter attacks on 18 July.

The first fell onto the beleaguered South Africans at 3.45 a.m. and the second during the afternoon. The preliminary bombardment alone lasted eleven hours before the Germans attacked. The South Africans were pushed back to the western corner of the wood where they managed to hold the line along Princes Street, a gallop that ran west to east and situated in the central part of the wood.

The Germans also retook most of Longueval where they managed to infiltrate as far as to the central road of the village. Even greater gains were made in the eastern part of the wood with the German 153rd Regiment pushing the South Africans right out of the wood and onto the Ginchy Road. Here they were stopped by British artillery and machine-gun fire from Longueval.

So, by dawn on 19 July, the South African Brigade were desperately low on ammunition and men, and it is here that we come back to the 8th Norfolk Regiment. On 18 July, the battalion had moved into the area of the old fron-line and ended up near to where they had initially had gone over the top as the war diary records them being situated in the 'Talus Bois Salient'.

It was here that they were warned at 1.30 a.m. on 19 July to proceed to the valley north of Montauban and prepare for an attack on Delville Wood. They along with the rest of the 53rd Brigade had been loaned to the now depleted 9th Division. It was the 8th Norfolks that attacked first. They went in at 7.15 a.m. and their orders had been specific:

> We are to take the whole of the South portion of the wood from West to East, as far up as Princes Street, the middle ride of the wood, and that while that operation was being carried out a barrage would be on the north portion of the wood, North of Princes Street and directly the South portion was cleared, the 10th Bn., the Essex Regiment and the 6th Royal Berkshire Regiment would form up just South of Princes Street, and the 8th Bn., Suffolk Regiment, in the village, and then take the north of the wood and the North of the village, and that then the 8th Bn., the Norfolk Regiment would take over the whole of the wood and hold it with 16 strong points around the edge.

There is an excellent after-action report for this engagement, and we will follow that as well as look at the narrative for what was reported later on. The after-action report was put together by the 8th Battalion's CO at the time, Lt-Col. Henry Gaspard de Lavalette Ferguson:

> Briefly, the task which confronted us on the morning of July 19th, was to clear the southern portion of Delville Wood, deploying at the one hand in the S.W. corner and attacking in one easterly direction. It was decided that two companies, 'A' & 'B', should make the attack, 'D' Company being held in reserve, 'C' Company providing protection on the flanks.
> Battalion Headquarters was established in the village of Longueval at the corner of Dover Street and Pall Mall. Proceeding in file, the one hand was reached by A the leading company at 6.30 a.m. and they at once deployed in four waves facing the direction of their objective. It was arranged that 'B' Company should be on the left but likewise machine gun fire and much sniping from the N.W. corner of the wood caused us to alter our plans and leave 'B' Company on the right. The latter company accordingly deployed on the N side of South St from its junction with Down St to Buchanan St.

Initially, the attack went in well, and 'B' Coy managed to reach Campbell Street. However, 'A' Coy, to which Herbert Cooper, a man from my village, was part of, had difficulty advancing when a German machine gun from the east of the wood above Princes Street opened up on them. 'A' Coy incurred heavy casualty here, including the loss of both their officers, Lieutenants H. M. MacNichol and B. W. Benn.

Herbert is known to have received a gunshot wound to the scalp. At this point, 'C' Company had to be brought up to support them. Both companies only managed to take part of the wood from the west of Buchanan Street

Campbell Street but could not cross over Rotten Row, nor get to Prince's Street owing to the British barrage and the machine gun firing from the edge of the wood:

At 7.15 a.m. the two companies advanced and met with stubborn resistance, particularly on the left flank. The officers leading the first two waves of A Company were killed, the men themselves suffering heavy casualties from machine gun fire and snipers concealed in trees. Several Germans surrendered as soon as we advanced but our men had become infuriated by the enemy's sniping methods and they were shot. A platoon from the reserve company having reinforced us on the left, we pushed forward to Buchanan St, which was occupied by South African troops. The forward movement now proceeded without serious opposition on the left until King St was revealed.

At Campbell St, however, strong position was encountered on the right where the enemy had dug-outs, machine guns and snipers in well concealed positions. All along the south edge of the wood our progress was hampered and at the junction of King St with south of South St. We again found the enemy well established. Having been reinforced, however, by a platoon from each of the two companies behind, we eventually overcame this resistance; our centre having advanced and outflanked the enemy's position.

About 30 surrendered, whilst the remainder threw down their arms and ran round to the N side of the wood, losing heavily from our fire, at this point we captured a machine gun after several unsuccessful attempts had been made.

At 10.45 a.m., having cleared the S.E. corner of the wood we took up a position some 100 yards from the edge of the wood whilst our artillery concentrated a heavy fire on our objective. As soon as the barrage lifted, we attempted to carry the edge of the wood by assault. On the right this was successfully achieved and trench occupied at the extreme S.E. of the wood. Our left was held up however by machine guns occupying positions at the points where Princes St and Rotten Row leave the wood. Several determined attempts were made by our bombers to dislodge these but without success.

Patrols were sent forward and reported small parties of Germans retiring to high ground between Ginchy and Flers. But outside the wood we found a South African hiding in a haystack where he had been for two days, needless to say he was more than pleased to see this portion of the wood again pass into our hands.

Meanwhile C Company had progressed on the left flank and took up defensive positions N & N.E. between Campbell St and King St, 20 yards or so to the S of Princes St. A reconnoitring patrol from this company actually penetrated the entire wood to the N of Princes St and reported all clear. By 12 O'clock noon, the whole portion of the wood assigned to the battalion was to all intents and purposes in our hands. The remainder of the reserve company had moved from the one hand and now occupied the centre of the wood.

'B' Company did, however, manage to gain a little more ground between Campbell and King Street, but it too started to suffer heavy casualties from another German machine gun.

This gun was silenced by a platoon under the command of Lt H. V. Hughes and 'C' Company, under the command of Lt L. A. Gundry-White, managed to get the second machine gun, which had caused so many casualties to 'A' Coy, to retire. By 11.30 a.m., the 8th Norfolks had managed to gain ground within the line from Buchanan Street in the west and King Street in the east and had got past Rotten Row and were just shy of Prince's Street, which was cleared of Germans at 12 p.m. In effect, the 8th Norfolks now controlled the extreme southern eastern part of the wood.

It was here that the rest of the 53rd Brigade was called upon to act and their attack went in at around 2 p.m. This attack did not gain much more ground and so the brigade concentrated on defending what ground had been taken by the Norfolks and the war diary notes that they concentrated on making strongpoints and sending out their snipers; the diary states: 'Made excellent practice from the South end of the wood from the North ridge of Guillemont'.

Apart from continuous bombardment of the southern part of Longueval, the afternoon passed quietly. By now, the battalion HQ had been brought up and positioned itself 100 yards north of Dover Street.

Further attacks were attempted by a battalion of Royal Welsh Fusiliers, who were guided by Lt S. N. Cozens-Hardy from the southern point of Buchanan Street towards Prince's Street, but they did not get very far past this position before being heavily fired upon and the Cozens-Hardy was wounded in this attack. The 8th Norfolks then took up positions to the south of Rotten Row. This aspect of consolidation and then eventual relief is clearly described in the report:

> A comprehensive scheme of defence was at once put in hand and a series of strong points constructed by all companies on the ground held by them. On the south side, these defences coincided with the edge of the wood and on the east, they were some 100 yards or so inside. This enabled the work to proceed unobserved by the enemy whilst on the other hand we commanded a clear view of the open ground on the E. S.E and south.
>
> Throughout the day, we were subjected to heavy artillery fire and were fired at by snipers on the ridge to the S.E. Occasionally, Germans showed themselves in this direction, providing opportunities for our own snipers of which they were quick to take advantage. As in the previous engagement, two Lewis guns were attached to each company & constituted an important item in the defence of our strong points. We also had the co-operation of the machine gun corps. In accordance with the pre-arranged scheme, the Essex Regiment attacked the northern portion of the wood about 1.30 p.m. but owing to heavy artillery fire, were obliged to retire, eventually conforming to our position to the south of Princes St, on our left. In the evening,

owing to heavy shelling, Battalion Headquarters was moved to a point about 100 yards N of Dover St.

The field cookers were brought to the valley between Montauban and Longueval, from where tea and rations were conveyed to the wood by fatigue parties. This route was continually under heavy shell fire, a factor which contributed in no small measure to our losses.

Shortly after midnight on the 19th, the Essex Regiment on our left reported Germans approaching their position and rapid rifle fire commenced which was taken up by our men. Whatever the nature of the enemy's attempt, he did not reach our position but several of his dead were observed, on the following morning.

Two attempts were made to bomb our advanced bombing post which we had established on the eastern side of the wood but both were successfully beaten off.

At 11 a.m. on the 20th 'C' Coy moved to the S.W. corner of the wood where they constructed and occupied a strong point. An adjustment of the positions of 'A' & 'B' Companies also took place, their left having been taken over by the Berkshire Regt.

'B' Company accordingly made a fresh strong point on the southern edge of the wood between Campbell St & King St, A Company moving to the junction of King St, with South St where they suffered severely in officers and men from artillery fire.

One of the casualties that day was a sixteen-year-old boy, Private Harry James Hood (3/8104). He was born in Rocklands and had enlisted in Norwich. He was killed in action on 19 July 1916, serving with the 8th Battalion. On his grave, he is listed as being seventeen years old. In reality, he was aged sixteen; one record also suggests he was born in 1899, which possibly makes him fifteen. Certainly, both the 1901 and the 1911 Census record him being born in 1900.

He had been a draft to the battalion and had landed in France on 2 November 1915. Furthermore, his service number intimates that he had joined up before outbreak of the First World War. Whether that is correct or not, what we can definitely say is that his age on the CWGC listing is not correct. Harry was the son of George and Emily Hood of Gressinghall.

Another man to die that day was Private Arthur Allison (13321) from Little Ryburgh. His company commander wrote to his parents:

His death is a great loss to me and to his mates in his platoon, with whom he always appeared to be a favourite. Private Allison was carrying a message to him when he was shot, and fell. Two of his mates went to see if they could do anything for him. He told them that he was done for, and then asked them to get the message out of his pocket to deliver it. Immediately after that he expired; and you could not need a better example than his devotion to duty and deeds of his description, which inspired everyone during these troublesome times. You may well be proud of your son, even as we, his officers and mates are.

Arthur was the son of Thomas and Elizabeth Allison and he is also buried in Delville Wood Cemetery.

The 8th Battalion stayed in a defensive position until they were relieved on the night of 21-22 July by the 1st Battalion Gordon Highlanders. This relief was described in the report:

> During the night of the 20th and the following day, heavy shelling continued and the junction of High Holborn & Down St, our only approach to the wood, came in for special attention. At about midnight on the 21st, 3 Companies, B, C & D were relieved by the 1st Batt Gordons. The half company which should have relieved A Company were taken to the position occupied by the Essex Regt. By arrangement with the O.C. the Gordons, however, on the following day, A Company were relieved at 9.30 p.m. on the 22nd, the route taken was by Montauban, skirting Trones Wood and Bernafay Wood on the left.

The wood was never entirely taken by the South African and British forces during this action. Despite determined efforts, the Germans always managed to hold onto portions of it.

It would take another month of fierce fighting before the wood was finally clawed from the Germans. On 25 August 1916, the 14th (Light) Division captured the wood and held it. The after-action report was very clear in describing how difficult it was to fight in a wood setting and had advice as to how best tackle that for future operations:

> I consider that the lessons learnt from this wood fighting are as follows:
>
> 1. A company should be told off from a reserve Battn to establish strong points as the fighting line clears the position as it is quite impossible for the attacking line to do this thoroughly as they are much too exhausted after the actual fighting. This company should follow the attackers closely complete with all material for this purpose. I would also be of advantage if the fresh troops were told off for holding of the captured positions.
> 2. Stokes guns, if the ammunition question can be solved, would be of great value in knocking out enemy machine guns where the wood allows of them doing so.
> 3. Artillery barrage should be put on wood for some considerable period before the infantry attack. Barrage should then be lifted at intervals of at least 150 yards, as else barrage is dangerous & detrimental to attacking live.
> 4. S.O.S. as for as possible should be arranged by FOO by telephone as rockets are difficult to see in woods and confusing to our artillery.
> 5. Best method of protection, over the position is taken is deep narrow trenches & shell slits. These trenches, if the wood is cleared, should be some yards on the outside edge of the wood if the digging is by night, if by day, just inside edge of wood.

6. I consider that should there be no danger of being driven out by counter attack, if the digging is good as this should give protection against artillery fire, the main course of losing captured positions to.

7. Enemy dug-outs in captured positions are certainly not desirable protection as they are well marked by the enemy and he can make it dangerous & costly for getting our troops to assist in counter attack.

8. Information, wherever possible should be sent by telephone or visual as the system of runners is both slow and costly if the firing is intense; although I might add, taking everything into consideration; runners work admirably in all our fighting if a little slow at times.

9. Every effort should be made by all units to establish touch. This is most important in wood fighting as where breaks occurred, enemy machine gunners and snipers slip through, causing several losses & confusion in our own ranks.

10. Good snipers are of immense assistance to the attacking line in dealing with enemy machine guns in wood fighting & should be attached to companies for this purpose. I should suggest their being kept with the company commander until such situations crop up.

11. Lewis Guns should be mounted in all strong points and machine guns used for the protection of the outside of the wood captured.

I always feel that this type of advice is such an excellent example of where commanders on the ground offered their professional advice in an effort to develop future operations, and this is not the last time we will see evidence like this.

Herbert Cooper was stable enough for him to be evacuated off the battlefield to a casualty clearing station (CCS); in this case, this turned out to be No. 21 CCS at Corbie. The CCS was the first type of medical facility that could deal with all medical cases and was designed to retain the more serious cases, until they could be evacuated, or treat and move the less serious cases to base hospitals either in France or England. In Herbert's case, he was not fit to move and he stayed at 21 CCS.

Tragically, he died of his wounds on 28 July 1916 at the age of twenty-three. As with all CCS, there was a burial plot nearby and he is now laid to rest in grave I. E. 17 of La Neuville British Cemetery along with a further 887 British and Commonwealth troops and twenty-seven German soldiers. Many of Herbert's comrades, including Lieutenants MacNichol and Benn, have no known grave and are now commemorated on the Thiepval Memorial.

Guidebook

On the Albert–Bapaume road, head for and park up in the car park for the South African Memorial at Delville Wood and walk onto the road that takes you to

Ginchy. At the gate for the memorial, walk into the grounds. On the right of the wood is the frontline for the 8th Battalion Norfolk Regiment on 19 July 1916.

As you walk toward the South African Memorial on your right, you will see Rotten Row and Prince's Street and all of the original rides are still listed as such by signposts. Both of these rides are where the 8th Battalion advanced on that day.

What3words: Rotten Row—alternately.resembled.easiest; Prince's Street—trilogy.experiments.accustom.

Optional Visit

Opposite the South African Cemetery stands Delville Wood Cemetery. Within the cemetery, there are thirty-seven men from the Norfolk regiment buried here, including Harry Hood. The rest of the men buried in Delville Wood come from the 1st, 7th, 8th, and 9th Battalions who were killed fighting in this sector between July and October 1916.

What3words: motorcycle.weaseals.kiosks.

10

The 1st Battalion, The Battle of the Somme, High Wood and Longueval: 21–27 July 1916

The 1st Battalion Norfolk Regiment had been positioned around Arras, and although they had seen localised action, namely when the Germans had attacked their positions in May and June, they had not seen anything like they would on the Somme since they had fought at Mons in 1914.

The 5th Division moved to that sector after the battle commenced and were in support of the 7th Division, who were facing Longueval, by 16 July. On 21 July, the 13th Brigade were ordered to attack High Wood. At 6.30 a.m., 'D' Company advanced in four waves, occupying the line that ran from the south-west corner of High Wood. 'C' Company occupied a trench north of Bazentin le Grand and 'A' and 'B' Companies remained in the old German frontline.

At 8.45 a.m., they relieved the 1st Battalion West Kents in the firing line, which ran from the south-west of High Wood running eastwards to Longueval. Here they remained and carried out work constructing a new trench and could not be relieved on 24 July due to heavy German bombardments, which were mixed with high explosive and gas shells. Eventually, they were relieved and ended up at Pommiers Redoubt. Their relief was short-lived because they moved to their start line where the 15th Brigade had been ordered to attack and capture Longueval.

By now, this area was a charnel house as described by a German soldier, Reserve *Leutnant* Walter Schultz of 8th Company Reserve Infantry Regiment 76, who was facing the British in the Longueval Sector:

It was foggy this morning [29 July]. After the sentries had been relieved I had sheltered in a corner of the front wall of the trench and slept a little. To one side, in the early dawn, I could hear someone speaking about machine guns, dead British soldiers, bread pouches and razors and I woke up. There was a thick layer of fog all around. The half company had left the trench and crossed the cover in front of the position. I climbed to join them. We looked around at the dead British soldiers. Most of them had appalling wounds, which had been made worse by the ceaseless drumfire of the past few days. Some skulls were only partly there.

Stomachs and chest were torn open and ripped apart. Arms and legs lay all over the place. Many bodies had received direct hits and were reduced shapeless lumps of flesh. Dreadful sights met our eyes everywhere we looked. Most of our soldiers were there to cut the ration pouches from the dead.

It was well known that the British had good things, such as binoculars, cut-throat and safety razors that we did not just want to leave lying around in the clay. I extracted some biscuits from a pouch, which was lying on the ground and a spoon and fork to replace my cutlery which had gone missing. I also took a tube of hand cream, but I could not bring myself to cut ration pouches off the dead like the others.

The battalion had to advance to their start lines through gas and a terrific bombardment, which took them five hours, and they did not reach positions facing the village until 2.30 a.m. on 27 July. The British opened their advance with a barrage that started at 5.10 a.m., but the Germans replied with a terrific counter barrage that decimated 'A' Company who could only muster one platoon, forcing the battalion to bring up 'C' and 'D' Company who simultaneously supported 'B' Company in the advance on the village along with the 1st Battalion Bedfordshire Regiment with the 23rd Battalion Royal Fusiliers on the 1st Norfolks' right.

The German counter barrage stopped 'C' Company from advancing in a direct line, and they had to move to the right. But the initial German trench, which ran towards High Wood, was soon captured. Yet German strongpoints in the houses around the village caused the battalion a number of issues as they advanced up the road that ran north towards Flers. This road was known as North Street to the British.

The after-action report for the battalion noted:

No opposition was encountered until they had advanced 75 yards north of the church. There was here off to the right a very strong redoubt in which was a small house and cellar.... The left centre of their line had advanced a little beyond the redoubt and killed several Germans trying to escape through the wood.

Much of the German resistance came from the left of North Street, but resistance was also met from German machine guns and snipers holding the sunken road situated to the north-west of the village and a German strongpoint that had been left behind. The Germans also launched a counterattack from the high ground to the south of Flers. This attack was stopped by British and German artillery falling short forcing them to fall back.

Herbert Reeve was present for this attack:

> Eventually our turn came for an attack, which was at Delville Wood. What a shambles
> it was, we were given no orders for our objective, the artillery Barrage dropped
> amongst our own troops or was 100 yards in advance of our forward positions. The
> Germans were fortified by steel defences from an old scrap yard dump. Two fellows
> were killed by my side. The Company Sergeant Major by the name of Moore was
> shot whilst advancing at my side, Captain O'Connor, our Company Commander,
> was also killed.

By now, only one officer was left to command both 'A' and 'C' Companies. This
was Lieutenant Windham who took command of what was left of them as they
advanced to the west of North Street.

'B' Company had initially advanced with no opposition until they came up
against heavy resistance from a redoubt by the church and had to be assisted by
'D' Company who helped with bombing parties in order that the redoubt was
cleared. This was captured with 100 Germans inside it. The war diary noted: 'The
prisoners taken belong to the 8th Brandenburg Regiment and the 12th Guard
Grenadiers. Those who had been at Douamont said that the artillery was worse
at Longueval'.

The advance was supposed to go 300 yards north of Longueval but this could
not be met and the battalion along with the Bedfordshires consolidated a line at
the northern edge of the village and the British artillery, which had supposed to
assist the battalion in further advances moved on leaving the infantry without
any support.

The CO of the battalion, Colonel Stone, noted in the after-action report:

> In order to make certain of my advance I ordered 'A' and 'B' to go through to the
> olive-green line and then let 'C' and 'D' pass through them to the red line, but these
> orders were sent out after arrival in Longueval and Company Commanders were
> unable to give out fresh instructions to their platoon commanders owing to the
> heavy artillery barrage.

The hardest fighting was described as being in the north-west end of Delville
Wood where the Germans were able to fire on the Norfolks from High Wood
and the Switch Line along with a number of strongpoints out of the wood, which
could also fire on the battalion. A witness on the German side, Reserve *Leutnant*
Walter Schultz of 8th Company Reserve Infantry Regiment 76, also noted the
terrible fighting, especially the artillery fire:

> This afternoon [29 July] the British laid on another murderous bombardment. Our
> own artillery had been firing short during the morning and had damaged the trench.

Now the British were trying to make a more thorough job of it. We ducked down behind the clay walls to get what shelter there was.

Brudereck and *Unteroffizier* Schnell arrived, somewhat agitated. Blood was streaming down Brudereck's face. Schnell was shot through one arm and had a splinter wound in the other. I took his field dressing off him and bandaged him up. I then went over to Brudereck, where another comrade was bandaging up his head wound. He also had splinter wounds to the chest and back. When the fire eased a bit, the two of them set off for the dressing station. That was another two men gone. How quickly the little band shrank. Fewer and fewer of the old hands were still around. Shortly afterwards, the feared British aircraft, 'Number 10' appeared. He flew so low over our lines that we could easily see the figure '10' underneath his wings.

A lot of brave actions took place that day, George Lark who had been with the battalion since December 1914 was acting as a battalion runner and volunteered to visit all the companies when all the other runners had been lost and assisted in dressing casualties as found them. He did this under heavy shellfire and machine-gun fire. Arthur Edwards collected water at Longueval and took them up to the firing line under heavy shell and machine-gun fire. For his bravery, he was awarded a Military Medal. John Ainsworth showed great coolness and initiative on the right of the Norfolk's advance and fought his way into a house where shot a number of the enemy before he had to retire due to machine-gun fire. But he then continued to snipe at the Germans until they surrendered. This was reported to be about 100 men.

The endeavours of the battalion along with the other battalions that took part in this advance were noted by the brigade commander:

> The Brigadier-General wishes to express to all ranks of the Brigade his great admiration at the magnificent manner in which they captured the village of Longueval yesterday. To the 1st Norfolk Regiment and the 1st Bedfordshire Regiment and some of the 16th Royal Warwickshire Regiment, who were able to get into the enemy with the bayonet, he offers heartiest congratulations. He knows it is what they have been waiting and wishing for many months. The 1st Cheshire Regiment made a most gallant and determined effort to reach their objective and failed through no fault of their own. The way in which troops behaved under the subsequent heavy bombardment was worthy of the best traditions of the British Army. The Brigade captured 4 officers and 159 other ranks.

Losses for the battalion were high. Eleven officers were killed or wounded and 257 other ranks were killed, wounded, or missing. William Brown, now a captain, was again wounded in action on 28 July 1916 when he received a gunshot wound to the leg that required his brief admission to the Red Cross Hospital in Rouen, from which he returned to duty on 31 July 1916.

In total, the war diary notes that with the fighting in front of High Wood and the capture of Longueval, the battalion lost 429 officers and men. Between 21 and 28 July 1916, a total of ninety-eight officers and men were killed in the fighting around this area. Many of these men have no known grave, although a few are buried in the cemeteries in the area including London Cemetery.

Sidney Smith, who had been with the battalion since the battalion had landed in France in August 1914, wrote to his mother on 29 July 1916 to report the loss of his brother, Bert:

> Well dear Mother I am sorry to tell you the sad news about poor Brother Bert he is missing, but do not worry as he may be wounded and sent to hospital. I asked his pals in his platoon if they had seen him, one of them said he saw him and he was alright on Wednesday morning the 27th July but I have not seen him since Tuesday night when we went up to the trenches. We had a long talk together and we shook hands when we parted and wished one another the best of luck.

Sadly, Sidney was killed in action two days later. Both brothers have no known grave and are commemorated on the Thiepval Memorial.

This action would not be the last time that they saw service on the Somme and they would serve in the trenches around Longueval until the end of July. At that time, the 5th Division was sent out of the line to reorganise.

Guidebook

On the D107 from Longueval heading toward Martinpuich stop at London Cemetery and Extension. Walk back with High Wood on your left. At the south-eastern tip of the wood, look toward Caterpillar Valley Cemetery, which can be seen in the distance to the south. Within the field between the wood and the cemetery is where 'D' Company were positioned when they relieved the 1st Regiment Kents on 21 July 1916. Then turn to your right and look toward Bazentin. In the field between you and the village is where 'C' Company were positioned.

What3words: hotspots.dissolved.squids.

Now head back toward Longueval. At the crossroads in the centre of the village, turn left heading toward the New Zealand Memorial at Flers. It was on this road and the houses on the right that the 1st Battalion advanced along on 27 July 1916.

What3words: mercy.zeal.gamed.

At the bottom the main road veers around to the right, the D197, and there is a track in front of you. From left to right in this area is where the 1st Battalion consolidated what they had captured and is also where they engaged the German counter attacks from in front of you.

What3words: vertigo.pylons.blinked.

11

The 6th (Cyclist) Battalion to the Somme and the 7th Battalion at Ovillers to 6th Avenue Trench: 3 July to 13 August 1916

At this point in the timeline, it would be remiss of me not to mention this battalion of the Norfolk Regiment.

The 1/6th (Cyclist) Battalion, a Territorial Force battalion, was mobilised at the start of the war, under the command of Lt-Col. Bernard Henry Leathes Prior (again, we will meet him later on the book). They spent time patrolling the Norfolk coast and over 90 per cent of the battalion volunteered for overseas service and another battalion, the 2/6th was formed at the end of 1914. This battalion was sent to Bridlington.

Examples of men who joined this battalion can be seen with the Durrant brothers, Sydney born in 1898 and Len born in 1896. They had two other brothers, Arthur and Victor, who did not go into the Norfolks but also served. Sydney joined up on 12 November 1914, attesting in Norwich. His given address was No. 4 Kent Square, the family home, in Great Yarmouth and he received the service number of 1761. Len joined up after him, receiving the service number of 1973. In 1915, the Territorial Force came into line with their Regular comrades and went to a four company and headquarters company formation. With this came a new service number, based on a Regular number. Sydney received the number 43099 and Len got 43182, just 83 numbers apart.

It is noted that during 1915 the 1/6th Battalion had amongst its ranks A1 men and many requested to go overseas but were turned down because it was noted that the battalion was doing important war work at home.

However, by the spring of 1916, drafts were sent overseas, some to become divisional cyclists, and another 126 men went to the Gloucestershire Regiment. In July 1916, virtually the whole of the 1/6th Battalion and a large proportion of the 2/6th Battalion went to France. Most of the 1/6th Battalion went to the 8th

Battalion and the 2/6th went to the 1st Battalion. At least 100 men also went to the 1st Battalion Northamptonshire Regiment.

Bertie Chenery, who had been with the 2/6th Battalion, noted in his memoirs:

> At Mametz we linked up with the remains of the 1st battalion Northamptons, they had been in action earlier and had lost a lot of men. I remember the horrible smell at Mametz and one of the Northamptons told me it was the usual smell of dead men, many were buried in shallow graves in Mametz, British and Germans, there also a hint of poisonous gas about.

Bertie would see action at High Wood and Flers and would eventually go on to serve in the Tank Regiment at Messines and Cambrai.

For the rest of the 1/6th Battalion, it would be service with the 1st and 8th Battalion. Sydney went to France on 26 July 1916, and became a draft for the 1st Battalion after it lost a number of men at Longueval. Len also followed Sydney into the 1st Battalion and it is more than likely he went to them at the same time due to the massed posting of the 1/6th Battalion to the Somme.

Both saw action throughout the war. Sydney contracted an inflammation of his hand while the 1st Battalion had a short period of time in Italy in late 1917 and early 1918. He was treated for this in No. 38 Stationary Hospital in Genoa and Len got trench foot in October 1917 and was sent home to recover from this at Spalding Hall Hospital near Hendon. We will catch up with both brothers later on in the book to see what happened to them in mid-1918.

Another soldier we can look at is Samuel Riches who was born in 1889, known as Sammy, he enlisted at North Walsham and went to the 8th Battalion in July 1916. A green grocer by trade, he was living at 73 South Quay in Great Yarmouth and he was related to Sydney and Len by the fact that his mother and Sydney and Len's father, Thomas, were brother and sister. Sydney initially started out as cook in the 6th Battalion, and although I cannot trace his original TF number, his Regular number was 43491. We will catch up with Sammy later on in the book.

Another part of the Norfolks should also be mentioned here, and we will see them later on in this book. Also seeing service were the Norfolk Yeomanry (The King's Own Royal Regiment). The regiment had been formed on the creation of the Territorial Force in April 1908 and came under the orders of the Eastern Mounted Brigade. Their headquarters were at the Cattle Market Street in Norwich. When war broke out, they had squadrons all over the county who then formed into the 1/1st and 2/1st Norfolk Yeomanry. The 1/1st went to Gallipoli in October 1915 and the 2/1st Norfolk Yeomanry remained at home. In 1915, the 3/1st Norfolk Yeomanry was formed as a training unit, although disbanded in 1917 with their personnel going to the 2/1st Norfolk Yeomanry. I make mention of this now because men from the Norfolk Yeomanry also found themselves being sent to the Norfolk Regiment around this time. An example of that being

Lewis Thaxter from Gresham who initially saw his service at home with the 2/1st Norfolk Yeomanry before going to the 9th Norfolks.

Moving back to the Somme

The 7th Battalion Norfolk Regiment had moved from the rear where it had been positioned around Hennencourt Wood, to occupy the intermediate line of trenches south-west of Albert at 6.50 p.m. in order to support the 8th and 34th Divisions who had gone over at Zero Hour on 1 July 1916.

But this all changed due to the 8th Division failing to capture Ovillers. Instead, on 2 July 1916, the 12th (Eastern) Division took up positions at the front with 7th Norfolks occupying the embankment of the Albert–Arras railway.

On 3 July, the division went over the top and Zero Hour was at 3.15 a.m. The 35th Brigade advanced on the right with the 37th Brigade on the left with the 36th Brigade held in reserve. The 35th Brigade advanced with the 7th Suffolks, the 9th Essex and the 5th Berkshires leading and the 7th Norfolks in reserve.

The battalion war diary is retrospective and was written up on 6 July 1916:

We got into these positions at 3.30 a.m. 2nd July and stayed there all day. At 11.15 p.m. that day we marched to the trenches in preparation for an attack on Ovillers, having previously been told that the 19th Division had taken La Boiselle that evening. We arrived in the trenches at 2 a.m. July 3rd. The attack was to take place at 3.15 a.m. that day, 35th & 37th Bdes on right and left respectively & 36th Bde in reserve. The 19th Division were on our right. At 2 a.m. July 3rd we reported all ready to the Brigade which was distributed for the attack front line Berks Right, Suffolk left, Essex support, Norfolks reserve with orders not to do over the parapet without a specific order from Brigade HQ.

The attack went in at night supported by artillery, but the advancing battalions soon came under machine-gun and artillery fire from the Germans. As the 7th Norfolks advanced via communication trenches in support of the other battalions they lost one officer, Captain John Tilley, and 100 other ranks killed or wounded. The leading battalions failed to take their objectives, losing a total 1,117 men killed, wounded, or missing and the 7th Norfolks were not allowed to advance:

At 3.15 a.m. the Division attacked & as the troops in front went over, we moved up until at 4.15 a.m. we were in O.B.1. We had sustained considerable casualties on our way up the communication trenches, about 100 men being killed wounded or missing. Only 1 officer, Capt J Tilly, being wounded. The battalion was not allowed to go over to the attack which had not succeeded although several of our troops got into the Hun trench. At 8 a.m. the Bn took over the whole of the Brigade front line from the other 3 regiments who went back into support to reorganise. The Germans shelled our line very heavily about this time with H.E. & shrapnel. The battalion now holds the line from Dorset Road (R) to Barrow Road (L).

Efforts to get Mills Bombs to the battalion failed when the bombing party carrying them was wiped out. Their CO, Col. Francis Edward Walter, was wounded by a piece of shell but remained at duty:

'B' Coy in front line, 'D' Coy in support, 'C' Coy in reserve & 'A' Coy doing a carrying party for bombs. About midday Lt Col F.S. Walter D.S.O. was hit on the back by a piece of shell which broke the skin & bruised his right shoulder. However, he did not leave the trenches. The remainder of the day, 3rd July was comparatively quiet on our front, though the 19th Division attacked La Boiselle again which they had been driven out of.

The 7th Norfolks now holding positions between Dorset to Barrow Road, had the task of holding the 35th Brigade front while the other battalions withdrew. They were heavily shelled and remained there all day of 3 July while the 19th Division attacked La Boisselle on their right:

The night July 3/4 was spent getting in wounded from between the lines and in connection with this work our M.O. Capt R.B. Lucas R.A.M.C. was reported missing & it is thought that he walked into the German trenches by mistake—anyway he has not been seen or heard of since. On 4th July at 10 a.m. the Germans put up a very heavy artillery barrage on our front, support 7 C.T.'s for half an hour, in consequence apparently to show their position. During the 24 hours ending 12 noon 4th there were about 8 casualties in the Bn. At 3.30 p.m. the same day 4th, the Germans again shelled our positions very heavily.

At 4 p.m. Major R.J.L. O Gilby 2nd in command of the Bn came into the trenches & relieved O.C. Walter of command who went back to the transport where a certain number of officers & NCOs have been left in order if the Bn is much cut up they may be of assistance in reorganising it. The transport lines are almost 1/2-mile E of Millencourt. The remainder of the day, 4th July, was quiet & during night 4/5 we brought in some more wounded from no man's land & the R.E. & Pioneers dug a fire trench linking up Argyll St and La Boisselle which latter village the 19th Division is now holding & consolidating.

The night 4/5 July was very quiet except for a heavy bombardment on our left opposite Thiepval. On 5th July at about 12 noon the Huns began shelling is again, one shell blowing in O.P. killing 1 officer and wounding another. At 1 p.m. 19th Division make another attack this time in a northerly direction with the intention of cutting off Ovillers in the rear.

Between 4 and 5 July 1916, the battalion suffered a number of heavy German barrages where they lost one officer killed, two wounded, and a further eight other ranks wounded. The officer killed was Lt Arthur Perceval Green, aged twenty-one, who was the son of the Rev. William Arthur and Alice Mary Green of Winterton Rectory. The war diary noted:

> In consequence of the attack we were again subjected to a heavy bombardment, which lasted for a couple of hours. During last night 5/6 we got in more wounded & the trench from Argyll St to La Boisselle was continued. This morning at 3 a.m. the enemy opened a heavy bombardment on our lines & one shell landing in the bay where 'D' Company HQ were killed one officer, Lt A.P. Green, & wounded two others, 2/Lt M.R. Allen, 2/Lt F.G. O'Donnell, in the same company.

German losses in this sector were also high, with *Oberst* Paul von Malmann of Lehr Infantry Regiment noting:

> 'What enormous sacrifices this battle demanded of the German infantry might have been describing the entire battle, but this was still the beginning'. On 3rd July, 1st Battalion Lehr Infantry Regiment arrived on the Second Position in Pozières and on that day did not suffer any casualties. So there remains only the outcome of just over four days of fighting to be counted. The calculation presents an appalling picture!
>
> What a state this superb battalion had been reduced to as a result of these few days of battle of changing fortunes under the violent fire of enemy heavy artillery! The battalion commander, *Hauptmann* von Schauroth, was wounded, but still with the troops.
>
> His Adjutant, Reserve *Leutnant* Kohbieter, was dead and left lying on the battlefield. His replacement as Adjutant, Reserve *Leutnant* Cann, was wounded and still at his post. From 1st Company. *Landwehr Leutnant* Verholen was wounded, *Leutnant* Behnke was wounded and missing, *Offizierstellvertreter* Staudtmeister was wounded. In addition, there were twenty-two dead, eighty-nine wounded and ninety-two missing. From 2nd Company, Leutnant Pielock was dead and *Leutnants* Collinge and Langhoff were wounded. There were also forty dead, seventy-five wounded and twenty-five missing. From 3rd Company, Reserve *Leutnant* Graw was wounded and there were thirty-eight dead, fifty-one wounded and seventy missing. From 4th Company, Reserve Lentnant *Burghardt* was dead and *Leutnant* Fiukenstedt wounded. To these must be added thirty-four dead, fifty-one wounded and ninety-eight missing the total amounted to nine officers, one officer deputy, and 685 other ranks.
>
> Again, and again the questions were asked: 'Where is this soldier? Where was so and so left? Who saw him last and where? Yes, where were they, all those whose name had to be entered in the nominal roll under that unholy heading, Missing?'
>
> That was a dreadful word for the parents and siblings, for all relations whose thoughts back in the homeland were directed day by day and hour by hour, waking

or dreaming, towards the hoped-for safe return of their father, uncle, brother, son, husband or grandson. Missing in other words, 'We do not know what has become of him.'

Perhaps he is lying in a hole in the ground, torn apart by a shell, perhaps he has been killed while acting as a runner and carrying a message through a hail of shells, maybe he was a signaller and died isolated and alone while out repairing a cable. He could have been buried alive beneath the ruins of a house or down in a dugout, which did not withstand the shock. Perhaps he sank exhausted into the wet clay. Possibly he was wounded and fell into the hands of the enemy when he had no means of returning. The hopes of many were concentrated on this last possibility and certainly one or two families were lucky enough to be reunited after the war with those who went missing on the Somme. But, sadly, it is certain that many of the missing never returned, could never return, because, soldiers brave to the last as they were, they had already spent years slumbering somewhere beneath foreign soil.

During the incident in which he was wounded, *Hauptmann* von Schauroth was Witless to several courageous acts by men of Infantry Regiment 190, who were supposed to be withdrawing, having been relieved. As soon as he was well enough in four days and not counting losses in the Machine Gun Company. To do so, he sent a full description to the commanders of 1st and 3rd Battalions Infantry Regiment 190, in order to ensure that those deserving of medals received them.

On 6 July, they were relieved by men of the 36th Brigade and went back to positions at Warincourt Wood:

At 2 p.m. today the Bn was relieved by 36th Inf Bde & went into the Intermediate Bouzincourt–Albert Line just N of Albert. The transport moved to Bouzincourt today. The last two days in the trenches, it was extremely muddy & wet & the men suffered to some extent from bad feet in consequence.

In total, during their three-day action, the battalion lost twenty men killed or who died of wounds and 110 men wounded or missing. Ovillers did not fall until 16 July 1916 when it was captured by the 48th (South Midland) Division.

Charles Edmonds, who wrote *A Subaltern's War*, described the area around Ovillers when he passed through that area on the day the village finally fell:

A little grass had still room to grow between the shell holes. The village was guarded by tangle after tangle of rusty barbed wire in irregular lines. Among the wire lay rows of khaki figures, as they had fallen to the machine-guns on the crest, thick as the sleepers in the Green Park on summer Sunday evening … the flies were buzzing obscenely over the damp earth; morbid scarlet poppies grew scantily along the white chalk mounds; the air was tainted with rank explosives and the sickly stench of corruption.

The medical officer who went missing was Capt. Robert Brockley Lucas who is listed as having died on 3 July 1916 and was the elder son of Mrs Lucas of 'Dereham' North Gate Street in Millswood in Adelaide in South Australia. As listed, he went missing and has no known grave and is commemorated on the Thiepval Memorial.

Lt Arthur Percival Green came from Winterton and was aged twenty-one. He was the son of the Reverend William Arthur and Alice Mary Green of Winterton Rectory and is buried in Grave I.I.22 in Albert Communal Cemetery Extension. If you would like to see an example of an original grave marker then you could go and visit Lt Green's original cross, which now rests in Winterton Church. The cross is at the left rear of the church opposite the main entrance and is immediately next to 'Fisherman's Corner'.

Guidebook

On the Albert–Bapaume road, coming from the direction of Albert you will enter the village of La Boiselle. Take the first turning on the left onto the D20. Turn right at the next junction and then park up at Ovillers Military Cemetery. Looking back toward where you came from you are looking at Mash Valley and also toward where Dorset Street was situated. If you walk to the top of the cemetery and look toward an area called le Haut Ovillers you are looking at the area where Barrow Street was. Between these two points is where the 7th Norfolks held the line on 3 July 1916.

What3words: gutter.spent.struggles.

* * * * *

The Battle of Pozières was launched on 23 July 1916, which saw the Australians, who had only arrived on the Somme two days earlier, and the British fight hard for an area that had the Germans controlling the high ground on the ridge. This meant they could observe everything around that area and places such as the windmill on the outskirts of Pozières was used as an observation post in which to do this. The ridge did not fall until 4 August, after almost two weeks of bitter fighting, and the Australians alone lost some 23,000 troops during this period. To the north-west of Pozières, Mouquet Farm, given the nickname of Moo-Cow Farm by the Australians, which was an enemy strongpoint, remained under German control.

The 7th Battalion Norfolk Regiment, along with the rest of the 12th (Eastern) Division, would take part in attempts to capture this area and they were put into the line on 10 August. Between 11 and 12 August, the battalion suffered casualties from enemy shelling including 2Lt Frederick Marcus Beck Case. Frederick was born in Caister on Sea and was the second of five children born to William and Muriel Jessie Case. He was educated at Yarmouth College and had entered the

National Provincial Bank in the city in 1912. He had been a pre-war TF soldier, enlisting with 1/28th City of London Battalion (Artist Rifles) in January 1913. He had landed with them at Boulogne on 26 October 1914. After being promoted to corporal in 1915, he had been recommended for a commission and had had joined the 7th Norfolks on 1 August 1916.

He was in support in the reserve trench at 4th Avenue when a shell hit his dugout showing that he lasted exactly ten days as an officer in the battalion before he was killed. Sadly, the Case family would lose another two sons in the First World War. Frederick was twenty years old and is now laid to rest in Bapaume Post Cemetery. Between 10 and 13 August, the battalion would lose ninety-two officers and men to shelling alone.

On the night of 12–13 August 1916, the 12th (Eastern) and the Australian 4th Division attacked the German lines in an attempt to capture 6th Avenue and the trenches in front of Mouquet Farm. This is what the Australian Official History noted about the orders for this advance:

> The formal second stage in the advance of I Anzac and the II Corps to the line of Mouquet Farm was fixed for the following night (August 12th), the 12th British Division assaulting Skyline Trench and the knot of German works at its south-western end, and the 4th Australian Brigade attacking (according to the Reserve Army's order issued on August 10th) the enemy's supposed line south-east of Mouquet Farm, however, the Australian line was already well beyond these objectives.

Depending on what history you read at this stage, you can become quite confused. So just to clarify things: if you looked at the war diary for the 7th Battalion you would see that they were positioned in a trench called 5th Avenue and faced a German frontline trench called 6th Avenue.

However, in both the British and Australian Official Histories, these have different names. In these accounts the 7th Battalion was positioned in a trench called Ration Trench and would be assaulting a German position called Skyline Trench, so called because it was positioned at the highest point on the crest of a spur. The highest point here, on the Pozières–Thiepval road, within the Australian OH also had a name, 'Point 81'.

At 10.30 p.m., the 7th Norfolks advanced with the 9th Essex on their left and the Australian 50th Battalion on their right marking the line between the Australian and British divisions. The Norfolks advanced with 'A' and 'D' Companies leading and 'B' and 'C' Companies behind them.

The war diary is again retrospective, written up on 13 August 1916:

> At 10.30 p.m. yesterday the 12th Division & 4th Australian Division attacked on a front of about a mile. The Norfolk Regt had its objective 6th Avenue, 4th Australian Division on our right, 9th Essex Regt on our left.

'A' & 'D' Companies were in front, 'B' & 'C' behind, each company forming 2 waves. By 10.30 p.m., zero, the battalion was ready in position in front of 5th Avenue on a tape which had previously been placed to form on.

At zero the line slowly advanced to when the artillery lifted, got into the German trench. Very little resistance was met with, the Huns being completely taken by surprise. Work was at once commenced clearing & bombing dug-outs, sending forward patrols to the next German line & consolidating.

The advance carried forward under the cover of a barrage and because of this the Norfolks managed to get into the German trench unopposed and caught the enemy by surprise capturing twenty out of the thirty Germans they encountered there:

At 11.10 p.m. a message was received at Bn H.Q. which had remained in 8th Street that the German trench had been captured. Soon afterwards, R.E. Consolidating Parties were sent to the captured trench to assist our men in the construction of strong-points, within also Vickers & a Stokes gun were taken. Very few casualties had been incurred going over, but in the German trenches there were several from shell-fire. The Germans during the night put a heavy barrage on all C. T.'s.

They then cleared out the dug-outs in the trench and consolidated their gains. They made contact with both the Essex and the Australians of which the Australian Official History notes: 'An hour later arrived news that the left company at 81 was in touch with the Norfolk Regiment in Skyline Trench'.

The Norfolk and Essex battalions sent out patrols who were held up by the British barrage although both managed to get into enemy positions where they captured six more of the enemy. Having consolidated their gains, most of the men were withdrawn and only two strongpoints were manned in Skyline Trench with one Lewis gun in each.

They continued to be harassed by German artillery, and it is also noted in the British OH that some of the shelling was caused by British heavy howitzer shells falling short on Ration and Skyline Trenches. In the final entry for the fighting, their war diary notes: 'By 12 midnight it was clear that the line attacked by 4th Australian Division & 35th Inf Bde had been taken & communication to the flanks ensued. 37th Inf Bde on the left of the 12th Division was held up by M.G. fire & made little progress'.

To give you an idea of the terrible fighting that went on here, we will look to the Australian OH, which details the 50th Australian Battalion's advance on Mouquet Farm:

As the II Corps had captured Skyline Trench, being held up only on the right, the total result was naturally announced by the higher staffs as a sweeping success.

Unfortunately, the line given by the 50th was, except as regards the left, incorrect. After advancing about 250 yards without opposition both flanks of that battalion had met some resistance.

The left company had pushed on to its objective-Point 81, where Skyline Trench was crossed by the Pozières–Thiepval road; but opposite The Quarry there had opened a gap of 350 yards. This was partly due to the operation orders not having got through to all the platoons.

Thus, in the line advancing near The Quarry, all that was known to the platoon commander, Lieutenant Hoggarth, was that he was to go forward under the barrage and more or less conform to the company on his right. This he did, crossing the dip, mounting the far slope (passing east of The Quarry) and reaching, just over the rise, some large mounds of earth and rubble, which-though he was not aware of it were the southern ruins of Mouquet Farm. No one moved in the place, which then lay under the British barrage.

Still with the notion of following the barrage, Hoggarth moved along a zigzag trench nearby (the German '*Grosser Riegel*') until he was wounded by one of the shells of his own side. Some Germans in a dugout were killed and others captured and sent to the rear, and a German bomber, who now emerged from the farm whirling a stick-grenade, was shot. Recognising that with Germans so near he could not hold an isolated position, Hoggarth returned, and dug in near Point 81; to his right was a wide gap, on the other side of which the centre and right of the 50th-still out of touch with the 13th-were established in detached bodies, 100 yards short of the objective.

Lt Hoggarth can be identified as William Paton Hoggarth who, it is later noted in the Australian OH, became the first Australian to reach Mouquet Farm. After being wounded, he was evacuated and eventually returned back to the 5th Battalion but sadly would not survive the war and he was killed in action at Noreuil on 2 April 1917. He was aged twenty-seven when he died and was the son of William Hanna Hoggarth and Helen Hoggarth and came from Adelaide.

On the morning of 13 August, the 7th Battalion was relieved by elements of the 48th Division and they marched to the rear. Their war diary noted the following:

Before dawn all the men except the garrisons of strong points (40 men at each, +1 L.G. & 1 M.G.) were withdrawn. At 5 a.m. in the morning the relief of 12th Division by 48th Division commenced & by 12 noon the battalion had been relieved by 1/4th Oxford & Bucks L.I. and marched back to bivouacs outside Bouzincourt. 18 Huns, all 29 Regt, were taken prisoner by us last night.

In the advance on Skyline Trench, they had lost six officers and 128 other ranks killed, wounded, or missing. An order of the day was issued by the 35th Brigade commander who noted:

Please convey to all ranks of the battalion under your command the brigadier's high appreciation of the way they have comported themselves in the recent operations. Whilst it may be said that the task set was not a hard one, and that the actual infantry fighting was but little, the fact of being able to form up for and execute an assault after the severe shelling they had endured for a night and two days points to soldierly qualities of the highest order.

The Australians continued to push forward towards Mouquet Farm but never fully captured it and lost 6,300 men in the process. They were relieved by the Canadians on 5 September 1916, who continued to fight over the ruins but the farm did not fall until the British 11th Division eventually captured it over the period of 26 and 27 September 1916.

A total of forty-one men were lost serving in the 7th Battalion Norfolk Regiment between 10 and 13 August 1916. On my travels, I have often came across them on the Somme. Two of them, Robert Chilvers Holden and William Robert Ecclestone now lie side by side in London Cemetery and Extension. Both were only twenty years old when they died.

Robert was the son of Frederick and Emily Holden of Dunstan Common and William was the son of Charles and Bertha Ecclestone of Moulton St Mary. Robert had the service number of 22704 and William the number of 22707, and I often wonder if they met when they enlisted and became friends afterwards.

The 7th Battalion Norfolk Regiment would return back to the Somme in October 1916.

Guidebook

On the Albert–Bapaume road heading toward Bapaume enter Pozières. On your left, there will be a turning signposting the Thiepval Memorial. Turn left and head toward Thiepval. On your right, after about half a mile, you will see the Australian memorial for Mouquet Farm. Park here and walk back toward Pozières. You will see that the ground rises gradually.

Walk up to the top of this rise. This is where Skyline Trench was positioned either side of the road. You can then look back toward Mouquet Farm to see where the Norfolks and the Australians advanced in an attempt to capture this area.

What3words: naivity.invalidate.neutered.

12

The 1st and 9th Battalions, The Battle of the Somme, Falfemont Farm to Morval: 4–25 September 1916

After their assault on Longueval, the 1st Battalion Norfolk Regiment had been moved out of the line on 2 August 1916 and had been sent to Le Quesnoy to rest and refit. Here they received drafts from the 2/6th Battalion Norfolk Regiment. Because most of these men had never served in the trenches, they had to undergo a period where they were trained in the type of fighting that was happening on the Somme. However, by 24 August 1916, they were back at the front and were initially placed in bivouacs around Bronfray Farm near Maricourt.

The fortified village of Guillemont had finally fallen on 3 September 1916 and the momentum of continuing to put pressure on the Germans in this sector of the Somme was not about to stop. Orders came down that the German Second Line to the east and south-east of Guillemont was to be captured on 4 September.

This task was given to the 5th and 20th Divisions who were to capture the line between Point 48, Wedge Wood, and Valley Trench. If favourable this advance was to continue to Leuze Wood. At this point in time, the British trenches were disjointed and not joined up. But the advance would have the French on the right of the Norfolks. One of the positions to be captured also included Falfemont Farm. This farm was actually called Faffemont Farm, but a spelling mistake on trench maps had it called Falfemont instead.

Zero Hour was set for 3.10 a.m. 'A' and 'B' Companies were to lead, and when they went over the top, they immediately came under heavy machine-gun fire. But Captain Francis and a few men reached the south-west edge of the farm before being ejected from that point by German grenades. By this time, all the officers but two in the initial attack had either been killed or wounded and the advance had was being held up by machine-gun fire.

George Lark who had been in the thick of it at Longueval was again in action and he kept messages going between Battalion HQ and the firing line under heavy machine-gun fire. For this act of bravery and his actions at Longueval, he was awarded the Military Medal. This had split the battalion up and these groups could only advance by crawling from shell-hole to shell-hole and any attempt at any proper advance was checked by machine-gun fire, the French were also having issues advancing, and although 'C' and 'D' Companies tried to capture the south-east part of the farm and Point 48, they were also stopped by machine-gun fire. The Norfolks lost touch with the Cheshires who had tried to work around the machine-gun fire from the west where the hill gave protection from the machine guns: 'Lt Brown was sent with the reserve bombing platoon and two Lewis Gun teams to go behind 'C' Company to capture the Quarry in an attempt to working round the west of the farm. This failed and, in the attempt, Lt Brown was killed'. This was 2Lt Thomas Brown, aged twenty-six, who was the son of Davis and Leonora Mary Brown of Marham Hall, now laid to rest in Delville Wood Cemetery.

In the attack on Falfemont Farm, John Ainsworth who had shown great bravery at Longueval, was wounded in the neck and arm and was evacuated. For his bravery at Longueval, he was awarded a Military Medal.

The 16th R. Warwicks were sent to the south-west edge of Leuze Wood to work a line from the wood up to the light railway. But the Norfolks informed their brigade commander that any attempt by the Warwickshires to do that would end in failure due to them not reaching their objective. At 5.30 p.m., 'A' Company was within a few yards of the farm, and at 6.40 p.m., the 15th Brigade commander ordered informed the Norfolks with the rest of their brigade that they would make a simultaneous attack on the farm with the 95th Brigade. The CO of the Norfolks asked the CO of the Warwickshires to order any Norfolks found in the advance to help him in the advance.

The ferocity of the desperate fighting in this sector be seen in this account of a German soldier, Reserve *Leutnant* Oschatz of 7th Company Fusilier Regiment 73 who faced these attacks:

Gefreiter Preul came charging down the steps (of a dugout near to Faffémont Farm] yelling, 'Here they come.' Because we had been sitting here all day long with our equipment on, we were able to man the trench swiftly. As I emerged, I saw the British advancing in broad dense lines out of the hollow about 200–300 metres to our front. We fired the previously agreed red signal flares to call down our artillery fire and battle as joined. Because the men clustered around the two entrances to the dugout, Neckel and I made them spread out. Initially, in accordance with orders, I ran through the craters to ensure that the right-hand platoon had stood to. I shouted briefly to *Leutnant* Dühr and hared back again. Bullets were flying everywhere and as I reached the dugout, I saw my old comrade Neckel, with whom I had passed many an hour, held in the arms of my batman with a serious neck wound. Blood was pumping in a thick stream from his severed artery; he was beyond help. I could not stop, duty called on the left. I grabbed my men, who were pinned down by heavy fire round the entrance to the left-hand dugout and led them through the craters to the left so as to fill the gap there. Once I felt that we had gone far enough.

I threw myself down and opened fire with a rifle that I had grabbed. Now for the first time in the full September sun I could see the battlefield that thus far I had only observed when it was dark. All around, as far as the eve could see, there was not a speck of green, just a broad brown crater field. In front of us, beyond the hollow, was the steep rise to the village of Maurepas, down which streamed dense enemy columns. There were countless aircraft in the air buzzing around just above the ground.

To our front and advancing in short bounds, were the British. I could see how, on the hand signal of an officer, the whole line rose and rushed towards us. They were about two hundred metres away. Our artillery fire was coming down brilliantly; the black fountains of earth were springing up all around the enemy. I could see men spinning up into the air. We shot as rapidly as we could. It was just a wild crashing and clattering. I was the furthest left. Left of me there was nothing. Immediately next to me was Musketier Mehrle. We shouted to each other every time we thought that we had scored a hit. Suddenly we came under heavy machine gun fire from a rise to our left. I could see the muzzle flashes and the crew of the gun, so I shouted to Mehrle to indicate the target. I did not receive a reply and spun round to see that he was already dead, killed by a head wound.

Now I was all alone and the machine gun fire was getting worse. I could not make up my mind if it was coming from the machine gun that I had spotted, or from one of the many aircraft that were still buzzing around overhead. The British attack had stalled. Individuals could be seen running to the rear. Suddenly there was another burst of machine gun fire and I received a heavy blow on the right thigh and noticed blood streaming down. I had just received a flesh wound. The bone was uninjured, so I was able during a quiet moment to make my way through the craters to the entrance to the dugout where I was met by our medical orderly Busse, who bandaged me up.

Records also show that British artillery had a part to play with the confusion and Sgt Walter Freeman had to work under heavy fire to keep communication open. He also had to organise orderlies' working parties under fire. When British artillery fell on the Norfolks, he went out alone through heavy fire to a friendly battery, which was stopping the advance. For this bravery, Sgt Freeman was awarded the Distinguished Conduct Medal.

From the Official History of the Great War:

The 15th Brigade accordingly prepared for another frontal attack on Falfemont Farm, the 1/Norfolk being now in actual touch with French troops. The latter, however, did not advance at 3.5 p.m. when the Norfolk left their trenches only to be checked by machine gun fire from Combles ravine. On the left, a party which entered the south west corner of the farm was bombed out again; but a company of the 1/Cheshire worked round under the shelter of the spur, whilst the 1/Bedfordshire, starting from Wedge Wood, began to bomb south-eastward along the German trench. The Bedfordshire gathered in over 130 prisoners, mostly 164th Regiment, together with several machine guns, and by 4 p.m. the northern and western corners of the farm enclosure were taken. Reinforced by the 16/R. Warwickshire, the Norfolk, who had been working forward from shell-hole to shell-hole, made another unsuccessful attempt to storm the farm at 5.30 p.m., so it was then decided that the 16/R. Warwickshire should sap forward towards the objective during the night. Patrols of the Bedfordshire and Cheshire on the crest of Leuze Wood spur had assisted to prevent the approach of German reinforcements, which were also caught by British artillery fire as they advanced from the direction of Combles.

Sadly, this attack also failed, so the order was given to dig in and the ground between the British trenches and the farm was a mass of shell-holes and heavy rain began to fall. By now, the men in the advance were exhausted although part of 'A' Company managed to reach the south-west edge of the farm so the Warwickshires started to dig communication trenches towards the 'A' Company.

At 3 a.m. on 5 September, the Norfolk Regiment war diary noted: 'Falfemont Farm completely occupied by "A" & "C" Coys.' And the Official History noted: 'In spite of the weather, the forward troops of the 5th Division were not idle during the night. The German resistance was obviously weakening, and by 3 a.m. on the 5th September Falfemont Farm was in the possession of the Norfolk, who pushed patrols towards Point 48'.

It is interesting to note that one observation of a 1st Norfolk man noted an unexpected surprise for some Germans as Herbert Reeve noted:

> Then came an attack on a place called, I think, Falfemont Farm at 3:30 in the afternoon. We were the fourth Regiment to attack this place, our losses were heavy, but we eventually broke through and surprised some Jerries who were having their clothes de-loused in the next village.

This victory did not come without a price and as the Norfolk Regimental history of the Great War noted:

> Such a feat as the capture of Falfemont Farm necessarily involved serious casualties. Of officers six were killed—Captain W.J.H. Brown; Lieutenants H.S. Cameron and E.P.W. Brown; 2nd Lieutenants L.C. Coath, T. Brown and W.F. Bice. Wounded, seven—Captains Sibree, Francis, Youell, Grover; Lieutenant Swift; 2nd Lieutenants Cullington and Watson. Of other ranks there were killed fifty; wounded 212; missing, believed killed, ninety-four.

Two brothers were killed in action during the fighting for Falfemont Farm. Second Lieutenant Edwin Percival Wildman Brown and Captain William John Henry Brown, who we know was wounded twice before serving with the 1st Battalion.

Edwin had enlisted with the Norfolk Regiment in 1914 at the age of seventeen. He initially served in the 3rd Battalion but had his service deferred while he attended Durham University where he received a commission into the Norfolk Regiment from Durham OTC. He joined the 1st Battalion on 13 July 1916.

Their loss was reported in the Shields *Daily News* on 16 September 1916:

NEWS OF LOCAL MEN.

Killed and Wounded in Action. SECOND-LIEUT. EDWIN P.W. BROWN KILLED. North Shields people will learn with regret that Second-Lieut. E.P.W. Brown, second son of the late Dr. W. H. Brown, was killed in action on 4th September. He was only 19 years of age, and was educated at Tenbury and Tynemouth.

A few days ago, we recorded the death, which occurred on the same date, of his elder brother, Lieut. W. J. H. Brown. They were both serving in the Norfolk Regiment. Their mother, Mrs Brown, who is now residing in Sydenham, has received the following letter from their commanding officer:—'It is with the deepest regret that I write to tell you that your two sons, William John Henry and Edward Percival, were killed in action during the attack on Falfemont Farm on 4th Sept.'

Both were excellent officers, and they are a great loss to us, and the whole regiment feel with you most deeply in your great loss. Both were leading their men with great gallantry in the attack, and were killed instantaneously. Severe fighting is going on, but we were able to have them buried, and as soon as possible, I will have their graves marked with a cross.

It was, I think, perhaps one of the finest attacks in the war, and carried out with the utmost gallantry, and I think its success will be a far reaching one. The regiment lost very heavily, but I hope that their great sacrifice may help to bring a speedy end to this war. No words of mine can express how deeply I feel for you, and with what reverence I shall for ever keep their names.

Sadly, William's grave was lost and he is commemorated on the Thiepval Memorial but Edwin now lies in grave XXVI.B.4. in Delville Wood Cemetery.

To me, Falfemont Farm is rightly sacred ground to the Norfolk Regiment. On 5 September, the 1st Battalion was relieved and went to Morlancourt to rest and refit, but it would not be long before they were back in the line.

Guidebook

From the Albert–Bapaume road, take the D20 from La Boiselle toward Longueval. Keep on the D20 and head through Guillemont to Combles. When you get to the centre of Combles, you will see a shop on the right called 'Proxi'. Turn right here. This will take you to the new Faffemont Farm, listed as Fme de Faffemont on a French IGN map. Go past the farm and you will see a dirt track on your right with a copse of trees. This is the original Faffémont Farm, listed as Falfemont Farm on a trench map. If you walk up to the copse of trees, it is wise that you ask permission from the farmer as you are walking on private land.

What3words: carriage.premiums.mantras.

* * * * *

The 9th Battalion Norfolk Regiment had not been on the Somme yet, but that all changed in August 1916. They arrived at Villers Candas on 3 August and arrived at Mailly-Maillet on the 5th. On 14 August, they went into the trenches and then spent time in and out of them until 5 September, when they moved to Flesselles to practice for their coming baptism of fire. On 8 September, they moved to the Sandpit and then Trones Wood. Then, on 15 September, they took up their positions facing the Quadrilateral, known to the Germans as the Sydow Hohe, between the Ginchy–Morval road and Leuze Wood.

Haig had planned a large-scale offensive for mid-September and this would involve eleven divisions, supported by the new weapon in the British armoury: the tank—a total of forty-nine were to be used in the offensive, and the advance would be on a front of 12,000 yards, from Courcelette in the north all the way to Lesboeufs and Morval in the south. There would be a preliminary bombardment, which began on 12 September. Attacks in this area had started on 13 September with the 9th Suffolk Regiment and the 2nd Sherwood Foresters attempting to capture position just to the north of the Quadrilateral. They had managed to get to within 250 yards but could make no further progress and were now waiting for the next attack, which would start at 6.20 a.m. on 15 September.

At the start of this attack, progress was made by the 47th (London) Division, although they suffered terribly capturing High Wood. However, the 50th and 15th (Scottish) Divisions captured all of its objectives and 2nd Canadian Division had occupied Courcelette by evening. In the centre, with the support of tanks, the 41st and New Zealand Divisions captured Flers.

But on the extreme right, where there were hopes of a breakthrough, both the 56th and 6th Divisions did not fare well and the Guards Division ended up short of its final objectives. We will now look at the 9th Battalion's experiences at the Quadrilateral.

As noted in the Norfolk Regiment History of the Great War, the commander of the 6th Division, General Marsden, noted this about the ground we were about to assault:

On September 9th a successful attack had given us Ginchy and Leuze Wood, but the Germans were holding very strongly the high ground which lies in the form of a horseshoe between the above-named points, and which dominates the country for some distances to the south. The trenches followed the slope of the spur roughly at the back end of the horseshoe, and covered access was given to them by a sunken road leading back to the deep valley which runs north from Combles. At the top of the spur just south of the railway was a four-sided trench in the form of a parallelogram of some 300 yards by 150 yards, called by us the 'Quadrilateral'.

Dennis Douglas who came from Cawston recorded this time in his diary: 'We were moved up in stages and by the 10th of the month, had dug in, at the appropriately named "sand pits". The shelling, which had increased with every day, now was like steam trains thundering over our heads. Sleep was something to dream about'.

The 71st Brigade would assault with the 9th Norfolks on the right and the 1st Leicesters on the left on a front of 500 yards. On the 71st Brigade's right would be the 16th Brigade. In this sector, the assault would be assisted by three tanks.

Dennis Douglas noted in his diary:

On the 14th we moved up to a once wooded area. It was a shell pocked landscape of half buried tree stumps. We had little or no cover and set about digging in. Major Turner and Captain Robinson were organising the effort to construct some kind of shelters, when a shell scored a direct hit on their, so called, command post. I noticed George had become seriously withdrawn and ghost like. This was the first action of any consequence he had been in. We had little time to collect our thoughts or dead and injured. At 10pm we were ordered to move up to our start line for the morning attack.

Both battalions had to assault the Quadrilateral up a slope. They passed through the remains of the 9th Suffolks and the 2nd Sherwood Foresters and advanced towards a German position called Straight Trench. They were seen to go out of sight over a crest. Once they reached the position, they found that the wire was uncut. This was due to a 200-yard gap in the bombardment to allow the tanks to push through. Neither the Norfolks nor the Leicesters could meet up and nor could the Guards be reached on the brigade's left. They took machine-gun fire from the front and the right.

Dennis Douglas recorded his experiences of the assault on the Quadrilateral:

September 15th 1916, 1 a.m.
Eventually we made it to the line of trenches held by the Suffolks. The chaos was total and it took our senior officers an age to get some sort of order. At 5.50 a.m. a strange mechanical thing ground its way through our line. Like some mobile pill box. Later I was told this new metal war machine was called a Tank.

Sometime later we were ordered to form up and prepare to advance; I kept a watchful eye on George. When the time came Lieutenant Garnham blew his whistle and we climbed over the top.

My heart was pounding fit to burst, and I was feeling light headed. I lost sight of George and just kept heading forward in a low, stumbling stoop. All around me was the whizzing of bullets and the crash of shell fire. The churned-up earth felt more like a porridge mixture. At last I caught sight of George in a group of men being led by Major Bradshaw. As I tried to reach them I felt a sting in my right leg and was spun round and fell to the ground. For a moment I looked up into the sky and wondered if this was my lot. I must have passed out, as the next thing I remember, two privates from the Suffolks were dragging me towards their trench.

Major Arthur Weyman, who was serving in the 1st Battalion Leicestershire Regiment, and who saw action with the battalion during the assault on the Quadrilateral, wrote to Captain Wilfrid Miles, the official historian who compiled the Official History of the Battle of the Somme, noting an incident that occurred with one of the tanks. One of two things were supposed to have happened:

> The tank which passed through the 9th Norfolk ... actually mistook the Norfolks for enemy and fired towards them. Capt Crosse, 9th Norfolks, who commanded one of the forward companies ran up to the tank and beat on the sides of it to attract attention. He told the driver that he was firing in the wrong direction, and pointed out the enemy position. As far as I know, the tank caused the 9th Norfolks no casualties but it undoubtedly upset them a good deal and they were furious with it. It was many months before the personnel of 71st Infantry Brigade wished to have anything to do with tanks after that. In fact, it was not till the Cambrai show that their confidence was fully restored in the tank.

This incident conflicts with Dennis Douglas, who makes no mention of a tank firing on the battalion. The Official History noted:

> The first movement on the 6th Division front was the advance of the single tank following the railway track along its northern side towards the Quadrilateral. The machine passed through the right of the Norfolk about 5.50 a.m. and, by mistake, opened fire on the waiting troops. This was stopped by the gallant action of Captain A. J. G. Crosse, 9/Norfolk, who approached the tank under heavy fire and pointed out its true direction. The machine was afterwards seen to turn north and move parallel to Straight Trench, firing as it did so.

It is also believed that the presence of this tank, which was alleged to have arrived too early, brought down German artillery fire of the 9th Norfolks.

So, did these incidents actually happen?

Zero Hour for the Norfolks and Leicesters was 6.20 a.m., and this incident is recorded as occurring at 5.50 a.m. The officer mentioned in the Official History account can be identified as Captain Arthur John Green Crosse. There is no mention of this incident in the 9th Battalion war diary and Captain Crosse does not get a mention in any Norfolk Regiment accounts either. In fact, it is not recorded in the Norfolk Regiment's history.

The tank in question was C22 from 'C' Company of the Heavy Section Machine Gun Corps, commanded by Lieutenant Basil Henriques. I find it interesting that Dennis Douglas gets his timing of the tank appearing at exactly the same time as the account where it says the 9th Battalion is fired on. Surely, he would have mentioned this incident if it happened?

Therefore, I think this must be questioned.

The time for Lieutenant Henriques's movements are also confusing. Various records, including the HSMGC war diary, state that he moved off to the front between 5.30 and 6.30 a.m. Could it have been one of the other two tanks allotted? These were C19 commanded by Captain Archie Holford-Walker and C20 commanded by Lieutenant George Macpherson. Both of these tanks did not reach the front. Holford-Walker's tank broke an axle and Macpherson's tank broke down with engine trouble. So, the only tank to reach their allotted point and to advance was Lt Henriques's.

Henriques also makes no mention of the incident himself and his timings also fit with Dennis:

> At five, I was about 500 yards behind the first line. I again stopped, as we were rather too early. There was to be a barrage of artillery fire through which a space was to be left for me to go through. At 5.45 I reached another English trench, but was not allowed to stop there for fear of drawing fire upon the infantry, so withdrew 20 yards and waited 5 minutes, but nothing happened and I decided to go forward.

Henriques's account puts him within the British line at 5.45 a.m. It is reported that the 1st Leicestershires saw him at 5.50 a.m. Lt Henriques noted he was at the German wire at 6.05 a.m. Accounts dispute he got this far, but the war diary for 'C' Company HSMGC reported that he got into the Quadrilateral where his tank was hit heavy by German fire who were using S.m.K. ammunition, which was a type of armour-piercing round used to fire through metal sniper shields. Lt Henriques's own account also describes what happened to him once he reached the enemy position:

> Then a smash against my flap in front caused splinters to come in, and the blood to pour down my face. Another minute and my driver get the same. Then our prism glass broke to pieces; then another smash - I think it must have been a bomb - right in my face. The next one wounded my driver so badly that he had to stop. By this

time, I could see nothing at all. AII my prisms were broken and one periscope and it was impossible to look through the other" On turning round I saw my gunners lying on the floor. I couldn't make out why and yelled to them to fire.... I could see absolutely nothing. The only thing to do was to open the front flap slightly and peep through. Eventually this got hit so that it was hanging only by a thread, and the enemy could fire in on us at close range.

The 9th Norfolks also saw him heading north up Straight Trench firing as it went and Royal Flying Corps' sorties in this sector also reported a tank just north of the Quadrilateral. But sadly, Lt Henriques had to withdraw:

As the infantry were now approaching and as it was impossible to guide the car and as I now discovered the sides weren't bullet-proof, I decided that to save the tank from being captured I had better withdraw. How we got back, I shall never understand. We dodged shells from the artillery and it was just a guiding hand which saved us.... It was like Hell in a rough sea made of shell-holes.

The way we got over the ground was marvellous; every moment we were going to stick, but we didn't. The sight of thousands of sur men dying and wounded was ghastly. I hate to think of it all.

Lt Henriques was wounded in this action and got sent home. His friend George Macpherson died of wounds on 15 September after he had been hit by enemy shellfire and this deeply affected him. His wife noted in a letter:

He was in a state of shock and nervous breakdown. In this condition he was firmly convinced that he had done badly and had disgraced his regiment, although he knew that he had been Mentioned in Despatches. It was some months before he could shake off the depths of despair in which he was submerged.

There is a suggestion that this is because he thought he had acted in a way with which had caused issues. But there is no record as to what that was. But this despair was ended when he discovered that different orders had been given placing his start point on the Guillemont crossroads and he would have set out ninety minutes before Zero Hour:

I have made a most wonderful discovery today whilst preparing for my lecture. Walker lent me all his Battle Orders which he has bound up. You know what I have been through, for thinking that I started too early on the day, thereby bringing a barrage down on our own troops. I had no written orders, as you are aware, and had to judge my own time. Well, today I have just seen that written orders were issued and that I was to have a starting point about 800 yards before the one I was verbally told, 90 minutes before the infantry. As it was, I left 40 minutes before, and calculating the 800 yards to take 45 minutes, which I did, I really left 5 minutes later than was intended by Divisional Orders! I don't know whether you can follow all this or not I was a fool to have made such a fuss, but any other conscientious person would have done the same, if only they knew the facts as I did.

This puts his start time at 4.50 a.m., meaning that he was only five minutes late at 5.35 a.m. where he would have moved up to where the 9th Battalion were positioned.

Timings aside, it is certain C22 is the tank that Dennis Douglas is talking about and that this incident must be called into question. Certainly, I agree with Trevor Pidgeon who has also challenged this narrative in his excellent book *Tanks on the Somme*. I put this story in the same category of football and the Christmas Truce.

There are others that believe this happened, but where I have seen accounts, I do not actually see them being backed up with any evidence. In fact, other than the primary account from Dennis Douglas, all of the others are third hand. If it did happen, I am inclined to go with Trevor Pidgeon's idea that one of the gunners in C22 in doing a final check of his gun accidently squeezed off a burst of machine-gun fire through excitement and nervousness.

Only forty men from the Norfolks, under the command of Major Bradshaw, could reach the German wire and the rest of the battalion ended up in shell holes and stayed there. Two brothers were killed in the assault; these were Herbert and William Aldis, who were the sons of Walter and Hannah Aldis of Alpington. Herbert was aged twenty-two and William was aged twenty-five. Herbert is now laid to rest in Guillemont Road Cemetery and sadly William has no known grave and is commemorated on the Thiepval memorial.

They became mixed with the Suffolks who had been holding Leuze Wood–Ginchy road; with all tank support gone, the area in front of the Quadrilateral became a killing ground for German fire. From the Official History:

> … the Norfolk and Leicestershire who lay scattered in shell-holes before the western side of the Quadrilateral and Straight Trench. The movement most gallantly carried out, only resulted in fresh sacrifice of life, German machine-gun fire remained unsubdued despite fresh bombardment of the Quadrilateral.

Brigade recognised that a frontal assault on the Quadrilateral was not going to work. They were ordered to outflank the position and the 18th Brigade was put into the fray and the 14th Durham Light Infantry were ordered to assist the Norfolks.

This attempt to capture the Quadrilateral also failed due to the fact that the trench that was fought over did not connect the position. Efforts to link with other battalions also failed and the attack foundered.

The attempt to capture the Quadrilateral also failed due to the fact that the trench that was fought over did not connect the position. Efforts to link with other battalions also failed and the attack foundered.

Both the Norfolks and the Suffolks were relieved in the evening and moved back to positions south of Guillemont. Casualties were terrible with the war diary noting that seventeen officers and 431 men were lost; of this total, 160 died and this can be counted as one of the worst days for the Norfolk Regiment on the Somme.

One of the men lost that day was Private Archie Ward from Roughton. His platoon commander, Lieutenant Claude Morgan, who was wounded in this action, wrote: '… I am unable to give you any details of Private Ward's death as I was myself hit that day. But may I say this of him that he was one of as fine a platoon of British lads, gentlemen every one of them, as any officer will ever command. Men of this stamp only die way'.

Archie has no known grave and is commemorated on the Thiepval Memorial. Also lost that day was the George, identified as Private George Dennis Douglas (40010), who was mentioned in Dennis Douglas's diary, this was his younger brother:

> Still today I do not know what has happened to George. Some of the lads who survived with me, believe he was lost with Major Bradshaw in front of the strong-point called 'Quadrilateral'. Before leaving France, I heard the battalion had been stopped by uncut wire and over half had lost their lives. So many friends and George were unaccounted for.

George has no known grave and is commemorated on the Thiepval Memorial.

Also lost this day was Frederick Howson, who by now was a sergeant serving in 'B' Company. He was wounded and died of those wounds in No. 1 (New Zealand) Station Hospital at Amiens on 19 September 1916. He was then aged twenty-six and was the son of George Howson and Sarah Howson who were then living in Trowse. He is buried in Grave IV.C.6. in St Pierre Cemetery.

Major Arthur Weyman had his own thoughts on why the attack here failed:

> I venture to offer a correction to page 5 [of the draft] of the 15th September operations, in that I am quite sure that the Quadrilateral which caused such terrible losses to 16th and 71st Brigades was situated not beyond the crest but down the slope on the British side of the crest.... The trench almost on the crest of the ridge was later found to be the rear face of the Quadrilateral ... I well remember that Brig Gen Edwardes, who commanded 71st Brigade, was not satisfied with the area selected for the British artillery preparation.... He wished it to be brought down on the near slope of the crest and not, as it was, on the crest itself or beyond the crest. Both 6th Division and XIV Corps were dead against him.... My diary for 29th September [after its capture] states 'I had a good look at the Quadrilateral—a fearful crest of the ridge rear face, and not the front face as was first thought.'... The Quadrilateral had, I think, eight deep wooden dugouts in its forward face of which one was badly done in and one damaged, the rest being hardly damaged at that date. Wire on the outside of the Quadrilateral 'was very strong and cut in not very many places by our shell fire'.

His thoughts were not put into the official history.

I have stood at the site of the Quadrilateral many a time and have looked out towards Leuze Wood into the field where so many 9th Norfolk men fell on that day. Therefore, it is rightly sacred ground for those men who laid down their lives in that field.

A reminder of that came in 2013 when Annette Burgoyne was walking the line of advance for the 2nd Battalion King's Shropshire Light Infantry who attacked and captured the Quadrilateral two days after the 9th Norfolks had been in action. The story is taken up by Annette Burgoyne, who gave me permission to tell the story:

> After following the line of the 1st K.S.L.I. attack has far has we could, crops stopped us just short of the Quadrilateral, we then made our way along crop line towards the Ginchy to Morval road, cutting across the 71st (15th Sept) & 18th (18th Sept) Brigade's sector.
>
> As I was walking I saw something a bit shiny in the ground, one part of my brain was saying it's just a pull ring from an old can or something like that but something made me bend over a pick it. I could then see it was disc looking, so I called Dave over and he confirmed it was a personal ID disc that would have been worn on the wrist.
>
> The dirt was removed to reveal that it had belonged to A. Copeman, 15369, of the 9th Norfolk Regiment. Tim was soon on the phone to the UK and within minutes we were told that 15369 Albert Copeman had been killed on the 15th Sept 1916. Also has the disc was being cleaned I noticed a small bone near to where I had picked up the disc, now I tend not to going around picking up old bones but again something just made me pick it up, after talking to some of the other I decided to put it back in the ground, we all had a good look around the area to see if we could find any other bones, only one tiny bit was found, it had been sliced off by ploughing (guess). We placed a cross to Albert in a tree on the road side and Tim quoted the Soldiers verse, very moving.

Guidebook

From Longueval, head toward Ginchy by starting from the South African Memorial. At the T-Junction, turn left and keep on this road until you see a hard standing on your right. This is where the Quadrilateral was positioned in 1916. If you look south, you will see Leuze Wood in the distance. Between the wood and the road, you are stood on is where the 9th Norfolks took shelter in shell-holes on 15 September 1916.

What3words: clarity.moonlight.lurched.

* * * * *

After this action, the 5th Division took over from the 6th Division and were ordered to capture Morval. The 1st Norfolks were ordered to advance as the lead battalion in this assault and Zero Hour was set for 12.35 p.m. The 1st Norfolks had spent a short while out of the trenches before being sent back to help build and restore positions close to the line. While that had gone on, they had received new drafts. None of these came from the Norfolk Regiment and they came from three regiments. Most in that draft had not seen any action. Knowing that the CO of the 1st Battalion requested permission to lead his battalion, which was granted. He then ordered all of his commanders to do the same. He also sent a special order to the men of the battalion:

Special Battalion Order
By Lieut Col. P.V.P. Stone—Comdg 1/Norfolk Regt 24 Sep 16
   Tomorrow an attack on a large scale takes place in co-operation with the French Army on our right. One more great effort is required from the 5th Divn. The C.O. and the higher Commanders thoroughly realise the strain that has been put on all ranks by their strenuous efforts during the past week under the most trying circumstances possible in war, but he wishes all ranks to thoroughly understand the vast importance that tomorrow's operation will have on the final issue of the war.
   The Bttn has earned undying fame at Longueval and Falfemont Farm where they have lost their bravest and best, and he is certain that all of us here now will do their utmost tomorrow in honour of our fallen heroes, who have paved the way for us, and the glorious name of the 1st Norfolk Regiment.
   All those who have been wounded and are now at home, and those who have been with the regiment from the start of the war, will look to the new drafts of the Territorial Bttns. Tomorrow uphold these magnificent traditions which they have made for them.
   We have the easiest of all the objectives, and it has to be taken at all costs. The remaining Regts of the Brigade will then go through you, and I am certain that no Norfolk man who is not wounded will be found in the rear of the objective.
P.V.P. Stone—Lt. Colonel
Comdg 1/Norfolk Regiment

Within five minutes of Zero Hour, the 1st Battalion had captured their objective with the loss of four officers and seventy other ranks, this loss is reported in the war diary as slight. The Official History of the Great War noted: 'The 1/Norfolk was led by Lieut-Colonel P.V.P Stone in person, and took the first objective in one rush, killing many Germans and capturing over a hundred'.

The Official History, as an added extra, noted this about the action led by Lt-Col. Stone:

Lieutenant Colonel Stone had obtained permission to lead the attack on the score that his battalion had recently received three large drafts composed of men of three other regiments, and that the new-comers had not settled down. He is said to have 'treated the attack as a pheasant shoot, with his servant loader, and to have accounted for quite a number of the enemy'.

That account captures all sorts of images in my mind. Lt-Col. Stone advancing with his servant acting as his loader? It is almost like a scene out of *Downtown Abbey*. And yet this was an action on the Western Front. It is an action that harks from another time involving men of a different calibre.

The 1st Battalion Bedfordshires moved past the positions captured by the Norfolks, and within ten minutes, they had captured their objectives. But it was not as simple as all of that and the battalion war diary noted that they came under machine-gun fire from all directions and had to deal with pockets of defenders who were in shell holes in front of their trenches. Acts of bravery were carried out here, including an action by Leonard Causton, who led a bombing party up a forward communication trench and drove the German defenders out while the area was still under heavy artillery fire. He then cleared out the trench and took his party out to the second objective. For this action, he was awarded a Military Medal.

Others were in the rear of their trench and also had to be dealt with. They captured three machine guns in the advance and estimated that their tally for prisoners was 150. This swift action saw a swift withdrawal, and by 5 p.m. on 26 September 1916, the battalion were out of the line and sent back to the rear, specifically to Arrow Head Copse. This would be the last action fought by the 1st Battalion on the Somme, and they had left their service there with glory. In all the engagements from Longueval to Morval, they had acquitted themselves with battle honours and this is noted in the Norfolk's history.

Lt-Col. Stone sent a battalion order to all companies, stating:

Before leaving the Somme, and all it will mean to us and to the history of the Regiment, I wish to convey my most sincere thanks to all ranks for what they have done. We were no new regiment, fresh and keen from home, who had rested in billets well at the back for months, but an old regiment who had been continually engaged since the start of the war with practically no rest at all, trench worn and suffering from overwork and over exposure. You had everything against you, but you have been through the heaviest fighting of the war and come out of it with a name that will live forever.

At Longueval, your first battle, you were given your first and severest test, and no praise of mine can be too high for the extreme gallantry and endurance shown on that occasion.

The severest test of discipline is for men to stand intense shell fire and to hold on to the ground they have won under it, and this you did. At Falfemont Farm you again had a difficult task and a severe fight, but you stuck to it and eventually captured it, a position whose importance cannot be overestimated. Then, during the most trying weather conditions, you were in the open making trenches, and at one time the limit of complete exhaustion had almost been reached, but when one final effort was asked of you at Morval, you carried out a brilliant assault. These things could have only been done by the finest troops in the world.

I cannot sufficiently express my admiration of your gallantry and splendid conduct throughout. You came to the Somme battlefield with a very high reputation, which you had rightly earned during twenty-five months of strenuous warfare, you leave the Somme with the highest reputation of the British Army.

[Signed] P.V.P. Stone

Commanding 1st Battalion the Norfolk Regiment

This had come at a high cost to the battalion. Between 16 July 1916, when they arrived back on the Somme, and 1 October 1916, when they entrained for Béthune, they left behind them 277 of their comrades in the fields of the Somme. Men like Thomas David Gage, who was awarded the MC, which was listed in the *London Gazette* on 18 August 1916, his citation stating:

> 8341 Coy. S./M. Thomas David Gage, Norf. R.
> For consistent gallantry and good work throughout the campaign, notably when he on several occasions set a fine example to his men in building up his parapet under heavy shell fire.

Thomas was a pre-war Regular who had landed with the battalion on 16 August 1914 so was one of the men Lt-Col. Stone was alluding to. He died of wounds at 2/2nd London CCS two days after they had assaulted Morval and is now laid to rest in Grove Town Cemetery.

Guidebook

From Delville Wood travel toward Ginchy and the T-junction turn left. Drive through the village and at the next junction carry straight on heading toward Morval. After about half a mile, you will see a small chapel on the right; stop here. With the chapel to your back, you are now stood centrally to where the 1st Battalion advanced over the high ground you see in front of you.

What3words: chivalry.starlight.tribunes.

13

The 8th Battalion, The Battle of the Somme, Thiepval to the Schwaben Redoubt: 26 September to 5 October 1916

On 26 September 1916, the 8th Battalion Norfolk Regiment assisted in the capture of French village that had held out since 1 July 1916. Thiepval had been an objective of the doomed 32nd Division on that day and had lost around 4,000 men killed, wounded, missing, or captured in the process. Thiepval had held out that long summer until the 18th (Eastern) Division made a last ditched attempt to capture it.

Supported by two tanks, the 53rd Brigade went over the top at 12.35 p.m. with the 8th Suffolk and 10th Essex Regiments leading the way with the Berkshires in reserve. The 8th Norfolks would follow up with a supply party from 'C' Company and a platoon from 'B' Company who advanced behind the lead battalions to act as 'moppers-up'.

The attack went in well and the lead battalions reached the village with little difficulty. The Norfolk element followed on and cleared the village and the trenches around it. It was not an easy task and the division lost 1,456 men killed, wounded, or missing.

Losses for the Norfolk element was light, although the war diary noted that two men were killed. After the capture, 'A' and 'D' Companies moved up to the old British line and then to the assembly trenches vacated by the advancing elements.

A witness to this was Lt Adrian Consett, MC, who had been sent up to sight his trench mortar battery, who watched the attack go in from high ground near Mouquet Farm:

> Noon on the 26th found me at the O.P. with the Captain. Zero was at 12.35, and as yet the trenches were silent and motionless. Then suddenly, at the appointed minute the slopes of Thiepval seemed to move with small brown figures, like a field alive

with rabbits, and the guns swept down on Thiepval and the country to the right of it. At first the men advanced in disordered masses, but gradually, taking their own time they opened out like a stage crowd falling into their allotted places. I could see the first wave walking towards Thiepval, and then a second wave sprang up and spread out behind them, then the last wave took shape and followed up in artillery formation; small bunches of men, with an interval between each bunch, or more often six men advancing in single file with a stretcher bearer in the rear. It was a wonderful sight. Never have I seen such a calm, methodical and perfectly ordered advance. It seemed incredible that this parade could be marching on Thiepval, the most sinister of German strongholds, yet hardly a man fell. The barrage was as perfect as it was terrible.

The white smoke of shrapnel ran like a rampart along the trenches that were the first objective, as clear as though it were made from tape carefully placed and measured. Indeed, the barrier of white smoke broken now and again by a black puff from an enemy gun, might have been an ermine fur with its little black tufts.

From my vantage point I could even look over the barrage on to the trenches beyond, but it was hard even for a moment to drag one's eyes away from the little brown figures that were slowly but steadily drawing upon Thiepval. Sometimes a wave of men would dip and disappear into a trench only to emerge on the other side in perfect line again. Now they are into Thiepval now the line suddenly telescopes into a bunch and the bunch scurries to right or left, trying to evade a machine-gun in front, and then with a plunge the first wave, broken now into little groups, vanished amidst the ruined houses. What desperate resistance they encountered in the dark and mysterious passages beneath those ruins, only the men who fought will know, but the other waves swept on up to the slope, till they too were lost amidst the village. Farther to the right, where the barrage had lifted, more brown figures streamed across the open. A black dog came out of a dug-out to meet them; a man stooped down and fondled it. When they drew near to a line of chalk heaps I saw black masses emerge and march towards our lines.

Prisoners were giving themselves up without a light. Prisoners were pouring in from all les sometimes in black batches, guided by a brown figure and a shining bayonet, sometimes a single Boche would race, hands above head, panic-stricken till he reached our lines. Thiepval was now a closed book, though runners would sometimes emerge and dash stumbling to our trenches. The Boche retaliation was feeble and badly placed. His barrage fell behind all our men, and very few shells had burst among them, and even then, never did they cause a man to turn his head or swerve out of place—unless he fell. At this stage a tank crawled on to the scene and crept laboriously, like a great slug, towards Thiepval. It disappeared among the ruins, puffing smoke. Subsequently it caught fire. Thiepval now became as stony, as devoid of life, as it was before the attack. Away to the right, however, a fresh assault was being launched. A new barrage opened, and our men swept forward to another objective, wheeling slightly as the trench in front ran diagonally across their path.

Suddenly, as though spirited away, they vanished, sank into the ground. Watching carefully, we could distinguish a movement among the long grass and wire, and sometimes a man would leap up, dash forward, or run backward. It seemed they were playing at hide and seek. Probably they were. It is certain they were held up by something, and the bitter fighting which continued the next day for Hessian Trench the trench in question—made one wonder how they ever got as far as they did. Yet all this time men were streaming backwards and forwards to the Zollern Trench just in the rear.

The tank action was also witnessed by a German commander, *Oberstleutnant* Alfred Vischer of Infantry Regiment 180, who watched the attack go in on positions known as *Braunerweg* (Brown Way), a communication trench linking their first and second lines to the south of another position called *Mauerweg* (Wall Trench):

On 26th September at 1.30 pm, drum fire came down along the entire line Thiepval–Serre and Thiepval–Courcelette. This was immediately followed by an infantry attack in an easterly direction on the southern flank of Thiepval. The left flank of the attack, which was organised in waves, was directed against C7 and the southern part of C6 at the junction with the road Thiepval–Authuille. As could not otherwise be expected the event of so strong an attack, the advanced triangle Mauerweg–Braunerweg, which was only defended by a platoon of 2nd Company and sentries from 2nd and 3rd Companies were lost. The first determined resistance was offered at Braunerweg.

The first wave of attackers was almost completely destroyed by rifle and machine-gun fire before it even closed up to the obstacle. The second denser, wave flooded to the rear with heavy casualties. Suddenly an armoured vehicle (tank) emerged out of Authuille Wood. It was followed and flanked by a third wave, which succeeded in checking the withdrawal of the second wave and, assisted by the tank, to work its way forward to the obstacle. There the attack stalled. Attackers and defenders engaged in a fire fight. The situation took an unfavourable turn when suddenly the left flank and almost simultaneously, the left flank and centre of the 3rd Company were attacked from the rear with hand grenades. The British seemed to have forced their way into the south eastern and eastern fronts of Thiepval and pressed with increasing strength from the direction of the church and chateau to the south and south-west. Attacked from the front and rear and threatened in the flank as well, the 3rd Company had to fall back, echeloned from the left, on C6. The enemy did not succeed in forcing a way via Mauerweg into C6 from the south, but the attacked unopposed from Thiepval until, finally, after the toughest defence possible, the barricade at the junction of C6 and Mauerweg had to be pulled back in order to avoid encirclement.

Although the 'moppers-up' were withdrawn, the fighting did not stop there. On 27 September 1916, the 8th Suffolks and the 7th Queen's from the 55th Brigade were ordered to attack and capture the trench to the right of the Schwaben Redoubt, which was another stronghold that had held out since 1 July 1916.

At 1 p.m. on 27 September 1916, the attack went in with the 8th Norfolks acting as the moppers-up again. This time 'D' Company took on that role and assisted the Queen's and another two platoons did the same for the Suffolks. The fighting here was terrible, with a big part going in by bayonet and bomb. The fighting here lasted for days, with a number of German counterattacks being fought off.

On 29 September 1916, the Norfolks were relieved and sent back to their original positions from the 27th. They were then withdrawn minus 'B' Company, who remained at Crucifix Corner who were engaged in the burying of the dead. Between 26 and 30 September 1916, the 8th Battalion lost 133 men killed, wounded, or missing.

One of the dead was Private George Alfred Catchpole (43581) from Salhouse, who was killed in action on 27 September 1916. George had come from the 1/6th Norfolk (Cyclists) Battalion when the majority of that unit had been sent to France to act as drafts for the 8th Battalion. He has no known grave and is commemorated on the Thiepval Memorial.

George Catchpole is one man of a total of 762 men from the Norfolk Regiment who are commemorated on the Thiepval Memorial. George was the son of John and Elizabeth Catchpole who lived at the Railway Cottages in Salhouse and he was aged twenty when he died. He is just a name on a panel of the largest Commonwealth war memorial in the world. It records the names of 72,397 men who fell in the Somme Sector before 20 March 1918. Behind the memorial are 300 British and Commonwealth and 300 French graves placed there in a symbol of unity between the two Allies. Within the 300 CWGC graves are a number of unidentified Norfolk Regiment men. I often wonder if one of those is George.

Guidebook

Park up at the Thiepval Memorial. Instead of walking into the visitor's centre turn right and walk toward the road that is listed as the D151 on a French IGN map. At the junction, turn left. Walk to the 18th (Eastern) Division memorial you will see on the right. Once there, turn around so the memorial is to your rear. You are now stood at the jumping-off point for the 53rd Brigade. You can now walk from the memorial to the church, which is roughly where the line got to and where 'C' and 'B' Companies were used in the initial advance.

What3words: family.heavy.makeups.

* * * * *

After the capture of Thiepval village and Thiepval Ridge, attention was put onto a position that had held out since 1 July 1916. The mighty Schwaben Redoubt had been assaulted on that fateful day by the 36th (Ulster) Division. They had managed to take the position, but after terrible fighting and the fact that both the 29th and 32nd Divisions on either side had failed in capturing their objectives, the Ulstermen had to give up most of the gains and had ended up retiring to the German frontline, which they held. And so now, after months of fighting, and with the recent fighting close to it, the next plan was to capture it.

Since 28 September, the fighting had intensified around the Schwaben Redoubt, which occupied high ground, and both sides knew it was an important position to hold or capture. The task of capturing it was given to the 8th Battalion Norfolk Regiment. The position they would assault is described as this on the CWGC website:

> The Schwaben Redoubt, formed from a roughly triangular shaped set of mutually supporting trench systems, was perhaps the most formidable in the German second line. An extensive arrangement of well-constructed field-works—effectively a battlefield fortress or 'redoubt'—it possessed all-round defences and was linked by a maze of subterranean passages and interconnecting tunnels. The position included medical facilities and a telephone exchange.

It is no wonder that it had held out for such a long time. So, the CO of the 8th Norfolks, Lt-Col. Henry Gaspard de Lavalette Ferguson, decided that the best way to assault this mighty fortress was to use his battalion bombers, his Lewis gunners, and his snipers under the command of his battalion bombing officer. It was planned to attack the position from both flanks with support waiting to make up for any losses in the assault. The idea was for the assault parties to work down trenches on either side of the redoubt, which correspond to Point 39 and 27 on the map I have supplied from the Norfolk Regiment history of the Great War.

As each trench was captured in the redoubt, blocks would be put on and the overall assault would be supported by a barrage to the west, the south and north of the position as well as it falling on communication trenches that the Germans might bring up reinforcements.

Zero Hour was set for 6 a.m. on 5 October 1916. But at this point in time, the autumn weather had set in and the trenches were flooding. It took a long time to set up the attack, which had to be postponed until 7.30 a.m.

As with the Norfolk Regiment history, we will look at the assaults separately.

On the left-hand side, the attack came in from three parallel trenches and started well until the left-hand party of a total of three got held up at Point 19 at Strasbourg Trench. Here they were counterattacked by German bombers and in attacks over open ground. The attacks over open ground were dealt with by the Lewis gun teams, but the trench fighting against the enemy bombers caused problems.

The main issue here being the fact that the German bombers could readily resupply their grenadiers where the Norfolk bombing parties could not. This forced the left-hand party back and another counterattack came in, although this was dealt with by Lewis gun teams under the command of Lt Arthur Gundry-White.

On the right, the attack met strong opposition and was driven back. The fighting here ended up in hand-to-hand with bayonet and bomb and Lt Thomas Whitty along with a number of men were killed in this fight. But they reached the northern part of the redoubt and managed to get within 50 yards of a position identified as Point 99, which on a map shows it faced towards the German second lines looking towards places such as Grandcourt. At 2.20 p.m., they consolidated their gains and waited for relief, which came in the form of the 39th Division. In the process of attempting to capture this area, the 18th (Eastern) Division, who had been fighting in this area since 26 September 1916, had lost 2,000 men killed, wounded, or missing.

But although they had captured Thiepval and Thiepval Ridge, they never fully captured the Schwaben Redoubt, and when they handed over their gains, Points 19, 39, 49 and 69 were still in German hands.

It would not be until 14 October 1916 that the entire position would fall. This was noted in the Official History of the Great War:

> … on the 14th, the 39th Division drove the Germans from their last hold on the Schwaben. The 4th/5th Black Watch and the 1/1st Cambridgeshire (118th Brigade), assisted by the 17/K.R.R.C. (117th Brigade) attacked over the open and, although the fighting continued until 11 p.m., the enemy's discomfiture was then complete. More than one hundred and fifty prisoners of the II./110th Reserve regiment were collected. Meanwhile, the 1/6th Cheshire (118th Brigade) had advanced the line on the left. Three counter attacks against the Schwaben, two of them with Flammenwerfer, were repulsed in the course of the following day.

If you visit either Connaught or Mill Road Cemeteries on the Somme, you will see that 8th Battalion Norfolk men lie next to 1/1st Cambridgeshire men along with the other regiments who fought so hard to take the Schwaben Redoubt off of the Germans.

In total, the 8th Norfolks lost ninety-one men killed, wounded, or missing and can rightly be classed as one of the many battle honours for the battalion, which had now been in the thick of the fighting since 1 July 1916. But this was not the last time that the battalion would see action on the Somme.

Guidebook

From the Thiepval memorial, head toward Hamel on the D73. In a little while you will see Connaught Cemetery on your left and a row of trees in front and to the right, which is part of the Ulster Tower. To your right, you should see a farm track with a sign for Mill Road Cemetery. Walk up this track to the cemetery. You are now stood on the site of the Schwaben Redoubt. With the cemetery to your right rear, you are looking toward to the extreme point to where the Norfolks reached before being stopped.

What3words: expired.operation.boggled.

Mill Road Cemetery is sat on top of the Schwaben Redoubt and holds the remains of three 8th Battalion men killed on 5 October 1916, and if you return to Connaught Cemetery, you will find another five 8th Norfolk men who died in the assault on the Schwaben Redoubt.

What3words: innate.zing.manager.

14

The 7th and 9th Battalions, The Battle of the Somme, Bayonet and Mild Trenches: 12–18 October 1916

On 2 October 1916, the 7th Norfolks moved to Bernafay Wood and went into the reserve with the rest of the 35th Brigade, while the 36th and 37th Brigades occupied the frontline facing Gueudecourt. On 10 October, the 35th Brigade relieved the 36th Brigade and were given orders to prepare for an attack on a German position called Bayonet Trench on 12 October.

By now, the autumn weather was setting in and the conditions in the trenches were terrible. Although you could define the line here, the actual trenches were by now flooded holes full of the dead on both sides and the smashed equipment of successive attacks that had failed.

The assault was timed to go in at 2.50 p.m. and would involve all four companies going in as 'D', 'C', 'B', and 'A' with the 7th Suffolks advancing on the Norfolk's right and a battalion from the 30th Division, namely the 2nd Battalion Royal Scots Fusiliers. They were to move to capture Luishof Farm after they had secured Bayonet and Scabbard Trench. They would advance on these positions under the cover of artillery:

Today, at 2.5 p.m. we attacked Bayonet Trench. Last night the assembly trenches were completed & all the battalion lay out in them from 5 a.m. This morning until the attack. The attack was carried out with all four companies in the line disposed in depth one platoon behind the other, D on the right, C, B, A. On our right 7th Suffolk Regt and on our left 2nd Royal Scots Fusiliers 30th Division. Bn H.Q remained in Bulls Road. The object was to attack was first of all to capture Bayonet & Scabbard Trench and then to sweep on to take Luishof Farm and establish a line beyond it.

The battalion had only advanced 50 yards when they came under machine-gun fire from both flanks, and as they continued onto Bayonet Trench, they came up against uncut wire:

> At 2.5 p.m. our artillery barrage commenced & our men advanced to the assault. After advancing about 50 yards the Hun opened fire with M.G.s from both flanks & from the front. Our troops continued to advance but before reaching the enemy's trench ran into barbed wire which had not been cut. This wire coupled with the M.G. fire prevented any further advance. And our men lay down in shell holes from where they brought rifle fire to bear on the Germans who were standing up in their trenches shooting at them. We caused considerable casualties in this way to the enemy. After dark we made a further attempt to cut a way through the enemy's trench but the wire proved too strong.

The 7th Suffolks fared better and managed to get into the German line, but were forced out by Germans, who bombed them. The Norfolks got close to Bayonet and Scabbard Trench and attempts were made to cut the wire here. But these attempts failed and they had to move back: 'The survivors then crawled back to our own lines & reformed. The 9th Essex Regt then relieved us & the Suffolk Regt in the front line near Flers which we are sharing with the Suffolk Regt.'

Losses here were nine officers and 212 other ranks killed, wounded, or missing. This left eight officers and 350 other ranks when they were relieved by elements of the 29th Division and marched to Mametz Wood. By 25 October 1916, they were away from the Somme battle area and had moved to Arras.

Guidebook

From the Albert–Bapaume road at Le Sars, turn right onto the D11 signposted Flers– Gueudecourt, if you are coming from the direction of Bapaume you will turn left. Keep on this road, which becomes the D74, until you come to crossroads. This is the D10, turn left, signposted Bapaume, and continue until you see a track on your left and a small layby next to it. You are now stood on the British frontline for 12 October 1916. If you continue toward Bapaume, you will come a natural piece of high ground in a slightly sunken road with a piece of hard standing on your right. From left to right of this road and through the hard standing is where Bayonet Trench was situated. Luishof Farm does not exist anymore, but the remains of it are where you are stood.
What3words: British Line—probability.antisocial.drove; Bayonet Trench and Luishof Farm—major.imitators.photograph.

* * * * *

Since their assault on the Quadrilateral, the 9th Norfolks had spent time resting and refitting. For the rest of September and the beginning of October, they were positioned in the rear and on 1 October 1916, a new CO, Lt Bernard Henry Leathes Prior, took command of the battalion from Major Frederick Lewis, 2nd Battalion Leicestershire Regiment, who became his second in command. You will remember that he was the CO of the 1/6th (Cyclist) Battalion.

Lt-Col. Prior wrote his memoirs after the war and noted his journey to the 9th Battalion:

> I was particularly anxious to get to the 8th battalion as a large proportion of my old 6th battalion men had re-enforced that unit. However, at the end of September, I got wire to proceed at once to take command of the 9th Norfolk Regiment. Rumours had reached the 7th Battalion that the 9th had been tremendously knocked about in the Somme battle but whether they were still in the battle area or had been relieved was not known.
>
> I was soon to ascertain that the first rumour was only too true and that 6th Division was still hard at it in the big battle. After detraining I joined a small party of officers, reinforcements for the 6th Division, amongst them two for my battalion, 2/Lieutenants Blackwell and Baningthwaighte.

The second officer can be identified as 2Lt Cyril Percy Bassingthwaighte, and we will hear from him later on in the book. Lt-Col. Prior continued:

> We boarded a motor lorry and proceeded on our way through Albert to the 6th Divisional rear Headquarters. On our way we passed the remains of the 1st Battalion marching out of the battle areas. There were several of my old 6th men in the ranks, some of whom recognised me as I passed and were not too weary to turn and give me a cheer, an incident which gave me intense pleasure.

He very nearly did not get to command the 9th Battalion, stating that his general said:

> 'I don't know why you have been sent to the Division. This is a regular Division. We have no Territorial commanding officers here and to be quite frank we don't want you.'
>
> I explained that I had been ordered to the Division to command the 9th Norfolk Regiment, that I had not asked to command them and that I had not the least desire to come where I was not wanted.

Luckily, the general cooled down and apologised for his outburst and Lt-Col. Prior was allowed to command the 9th Battalion: 'I found that there were only three officers left who had taken part in the quadrilateral battle, namely the Adjutant Everitt and 2/Lts Huntshall and Jones'.

Lt-Col. Prior made note of the fact that his battalion was made up of new drafts of men and very few of the original men were left from before that time.

But that held no sway, and by 16 October, they were back in the trenches north-east of Gueudecourt.

The fighting around Gueudecourt had not stopped with the recent assaults made on 12 October 1916, and the 6th Division were positioned to the right of the 12th (Eastern) Division. They were ordered to advance and capture Mild Trench and then to capture Cloudy Trench. This would then afford the British the ridge that then led to Le Transloy:

> Battalion Headquarters was placed in Rainbow Trench, at least it had at one time been a trench but was so blasted by shell fire that very little of the original line was left. The front line was located in Shine Trench and between the two there was no continuous communication trench. Our left flank was entirely open and rested on a road leading from Gueudecourt. Immediately behind us was the valley in front of the village of Gueudecourt, the ground rising sharply as it crossed Rainbow Trench and forming a ridge, the front line (Shine Trench) being on the far, or enemy side of the ridge. From the front line the ground was fair level but sloping slightly away until it rose again to the Bapaume–Le Transloy road. Le Transloy when I first saw it was a charming little red-roofed village standing amongst trees and scarcely touched by shell fire.
>
> One could follow quite clearly the road to Bapaume, past another small village and in the extreme left distance one could just see the spire of a church which was reported to be Bapaume itself.

The attack would go in at night and would be supported by artillery. But as noted in the chapter on the 7th Norfolks's attempts to capture Bayonet Trench, the weather now was atrocious. The ground was described as being a quagmire and the parapets were slippery. This would have a bearing on the attack:

> The trenches and shell-holes very speedily became knee-deep in liquid mud and the sides of the trenches so slippery that it was often a physical impossibility to get on top. Add to this a night of the most intense blackness and one gets but a faint glimmering of the difficulties of getting men unused to trench warfare into their assembly position. Never before nor since have I experienced so bad a bombardment, I have known a more intense shelling but never one so continuous and so accurate.
>
> Ongoing around the trenches I was dismayed to find how backward the companies were with their arrangements. I could not find the commander of 'C' Coy but his men had not received their instructions, 'B' Coy had not yet moved into their positions in the front line nor could I find, with the exception of 'D' Coy, that any arrangements had been made to collect and bring up rations.

What also complicated the plan was that the Norfolks would have to fight on their left flank until supporting troops came up and the Germans were pouring fire onto their positions. The attack went in at 3.40 a.m. on 18 October 1916.

The initial problem was not the enemy but the conditions, and the Norfolks had difficulty on getting out of their trenches due to the slippery conditions. Men who managed to get out often then slipped back and the protective barrage was lost and the battalion also suffered from the German counter barrage, the war diary noting:

'A' and 'B' Companies led the attack and were followed up by 'C' and 'D' Companies. 'D' Company had the job of protecting the flank. But due to the night being extremely dark cohesion was lost and 'A' and 'B' lost each other and left a gap which C Company could not fill. 'B' Company managed to capture Mild Trench and under the command of Lieutenant Terence Algernon Kilbee Cubitt who blocked the right-hand trench. 'A' Company overshot their objective and were lost. All other attempts by other battalions also got into trouble.

Lt-Col. Prior stated:

The front-line trench was very narrow with steep sides and full of thick clinging mud. Time was getting away and to my consternation I found that instead of 'B' Coy being in touch with A there was a big gap between them. I saw Hartshall and Page, a subaltern in 'A' Coy, who was subsequently killed and they agreed to mutually extend so as to join up. I could not find the company commander of C. I found, however, a platoon of his men, under a Sergeant, explained the position and the told the sergeant to give my orders to the company commander.

Just as I was starting I met a runner from 'B' Coy with a report that they had gained their objective and though counter attacked had driven the Boche out of the trench and had been holding it since. The runner informed me that 'B' Coy were in touch with the Hampshires on their left but their right was open the attack having failed. I went on and saw Blackwell, reported the situation to him and told him to organize a party from his company, reinforce 'B' Coy and take command of the position. I then went along the line and here the news was not so good. The right of 'B' and 'A' Companies had apparently failed. There were stragglers of both companies who had got back to our original front line but they had missed their direction, got caught in the Boche barrage and those who were not killed or wounded had eventually got back to their own line.

We also have an excellent account of this action from a Norfolk Regiment officer:

Precisely to the minute the great British barrage opened, the whole earth shook, the noise was deafening, and the sky was lit up with the flash of guns. I clambered over the top and walked slowly forward till I fell in a shell hole. I crawled out of the shell hole, then walked blindly forward again until I came to the Bosche trench, shattered and with many dead.... There was one live German in that trench, a few yards from me, with a bomb in his hand; but when our boys came over the parados and leaped into the trench, up went his hands and he shouted '*Camerade*! *Camerade*!'... I felt exceedingly tired and would have liked to have slept, but we got that trench and I wasn't keen on losing it.

The account comes from Lt Cubitt who, we have already noted, was setting up blocks in the captured trench. He was aged twenty-one when this action took place and he rightly won a Military Cross; his citation, which appeared in the *London Gazette* on 24 November 1916, stating:

2nd Lt. Terence Algernon Kilbee Cubitt, Norf. R.
For conspicuous gallantry in action. He led his platoon in the attack with great courage and determination. Later, with a few men, he formed a strong point, which he held till reinforcements arrived.

A series of German counterattacks supported by their artillery ensued. Snipers picked off Cubitt's men and he makes mention of one sergeant being wounded when a round ricocheted into his cheek just below his eye.

The sergeant, it was reported, smiled through the helmet as a joke. But the trench was held, and at midnight on the night of 19–20 October, this small group was relieved.

Algernon Cubitt's account of this action also has this to say about his men:

The Bosches were coming down the communication trench towards us, but my little party of bombers-only seven men strong-bombed them back, three being killed in doing it. That left me with one Lance Corporal and seven men to hold the trench. Picking up captured German rifles (our own being caked with mud and it raining in torrents) we sniped over the parapet. I called for a volunteer to take a message back to Headquarters for reinforcements. Within five minutes one was on his way.

We recommended him for the Military Medal ... I saw an officer and four men crawling towards me under heavy fire; two of the party were killed, but the officer (Lieutenant Blackwell) got there with the other men. He took over, and I went to sleep in the mud! Subsequently others came to our assistance and forty-eight hours, with water up to our knees, soaked to the skin, practically no water to drink, and dead beat, those splendid boys 'stood to', fought, and bombed, and held on. It was glorious to see how when one man was killed, another took his place, and, when he fell, a third man. They were all heroes.

This, to me, epitomises the men of the infantry who fought on the Somme in 1916. One of those men was 2Lt Harold John Badcock. Harold had served as a constable in King's Lynn borough police prior to joining up.

He had joined the battalion on 30 September 1916 and lasted just eighteen days before he went missing in the assault. He, like Algernon Cubitt, had been sent to the 9th Norfolks from the 4th Battalion. He was aged twenty-eight and was confirmed as being killed in action and was the son of F. St John Badcock and the husband of Hilda Gladys Badcock of 'Hillside' George Street in Hemel Hempstead and a native of Boxmoor. He is now buried in Bancourt British Cemetery.

Information was received that 'A' Companyy had advanced past the objective, which gave hope that the attack had been successful and Lt-Col. Prior wanted to confirm this:

> I then went along the left flank, got the direction of the trench we had captured and went over. The garrison holding the trench were in the best of spirits, despite many casualties. They had been heavily shelled, sniped at and machine gunned and at least once seriously counter attacked. Blackwell had put in a block on his right flank. On his left was the Gueudecourt road on the other side of which were the Hampshires.

The Germans put in localised counterattacks and one of the men who took part in this was *Leutnant* Meyer of the 3rd Battalion Infantry Regiment 64:

> Well equipped with hand grenades—the previous night 5.000 had been brought forward to the battalion staff—I went with some men of 10th Company to the left. One hundred metres this side of the sunken and we met up with the last man of the company. We took it a step at a time, always after having thrown several grenades. So gradually we worked our way forward until we could reach the sunken road with our grenades. After we had thrown half a dozen, panic set in amongst the British who were packed in there tightly. Without offering resistance, they attempted to flee the sunken road and were shot down by fire from all sides; we then left a small party to guard the sunken road. Because this had been so successful, we attempted to do the same thing on the right Dank of the battalion in the 11th Company area. Step by step, the trench was rolled up. The only difference was the fact that hardly a man who attempted through flight to avoid the hand grenades escaped with his life. The machine guns, which were back in action, shot down from the all who attempted to get to the rear.
>
> Only the first British soldiers that I met attempted to resist. Out of a group of about twenty Tommies who were sheltering in a tight group behind the parapet of an intact section of trench, most raised their hands. The commander, on the other hand, fired his revolver at me without hitting me. A few hand grenades swiftly put an end to resistance. In a rather cowardly way those who had not been hit by grenade splinters also surrendered. Further on around the right flank of the old company position, we did not need to use grenades any more. We just shouted 'Hands up!' and they raised their arms high and surrendered.

Lt-Col. Prior was present for these counterattacks:

> The Boche was quite close in front and we could see spade fills of earth coming up from a trench not more than 80 yards or so on our front. I directed him to make a

reconnaissance to his right flanks as soon as he could reasonably do so and in the meantime to use every available man to dig back a communication trench to join up with one I had already started from our old front-line.

Lt-Col. Prior then returned back to the original frontline. When he got back, he could see a number of the enemy sat up on a parodos:

> They were in close range and easy targets but no-one was firing on them. The 1st Leicestershire subaltern from whom I asked for an explanation gave his excuse that he had no snipers and it is a fact that after so a period of trench warfare the troops had come to look on a rifle as a specialist's weapon.

Lt-Col. Prior then accounted for two of the enemy, which in turn rallied the Leicestershires to fire at the Germans who dropped into cover. An enemy aircraft then flew over, and soon afterwards, a heavy bombardment supported with rifle and machine-gun fire started; Lt-Col. Prior expected an attack, which luckily did not materialise. Lt-Col. Prior put his thoughts down on paper as to what he thought had gone wrong:

> The failure of the attack on our right I put down to the following causes:
> First and foremost, the troops were largely composed of new drafts, with officers and n.c.o.s they did not know and were, I think, totally unfitted for a night operation, secondly, three of the four company commanders had never had experience of this onerous position in trench warfare. Through this lack of knowledge and experience much valuable time was wasted which should have been employed in systematically organising their companies for attack and as a consequence, in the end, a large proportion of the ranks under them did not know the role they had to play. Thirdly though the rations came up to the dump, some companies failed to draw them, or if drawn, failed to them issued. Fourthly the attacking line companies failed to get out of the trenches quickly enough to fill the gap. However, these causes of failure can be boiled down to one word, inexperience. When the circumstances are recalled under which the battalion was reformed and replenished with officers and n.c.o.s and men, the marvel is that they should have gained even a partial success.

Two other awards were given that day. The DSO went to Lt Frederick Blackwell, his being listed in the *London Gazette* on 27 November 1916, which stated:

> 2nd Lt. Samuel Frederick Baker Blackwell, Norf. R.
> For conspicuous gallantry in action. He led a reinforcement party over the open under very heavy fire, bombing back the enemy and maintaining his position against three enemy counter-attacks for 36 hours. Later, he led a daring patrol, and proceeded over 100 yards along the enemy line and obtained valuable information.

And Sgt Walter Gould (14104) who won a DCM, his citation listed in the *London Gazette* on 24 November, stating:

> 14104 Sjt. W. Gould, Norf. R.
>
> For conspicuous gallantry in action. During the day he three times went back over open ground swept by heavy fire and brought up reinforcements, ammunition and a machine gun.

But, as the Norfolk Regiment history noted about this action, 'The equally grand work of the platoon of "A" Company, who fought the Bosche to a finish, remains but an incident hitherto unrecorded and unsung'. A total of 248 unsung heroes were killed, wounded, or missing in the assault on Mild Trench, of which a total of ninety-eight can be confirmed as being killed in action or dying of wounds.

Two men that died that day were brothers. Pte Thomas Ducker (5/3239) enlisted at East Dereham in the 1/5th Battalion on 2 November 1914. He volunteered for Imperial Service Obligation on 18 June 1915, meaning he was prepared to serve overseas and remained on Home Service for the rest of 1915, being posted to the 3/5th Battalion Norfolk Regiment where he remained in 1916 until he embarked from Folkestone landing in Boulogne on 9 September 1916. He was given a new number (40205) on 25 September and was posted to the 9th Battalion on 27 September. Aged twenty-nine, he was the husband of Ellen Ducker of Fox Loke in Aylsham and also left a daughter, Mildred. His brother, Edward James Ducker, had the service number of 40204, which says to me that he went to France at the same time as Thomas as it is one number less sequentially. Both were the sons of James and Letitia Ducker. Both now lie next to each other in Graves VII. B. 9 and 10 in Bancourt Military Cemetery where many of the 9th Battalion men who died on 18 October 1916 now lie.

After they had captured part of Mild Trench, the battalion assisted in digging a communication trench to it and were then relieved. They then moved to Annezin near Béthune and their time on the Somme ended.

Guidebook

From the Albert–Bapaume road at Le Sars, turn right onto the D11 signposted Flers- Gueudecourt, if you are coming from the direction of Bapaume, you will turn left. Keep on this road until you enter Gueudecourt and you come to crossroads. Turn left here, signposted Beaulencourt, which will put you onto the D574.

Continue on until you see a small white shed on your left. This is where Mild Trench started, running parallel with this road on the right-hand side of the road. Continue on, and before the Canadian Memorial, you will see a turning on the left. Mild Trench now goes right of the road heading east.

What3words: objecting.elaspse.elimination.

15

The 8th Battalion, The Battle of the Somme, Regina Trench: 21–23 October 1916

It seems fitting that the battalion that had been there on the first day of the Somme should be the last battalion I write about in that campaign. The 8th Battalion Norfolk Regiment had been in and out of the trenches since their action on 5 October 1916 and had been employed in trench digging.

But on 21 October 1916, it was again asked to participate in an action with 10th Battalion Essex Regiment and the 11th Battalion Lancashire Fusiliers. They were given the task of capturing Regina Trench. This was so named because it had been captured for a time by the 5th Canadian Brigade on 1 October 1916 and further attempts were made to capture it by the 1st and 3rd Canadian Divisions on 8 October 1916. On 21 October 1916, an attempt would again be made by the 18th (Eastern) and the 4th Canadian Divisions.

Regina Trench is described as thus in the Norfolk Regiment History: 'This was a long trench running from the sunken road to Grandcourt, some 1,100 yards east of the Schwaben Redoubt, eastwards as far as the Courcelette–Miraumont road, a length of about 3,000 yards'.

The objective of this action was to capture Regina Trench from a point 150 yards west of the Miraumont road, where strongpoints would be made at the junction of Courcelette Trench, Twenty-Three Road, and Left Trench. 'C' Company was given the task of capturing the point west of Miraumont and 'B' Company would attempt to capture Left Trench. 'D' Company would follow in support and help to consolidate any gains. 'A' Company would remain in reserve.

To get an idea of the conditions and fighting going on at this time, we can look at accounts of *Gefreiter* Fritzsche, 6th Company Infantry Regiment 179, who was positioned around Regina Trench in October:

The firing increases in intensity. Shrapnel rounds burst and shells explode sending columns of mud flying into the air. The giant coal boxes of the naval guns roar past overhead. Steel fragments whiz through the air and we are deluged with clods of clay. We sit there and stick it out. Suddenly one of us falls dead, pierced through the chest by a shell splinter. Time passes agonisingly slowly. We realise that the enemy could appear at any minute. During the evening we try to improve our holes and to establish a link with our neighbours.... Further to the rear is the village of Avesnes, where the Second Position runs. Our heavy artillery is located here.

When it fires, the houses creak and the walls crumble. The air is full with countless enemy shells, which are seeking out the guns. There are still some rooms in these houses, even though the windows and doors are smashed and there are shell holes in the walls. These rooms provide at the illusion of security and those holding out in mud-filled or smashed dugouts or lying in the filth and squalor of the front line long for them for what is danger to us!

Both of the lead companies formed up in Hessian Trench and Zero Hour was at 12.06 p.m.; within six minutes, the Norfolks were in Regina Trench. There is an after-action report for this engagement. This describes the battalion plan of attack and who would be used where. It also notes the battalion strength, which is quite telling:

Regina Trench
Short History of Regina Trench Operations
1. On the 20th October 1916, the Battalion was ordered to attack Regina Trench on the following day.
   The objective of the battalion's attack, which was in conjunction with the 10th Essex Regiment, 53rd Infantry Brigade, on the right, and the 11th Lancashire Fusiliers, 74th Infantry Brigade on the left, was to take and occupy
   Regina Trench from a point 150 yards S.W. of the West Miraumont Road to its junction with left trench and to establish strong-points at:
   (a) Junction of Regina and Courcelette Trenches.
   (b) Junction of Regina Trench and Twenty-Three Road.
   (c) Junction of Regina and Left Trenches.
2. Attached Units
   To the Battalion were attached:
   (a) 2 Guns, 53rd Machine Gun Company.
   (b) 2 Guns 53rd Trench Mortar Battery.
   (c) A few sappers from the 79th Field Company, R.E. to be used in construction and improvement of dugouts in Regina Trench
3. Disposition of Battalion
   (a) 'C' Company

The right attacking Company with objective from a point in Regina Trench 150 yards S.W. of the West Miraumont Road to the junction of Regina and Kenora Trenches to include the strong point to be made there.

(b) 'B' Company

The left attacking Company with objective, from the junction of Regina and Kenora Trenches (exclusive), to the junction of Regina and Left Trenches, (inclusive).

(c) 'D' Company

The Support Company. To proceed to Regina and help to consolidate and to return, immediately Regina had been deepened, to Hessian Trench via Kenora Trench, leaving one platoon in Kenora to open it up.

(d) 'A' Company

To act as reserve Company.

4. Forming Up of the Battalion

'C' and 'B'—Hessian Trench—2 waves each.

'C' and 'B'—Vancouver—1 wave each

'D'—Sudbury Trench—

'A'—Zollern—to move up to Vancouver at Zero Hour.

1 gun 53rd Machine Gun Company, and Stokes Mortar 53rd Trench Mortar Battery, were allotted to both 'B' and 'C' Companies. Battalion Headquarters, Headquarter Company—R.29.c.9.9.

5. Strength of Battalion

Strength of Battalion proceeding into action—18 Officers, 540 Men.

This shows that, even though the battalion received drafts from the time it went to France in July 1915, it had lost over half of its complement of 1,031 officers and men killed, wounded, or captured, and they had seen and had been used as shock troops time and time again. This is a good example of the attrition rate for a battalion that had not left this sector since the start of the campaign in July.

Once the attack started, the response from the enemy was mixed. The Germans facing 'C' Company surrendered, but 'B' Company met with strong resistance and those met were either killed or captured. Captain F. J. Morgan led 'B' Company and fought his way through using bombs. While advancing, he found a waterproof sheet, which led to an entrance to a dugout. The Norfolk history stating:

On each step sat a couple of Germans, their backs to the entrance. When Captain Morgan called them to come out, they came unarmed. When the Norfolk and Essex were in full possession of Regina, a dozen Germans who had lost themselves descended into the trench, not knowing it had changed hands. They did not seem unduly depressed when they found themselves prisoners.

The report also notes the initial advance and first contact with the enemy:

6. First Phase—Zero to 2 p.m.

Punctually at Zero hour (12.6 p.m.), 'C', 'B' and 'D' Companies left our trenches and Regina was entered about 12.12 p.m. Germans holding it adapted different attitudes. So far as can

be gathered, those opposite 'C' surrendered easily: those opposite 'B', especially in a gap of about 100 yards between the left of 'B' Company and the right of the 11th Lancashire Fusiliers, showed fight and put up a good resistance, but were finally either killed or taken prisoners.

We lost four officers in taking the trench:

2nd Lieut H.W Case   Killed

2nd Lieut H.V. Marsh Wounded (Since died of wounds)

Captain C. Shelton   Wounded (This officer had been with the Bttn since September 1914.)

2nd Lieut S. Darrington   Wounded

About 90 Other Ranks were casualties.

One machine gun was knocked out on the way over.

Information was slow in coming back, (Due to the fact that a German barrage opened on Zollern, delaying the runners), the first intimation of things mentioned above was at 1:53 p.m. (1 hour. 47 minutes. after zero) when Captain F.J. Morgan D.S.O.

Commanding 'B' Company, stated that the objective had been reached, and that he was in touch with the 11th Lancashire Fusiliers, 74th infantry Brigade, on his left and the 10th Essex Regiment on his right.

Second Phase—2 p.m. to 6 p.m. 21st October

A considerable amount of consolidation was necessary and 'D' Company remained in Regina. Owing to the casualties and the amount of work had to be done, I decided that 'D' Company should remain in Regina and not return. At the same time I issued orders to 'A' Company to be in readiness to move to into Regina should Captain Morgan require them. (Message sent 2.43 p.m.)

At the same time the 53rd Infantry Brigade allotted me two more machine guns, 53rd Machine Gun Company, which were situated in Zollern, and informed me that the 6th Royal Berkshire Regiment had been ordered to place a Company in Vancouver and Hessian, should my 'A' Company move up to Regina.

On receipt of my message 'A' Company moved into Hessian and sent out a liaison officer to get into touch with 'B' Company. Capt Morgan informed this officer, however, that he did not require more troops in Regina, and 'A'Company moved back into Vancouver.

In the meantime, however, the 6th Royal Berkshire Regiment had commenced to move up a company. This company finding Hessian empty—'A' Company having moved back to Vancouver—moved into it. (Message was received from 6th Royal Berkshire Regiment to this effect 4:7 p.m.)

I immediately got into touch with liaison Officer, 6th Royal Berkshire Regiment, and arranged that this Company should be withdrawn. Orders to this effect were issued at 5.20 p.m. to the O.C. 6th Royal Berkshire Regiment and their company in support to my Battalion moved back to Zollern.

The situation was, therefore, as follows:

At 6 p.m.

'B', 'D', 'C' Companies, Regina Trench, from a point 150 yards S.W. of the West Miraumont Road to just East of the junction of Regina and Left Trenches. 'B' Company in touch with the Battalion on the left and 'C' Company in touch with the Battalion on the right.

3 Machine guns 53rd MGC (One had been put out of action) and 6 Lewis Guns in the front line. The approximate strength of Companies at this moment was:

'B'—50 ORs

'D'—60 ORs

'C'—50 ORs

'A2' in Vancouver with two posts in Hessian. Approximate strength—80.

This aspect of the report shows you that the attack was put into two phases and the second phase started at 2 p.m. whereby 'D' Company occupied Regina Trench and 'A' went to Hessian Trench to assist 'D' Company if required. At 6 p.m., all three of the attacking companies were in Regina Trench and 'A' Company went to Vancouver Trench.

The battalion had to withstand heavy German bombardments and took part in occupying Regina Trench throughout the night, remaining there until 23 October 1916 at 11 p.m. This consolidation is described in depth in the report:

Strong points had been established in Regina at the junction of Kenora and Regina Trenches and Twenty-Three Road and Regina Trench.

Third Phase

6 p.m. 21st October to 6 a.m. 22nd October.

The night was comparatively quiet, patrols sent out reported that the Germans did not appear to be closer than Grandcourt Trench. Two hostile patrols which approached were completely wiped out every man killed.

Fourth Phase

6 a.m. to 6 p.m. 22nd October.

The enemy shelled Regina more or less steadily throughout the day, but did not put up a heavy barrage on it. He also shelled Vancouver and Hessian, generally with 5.9, most of these shells appeared to come from Loupart Wood. Consolidation was pushed on with throughout the day.

Fifth Phase

6 p.m. 22nd October to 6 a.m. 23rd October.

At 6 p.m. I decided to make the following changes in my line

'A' Company from Vancouver to Regina relieving 'B' and 'D'.

'B' from Regina to Hessian relieving posts of 'A'.

'D' from Regina to Vancouver relieving 'A'.

'C' Remained in Regina.

This relief was completed about 8 p.m. and 'D' Company immediately commenced work on Kenora Trench to open up communication between Hessian and Regina. This company worked exceedingly well throughout the whole night and by 3 a.m. Kenora was completely opened up, this, in spite of the fact that the Company was subjected to a very large amount of whizzbangs. Between 5 a.m. and 36 a.m. 23rd, our guns opened a very heavy bombardment along the whole Army front. The Boche retaliation was conspicuously feeble.

Sixth Phase

6 a.m. to 1 p.m. 23rd October.

Consolidation continued on Regina which had been blown in in places by German shells. A thick mist lasted to about 11 a.m. and probably on account of this making it difficult to observe the Boche artillery was very quiet. At 12.30 p.m.

Battalion Headquarters moved back to MacDonnell Road.

Seventh Phase.

1 p.m. to 3 p.m. 23rd October.

At 1.45 p.m. Captain RHR Nevill commanding 'A' Company, reported that several parties of Germans, numbering about 50 strong, could be seen in the vicinity of the Ravie in R.17.c., and that about 100 Germans appeared to be forming up, 250 yards north of Regina. A barrage was opened by our guns 250 yards north of Regina at 1.51 p.m. The Ravine in R.17.c. being shelled by our heavies. At 3:7 p.m. Nevill requested that this barrage be stopped having previously asked that its intensity should be halved at 2.50 p.m.

I am of the opinion that the Germans had hoped to dig a trench at this spot under cover of the mist which again had come on, but finding it difficult to see in the mist had come too close to Regina Trench.

A noteworthy fact is that a line laid to Regina on the top of the ground remained open throughout the whole afternoon. This line ran right up from MacDonnell Road.

At 6 p.m., the eighth and final phase took place when the battalion was relieved by the 11th Royal Fusiliers, 54th Infantry Brigade and they moved back to Albert. However, even though this assault had been successful, Regina Trench in its entirety was not finally cleared until 11 November 1916 by the 4th Canadian Division.

During this action, the battalion lost a total of 140 officers and men killed, wounded, or missing, and this came from a total of 558 officers and men who had started the attack. The report notes their casualty total as four officers killed or wounded and 136 men killed, wounded, or missing.

They had fought at Montauban, Delville Wood, Thiepval, the Schwaben Redoubt, and finally Regina Trench. The Norfolk Regiment history notes that in this period the battalion had won one DSO, six MCs, six DCMs, thirty-one MMs, and thirty-seven Parchment Certificates. In total, between 1 July 1916 and 23 July 1916, they had lost 336 men killed who now lie in the cemeteries on the Somme.

Guidebook

From the Albert–Bapaume road, if you are coming from the direction of Bapaume, turn right onto the D107, signposted Courcelette–Miraumont. Continue on until you see a turning on the left signposted Courcelette. Continue through the village and keep going until you see a turning on the right with a CWGC sign for Regina Trench Cemetery. Keep going until you come to a fork in the road and take the right-hand fork. This is the old Grandcourt Road, but it is now a dirt track so take care! Eventually you will see Regina Trench Cemetery on your right.

Stand on the track with the cemetery to your right. The trench itself ran through where you are standing and then back towards the cemetery, which it passes through heading east. Hessian and Vancouver trenches are about 100 yards behind you, again running east. Kenora trench is to your right, beyond the cemetery and runs back towards Courcelette. If you retrace your steps the next crossroads you come to is Twenty-Three Road. This ran off east. I recommend that if you visit this area, you take a copy of the trench map that can be found in the 8th Battalion's war diary.

Within Regina Trench Cemetery, there are twenty-seven men from the Norfolk Regiment from the 8th Battalion who died between October 1916 and February 1917.

What3words: handfuls.wifely.fumble.

16

The 8th Battalion, Operations on the Ancre, Boom Ravine to Irles: 17 February to 10 March 1917

After a period of time out of the line, the 8th Battalion went into trenches facing a German position known as Boom Ravine. Here they would take part in an attack to capture this position. The attack was due to go in on 17 February 1917.

The overall plan was to use the 2nd, 18th, and 63rd divisions, on a 3,000-yard front. With the ground still frozen, assembly trenches could not be dug, so it was decided that the troops would assemble in the open for the attack. However, the day before the attack, there was a thaw. This would cause issues for the attackers.

The 18th (Eastern) Division employed the 53rd Brigade for the attack and they would face Grandcourt with Boom Ravine, known as '*Baum Mulde*' to the Germans, situated to the north east. The 54th Brigade would be on their right, with the 2nd Division on their right. The Norfolk's history describes Boom Ravine as 'leading down like the stem of a T, the head of which was formed by its branches to the right and left'.

The position of Boom Ravine enabled its defenders to pour enfilading fire into the advance as well as taking fire from the front on the other side of the River Ancre, which would cause issues; the 53rd Brigade also had to contend with a wider front where they were due to advance. On their left would be the 63rd (Naval) Division who were expected to capture the north bank. The main attack had three objectives, the first about 600 yards forward along the southern slope of Hill 130, the second at South Miraumont Trench required an advance of another 600 yards to the north slope of Hill 130 on the right and the railway between Grandcourt and Miraumont on the western flank; the final objective was the southern fringe of Petit Miraumont.

The orders report for the 8th Battalion also confirms the positions for the attacking units:

On Z Day the 8th Norfolk Regiment will take part in an attack on Grandcourt Trench and the area north of it.

The 2nd Division will co-operate on the right and the 63rd Division on the left. The 18th Division will attack on a front of two brigades; 54th Infantry Brigade on the right and 53rd Infantry Brigade on the left.

The 8th Battalion would be on the left of the 53rd Brigade boundary with 'A' Company, next would be the 6th Royal Berkshires, which had 'B' Company Norfolks attached to them and then the 8th Suffolks on their right, who would have 'D' Company Norfolks attached to them. 'C' Company were to be employed carrying bombs and ammunition. A creeping barrage would be fired in an attempt to protect the advancing infantry.

The Germans, who it is said got wind of the attack from two deserters, opened up a bombardment at 4.30 a.m., which caused casualties to the assembled infantry. For this chapter, we can look at the after-action report for the 8th Battalion. This enemy barrage fell on 'A' Company, who were forming up for the attack:

> At 5.30 a.m. the Company was formed up in position. Considerable difficulty was experienced owing to the facts that:
>
> (i) A heavy hostile barrage, consisting chiefly of 5.9 shells was directed on the forming up line. This barrage started at 5 a.m. and continued until 5.45 a.m. (Zero-Hour).

The report also noted that this company had difficulty advancing due to the slippery state of the ground and the intense darkness. This was caused by the thaw, with the 18th (Eastern) Division's history noting: '…the hard surface of the ground turned first into one big slide, and then became a sea of mud, in which rifles and machine guns got clogged and through which the infantry pressed a slow, floundering stamina testing way'.

Sadly, the speed of the creeping barrage, which started at Zero Hour at 5.45 a.m., had been based on the infantry crossing frozen ground and was too fast for the conditions. 'A' Company had issues advancing due to the darkness and lost direction, which was also attributed to confusion between friendly and enemy artillery fire and the flashes from guns dazzling the advancing sections:

> Those troops who lost direction commenced to advance on Grandcourt with their right on the Grandcourt road. Capt. C.F. Ashdown, M.C. immediately went forward himself and collected all men whom he could see irrespective of their waves, led them back again into the valley and up to the first intermediate objective where he succeeded in gaining touch with a few men of his own Company under 2nd Lieut. D. A. Leamon and which had advanced in exactly the right direction.

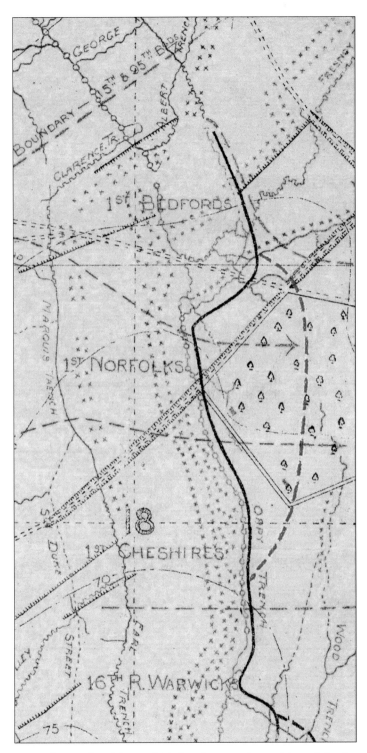

A trench map dated June 1917 showing you the position of the 1st Battalion Norfolk Regiment for the assault on Oppy Wood. You will see their main line moves north in Grid 18b. Oppy Wood is situated to the east. (*Author's collection*)

Above: Men of the 1st Battalion at Palace Barracks at Holywood at County Down in Ireland. This image was taken in 1913. (*Author's collection*)

Left: A sketch painting made by a Norfolk Regiment Officer. This depicts the 'B' Company reserve line for Mons. (*Norfolk Regiment Museum*)

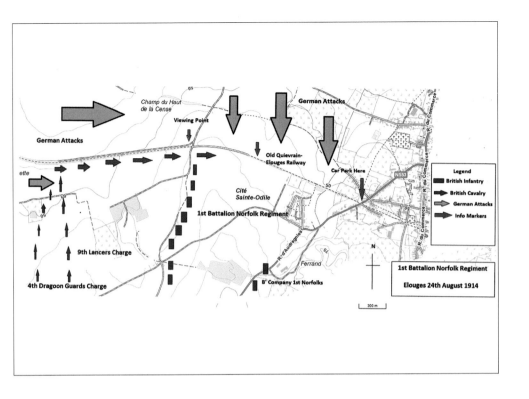

Above: The situation for the 1st Battalion Norfolk Regiment for the Battle of Mons, 24 August 1914. (*Author's map*)

Right: Capt. Francis James Cresswell, who was killed in action on 24 August 1914. (*IWM*)

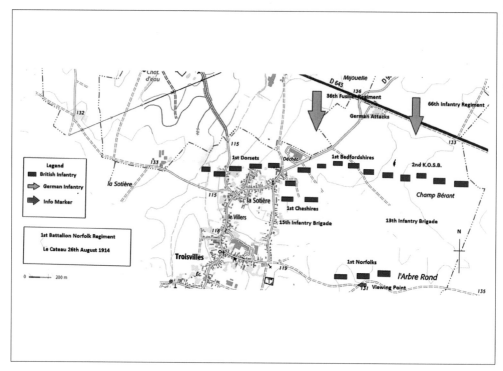

The situation for the 1st Battalion Norfolk Regiment at the battle of Le Cateau on 26 August 1914. (*Author's map*)

The position for the 1st Battalion for the Battle of Le Cateau, 26 August 1914. (*Author's collection*)

Above left: Maj. Charles Elmhurst Luard, DSO, who was killed in action during the fighting for the high ground around Missy sur Aisne. (*IWM*)

Above right: The church at Missy sur Aisne seen in 1919. This is where Herbert Reeve stood to distribute 303 ammunition. (*IWM*)

Above left: The ravine above Missy sur Aisne where Robert Sheldrake fought and was later captured. (*Author's collection*)

Above right: Albert Wyatt, seen later in the war when he was serving in the Bedfordshire Regiment, who was present for the Christmas Truce of 1914. (*Author's collection*)

Above: An early image of some men from the 8th Battalion. Note that their uniforms at this stage of the war are dark blue. (*Author's collection*)

Below: Recruits being processed at Britannia Barracks in August 1914. (*EDP Archives*)

RECRUITING AT NORWICH.

(1) A COMPANY OF NORWICH BUSINESS MEN AT BRITANNIA BARRACKS WAITING TO ENLIST.
(2) & (3) RECRUITS FOR LORD KITCHENER'S ARMY LEAVING BRITANNIA BARRACKS.

NEW N.C.O.'S AT BRITANNIA BARRACKS.

RECRUITS FOR KITCHENER'S ARMY, ATTACHED TO THE NORFOLK REGIMENT, WHO HAVE RECEIVED THEIR FIRST STRIPES. INCLUDED IN THE GROUP ARE THREE MEMBERS OF THE "EASTERN DAILY PRESS" STAFF.

An image from August 1914 noting new recruits to the Norfolks who were being promoted to lance corporal. (*EDP Archives*)

Hill 60 near Ypres, which was the scene of heavy fighting between April and June 1915 and a position the 1st Battalion were positioned in that time. (*IWM*)

Above: The trenches at Vebranden-Molen, which was close to Hill 60 and where the 1st Battalion also served in 1915. (*IWM*)

Below left: William Drewery, who served in both the 9th and 7th Battalions, being inoculated after joining up in 1914. William kept notes on a number of things, including the art of being a bomber, and was eventually given a commission. (*Wendy Salmon*)

Below right: Jack Paul seen with his sisters. Jack served in both the 8th and 9th Battalions and wrote many letters home describing his time on the Western Front. (*Margaret Sowter*)

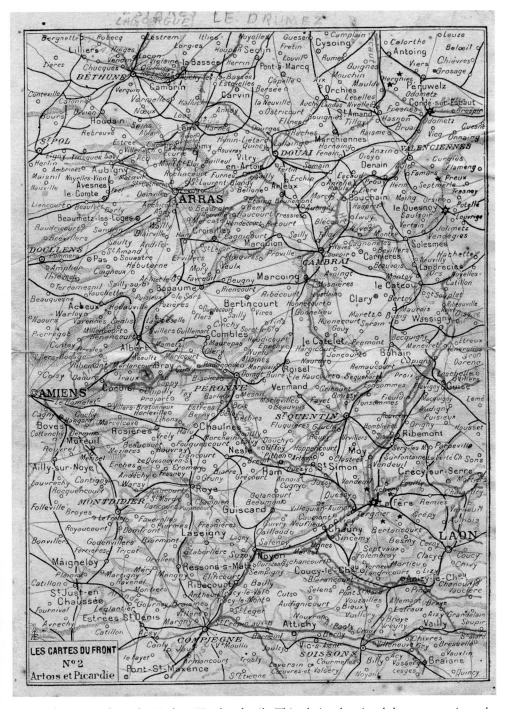

The postcard sent by Herbert Head to family. This obviously missed the censor as it marks
where he had been on the Western Front. (*Ady Church*)

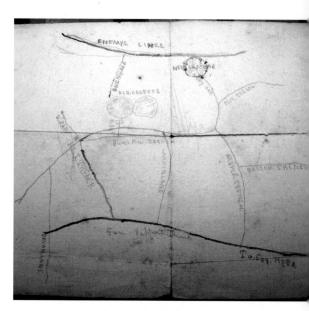

Above left: The position known as the Quarries. Both the 7th and 9th Battalions saw action here during the Battle of Loos fought between September and October 1915. (*Author's collection*)

Above right: A sketch map made by William Drewery while he was serving in the Loos Sector. This position equates to the same area assaulted by both the 7th and 9th Battalions in 1915. (*Wendy Salmon*)

Below: Sidney Smith, seen extreme left, who served on the Somme with the 7th Battalion. (*Norfolk Constabulary Archives*)

Sketches of Tommy's life 'p the line — N° 5

The main duties in the Front Line in the daytime are watching the periscope, and looking up in the air for «trench mortars», with a whistle ready to blow for a warning.

A postcard sent by Herbert Head to family, one of a series like this, detailing trench life, including the dangers of mortars and artillery. (*Ady Church*)

No. 15 Platoon 'D' Company from the 8th Battalion. Sat centrally in the second row is Capt. Bernard Pitts Ayre who was killed in action on 1 July 1916. (*Author's collection*)

Above left: Part of the start line for the 8th Battalion for 1 July 1916. Their objective, Montauban, can be seen in the distance. (*Author's collection*)

Above right: The line in Delville Wood that the 8th Battalion reached on 19 July 1916; this ride is still known as Prince's Street today. (*Author's collection*)

Above left: Harry Hood, who was aged sixteen when he was killed in action on 19 July 1916 at Delville Wood. (*Author's collection*)

Above right: Herbert Cooper's brief obituary in a local paper. (*Author's collection*)

The remains of Longueval, which through artillery, has been turned into matchwood. This road is the main high street, known as North Street to the British, which the 1st Battalion fought through on 27 July 1916. (*IWM*)

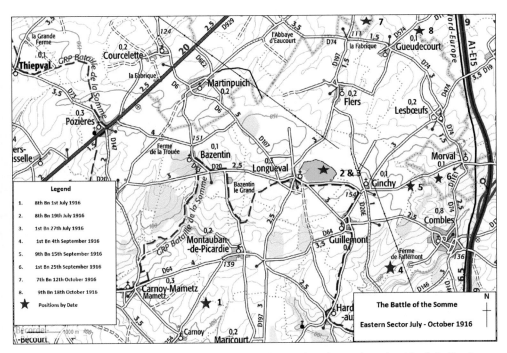

An overview of the Somme battlefield marking the places that the Norfolk Regiment fought over. This map looks at the eastern sector of the battle area. (*Author's map*)

Samuel Riches, seen fourth from left, who would go from the 1/6th Battalion to the 8th Battalion in June 1916. (*Chris Durrant*)

Lieut. A. P. GREEN,
Norfolk Regiment.

Above left: Arthur Green who was killed in action serving with the 7th Battalion at Ovillers on 6 July 1916. This was originally printed in the *London Illustrated*.

Above right: An artist's impression of the capture of Falfemont Farm in September 1916; this was originally printed in the *London Illustrated*.

Above left: Inside the copse of trees where Falfemont Farm once stood you can still find the remains of the war. (*Author's collection*)

Above right: This image looks back towards Ginchy from the Quadrilateral, which the 9th Battalion tried to capture on 15 September 1916. Most of the survivors of this assault ended up in shell holes in the field on the left. (*Author's collection*)

Below: Frederick Howson, stood extreme right, known as Freddie. (*Roger Howson*)

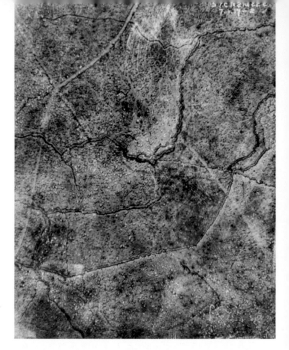

Above left: The mighty Thiepval Memorial. The 8th Battalion assisted in the capture of Thiepval Village in September 1916. The memorial records the names of 72,158 men who have no known grave in this sector before 21 March 1918. It also has a cemetery at the back of the memorial that holds the remains of 600 Commonwealth and French soldiers as a symbol of unity. Many of them are unknown and that includes five unidentified men from the Norfolk Regiment. (*Author's collection*)

Above right: Mild Trench seen from the air. The trench can be seen as the dark line heading from west to north. Part of Gueudecourt can be seen in bottom left; like all of the villages in this area, it was completely destroyed. (*IWM*)

Below: An overview of the Somme battlefield marking the places that the Norfolk Regiment fought over. This map looks at the western sector of the battle area from 1916–18. (*Author's map*)

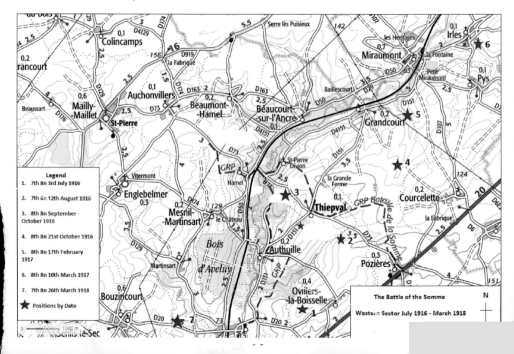

The start line for the 8th Battalion at Irles on 6 March 1917. The bridge spans the stream, which was known as 'The Ditch' where they jumped off from. (*Author's collection*)

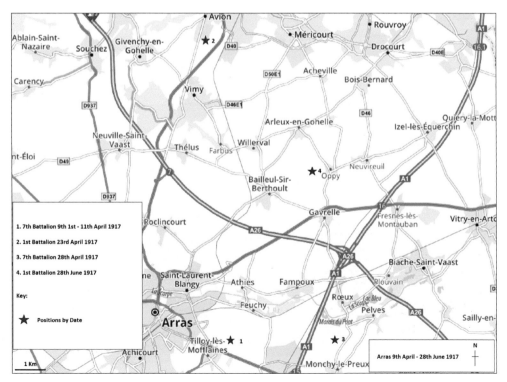

An overview of the Arras battlefield marking the places that the Norfolk Regiment fought over between April and June 1917. (*Author's map*)

Maison Rouge, which was one of the positions used by the 7th Battalion between 9 and 13 April 1917. (*Author's collection*)

The 1st Battalion crossed this road to enter Oppy Wood seen on the right on 28 June 1917. (*Author's collection*)

Above left: James Cooper who served in the Norwich Volunteer Corps prior to being sent over to the Western Front where he served with the 9th Battalion from January 1917 to the end of the war. (*Nigel Cooper*)

Above right: The postcard that James Cooper sent home on 3 September 1917 describing what he witnessed when the 9th Battalion were shelled at Maroc, killing and wounding a number of soldiers. He noted: 'They had to pick up the pieces and put them in blankets, some could not be recognised'. (*Nigel Cooper*)

Right: Arthur Patten. He was instrumental in the defence in front of the newly formed line in front of Glencorse Wood, for the opening on the Third Battle of Ypres on 31 July 1917. (*Author's collection*)

Above: Seen from a reconnaissance flight, Inverness Copse, bottom right, Clapham Junction, seen as the central white line that intersects the Menin Road and Glencorse Wood, seen at the top as the darker patch. The 8th Battalion saw heavy fighting in this sector between 31 July and 17 August 1917. (*IWM*)

Left: James Andrew Lewton-Brain who served with the 8th Battalion and who died from the effects of a gas attack on 14 August 1917. (*Author's collection*)

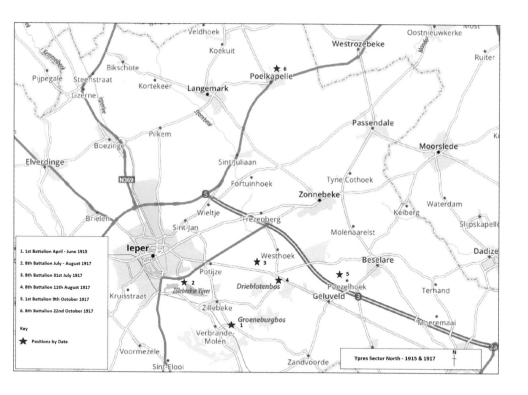

Above: The northern sector of the area around the Belgian town of Ypres. This covers the main Norfolk Regiment sites between 1915 and 1917. (*Author's map*)

Right: Polderhoek Chateau prior to the First World War. (*Author's collection*)

Polderhoek Château in 1917. By this time, it was completely destroyed and had been used an impregnable strongpoint by the Germans. (*Author's collection*)

Part of the area assaulted by the 8th Battalion at Poelcappelle. This looks at the position known as the Brewery, which was situated where the large white barn now stands and the battalion moved from right to left of this photo. (*Author's collection*)

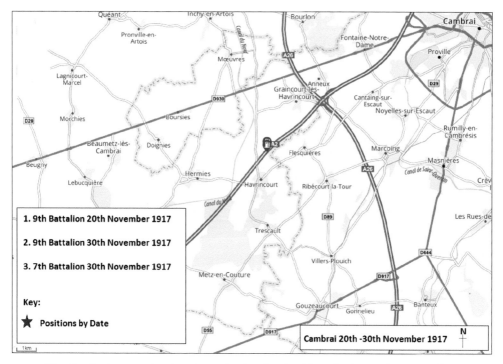

The Cambrai sector showing the main sites for the 7th and 9th Battalions. (*Author's map*)

Within the map:

1. 9th Battalion 20th November 1917

2. 9th Battalion 30th November 1917

3. 7th Battalion 30th November 1917

Key:

★ Positions by Date

Cambrai 20th -30th November 1917

Elements of the 1st Battalion Leicestershire Regiment stood with the Male tank called Hyacinth. The 1st Battalion assaulted Ribecourt with the 9th Battalion. This image shows you just how formidable the Hinderburg Line actually was. (*IWM*)

Lewis Thaxter, seen in the front row on the far right. Lewis initially served in the Norfolk Yeomanry and like many of his comrades would be sent to the Western Front in 1916 and 1917 to serve with the Regular battalions. Lewis was sent to the 9th Battalion and was killed in action on 20 November 1917. (*Brian Thaxter*)

One of a number of bunkers that can still be found in Nine Wood. The wood was occupied by the 9th Battalion after the initial assault at Cambrai and these structures were used by them while they occupied and defended the wood. (*Author's collection*)

Above left: Lt-Col. Henry Lex Francis Gielgud who was the CO for the 7th Battalion for the German counterattack at Cambrai. He was killed in action in the ill-fated defence of their positions around Gonnelieu. (*Aldenham School Archives*)

Above right: The sunken lane off Bouzincourt Ridge where the 7th Battalion were involved in heavy fighting on 27 March 1918. (*Author's collection*)

Crucifix Corner where the 9th Battalion fought off a series of German attacks and then were involved in counterattacks themselves in order that they pushed the enemy off high ground in this area. (*Author's collection*)

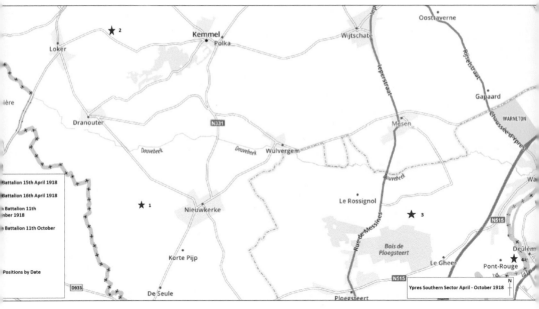

The southern sector around Ypres, which shows you the main positions for the fighting that took place in 1918 involving the 9th and 12th Battalions. (*Author's map*)

Above left: Gerald Failes who was instrumental in leading rearguard actions at Lagnicourt on 21 March 1918. He was awarded a posthumous DSO after he was sadly killed in action on 15 April 1918 leading counterattacks at Crucifix Corner. (*Author's collection*)

Above right: The ruins of Château Segard, which every battalion of the Norfolk Regiment who served around Ypres were positioned around between 1917 and 1918. (*IWM*)

Above left: The grave of Jack Paul in Voormezeele Enclosure No. 3. Jack had served in both the 8th and 9th Battalions and was killed in action in a localised defence of the Ypres–Comines Canal close to Château Segard. (*Author's collection*)

Above right: One of the bridges that formed part of a number of trench raids carried out by the 12th Battalion in June 1918 around the frontline of the Nieppe Forest. (*Author's collection*)

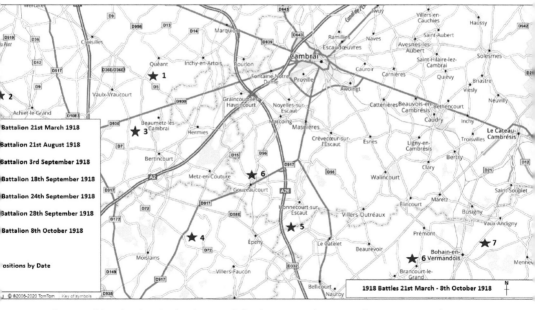

The initial battles fought by the Norfolks from March to October 1918. (*Author's map*)

NORFOLK PIONEERS.

Pioneers. — Battalion, Norfolks, with their trench-worn dog Pedro, who is suffering from wounds caused by contact with barbed wire entanglements.
Standing :— E. Denham (Norwich), H. Francis (Shotesham), Lance-Corporal Williams (Yarmouth), W. Russell (Norwich).
H. A. Dunnett (Downham), Sergeant Gilham (Dereham), C. Russell (Lynn),
A. R. Dunnett (Cambridge), Pedro, J. Ringer (Gissing).

Above left: Cecil Frederick George Humphries who was killed in action on 22 August 1918 serving as the CO for the 1st Battalion. (*Author's collection*)

Above right: A newspaper cutting from the *Weekly Press* in 1916 looking at a group of 1st Battalion Pioneers. By August 1918, four of these men had died serving in either the 1st or 9th Battalions. (*Norfolk Record Office*)

Below left: George Bede Hornby Plant, 7th Battalion, who was killed in action on 5 September 1918 in the fighting around Nurlu. George was twenty years old and is now buried in Grave I.I.1 in Épehy Wood Farm Cemetery. (*Author's Collection*)

Below right: Albert Arthur Walsha who was killed in action on 18 September 1918 during the fighting for Holnon. His CO noted that before he died, 'He led his men forward splendidly'. (*Author's collection*)

The ruins of Gonnelieu in 1918. This image was taken while it was still in German hands. (*IWM*)

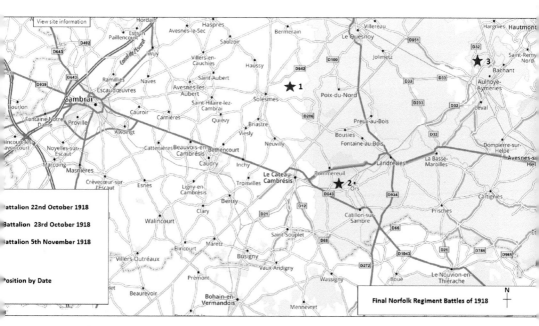

Some of the final battles fought by the Norfolk Regiment between October and November 1918. (*Author's map*)

Above left: The Reverend Richard William Dugdale, MC. He had been the chaplain for the 1st Battalion since June 1918 and was killed by shellfire on the night of 22–23 October 1918. (*Author's collection*)

Above right: The remains of Hirson Mill, which was used by the 1st Battalion as a Battalion HQ and formed part of the line of advance on 23 October 1918. It is an incredibly peaceful place to stand and reflect on the fighting took place around here. (*Author's collection*)

Below left: Albert Humphrey from Gorefield, who is seen sat centrally in this image. Albert served with the 12th Battalion from their time as Yeomanry in Gallipoli and Palestine to their time when they were sent to the Western Front. (*Peter Thatcher*)

Below right: Charles Neve, one of a number of men from the 12th Battalion who died in a fighting patrol around Ploegsteert in October 1918. Charles is buried in Strand Military Cemetery. (*Author's collection*)

Above: The lock at Pont sur Sambre seen from the bridge at the town. Both were found to be destroyed when the 1st Battalion assaulted this position on 6 November 1918. (*Author's collection*)

Right: George Wooden with his wife, Agnes, who served in the 8th Battalion and who returned to the Western Front in 1931. It is a myth that men did not ever return to the battlefields after the war was ended. (*Nic Blythe*)

Above: Another image taken by George Wooden of the Menin Gate at Ypres. This is a place I have stood at on many occasions where the ceremony that is held each night at 8 p.m. has become a focal point of remembrance. (*Nic Blythe*)

Below left: Delville Wood, which was visited by Lieutenants Sutcliffe and Ewart who were serving in the 2nd Battalion in 1923. (*Author's collection*)

Below right: Fred Gibbs who served in the 8th Battalion and saw the horrors of places like Delville Wood. This is my favourite image of a Norfolk Regiment man and he epitomises the spirit of the men who served on the Western Front. (*Author's collection*)

The first objective for 'A' Company was reached at 6 a.m., and by 7 a.m., they along with the Royal Berkshires were at their final objective. Here they consolidated their gains by making two strongpoints on the Grandcourt–Petit-Miraumont Road. 'B' Company moved forward into Grandcourt Trench and remained there. It sustained several casualties and stayed there until 19 February when it was moved back to Hessian Trench.

Although 'C' Company was employed in carrying supplies of bombs and small arms ammunition, it can be noted from this report that their participation, mainly due to the terrible conditions, was extremely taxing:

> The going was exceedingly bad and got worse as the day wore on. The right party came under some shell fire and sustained about 7 casualties. The left party was more fortunate as it was enabled to move along the Grandcourt road for some way and although this was heavily shelled by 5.9 shells from the direction of Loupart Wood it was rarely that a direct hit was obtained on the road. Owing to the greasy state of the ground and mud there were a considerable amount of sprained ankles and knees.

On 18 February, the continued difficulties of moving ammunition to the front was noted in the report: 'At one spot the left party, consisting of about 30 men, took 21/2 hours to cover a distance of about 200 yards. At this time the load was one box of S.A.A., 2 boxes Mills grenades to two men'. On 19 February, two officers were praised for their leadership with this group: 'Considerable praise is due to 2nd Lieut. A. Bentley and 2nd Lieut. A.F. Sherlock who carried out a very monotonous and wearying duty, often under very heavy shell fire, with unfailing cheerfulness and resource. This was the first time either of these officers had been under fire'.

Finally, 'D' Company stayed under the cover of a ravine but were continuously shelled. They assisted the 8th Suffolks by supplying carrying parties to Grandcourt and Coffee Trench as well as Boom Ravine. By the end of 18 February, they had been fully withdrawn back to dugouts in Hessian Trench.

The 54th Brigade had found uncut wire at Grandcourt Trench and lost the barrage while looking for gaps. The German garrison was able to emerge from cover and engage the British infantry, holding them up on the right. The left-hand battalion found more gaps but had so many casualties that it was also held up.

However, at the end of this advance, the outcome of the 18th Division attack in this area was that the Germans in Boom Ravine were engaged from the flank and three machine guns silenced, before the advance in the centre resumed and infantry found their way through the wire at Coffee Trench and captured it by 6:10 a.m. Boom Ravine was eventually captured at 7:45 a.m.

The 2nd Division managed to capture their first objective, but fell short of their second objectives and suffered with German counterattacks. With what was captured, they concentrated on forming a defensive flank. The 63rd Division advanced and captured their objectives.

At the end of the fighting, Boom Ravine had been captured, but the Germans had retained Hill 130 and between 10 January and 22 February, the Germans had retreated 5 miles. The advance of 17 February forced the Germans to begin their withdrawal from the Ancre valley, and on 24 February 1917, it was ascertained that the enemy had withdrawn. Although they did not know it yet, the Germans had given up all of this ground and had moved to pre-sited and well-defended positions to the north. It would become known as the Hindenburg Line.

The decision to build the line was made by Field Marshal Paul von Hindenburg and General Erich Ludendorff, who had taken over command of Germany's war effort in August 1916. The Hindenburg Line was built across a salient in the German front, so that by withdrawing to these fortifications, the German Army was actually shortening its front. The total length of the front was reduced by 30 miles and enabled the Germans to release thirteen divisions for service in reserve. The fortifications included concrete bunkers and machine-gun emplacements, heavy belts of barbed wire, tunnels for moving troops, deep trenches, dug-outs, and command posts. At a distance of 1 km in front of the fortifications was a thinly-held outpost line, which would serve a purpose comparable to skirmishers: slowing down and disrupting an enemy advance. In addition, villages (called 'Outpost Villages') immediately in front of the outpost line were sometimes fortified and used to reinforce the main defences.

The British advanced, finding that the Germans had carried out a 'Scorched Earth' policy as they had retreated and areas that had not fallen in 1916 were taken without a shot being fired. An example of this was that a number of patrols, including one from 'D' Company, from the 8th East Surreys, were sent out and they made contact with the enemy to the north of Irles where they established an outpost in a goods shed on the main line between Miraumont and Achiet le Grand.

In this action, the 8th Norfolks lost ninety-three men killed, wounded, or missing, the majority of which came from 'A' and 'B' Companies. In total, between 17 and 20 February 1917, the battalion lost twenty-six men killed.

Guidebook

The best way to get to the viewing point for the jumping-off point of the 53rd Brigade is to take the D151 from Thiepval. You will come into Grandcourt and you want to turn right onto the Rue de Courcelette. You will see an electricity substation on your right and two Commonwealth War Graves Commission signs, turn right here. Continue of this road and this road turns into a track. You will come to a hard standing, which is also a crossroads. I advise that you park up here, facing towards Courcelette, and then take the left-hand track and eventually you will come to a fork in the road. Grandcourt Trench and the point where 'B'

Company went over the top is 500 yards down the left-hand track. Boom Ravine can be seen as the tree line you will see from this position.

What3words: amply.grilled.warms.

There is an option to return to the D151 and then turn right towards Petit Miraumont. You will come out of Grandcourt and will see a dirt track on your right. If you stop here and then look towards the railway line, which would be on your left, you are now on the line where the 53rd Brigade ended up.

What3wors: nutrient.outer.albatrosses.

* * * * *

After Boom Ravine, the 8th Battalion spent time in the rear and then went back into the line on 6 March 1917. They were to participate in the capture of Grevillers Trench and the village of Irles.

After the massed German withdrawal to the Hindenburg Line, it was believed the Germans would withdraw from the village of Irles, but by 1 March 1917, it was clear they still occupied the village, although on the day of the attack, the Germans were preparing to vacate it. On 6 March 1917, Resurrection Trench was captured by the 8th Suffolks.

The 10th Battalion Essex Regiment occupied Resurrection Trench, which faced the entire west side of Irles and the 8th Battalion were positioned facing Irles from the east in a trench called the Ditch. In the coming attack, the 10th Essex would attack to the east and the 8th Battalion would come in from the north-east, wheel left, and then meet up with the 10th Essex.

Orders to Battalion

The orders issued by the GOC 53rd Infantry Brigade were to the affect that the battalion would attack and capture Grevillers Trench and push out certain strong points. In accordance with these the following orders were issued to companies:

'D' was to capture Grevillers Trench from G.32.d.4.2. to G.32.d.0.7 and to establish a strong point at G.32.b.9.3.

'B' was to capture Grevillers Trench from G.32.d.0.7 to G.32.a.55.15 and establish a strong point at G.32.b.6.4.

'C' was to clear the quarry in G.32.a. strong points at:

G.26.d.70.15.

G.32.a.8.9.

and to push forward a post to G.26.d.5.4.

'A' was to remain in reserve.

Zero Hour was set for 5.14 a.m. and would be supported by artillery. At Zero Hour, 'A' and 'D' Companies of the 10th Essex attacked the Irles from the north and the barrage for this attack was able to protect the troops as they rushed the village. The 8th Battalion war diary has a report for their participation in the attack:

'D' Company.

This Company got off punctually at Zero hour and arrived at its objective at 5.21 a.m. One platoon was immediately pushed out to make the strong point and touch was obtained with the 2nd Division at about 5.25 a.m. At 6 a.m. the Company was in touch with my centre company and a report to this effect was received from Capt Beckerson at 7.5 a.m. This was repeated to Brigade at 7.10 a.m.

At this time the Company had captured 30 prisoners and 2 machine guns. At 9.30 a.m. 'D' reported that another machine gun had been taken in Grevillers Trench and that a strong point had been commenced...

'D' Company continued to consolidate their part of Grevillers Trench and came under continuous shellfire but luckily did not take any casualties and by 4 a.m. on 11 March was relieved and ended up at Mouquet Farm:

'B' and 'C'

At Zero Hour 'B' Company, less one platoon left behind in the Ditch, to hold posts and 'C' Company less two sections left behind in the ditch to clear the southern portion of Irles at plus 11/2 hours when the 4.5 howitzer barrage would lift, advanced to the attack. At about 5.35 a.m. the O.C. 'B' Company noticed that his men had halted; he therefore advanced to his first wave and discovered that someone had given the alarm of gas and that the men were putting on their box respirators. He himself noticed a sweet smell in the air but states that it appeared to have been quite unlike the smell of pear drops which is usually to be associated with German Lachrymatory shells, neither did he feel any irritation of the eyes.

This hold up was rectified and the advanced resumed, but the CO of 'B' Company noticed that objective had been outstepped. From the after-action report:

He therefore halted his Company and reviewed the situation which was as below:
   (a) He had crossed no trench.
   (b) He had been advancing for half an hour.
   (c) The line of his advance—checked by the compass had been NE
   (d) He had not encountered the Irles–Loupart Wood road.
   (e) He appeared to have reached higher ground that that on which he estimated
    Grevillers Trench to be.
   (f) He was not in touch with the right or left.
   Captain Morgan concluded that his company had lost direction but checking a compass bearing that they were on the right track and Grevillers Trench must have been destroyed in this area. It later transpired that the man who was supposed to

check the advance had missed the Irles–Loupart Wood road and Captain Morgan had correctly guessed that the Grevillers Trench was completely destroyed.

Immediate action was necessary and he therefore ordered 2nd Lieut V.M. Harrison to move one platoon forward to just out of seeing distance of the remainder of the Company and to dig in at where he considered the strong point allocated to the Company should be sighted. Immediately this platoon was out of sight of the rest of the Company he ordered the remainder of the Company to about turn and move back in a SW direction.

Scarcely had he begun this when he struck a bank and little further on Irles–Loupart Wood road became recognisable. By this time, it was getting light but was still very thick.

'C' Company advanced on Irles and cleared the eastern part of the village. At 5.20 a.m., they came up against uncut wire. The leading platoons, which had extended just before crossing the Irles–Loupart Wood road, pushed on to make the two strongpoints allotted to the company and supporting platoons went on to start the consolidation of Grevillers Trench. While these posts were being made, figures were seen in the distance and OC Company called out to them and was fired upon.

Fearing that 'B' Company was mistaking his party for Germans he again called out to them and was again fired on. It was therefore apparent that these figures were Germans but owing to the exceptionally bad light conditions it was impossible to estimate:

(1) Their exact position

(2) Their number.

His party was at the time in a very shallow portion of the trench, about 2 feet deep, and was being subjected to a considerable amount of rifle fire. At 5.45 a.m. the firing appeared to slacken and he was on the point of rushing the position where he judged the Germans to be when he saw a large body of men advancing from a NE direction on either side of the Irles-Loupart Wood road. It was now lighter and he was able to see the shape of their steel helmets which proved to be English troops. The was 'B' Company returning. Caught between two bodies of English troops the Boches surrendered.

After capture these prisoners expressed astonishment at being taken in the rear and had not seen 'B' Company crossing Grevillers Trench. Captain Morgan made contact with 'D' Company and consolidated his position; as they did so, stray prisoners were found. Captain Morgan was ordered to plug a gap between him and 'C' Company.

Strongpoints were built and patrols were pushed out. These patrols had issues with snipers until some of the 8th Battalion snipers were pushed out and it is estimated that they dealt with twelve enemy snipers, which were all found to be lying out singly in shell holes. 'B' Company were relieved on 11 March 1917 and went back to the Gravel Pits.

'C' Company reached its objective and worked on consolidating their position, under the command of Lt Dillon, they found out that the quarry marked on their maps was not as big as big as thought. Patrols were pushed out and Lt Dillon arrived and his company got in touch with the 10th Essex. He then sent out two platoons to clear out the eastern edge of Irles, where they captured some prisoners, noted as being chiefly old men, and a wounded German officer and seven men were found in a shell hole.

Second Lieutenant Sherlock, with two sections, entered the southern part of Irles from the Ditch and came under fire from a machine gun near Irles Church. This was dealt with and they were then joined by a clearing party from the 10th Essex who captured the gun. A large number of Germans, described as being in groups of three or four, were found in the village.

These Germans told their captors that they had been in the village for three days, having been told to offer strong resistance to any attack, but another 100 men had been sent to support them on the day of the attack. The Germans stated that they had expected the attack to come from Resurrection Trench and were surprised when it came from the Ditch.

The company then came under attack: 'Consolidation was in progress when at 7.15 a.m. a large party of Bosches, about 30 strong with 2 officers and wearing equipment, was seen advancing NE up the valley from Irles firing at Nos 3 and 8 Strong Points as they came'.

This group was also seen by 2Lt Sherlock:

At 7.10 a.m. a large party of Germans were caught in flank. They offered a good resistance and refused to surrender but finally turned and retreated along to valley running NE from Irles. This was the party seen by Lieut Dillon at 7.15 a.m. Lieut Sherlock realised that this party would encounter No 3 Strong Point and therefore pushed after it. Caught between two fires the Boche stood little chance but he fought exceptionally bravely until ten of the party had become casualties. The officers then advanced with their hands up and the whole party was captured.

It was ascertained that the main line of retreat was from this valley so 2Lt Sherlock extended his line out and captured a large number of the enemy in doing so. By noon, the village was cleared and the rest of the day was spent consolidating their gains. They were relieved at 3 a.m. on 11 March.

The report notes that the enemy fought well and were in good shape, clean, and well-clothed and in possession of good rations, with their water bottles filled with coffee. It notes that they counted forty-seven dead, forty of whom who had did through rifle fire. Some 114 prisoners went through Battalion HQ, including two officers, which included one from the 9th Battery of the 60th Artillery Regiment and one from the 75th Infantry Regiment. Ten to fifteen Germans were also evacuated through the battalion Regimental Aid Post.

Another after-action report has some interesting conclusions that are worth noting, again made by Lt-Col. Ferguson:

In conclusion I would state:

i. That the experiment of pushing my Regimental Aid Post as close up as possible proved successful, the battlefield being cleared by 6.10 a.m. I am of the opinion that the work of the Regimental Stretcher Bearers should if possible always be restricted to these short journeys, the long carry's being done by the RAMC and Bosche prisoners. With the object in view all men told off as escorts should whenever practical return with their prisoners via the Regimental Aid Post.

ii. Zero was undoubtedly too early, the difficulties of forming up a company in the dark are very great indeed and the keeping direction is a very hard problem. It is thought that perhaps it is considered that officers will see to this, but it should always be borne in the mind that Officers may become casualties too early to be able to check this and also that this is of unimaginable difficulty in darkness and when the noise of barrage prevents one's voice being heard.

iii. To be really affective, counter battery work must be heavy and continuous. A strafe of halt an hour is useless. It merely gives the Boche a rest and he returns to his gun on concluding.

iv. Battalions must be allowed to train Lewis Gunners when resting and the Battalion classes should not be included in the Battalion strength when detailing it for fatigues. The supply of really efficient Lewis Gunners must be maintained, no matter what expense is incurred by working parties. Partially trained me are apt to lose their heads if stoppages occur during an attack.

v. An hour and a half appears to be a very long time for a Battalion to be formed up before assaulting. If as in this case a Company has come some way this means that the last hot tea issued to the man is probably given them four or five hours before which is too long. Also, the nerve strain of men lying out waiting to attack is very great. I suggest half an hour be ample time.

vi. Sufficient accommodation for Battalion Headquarters must be provided. A large number of runners has invariably to be maintained at Battalion Report Centre and unless accommodation is provided they crowd the stair (especially when shelling is in progress) having nowhere else to go. Again, it is of paramount importance that runners who have had a hard journey should have somewhere to rest; otherwise they will not be fresh when called for.

vii. The best hours for relief appear to be between 6 p.m. and 10 p.m. I am of opinion that during this period the Boche is engaged in getting up ammunition and therefore fires little. The early hours of the morning (4 a.m.–6 a.m.) are not so quiet as they used to be, owing to the fact that the Boche is always on the lookout for an attack at this time, having been so frequently assaulted at dawn.

In total, the battalion lost thirty-four men killed, wounded, or missing. From this total, nine men died between 9 and 12 March 1917.

The good work of the 18th (Eastern) Division did not go unnoticed at a higher level, and the II Corps Commander Field Marshal Sir Claud William Jacob, GCB, GCSI, KCMG, sent a message on 23 March 1917:

18th Division

Before leaving the region of the Ancre the Corps Commander desires to thank the 18th Division for the consistently fine work it has accomplished during the past two months for the consistently fine work it has accomplished during the past two months.

The action of Boom Ravine and the capture of Hill 130 gave us possession of Miraumont and weakened the enemy's morale. The brilliant assault on Irles and on the Grevillers line upset the enemy's plans, and the evacuation of the Loupart Line—the first considerable retirement made by the enemy on the Western Front since trench warfare began—was its direct result.

The subsequent advance made by the 18th Division gave rise to several difficult situations, but all ranks rose to the occasion, and the pressure on the Germans never slackened

The enemy was compelled to evacuate Achiet Le Grand before he had any intention of so doing, and gave up several strong lines of defence where, had we shown less resolute action, he could have delayed our advance for a considerable time.

The 16th Division has every right to be proud of its achievements and the Corps Commander is glad to think that he is still to have the honour of retaining then under his command.

Guidebook

From Miraumont, having come in on the D151, take the D163 towards Irles by turning right at the crossroads. Keep on this road until you come to the fork in the road at the entrance to Irles, take the right-hand fork 'Bonne Rue'. You will take a sharp turn to the right and then come to a fork in the road. The ditch that can be seen at the small bridge runs left to right just after this fork. This is the start line for the 8th Battalion if you turn back and look towards Irles. Now head back into the village and take the Rue de Marais. Take the first right and at the fork in the road take the left turn. You will come to a small crossroads. Stop here and then look right, this is the valley from where the Germans launched their attack against 'C' Company.

What3words: impoverished.derailed.pledged.

17

The 7th Battalion, First Battle of the Scarpe, Maison Rouge: 9 April 1917

On 16 November 1916, the Chantilly Conference had seen the Allies decide their strategy for the following year, drawing up plans for a combined action to breach the German line. The area around Arras was chosen for a diversionary offensive to draw German reserve troops away from the main offensive at Chemin des Dames.

Their plans were disrupted in mid-March when the Germans conducted Operation Alberich, which saw their troops withdraw to the new fortifications of the Hindenburg Line. Conducting a scorched earth campaign as they fell back, the Germans managed to shorten their lines by approximately 25 miles.

Nevertheless, the Allies elected to move forward as planned. The main assault was to be led by the French under the command of General Robert Nivelle who had the task of capturing the ridgeline along the Chemin des Dames.

To support the French effort, the British planned to attack the Vimy-Arras sector a week earlier, where it was hoped that the attack would draw troops away from the French. The British would use the 1st, 3rd, and 5th Armies, running north to south respectively. Also, the offensive would utilise a vast network of underground chambers and tunnels that had been under construction since October 1916.

Taking advantage of the region's chalky soil, engineering units had begun excavating an elaborate set of tunnels as well as connected several existing underground quarries. These would allow troops to approach the German lines underground as well as the placement of mines. When completed, the tunnel system allowed for the concealment of 24,000 men and included supply and medical facilities.

To support the infantry advance, artillery planners improved the system of creeping barrages and developed innovative methods for improving counter-battery fire to suppress German guns. Rather than firing on the entire front as in the past, the preliminary bombardment would be focused on a relatively narrow

24-mile section and would last over a full week. During the bombardment, over 2,689,000 shells were fired.

On Monday 9 April 1917 at 5.30 a.m., after an intensive bombardment lasting four days to preclude any retaliation from the enemy, the British 1st Army comprising four Canadian divisions under the command of General Henry Horne set out to capture Vimy Ridge.

Taking control of this height from the Germans would allow the 3rd Army under General Edmund Allenby to advance on Douai, an important road and rail junction, and liberate the coal-mining region.

Allenby was also expected to take Monchy-le-Preux, a village lying a mile to the east of Arras, which gave a commanding view over the Scarpe Valley and, because of this, could hinder the second arm of the offensive directed at Cambrai. Finally, the 5th Army under General Hubert Gough, placed on the southern wing of the offensive, was given the task of taking the village of Bullecourt.

The 12th (Eastern) Division, part of VI Corps, was positioned to the north of St Saveur facing Tilloy-lès-Mofflaines on the Cambrai road. They would have the 3rd Division on their right and the 15th Division on their left. The division would attack with the 36th and 37th Brigades leading the advance and the 35th Brigade kept hidden in cellars near to the tunnels were in reserve. The 6th Queens on the right and the 7th East Surrey on the left (37th Brigade) and the 11th Middlesex on the right and the 7th R. Sussex on the left would start the initial advance at Zero Hour. They would be followed by the 8th and 9th Royal Fusiliers for the 36th Brigade and the 6th R. West Kent and the 6th Buffs for the 37th Brigade. The advance would be covered by twenty-four machine guns.

The initial timeline for the 7th Battalion was as follows: Battalion reached Arras on 6 April 1917 and was billeted in cellars under the museum; on 7 April 1917, the CO and his company commanders reconnoitred the route the battalion would take, which would be by sewers to St Saveur and final plans were made on 8 April; on 9 April 1917, at 4.20 a.m., 'C' Company led the way in the sewers with HQ, 'D', 'A', and 'B' Companies following (they ended up in the reserve line and then waited for Zero Hour).

The objectives were the German first, second, third, and fourth lines known as the Black, Blue, Brown, and Green Lines respectively. At Zero Hour, the Black Line to the north of Tilloy was captured but the advance on the next two lines met with heavy machine-gun fire as well as fire from the ruins of Tilloy.

The Blue line was eventually captured, but the 6th Buffs and 6th R. West Kents were checked and the 8th and 9th Royal Fusiliers were delayed. The line was eventually taken with over 300 prisoners captured. But the advance was at risk of being stalled so the 35th Brigade was called upon to support the advance:

> At zero the 36th and 37th Infantry Brigades attacked the enemy's first & second systems of defence. Their final objective being to capture the high ground known as Observation Ridge and for the purposes of these operations the 'Blue Line'. The 7th

Norfolk Regt had for its objectives the gun pits & trenches just east of the junction of Tilloy Lane and the Cambrai Road, and the Maison Rouge. The objective of the 35th

Infantry Brigade was the Feuchy–Wancourt Line about Feuchy Chapel & known for the purposes of these operations as the 'Brown Line'.

The 7th Norfolk Regt moved into the front-line trenches when they were vacated by the leading Brigades and Battalion Headquarters was established in Ink Street. Two machine guns from the 35th Machine Gun Company were attached to the Battalion and the officer in charge from the Suffolk Regiment also reported here. An officer was sent to the 7th KSLI, the left Battalion of the Division on our right, to maintain liaison between the 35th Infantry Bde and 5th Infantry Bde.

The 7th Norfolks on the right, along with the 9th Essex on the left, led the way up to the Blue Line and was given the task of capturing Observation Ridge as at this point it was learnt that the 3rd Division had still not cleared the position of opposition. The position was cleared with the assistance of the 7th Norfolks. Their advance was given special mention in the Official History of the Great War:

> The 7/Norfolk, the only battalion of the 35th Brigade to go forward from the Blue Line up to time, had as its final objective, the 'Maison Rouge' on the Cambrai road and some trenches north of it. It captured this without difficulty. Such Germans as were encountered put up their hands and 'only wanted to know where they ought to go'.

The battalion war diary records the loss of Lt Bolland and also notes their experiences in the advance:

> Up to this time the Battalion had only sustained two casualties which were two other ranks wounded. About 10.50 a.m. orders were received for us to attack from the Blue Line. On arrival at the junction of Haucourt Trench and Havant Lane it was evident that the Blue Line had not been taken. Houlette Work and the trenches running north and south had still to be taken. The 37th Infantry Bde were occupying the line Haucourt–Hangest Trench.
>
> The commanding officers got into telephone communication with Brigade Headquarters and informed them of the situation. There was a fair amount of machine gun fire and rifle fire during the forward movement from the old British front-line to the Haucourt–Hangest Line, especially from the ruined houses of Tilly, which caused a few casualties
>
> 2nd Lieut J.W.C. Bolland of 'C' Company was killed during this part of operations. On receipt of orders, our attack was launched about 12.8 p.m., and within a few minutes the machine guns & snipers were silenced.
>
> Our men went forward with great dash and the enemy began to surrender freely. A batch of about 90 were taken in Tilloy Quarry where they stood collected together with their hands above their heads. At this point, touch was established with the 3rd

Division on the right. The first objective was captured practically without fighting. Those of the enemy who did not surrender, ran, pursued by our men with all possible speed. In a camouflage trench running N from the Cambrai Road we took 15 Huns and 3 machine guns and established Battalion Headquarters in a good dug out which it possessed. There was a pause at the first objective, the troops proceeded straight on to the 2nd objective which they took without opposition gathering up more prisoners as they went. Some gunner officers were captured here in a gun pit.

The battalion pushed on and in total it captured at least 250 prisoners, and by the time they stopped, they had also captured seven 77 m.m. guns and six machine guns. They stopped to allow the 7th Suffolks and the 9th Essex to pass them in order that they capture Feuchy Chapel Redoubt. The battalion supplied a platoon to mop up German stragglers.

The line now held at Feuchy Chapel with the Suffolks and the Essex battalions digging in either side of the Cambrai roads. One objective still held, which was the Chapel Redoubt on the Brown Line and the 35th Brigade were ordered to capture this on 10 April 1917.

At 8.15 a.m., the 7th Norfolks formed up on Chapel road and either side of Tilloy Lane trench, they were supported by two machine guns. They would advance with the 9th Essex on their right and the 7th Suffolks on their left and would cross the Cambrai road to take their objective. Casualties, especially in NCO's were caused by snipers as they formed up and the attack was postponed until 12.30 p.m. The 5th Berkshires were to push onto the Brown Line from the left and if the wire was found to be uncut the Norfolks would be used in a feint to distract this advance. The wire was uncut and so the Norfolks went in as ordered. They pushed up Tilloy Lane using bombs and the fact that the Berkshires turned the Germans forced them to retire.

The finishing point for the 7th Battalion on 9 April 1917 and you are looking towards Feuchy Chapel, which was assaulted by 9th Essex and the 7th Suffolks on 10 April 1917 supported by a platoon from the Norfolks. The 37th Brigade now pushed onto Monchy-le-Preux, part of the Green Line, and the 7th Norfolks assisted in consolidating what had been captured at Maison Rouge. Between 10 and 12 April, the war diary notes:

10th April 1917

At 3.15 a.m. this morning an order from Brigade was received that the 35th Infantry Brigade with 2 companies of Queens and 6 companies of 36th Infantry Bde will capture the Brown Line. The assault was timed for 8.15 a.m.

The Commanding Officer moved up immediately to Maison Rouge and detailed the plan of attack to Company Commanders. The 7th Norfolk Regiment, with 2 M.G.s attached, assembled along the Chapel Road on either side of Tilloy Lane in touch on the right with the 9th Essex Regiment, the objective was the Brown Line from the Cambrai Road to H34 c.7.1.

The 7th Suffolk Regt, with two Coys Queens, 2 M.G.s and 1 T.M. had for its objective Church Redoubt and Brown Line from right Divisional Boundary and 6 Coys 36th Infantry Brigade were ordered to do a turning movement by crossing the Brown Line where the 15th Div on our left had already opened it & proceed southwards on the eastern side of it.

While getting into position the Battalion was greatly troubled by sniper fire who appeared to be shooting from the junction of Tilloy Lane & Brown Line. It was getting light rapidly and he inflicted a few casualties upon us before the men were under cover & ready for the assault.

About two hours later an order was received postponing the attack until 12.30 p.m. The Brigadier also directed that unless the wire in front of the Brown Line was cut no assault would be made frontally but a demonstration would be made & every support given to the turning movement of the 5th R. Berks.

The enemy evidently fully appreciated the situation as the 5th R. Berks advance was quite unhampered by any opposition and it was found that a retirement had been made. Only a few Germans had been left behind & these were taken prisoner. Cavalry patrols were pushed out and the 37th Division passed through to make their attack on Monchy le Preux and 'Green Line'. Consolidation of the Brown Line was commenced. The 7th Norfolk Regt taking up an outpost line along the high ground from Orange Hill to about 800 yds S of the Cambrai Road.

On 11 April 1917, the battalion was relieved along with the rest of the 35th Brigade and went back to the rear but were then again ordered back to the Brown Line so that another relief could be made for the 37th Division.

Eventually, they were relieved in terrible conditions on 13 April 1917 after snow had fell in the afternoon, with the war diary reporting: 'There was no accommodation here, all dugouts etc being occupied by the gunners and the men and officers have had to make what shelter they con of shell holes and pits'. Casualties between 9 and 13 April were five officers killed and wounded and 162 other ranks killed, wounded, or missing.

The initial stages of Arras were a stunning victory, and this was the beginning of a sustained offensive that would run into May.

Guidebook

Coming out of Arras, on the D939, heading towards Cambrai you are actually on the main line of advance for the Norfolks. They moved eastward in the field to your left moving through Tilloy-lès-Mofflaines up to Maison Rouge. Maison Rouge can be found as the derelict barn and new farm house you will come to on your left prior to the roundabout for the D37.

What3words: success.arrived.zipped.

18

The 1st Battalion, La Coulotte: 23 April 1917

After Vimy Ridge was captured by the Canadians on 9 April 1917, other units took over, and by 13 Aprilm the 5th Division relieved them and took over what had been taken. Hostilities were resumed here on 23 April 1916 when the 15th Brigade were ordered to capture German positions in front of La Coulotte. The war diary records that the specific objectives for the 1st Battalion Norfolk Regiment were Cyril Trench to the Lens–Railway line. The CO of the time, Lt-Col. John William Vincent Carroll, wrote an after-action report:

22nd April 1917
1. The Battalion strength 24 officers & 745 Other Ranks marched at 6 p.m. from Berthonval Wood and by 2 a.m. had taken up position extending from T8.C.6.8 TO T1.C.7.7

    The Batt was formed up A&C Coys on the right with two platoons inside the German wire & two platoons to halfway between the 45 & 50 contours. B & D Coys on the left in touch with A & C Coys & with their left about T1.c.8.7 in touch with the right of the 1/Bedford Regiment.
2. I had sent an officer from A & B Coys to report on the German wire, these officers who were accompanied by an officer of the H.A. Group reported to me at my Hd Quarters at T.13.a.3.7 by 11 p.m. on 21st that the German wire was uncut though slightly damaged in one or two places, this was reported by me to the 15th Bde.

Zero Hour was at 4.45 a.m. and the infantry followed with the 1st Norfolks leading the way. The war diary notes that their battalion strength was twenty-four officers and 743 other ranks. To the right of the 15th Brigade was the 52nd Canadian Battalion. 'A' and 'C' Company led the advance and 'B' and 'D'

Company followed up in support. As the Norfolks got to the German trenches, the enemy began to surrender but came under heavy fire from machine guns hidden in the railway cutting:

23rd April 1917

3. At 4.45 a.m. the artillery barrage was started & from what I can gather was quite good, very few shorts. The Batt closed in on the German wire under the barrage. A & C Coys right platoons advanced to their 1st objective & then came under a very heavy M.G. fire from the houses on the railway at T.2.d.1.3 & T.2.b.3.1 also from the railway cutting between these points & the houses in the south side of Avion & were unable to advance further.

The two left platoons of 'A' & 'C' Coys were unable to get through the uncut German wire and were held up by M.G. fire in shell holes in the open.

Both of the rear companies came up against uncut wire, but the 1st Bedfords found a way in and began to bomb along the trench. Both the lead Norfolk companies got elements into the trench who also began bombing, and they captured four machine guns.

'B' & 'D' Coys on reaching the German wire found it absolutely uncut, the O.C. 'B' Coy ran up & down the wire to try & find a gap but was unable to do so except on his extreme left, where a zig zag gap left in the wire for the use of German patrols. The left platoons of 'B' Coy & the right platoons of the Bedford Regt forced a way through this gap in the face of very heavy M.G., rifle & bomb fire & proceeded to bomb out towards & up the trench running from T.1.b.4.0 to T.1.b.5.8. The party of 'A' & 'D' Coy bombing along the German front line captured 4 M.G.s & bombed 5 or 6 dugouts but were held up about T.1.d.7.8 by a German strong point & could make no further progress. The 4 M.G.s captured were afterwards destroyed by firing a rifle grenade into the lock when it was found we could not withdraw them. The detachment which penetrated as far as the German support line found little opposition but were badly enfiladed by Machine Guns from the houses & railway cutting. The German barrage became very heavy about 10 a.m. & continued until about 7 p.m. when the remainder of 'B' & 'D' Coys were withdrawn to the original outpost line. About 7 prisoners of the 266 R Regt were captured.

Other parties also got forward and into the second trench but came under fire from enfilading fire even though this trench was poorly manned. This is where Captain Frederick Magnay was killed, and in a letter to his parents, his CO stated: 'He was killed when most gallantly leading his company into the German second line against heavy machine gun and shell fire. He was an officer of very great ability and promise, and had endeared himself to all ranks, his loss is very deeply felt'. Frederick had been with the battalion since 1915 and Second Ypres.

The detailed after-action report went through the process of noting a number of issues as to why the attack failed here:

Notes

German strong point at T.1.d.8.8 M.G. enfiladed front line to the west support line from contour 45 to where it joined trench from Fosse 7 is a dummy trench about 2 feet deep. The M.G. from the strong-point commands the ground up to the water tower. The German 77 fires on & commands the trench from the N.E. possible Avion Switch. Front Line trench is deep & not revetted. There is a big dug-out at T.1.d.5.8 with 2 entrances on the left of communication trench about 20 feet down with a brick tunnel & concrete steps, garrison retired to apparently Fosse 7 up communication trench. There is a high mound at T.1.d.6.8 all the ground to the N & W and as far as the strong-point on the E this would make a good position for us when consolidating. Two M.G.s which were enfilading us were captured & destroyed here.

Wire is 15 yds to 20 yds deep on wooded stakes & in very good condition. Water Tower is flat, but the buildings round Fosse 7 are standing & afford good cover for M.G.s. Ground is not much churned up not cut up between the outpost line trenches and the German wire. German shelling seemed to come from the N.E. The 77 seemed to do most damage. Cyril Trench is in fair condition but low at junction with the Hun line. After we retired the Germans advanced from Avion in open order. Our barrage was chiefly over. Large supplies of bombs were required as bombing went on all day. 30 sandbags of bombs were received about 6 p.m. by B & D Coys & enabled us to hold out. Rifle grenades were also required especially for the strong-points, our supplies proved inadequate. Heavy 5.9 fire on Lens-Arras Road where Cyril Trench crosses it.

Uncut wire not marked on map from railway to T.2.c.3.5 held up the right Coy from here to Avion the railway appeared to be organised for defence. I account for the failure of the attack to the uncut wire, even if only the artillery had cut two or three gaps in the wire where we could have got in the Germans would have surrendered, as on our reaching the wire the occupants of the German front-line all held up their hands. My casualties are 7 officers killed, 8 wounded & roughly 220 other ranks casualties.

Acts of bravery here can be listed such as the action by Lance Corporal Matthews was a No. 2 on a Lewis Gun team and assisted Lance Corporal Stewart with collecting his platoon but lost his gun team. He therefore found another disabled gun team and repaired the gun and pushed forward. He then opened fire on the enemy who were retiring with good effect. He then heard that the battalion on his left needed assistance so he pushed towards the flanks and selected targets that assisted that battalion who were consolidating their position. For his bravery, he won the MM.

Private Ernest Hall showed great initiative and courage during the advance and found an abandoned Lewis Gun. He used this to rush up a German communication trench and seized an advanced post. Firing on a strongpoint, this allowed his company to advance. It is noted that he was not trained in the Lewis but had been shown the method of firing. For his actions that day, he was awarded the MM.

The casualty return in the report can be amended to sixty-four killed, most of whom have no know grave and are commemorated on the Arras Memorial.

One of the officers to die here was 2Lt Fred Creighton Coleman, aged nineteen, the son of Dr Percy and Mrs F. M. H. Coleman of Riemore Lodge at Clacton-on-Sea in Essex. His CO stated in a letter:

> I had the very highest opinion of your son, and am deeply grieved that he has not been spared to meet the reward for the keen, zealous and splendid manner in which he prepared himself for his duty to his country. He was one of the best lads I have had under me during the whole of my experience in the training of young officers. Although so young I cannot say how splendidly he did the special work I gave him. We all feel the loss very deeply.

A fellow officer noted: 'He was killed at 5 a.m. whilst gallantly leading his platoon into the German second line. He was always cheerful, very brave and very cool, and by his fine example kept his men going'.

Another man to lose his life that day was Private John Ainsworth (13015) from Heigham, who had won the MM at Longueval and who had been wounded at Falfemont Farm. He is buried in Grave III.D.1 at La Chauderie Military Cemetery.

Guidebook

The best way to get to this position is to head to Vimy and to take the D51 out of the village heading towards Givenchy-en-Gohelle. You will pass under the N17. As soon as you do, you will see a turning on the right. Take this and you are now on the road heading towards La Coulotte, this eventually joins up with the D55. Prior to reaching the village look to the right. This is where the Norfolks advanced in this field.

What3words: screwball.veto.overgrowth.

19

The 7th Battalion,
The Battle of Arleux, Rifle Trench:
28 April 1917

After ten days out of the line, the 12th (Eastern) Division went into forward positions between the north-east of Monchy and the River Scarpe. On 27 April 1917, the 35th Brigade were given orders to capture Bayonet Trench and Rifle Trench situated to the south of Roeux:

> 27th April 1917
>   Orders were received about midday for an attack on Rifle and Bayonet Trench
>   1st Objective (Black Line) Capture of Rifle Trench and Bayonet Trench
>   2nd Objective (Blue Line) Consolidate a line from about I32c3.5-I32.a.2.2-I26c1.3-I26a.3.7 Zero Hour will be at 4.25 a.m. 28th inst. About Midnight the 2 front companies reported an enemy attack & sent up the S.O.S. signal.
>   Some artillery support was obtained and rifle & machine gun fire entirely checked the movement, no Germans reaching our trenches.

The 7th Battalion Norfolk Regiment, along with the 5th Battalion Royal Berkshire Regiment, were given the task of leading the attack. After the first objectives were taken, the 7th Suffolks would pass through to the second objective and the 9th Battalion Essex Regiment were placed in reserve.

Zero Hour was at 4.25 a.m., and it began with a two-minute intense artillery bombardment to which the Germans made a furious response and the 5th R. Berks advanced close behind the barrage and captured their objectives in Bayonet and Rifle Trenches without difficulty and began consolidation:

> At 4.25 a.m. this morning C & D Companies—C Coy on the right, advanced to capture Rifle Trench and join up with A & B Companies. In conjunction with the attack of the 5th R. Berks Regt this would establish the Black line.

At zero = 50 minutes, the Black Line being captured, all four companies of the 7th Norfolk Regt, with the 7th Suffolk Regt on their left, should have proceeded to establish a map line according to map references given above, to be called the Blue Line.

The 7th Norfolks were less successful. They had 'A' and 'B' leading with 'C' and 'D' attempting to gain contact with the lead companies. This failed, and the Norfolks came under heavy machine-gun fire from their flanks:

At 2 p.m. no definite news had been received regarding the attack. It appeared that 'A' & 'B' Coys went over the top at zero + 50 mins without gaining touch with 'C' & 'D' Coys and were lying out in front in shell holes having been entirely held up by M.Gun fire with both their flanks unprotected.

'C' & 'D' Coys are unlocated. Some men of A & B Coys began to crawl in back to our line but were at once sniped. At 11 p.m. the situation is as follows.

The attack by 'C' & 'D' Coys was held up by M Gun fire, none of our men reached the German line. The trench had not been touched by artillery and there was some wire. For the remainder of the day our men lay out in shell holes being sniped by the enemy. As soon as it was dark all those that could returned to our lines & stretcher squads went out to bring in the wounded. During the whole of their work they were continually under enemy M Gun & rifle fire which was done with the aid of extremely bright Very Lights.

This fire was so heavy & so accurate that it was impossible to bring in many of our men who were badly wounded and close to the enemy's trenches.

The 7th Suffolks also found themselves unable to proceed against heavy machine-gun fire when they attempted to pass through the 5th R. Berks lines at 5.05 a.m. At this point, the Berkshires still held Bayonet Trench and 150 yards of Rifle trench but the Germans still held Rifle Trench as far as Harness Lane.

Due to the heavy fire, both the 7th Norfolks and the 7th Suffolks were still in their original positions. One company of the Essex was sent to help the Berks hold on to their gains. Attempts to capture the rest of Rifle trench with bombing from both flanks failed.

An SNCO in the 5th R. Berks noted:

As we had lost all our officers in my company except one I was detailed with my platoon to take up bombs, ammunition, rifle grenades etc to another company of ours (C Company) Having collected all my men together and issued to them these different stores we left our trench at about 3 am under very heavy shell fire. I had been given orders by my company officer to get there at all costs as they had run short of nearly everything. I succeeded in reaching them after a very hard struggle as the Boche were giving us hell with his shells and machine guns. C Company were greatly relieved when they heard that I had arrived with a fresh supply of trench stores, which were quickly issued out.

I discovered on my way that there were a lot of bombs, shovels and picks lying spare in a trench that I passed. I succeeded in collecting them and was waiting to get through again to C Company when the Germans succeeded in blowing part of the trench in, cutting us off from C Company. We had to remain in this trench, where I had got my men, when the Germans started to shell us unmercifully, and continued at it all day long without a break, causing a good many casualties. I told my men to stick it and that as soon as it became dark we would chance it and make another attempt to reach C Company. I had succeeded in dodging these shells all day and was just on the point of starting to C Company when a big shell burst about six yards in front of me, which wounded me and also buried me.

'D' Company from 7th Norfolks had come up against uncut wire and 'A' and 'B' Companies had to take cover in shell holes. The war diary noted:

The remainder of the day our men lay out in shell holes being sniped by the enemy. As soon as it was dark all those that could returned to our lines and stretcher squads went to try and bring in the wounded. During the whole of their work they were continually under enemy M. Gun and rifle fire which was done with the aid of extremely bright Verey Lights. The fire was so heavy and accurate that it was impossible to bring in many of our men who were badly wounded and close to the enemy's trench.

The war diary noted that casualties were especially heavy in 'C' and 'D' Companies.

Another attack was ordered on 29 April and the 9th Essex advanced and took Rifle Trench supported by flanking fire but were driven out by two German counterattacks:

29th April 1917

The 35th Infantry Brigade has been ordered to capture Rifle trench tonight. The operation will be carried out as follows:

(i) Bombing Rifle grenade & Stokes Mortars attacks from another flank.

(ii) A frontal attack by two companies of the 9th Essex Regt

Rifle Trench has been bombarded throughout the day by heavy & field artillery.

30th April 1917

At 3 a.m. this morning the attack on Rifle Trench was launched. It was successful. The objective was taken & consolidation commenced but 2 bombing attacks, the first of which was repulsed, drove our infantry from Rifle Trench.

A few prisoners were taken.

On 1 May, the battalion was relieved by the 6th Buffs. In this attack, twelve officers and 223 other ranks were lost. In total, the CWGC records the loss of ninety-two men killed on 28 April 1917. Like the 1st Battalion at La Coulotte, many of them have no known grave and are commemorated on the Arras Memorial.

One of the officers lost that day was 2Lt William Gilbert Elphinstone Clapp who was wounded leading his platoon in the attack; he died of wounds the next day in No. 41 CCS. He was aged twenty-three and the son of Rev. W. S. Clapp, who was the Rector of Ashley at Stockbridge; 2Lt Clapp is buried in Grave III. H. 38. Duisans British Cemetery. His CO said of him: 'He had done very good work with this battalion and although at first things were a little strange to him, coming from the Yeomanry, he soon settled down, and was one of my most promising officers. He was very popular alike with officers and men, and his place will be very difficult to fill'.

Guidebook

The best way to come in is via the D939 Arras–Cambrai road. Take the D33 signposted for Monchy-le-Preux and go into the village. You then want to continue on the D33, which takes you to Pelves and Rouex. The British line crossed this road about half a mile out of the village and Rifle Trench originally crossed this road from east to west roughly half a mile out from Monchy. There is a track on the right that gets you into position for this.

What3words: greets.scholarships.unity.

20

The 1st Battalion, Oppy Wood: 28 June 1917

After the Arras Offensive had ended, the Germans still held Oppy Wood, situated to the west of Oppy village and to the south-west of Fresnoy. The wood was approximately 1 acre square and was heavily fortified. Attempts were made to capture it on 27 April and 3 May 1917 (the Third Battle of the Scarpe), though both of these attacks had failed during terrible bouts of heavy fighting, with the Germans counterattacking and pushing the British out of the wood on each occasion.

During this period, Lance Corporal James Welch (8763) of 'B' Company, the 1st Royal Berkshire Regiment, won the VC on 27 April and Lt John Harrison of the 11th (Service) Battalion of the East Yorkshire Regiment was awarded a posthumous VC during the fighting on 3 May. On this day, the 31st Division lost 1,900 casualties and the 2nd Division's composite brigade lost 517 officers and men.

The next attack, planned for 28 June, would be carried out by the 15th Brigade of the 5th Division and the 94th Brigade of the 31st Division. Their line would extend from Gavrelle in the south to the north of Oppy Wood.

By this time, the Army was operating under a new training pamphlet entitled *SS143-Instructions for Training of Platoons for Offensive Action 1917*. This booklet would pave the way for the way the infantry would fight until the end of the war. In this book, the infantry was expected to be able to fight its way forward independently of artillery support as a battle developed. Its doctrine taught that there were advantages for different weapon types being brought to bear on the enemy as and when needed.

In the place of a single line of riflemen, SS143 promoted the self-contained platoon comprising a small HQ and four sections of specialists. In simple terms, the attack was to be led forward by bomb and rifle sections, with the rifle grenade and Lewis gun sections following close behind. Upon contact with the enemy, the rifles and the bombers were to seek out the enemy flank and attack with fire, bayonet and bomb. The rifle grenadiers and Lewis gun team were to attempt to suppress the enemy, allowing the other sections to press home their attack. This flexible use of arms also passed a degree of initiative to the junior officers down the chain of command and was used to promote an *esprit de corps*.

SS143 taught a platoon to lead by its sections of riflemen and bombers with the platoon sergeant between, it is followed by the platoon commander then the Lewis gun and rifle grenade sections. The platoon has a prepared and hopefully rehearsed drill for reaction to coming under fire. In this moment of chaos, having a pre-programmed reaction is critical to overcoming the perfectly human reaction to hide.

It would be too easy for the platoon to fragment into cover and the attack to lose its momentum. From *SS143*, all members of the platoon would know what would be happening around them. On being engaged the Lewis gun section should find the first available cover and engage the point of resistance, this is accompanied by a barrage of rifle grenades. Under the cover of this direct and indirect fire, the rifle and bombing sections are to deploy to a flank and pursue the attack.

This was how the battle for Oppy Wood would be fought.

At 5.30 p.m., German artillery bombarded the British jumping-off trenches for ten minutes and caused around 200 casualties in the two attacking brigades. At 7 p.m., a British hurricane bombardment began from Gavrelle to Hulluch, along the 14-mile front of the XIII Corps and I Corps, as part of a feint against Lens. Howitzers fired smoke-shell to create a screen, to the north of the 5th Division attack and then a thunderstorm began, the infantry advancing at 7.10 a.m. amid lightning and torrential rain.

In the XIII Corps area, the 94th Brigade of the 31st Division advanced north of Gavrelle and the 15th Brigade of the 5th Division attacked Oppy on a 2,300-yard (2,100-metre) front. Despite the German bombardment on the jumping-off trenches, the British troops advanced swiftly across no-man's-land behind a creeping barrage, before the German counter-barrage fell three minutes later.

There is an after-action report for Oppy Wood, which was written on 3 July 1917:

> The task allotted to the 15th Infantry Brigade in the series of operations prepared for the 28th June 1917, was the capture of the German trenches from B.18.d.75/15 to B.12.d.45/10 and the consolidation of this of this line of posts from North and South through the Western end of Oppy Wood. The 94th Infantry Brigade attacked on our immediate right.
>
> The brigade had been training hard for five days over a prepared course at Brunhaut Farm and the troops were in their finest trim when they moved up into battle positions.

On the night of the 27th/28th June the order of battle from right to left was: 16th Warwickshire Regiment, 1st Cheshire Regiment, 1st Norfolk Regiment and 1st Bedfordshire Regiment with the 1st Royal West Kent Regiment (13th Infantry Brigade), in Brigade reserve in the Red Line.

At 5.10 p.m., when attackers were all in position, in their assembly trenches, the enemy put down a heavy barrage for about 15 minutes and fairly heavy casualties were sustained. However, the spirit of our troops remained undaunted and in less than two hours they were given the long-waited opportunity of showing what they could do.

The previous operation in which the Brigade had taken part was not successful. It was impossible to forget the fact that they had been set an impossible task at La Coulotte on the 23rd April, when artillery preparation was incomplete and the wire in front of the trenches was very strong and uncut.

However, on this occasion, a thorough preparation had been arranged and the results established by careful observation, patrols and raids, which were carried out. Nothing, in fact, was left to chance and, knowing the spirit of the officers and other ranks carrying out the operation, the result was a foregone conclusion.

On the 5th Division front, the 15th Brigade had the task of advancing on Oppy Wood to the north of the 31st Division. The 1st Norfolks would advance centrally with the 1st Cheshires on their right and the 1st Befordshires on their left. All three battalions went over at 7.10 p.m., moving out of Maquis Trench in two waves advancing within 25–30 yards of the creeping barrage and took some casualties from this:

Precisely at 7.10, a magnificent barrage was put down on the German front line and the wire in front, and our troops advanced to the attack, each Battalion attacking on a two-company frontage. Our troops advanced rapidly, keeping as close in as they possibly could to our barrage, in which they had the greatest confidence. The Battalion on the left was met at once by machine gun and rifle fire but the but down the enemy's artillery, which did not begin firing till 7.15 p.m., put down a very feeble barrage. The front-line was charged and carried and at 7.16 p.m. the first white 'Very' Light, (the pre-arranged signal for successful entry into the enemy's defences), was observed on the left of the attack. At 7.18 p.m. a similar light was sent up all along the line. At 7.32 p.m. the first message was received, from the 1st Cheshire Regiment, stating that they and the 16th Warwickshire Regiment had affected an entry into the enemy's line and that prisoners were being sent back by the battalion on their left. Six minutes later the right and left companies of the 1st Norfolk Regiment were reported to be in, but with slight casualties.

They also reported that the 1st Bedfordshire Regiment had carried their trenches. At 7.40 p.m. the 16th R. Warwickshire Regiment had taken all their objectives and by 8.20 p.m. had established touch with the battalions on their right and left. Few casualties were incurred and 40 or 50 prisoners were reported taken.

They got into the first German line with opposition from a group of Germans that numbered around thirty in a concrete pillbox. This defensive position was dealt with by Mills Bombs:

> At 8.24 p.m. the enemy began a heavy bombardment of our support lines. At 8.40 p.m. the 1st Cheshire Regiment had gained all their objectives and had captured 34 prisoners and a machine gun, and five minutes later the 1st Norfolk Regiment reported that the 1st Bedfordshire Regiment had reached their objectives and taken 63 prisoners, besides killing numerous Germans, several of whom were shot through the head. By this time the hostile shelling was pretty severe but our casualties were still light. A 9.50 p.m. the 1st Cheshire Regiment reported that they were consolidating the captured line and soon after all battalions were busy digging in and strengthening the captured positions.
>
> At 10.10 p.m. a report was received from the Brigade on our right that the enemy was massing prior to delivering a counter attack on their left flank. The 16th R. Warwickshire Regiment were informed and stood to, but no such attack followed then or afterwards at any time.

The brigade got into Oppy Wood with little opposition and a line was established 80 yards into it, with outposts placed further onward. By 9 p.m., this line was being consolidated and the battalion had captured one officer and seventy other ranks and two machine guns.

> All battalions settled down to the task of consolidating which they did without being molested. In this most successful attack 2 officers and 141 other ranks were taken prisoner and the number of German dead was considerable, including 4 officers who were killed in a dug out two of which were artillery officers. The total number of German dead on our front is estimated at not less than 150. We also captured 8 light machine guns, 4 light trench mortars, 5 bomb-throwers, 60 rifles and a quantity of ammunition, ammunition belts, pouches, etc., and re-captured Lewis Guns.
>
> The artillery barrage was intensified by the cooperation of the 13th and 15th Trench Mortar Batteries, which fired from zero to zero plus 2, at the rate of 28 rounds per gun per minute. A machine gun barrage was arranged, which undoubtedly inflicted further heavy casualties on the enemy, who were observed clearing out the trenches beyond our final objective.
>
> The 15th Machine Gun Company cooperated with the attacking troops and moved forward as soon as the objective had been captured and placed guns in positions, from which they would have dealt effectively with the enemy had they attempted a counter attack. Every precaution was taken to deal with a hostile counter-attack, which, however, was not attempted. A smoke barrage on our left flank had been arranged and effectively obscured the view from the high ground held by the enemy. About 20 minutes after the attack was launched it commenced to thunder and very

heavy rain fell. This added to the discomfort of the attackers, but in spite of this the way in which the troops dug a new line was beyond all praise. As soon as it was dark parties of Pioneers, 1/6th Argyll and Sutherland Highlanders, moved up and dug two excellent communication trenches across what had recently been 'No Man's Land'.

The morale of the troops in the Brigade was always good, but after this operation it attained a standard of perfection, and all the troops are satisfied to know that they accomplished, in magnificent style, all that was asked of them, although expressing regret that the pursuit of the Bosche was not permitted.

Fighting patrols put out the next day were repulsed as they entered Oppy village.

Burning oil was also used in the attack to draw the enemy away from Oppy and toward Fresnoy. This is thought to have helped and was used as a deterrent against the German flamethrower. Herbert Reeve had this to say about Oppy Wood:

> The two dots are fortified redoubts covering the entire defence of the wood. It was, of course, daylight at this time. We caught them on the hop. I fired a Lewis Gun from the hip at those in the trenches. We captured the Wood and 34 prisoners from each redoubt. Another Battalion passed through us to capture much valuable ground. That night we had a terrific thunderstorm, which helped us against any counter-attack. It was in this Action that I was awarded the Distinguished Conduct Medal. My Platoon Commander, Captain Joe Brewster, was delighted. He purchased an abundance of cigarettes for the whole Platoon.

In the attack of 28 June, the 31st Division lost 100 men and the 5th Division casualties were 352 men. From this total, seventeen men died serving with the 1st Battalion Norfolk Regiment.

Guidebook

From Thelus, head towards Bailleul-Sur-Berthoult on the D49. In this village, and before you exit it, you want the Rue D'Oppy, which will be on your left. Take this minor road and you will see Oppy Wood coming up on the right. The Norfolks were in the field on your left and then crossed the same road and then went into the wood.

What3words: descending.regretfully.erode.

21

The 9th Battalion, Hill 70, Loos: 1 July to 3 October 1917

To divert German reinforcements away from the Third Ypres battlefield, Haig ordered attacks further to the south. One of these, involving the 1st Army, would see the Canadian Corps attack at Lens.

Haig ordered Sir Arthur Currie, who in June had been placed in command of the Canadian Corps, to launch a frontal assault on the city of Lens. Instead of attacking the heavily fortified city directly, Currie, after studying the ground, convinced his British superiors that a better plan would be to capture Hill 70, directly to the north. If this dominating hill could be taken, the Germans would have no choice but to counterattack. Currie planned for artillery and machine guns to smash these German concentrations, thereby weakening their hold on the entire sector.

The Canadians attacked on 15 August 1917 and captured many of their objectives, including the high ground. They then held their positions against twenty-one determined German counterattacks over the next four days. Canadian probing attacks against Lens on 21 and 23 August were unsuccessful, but Currie's forces had inflicted severe casualties on the enemy and gained the high ground overlooking the city.

The Canadians lost more than 9,000 soldiers at Hill 70, but killed or wounded an estimated 25,000 Germans. Currie proved an able and innovative commander. His Canadian Corps would soon move north to help Haig and his faltering Passchendaele campaign.

This is what Col. Prior had to say about this sector:

Two companies from the battalion were loaned to another unit in the brigade and moved to Cite Joan d' Arc to make a counter attack on Lens. This however did not materialise. Cite Joan d' Arc being south of cite St Pierre was in consequence nearer to Lens where shells of every calibre were being hurled incessantly day and night.

The area was by no means healthy and the quick and sudden departure in omnibuses of the whole battalion on July 18th up to Laventies and Armentières was a welcome relief. Here the battalion found a veritable Garden of Eden, where peace reigned. The trenches seemed miles apart, with a water logged 'no man's land' and except for an occasional shot everything was decidedly quiet.

This paradise was not for the battalion; for on Aug 26 they were back at Noeux les Mines in Divisional Reserve. News of the great Canadian advance on Lens, on 15th August had leaked through all ranks did not relish returning to the Hill 70 area.

August and part of September saw the battalion in and out of the line, if line it could be called, as owing to the rapid advance, the situation was extremely difficult. Trenches were shallow, shell holes in abundance, which more often than not were linked together to form part of a trench.

Approaching Cite St Auguste one's ears were deafened by many machine guns that were actually firing millions of bullets over the heads of the men as they went forward to take up their positions.

Two industrial suburbs, Cite St Emile and Cite St Laurent had been captured and the battalion played a gallant part on holding the line recently won by the Canadians.

During the month of August and it seemed uncanny to be but a few yards from a city bearing that name, the country was literally covered with the dead of friend and foe. To reach battle positions one had to pick one's way across hundreds of bodies and limbs that were fast rotting in the summer sun.

The bayonet had been used to advantage and the writer well remembers a dug out in the quarry at Cite St Auguste where some twenty or thirty Germans had been bayoneted.

The Germans knew every inch of the country and their old headquarters were subject to heavy bombardment and in one instance a whole platoon was annihilated by a heavy shell bursting in their midst. The ground was churned over and over, communication trenches but a few feet deep, that one had to practically crawl on all fours to obtain cover from the whizz bangs that hampered movement.

Battalion and Company runners certainly had their baptism of fire whilst the transport night after night bringing up rations had to run the gauntlet of heavy artillery fire. The horror of Hill 70, its ghastly explosions, death traps where men fought and died, can never fade from the memory of survivors if the old ninth.

At the end of June 1917, the 9th Norfolks, along with the 2nd Sherwood Foresters, were loaned to the 46th Division. The reason for this was that they were to assist in the fighting around Lens. Col. Prior noted that he spoke to the GOC of the 46th Division, who told him they were going to attack the enemy and the division was weak so he had requested battalions to support the division.

The battalion would support the Sherwood Foresters who were given the task of being part of the left brigade who would assist in attacking the Cites, which were all suburbs of Lens that had been built for the workers who were employed on the coal mines around the area.

> There was a certain amount of open ground between each Cite but for the most part suburb ran into suburb and made it a most difficult fighting area. The feature of French domestic architecture is that every house however small is provided with a cellar and naturally cellars in this sort of fighting played an important part. The cellars, even without preparation, gave a certain amount of protection from shell fire and when well shored up and covered with rubble and cement made excellent dugouts.
>
> With cellars and the walls of houses to screen them it was difficult to know where the enemy was, what his strength was and altogether it seemed a risky undertaking for one weak and very highly tried division with no troops to back them.

Due to the weakness of the 139th (Sherwood Forester) Brigade, the 2nd Sherwood Foresters were put in the line and the 9th Norfolks were placed in support. The initial attack went well and all of the objectives were captured. But the Germans launched a heavy counterattack and hand-to-hand fighting took place. The 9th Norfolks stayed in support and expected to either counter attack or to move up to a rallying point. Neither happened and ground was lost but in other areas it was held. The confusion here can be seen with Col. Prior's experiences of eventually being called up to assist.

> About midday I received a message that it was believed that the Brigade on the right of the Foresters, 137th N. Stafford Brigade, had succeeded on their attack and were holding a line of houses on the Cite du Moulin and that when this had been definitely determined I was to send a couple of companies to report to Colonel Bradshaw, commanding the 2nd Foresters, who was to arrange an attack so as to bring the Sherwood Foresters front in line with the 137th Brigade front.

Col. Prior was not happy with this plan and thought it better that the entire battalion attack, he put these concerns to the brigade commander who initially noted that he still wished Col. Bradshaw to carry out the original plan. However, Col. Prior persisted:

> I then asked whether definite news of the 137th Brigade on our right had been received and finding that it had not, pointed out to the General that it would be suicidal to attempt the operation if the enemy and not our men held the Cite du Moulin houses. The General agreed to this and said that he would not permit the attack until this fact had been definitely established.

Col. Prior then tried to ascertain this himself, which he found difficult to do in light of the fact that he saw very little movement and could not identify if the troops he saw were friend or foe. Eventually, he was able to identify from the style of helmet that the position was held by the Germans. This was reported back to the brigade commander who agreed that the attack would not happen unless there was a definite confirmation that the position was held and eventually this was confirmed that the 137th Brigade had been ejected from their positions. The 9th Battalion did not attack. Col. Prior concluded:

> If, therefore, our attack had been successfully made it must have ended disastrously as the flank would have been open and under hostile enfilade fire. Despite the great difficulties of the ground there seems to have been some very bad intelligence work that the position had not been cleared up and the G.O.C. of the 138th Brigade informed.

This area was renowned for its ferocity in the way both sides fought each other. There was no live and let live here and this can be seen in James Cooper's diary entries. James had initially served at home in the Norwich Volunteers, but by January 1917, he was serving with the 9th Battalion as a bandsman:

Sept 4th

Up at 4.30 left billet at 6 and move by way of Maroc, It's the worst place I have been through. Streets of houses all knocked down and shells bursting over us as we went along. Passed a guard with some German prisoners evidently taken during the night. They looked very depressed. Got into the crater about 8 o'clock (...crater) It's now about 12 and they have been shelling all the time mostly shrapnel, large pieces keep falling all around us, have kept one piece. Cooks made a fire and too much smoke, Fritz spotted it and sent a shell very close. Plenty of aircraft. It seems likely to be very lively shortly. This is really being in the midst of it, especially day time. This crater is like a large shell hole 100 yds across it and all chalk. Fritz have been shelling Loos. It's only about 200 yds away and we have a battery of guns there, that is what he's after. Just seen seven of the Durhams carted away dead.

Sept 5th

Very rough journey last night and early this morning. 10.30 a.m. cleared the rations off the limbers. 11.15 fell in to take them to the companies. I and Micky told off with A Coy. We hadn't got more than 200 yds when Fritz started shelling and killed one of our party, Sergeant Rush, a good start. A piece of shrapnel caught him in the side and tore all one side away, he died almost instantly. We got under cover for a bit. Then he started sending over gas shells so on with our gas helmets and we started off again. It was rotten, didn't know the way and rough country, tripping over wire one minute, slipping over a shell hole the next and what with rifle and two sacks of rations and shells of all sorts coming over as last as he could send them, it was a night never to be forgotten and to make it worse our guide lost his way. Anyway, we managed to find again as it as it was a full moon and beautiful and clear. Could see some dead Fritz lay on the side of the trenches just with a little bit of chalk we covered over them.

We knew there was something up about as the smell was awful. As we went along it was a sight to see, Fritz concrete emplacements and snipers' huts simply blown to pieces by our artillery which showed that he had no earthly chance to stand against us and was forced to clear out. What were once trenches were simply shell holes. Anyway, we got back at 3.30 a.m. so finished the first night in the trenches between Lens and Loos. Just heard there were two more wounded. We had bad luck today, rations on the dump to take up tomorrow, while gone Fritz sent some shells and blew the lot up. He doesn't have his aircraft dump, or it might have been an accident. Had to go up to B.H.2 with the Major. Brought a message back from the Colonel that his wishes were that the band were not to be runners or carriers but to act as a nothing he had spotted salvage party, so we shall have to go and search all the dugouts and see what's lying about that's any good. Anyway, it done us a good turn, instead of turning in at 3.30 in the morning we got down about 10 o'clock at night.

September 6th

Up about 8.30. My pal Micky had to go to Philosophe so slept alone, expect he will come back this morning. He has just come back. He had to take the body of Sergeant Rush to Philosophe for burial. 1 am just put on sentry to keep all troops in the trenches under cover such as there is. Fritz has his observing balloons and can spot anything above here. I have a good position and can see for miles around Cite des Brebis, Maroc, Philosophe, the Old Hullo Road where we used to run like hell after taking the rations to Vermelles Dump and in the distance the village of Hulluch. It's a lovely morning but it rained hard last night and it's all white chalk, mud and slush. Old Steve just sent me up a tin of Woodbines from up Cite des Brebis as he thought I had run out.

Went up to the front line and looking over the top you could see several dead bodies lay there. These looked like ours so l expect they were the Canadians and there had been no chance to bury them. I could see one lay there with no head or shoulders. Came back and helped to take the rations off the limbers and that finished another day.

September 7th

Fritz tried to come over last night but did not succeed. There was a terrible bombardment for an hour so I expect we were ready for him., No casualties, only a few of them got buried but were soon got out. Fritz just sent in am and killed one and wounded three of our bombers.

Found some of Fritz's bombs, took out the fuses and hope to get them home. While going up the line looking for machine gun belts, which we are short of, came across two Fritz. Evidently, they had been on sentry for they laid there in the trench (a side one) the flesh was turning black and covered with flies and maggots and the stench was awful. A little further along one laid across a dugout, evidently, he had made a dash to get in but was caught before he could get down. A little further on we trod on another body with his leg sticking out and a little further on saw a Jack boot with half a leg in. Then we came back, had quite enough for one day.

Took rations off the limbers and brought them in then off to kip.

In October, he was witness to a terrible incident, while men from the battalion were getting ready to take part in a working party:

Wednesday October 3rd
While some of our boys were lined up in Maroc ready to move Fritz sent over a couple of shells and killed 9 right out and wounded 30. Some of those killed were going on leave tomorrow. Hadn't been home for 17 months, hard luck. Just been up to Maroc with some field (shell) dressings for the Dr. Saw where the shells fell. Up to the present there are 11 dead, awful lot of blood about. They had to pick up the pieces and put them in blankets, some could not be recognised.

This incident obviously affected him because he sent a postcard home to his family, which still exists today. On the front is a picture of a cemetery in Maroc for the French 152nd Division, a card that is very typical of the time. On the back, he has written the following: 'We had 9 killed and 30 wounded quite close to here yesterday. Enemy threw over two shells. Two of those killed were down for leave and would have gone home tomorrow. Hard luck'.

In total, the battalion lost twelve men killed in this incident.

It would not be long after this that the battalion was taken out of the line and spent some time in positions around Armentières and then away from the front, having spent over six months constantly in and out of the Hill 70 area; although this would not last for long. Col. Prior noted that he spent this period of rest reflecting on what had occurred previously, and with this, he involved the entire battalion:

I set to work deliberately to induce all ranks to think out the 'whys and wherefores' of their actions in the field. I had really a rather difficult task and it certainly involved me in a lot of heavy work but I believe in result I sowed the seeds of an honest endeavour to appreciate the situation and a determination not to be entirely guided by rule of thumb but to use common sense and initiative.

Guidebook

My advice on this aspect is that the memorial to Hill 70 is your best bet if you want to visit the area where the 9th Battalion served during this period. This memorial can be accessed by coming off the A21 at Junction 8 signposted Loos-en-Gohelle. At the roundabout, turn right and take the D943. Continue on this road until you come to the roundabout and then turn right signposted Wingles. Take the next junction on your right, Rue Mirabeau, you will go straight over two small roundabouts. At the third roundabout turn right on Rue Louis Faidherbe and the memorial will then appear on your right.

What3words: forbid.leaky.codifies.

Your other option here is to visit the men who were killed in October 1917. Most of them are buried in Maroc British Cemetery, which is located in the village of Grenay. To get to the cemetery, you need to backtrack and return to the D943. When you get back to the roundabout turn right signposted Béthune. Continue on this road until you come to the next roundabout. Turn left here. Keep on this road and the cemetery will appear on your right. There are eight casualties buried here from the incident written about by James Cooper in his diary.

What3words: rehearsals.mercies.margarine.

22

The 1st and 8th Battalions, The Third Battle of Ypres: 31 July to 22 October 1917

By July 1917, they were in Flanders and trained for their participation in what would become known as the Third Battle of Ypres. This offensive came after the major success at the Battle of Messines, which was fought between 7 and 14 June 1917. This offensive's objective was to relieve the pressure on the French Army who had suffered greatly after the failed Nivelle Offensive and were now at risk of collapse after a series of mutinies. Haig planned a new summer offensive on the Ypres Salient and he appointed General Sir Hubert Gough, commander of 5th Army, to plan and implement an attack. The initial attack would fall on Messines Ridge, which dominated the area to the south of Ypres.

This plan utilised the firing of nineteen of twenty-one mines under the German lines and a preliminary bombardment that began of 21 May. Nine divisions, including the 3rd Australian and the New Zealand Divisions, attacked after the mines were fired. The battle is generally considered one of the most stunning victories of the war and caught the Germans completely by surprise. They lost well over 25,000 men in the seven-day battle but recovered enough to bolster their defences and the battle came to an end on 14 June with the British now holding the Messines Ridge.

The successes at Messines should have been carried, but there was a halt and the German 4th Army, which was on full alert, soon guessed that there was going to be second offensive on their front. The architect of Messines, General Herbert Charles Onslow Plumer, advocated continuing the attack immediately into Passchendaele ridge, arguing that the morale of the German troops was, for the present at least, broken, and that this combined with a shortage of forces would virtually guarantee Allied capture of the ridge. Haig, however, disagreed, choosing not to bring forward his plans from the end of July.

The defences here were built upwards due to the high water table, the origin of the word Flanders can be traced to medieval times and it can be translated to the term 'Flooded Plain', and the German trenches were interlaced with machine-gun positions protected by concrete pillboxes. The Allied offensive was hampered by delay, and the artillery bombardment did not start until 18 July, ten days prior to the launch of the attack, and it made use of 3,000 guns, which expended four and a quarter million shells. This led General Friedrich Bertram Sixt von Armin, the commander of the German 4th Army, to fully expect that an imminent offensive was on the cards.

The Third Battle of Ypres was opened by Sir Hubert Gough's 5th Army, with 1st Corps of Sir Herbert Plumer's 2nd Army joining on its right and a corps of the French 1st Army, led by General Francois Paul Anthoine, to its left, in total twelve divisions, and did not start until 31 July when they pushed outwards of Ypres towards the north-east.

However, the Germans soon recovered and counterattacked. The advance was also hampered by rain, which fell on the first night. This rain, the heaviest of the war, flooded friend and foe alike and the offensive could only make a gain of 2 miles before grinding to a halt.

The 18th (Eastern) Division had the job of following the 30th Division who were given the task of advancing on Glencorse Wood and stopping midway through the wood on what was called the 'Black Line' and then capturing and consolidating the 'Blue Line', which ran parallel and intersected Nonne Bosschen. The 53rd Brigade, to which the 8th Battalion were part of, was placed on the left of the 30th Division and would leapfrog them when they had reached their objective. There is a detailed after-action report for this day:

31st July 1917

The part played by the 8th Norfolk Regiment in the attack on the 31st July can be divided into two phases:

1. The advance (in accordance with programme already issued) from the assembly positions in West Bund of Zillebeke Lake and Railway Dugouts to the R.E. Dump in Zillebeke Village and Ritz Street area beyond.
2. After 'A', 'B' and 'D' Companies had been ordered to 'Stand-Fast' and c Company had proceeded on to the firing line and had become involved in the fighting.

First Phase

The Battalion proceeded to the assembly positions during the night of 30th/31st July as below:

'A' and 'D' Companies—Railway Dugouts

'B' and 'C' Companies—Zillebeke Bund

Battalion Headquarters at Chateau Segard at 10 p.m. with Advd. Battalion Headquarters in Zillebeke West Bund.

In accordance with the Brigade programme 'C' Company advanced from West Bund of Zillebeke Lake at 8.50 a.m. on the 31st July, and proceeded to the R.E. Dump and Zillebeke; 'B', 'A' and 'D' Companies following in order at 10-minute intervals.

'C' and 'B' Companies having drawn their stores at the R.E. Dump proceeded to the Ritz Street area.

In reality, the 30th Division attacked Chateau Wood and the 53rd Brigade moved into the gap they made; the lead battalions, the 8th Suffolk and 8th Berkshire Regiments, met strong German fire and suffered heavy casualties from German strongpoints at Clapham Junction and Surbiton Villas:

Owing to the fact that the 30th Division had failed to get their first objective (Blue Line), at about 10:10 a.m. a message was received from the Brigade by Capt. F.J. Morgan, who was commanding 'B' Company ordering companies not to advance any further and to get under cover.

On receipt of this order B.H.Q. moved up from Chateau Segard to the Advd. B.H.Q. in Zillebeke Bund arriving there about 12.45 p.m.

'C' Company, however, in accordance with their timetable had left the line of Stanley Street at 10 a.m. and had proceeded towards the Blue Line.

'A', 'B' and 'D' Companies having halted on receipt of the message from Brigade and got their men under cover, remained in the Ritz Street area and the Promenade until 5 p.m. in the afternoon when they were ordered by Brigade to withdraw to their original assembly positions.

On arrival of these companies in their assembly positions B.H.Q. was withdrawn again to Chateau Segard, leaving Advd. B.H.Q. in Zillebeke Bund.

The 8th Battalion started to the west of Zillebeke Lake along a long from south to north from Railway Dugouts to the western bank of the lake (Zillebeke Bund). At 10 a.m., 'C' Company advanced as per their timetable and moved through a heavy barrage under the command of Captain Arthur Patten. They reached the Blue Line at 10.55 a.m. and found out that the 8th Division was held up. He then came under heavy fire from the north-west edge of Glencourse Wood:

Second Phase

'C' Company in the meanwhile had proceeded to the Blue Line through a fairly heavy barrage in No Man's Land.

This company crossed the Blue Line at about 10.55 a.m. at the point where the 'A.T.N. Mule Track' was to have cut the Blue Line Capt. A.J.H. Patten met the Brigade Intelligence Officer who informed him that the Brigade had been held up on the left. Capt. Patten therefore continued straight on the left boundary of the Division up to the point J.7.d.88.10, where his company came under heavy rifle and machine gun fire from the N.W. corner of Glencorse Wood. He therefore extended the three [platoons who were with him, on the line J.7.d.88.10–88.20 and j.7.d.83.10–83.20 and proceeded forward himself to make a reconnaissance and find out the situation.

Capt. Patten discovered Capt. A. Hudson who was then commanding the left company of the 6th Royal Berkshire Regiment with a very weak company holding the line J.7.d.95.10–95.20.

It was then noticed that the enemy were advancing in extended order east of Stirling castle and also in artillery formation behind the N.E. corner of Glencourse Wood. Capt. Patten at once decided to bring up his company owing to the weakness, through casualties, of the left Coy, 6th Royal Berkshire Regt and also to the fact that the 2nd Lincolns of the 8th Division on our left were approximately 350 yards from the Boundary-Line between the 8th and 18th Divisions, presumably owing to machine gun fire from Glencorse Wood.

The necessary details having been arranged between Capt. Hudson and Capt. Patten, C Company moved up to a line J.7.d.88.14–88.35 which placed the company of the Berks slightly to the right of 'C' Company. This move was necessary owing to the fact that previously 'C' Company's fire had been masked by the company of the Berks in the shell holes in front.

Immediately this move had been completed 'C' Company opened fire on the enemy, who could clearly be seen east of Stirling Castle and in Glencorse Wood, with 3 Lewis Guns and all available rifles.

At about 12.30 p.m. the 4th platoon of 'C' Company together with the attached R.E. sections and attached infantry platoon arrived under the command of 2/Lieut A.E. Bentley, and were placed by Capt. Patten on the left flank, on a line J.7.d.83.35–83.45. This move enabled the troops under Capt. Patten's command to cover practically all the ground between the left of the 6th Royal Berks and the right of the 2nd Lincolns of the 8th Division.

A patrol was then sent across to the 2nd Lincolns to get into close touch with the 8th Division, but this patrol was unfortunately shot down by the enemy and subsequently attempts to send men across met with similar results.

It was then noticed that the Germans were preparing to attack from Stirling Castle and the north-east corner of Glencorse Wood:

Throughout the afternoon and evening 'C' Company with the attached section of R.E. and attached infantry platoon kept up a steady rifle and Lewis Gun fired on any enemy who appeared in the vicinity of Glencorse Wood and this fire appears to have had a very harassing effect on the enemy, since although many of them were seen attempting to form up in parties they were invariably driven back under cover again by this fire.

During the afternoon the enemy directed a very heavy and accurate bombardment on the line of shell holes held by 'C' Company.

Patten identified that there was a gap between him and the 8th Division after the 2nd Lincolns had been forced back 350 yards by determined enemy fire from Glencorse Wood. He therefore attempted to plug that gap by slotting in next to the reduced company of Berkshires. He then ordered his platoons to open fire on the Germans.

At about 3.30 p.m. the left company of the 6th Royal Berkshire Regiment had lost all their officers and were reduced to about 21 O.Rs, so Capt. Patten took command of these and informed a Sergeant who he found in charge of them that he was to act under him.

A platoon of King's Liverpool Regt (30th Division) and few of the 10th Essex (Moppers-up) who had been in the vicinity the whole time, were taken command of by Capt Patten, owing to the fact that both the left company of the Berks and his company had suffered a considerable number of casualties.

As soon as it was dusk, and machine gun and rifle fire of the enemy became less accurate, Capt Patten made a personal reconnaissance of the whole of his front and reorganised all troops then under his command into 4 strong points as below:

The left company of the 6th Royal Berkshire Regiment J.7.d.95.10

Half of C Company, 8th Norfolk Regt J.7.d.83.20

The remaining half of C Company 8th Norfolk Regiment J.7.d.85.35

The platoon of the King's Liverpool Regt (30th Div),

1 section of R.E. (79th Field Coy), 1 Composite

Infantry Platoon attached to the R.E. J.7.d.85.45

Some 'Moppers-up' of the 10th Essex Regt (53rd Inf. Bde) were disposed to the left and right rear of the above 4 strong points.

Consolidation had already been started during daylight but after darkness considerable work was done since the enemy could no longer direct accurate machine gun and rifle fire on men moving about in the open. This consolidation was carried out throughout the night and at about 3.30 a.m. C Company and attached troops were relieved and returned to the West Bund of Zillebeke Lake.

They carried on in the same light all day whilst constantly under the fire from German artillery. Casualties were high and Patten eventually ended up with a mixture of Berkshire, King's Liverpool and Essex Regiment men.

The war diary noted that all of the casualties for the day were from 'C' Company and that amounted to three officers wounded and forty other ranks killed, wounded, or missing. The battalion would now go into a period of rest and would not go back into action until 10 August 1917.

Guidebook

From Ypres, take the N336, Rijselweg, and turn left before the railway crossing, which takes you onto Komensweg. You will pass Railway Dugouts Cemetery and then on your left will see parking area for mobile homes. You can take the track here that takes you up to a B&B called Vijverhuis. With the lake on your right you can look to the left and the area running on that side of the road as you look up toward the Vijverhuis is situated is where the 8th Battalion were positioned for the start of 3rd Ypres.

What3words: feel.saunas.enhances.

Now travel toward Verbranden–Molen and turn left at the next junction signposted Zillebeke. Drive through Zillebeke until you come a junction with a signpost on the left for Menen. Take this road which will bring you up to a large roundabout, which was once a large crossroads known as Hellfire Corner. Take the road signposted Geluveld.

An optional visit can be taken here if you want to look at the Hooge Crater Cemetery. Eighteen men from the Norfolk Regiment are buried here from the 1st and 8th Battalions.

What3words: properly.surrendered.tadpoles.

* * * * *

At Zero Hour, set for 4.35 a.m. on 10 August 1917, in what became known as the Capture of Westhoek, II Corps attacked. The initial advance on all fronts was successful with the left flank and the village of Westhoek being captured by the 74th Brigade of the 25th Division. The 8th Battalion after-action report picks up the story:

10th August 1917,

At about 7.30 on the 10th August, a warning message was received from the brigade to the effect that the Battalion was to be ready to proceed to the Chateau Segard area and possibly up to the trenches in front of Inverness Copse, to take part in an attack about 7 p.m. in order to capture the N.W. corner of this wood, which objective, the 55th Infantry Brigade had been unable to take in their attack that morning. At about 8:30 a.m. orders were received for the Battalion to move at once to the Chateau Segard area. This move was completed by 11.30 a.m. The Battalion remained in this area until 2 p.m. with the Commanding Officer and Adjutant at Divisional Headquarters. We were then ordered to move to the Ritz Street area where we would come under the orders of G.O.C., 54th Infantry Brigade. This move was completed by 3.30 p.m., the Commanding Officer and Adjutant joining the Battalion at about 6 p.m. at 54th Inf. Bde. H.Q.

Orders were then received from G.O.C. 54th Inf. Bde. that the Battalion, together with the 6th Royal Berkshire Regiment, was to take over the front of the 54th Inf. Bde. with as little delay as possible. Company Commanders were therefore sent off at once to reconnoitre the line. On their return the G.O.C., 54th Inf. Bde, owing to a report that the enemy were concentrating for a counter attack, ordered two companies to move at once to the line. This move was carried out by one company of the 8th Norfolk Regt. Owing to the difficulty of the 54th nf. Bde in supplying guides, the remainder of the Battalion did not move up until 7.30 p.m. Orders were then issued to the Commanding Officer to the following effect:

(i)   That on arrival at the front line, he was to take command of all units then in the line.

(ii) In event of the situation becoming critical and the enemy developing an attack or capturing any part of the line then held, he was to counter attack with the 6th Royal Berkshire Regiment, holding the 8th Norfolk Regiment in support.

(iii) That the Jargon Trench line as far as J.14.a.5.6—the strong point J.14.a.3.2—and thence to J.13.d..9.9. (The Ypres–Menin Road exclusive, was to be held at all costs.

(iv) That he was to remain in command until the completion of the relief, when he would come under orders of the G.O.C. 53rd Infantry Brigade.

On receipt of these orders, the Commanding Officer at once moved up to the forward Battalion Headquarters, situated in the tunnel at the bend in the Ypres–Menin Road. On arrival he found that the O.C. of the 6th Royal Berkshire Regiment had been brought up a short time previously by a guide of the 54th Infantry Brigade, had commenced to take over the Jargon Trench line as far as J.14.a.5.6. and had sent on 'A' Company of the 8th Norfolk Regt. to endeavour to take over the strong point at J.14.a.3.2 and the switch trench between this strong point and Jargon Trench at J.14.a.5.6.

The Commanding Officer had previously decided that the dispositions of the battalion were to be as follows:

'A' Company in the front line from J.14.a.5.6, to the strong point (inclusive) at J.14.a.3.2.

'D' Company in the front line from the strong point (exclusive) to J.13.d.9.9 (The Ypres–Menin Road exclusive), 'B' Company in support and C Company in reserve in the trench system around Surbiton Villa.

The remaining companies, therefore, followed after 'A' Company but owing to the darkness, the lack of guides, and the confusion in the trenches held by the 54th Infantry Brigade, due to the heavy fighting which had taken place that day, the relief was carried out under very trying conditions, and although the relief was reported complete at 3 a.m., it would appear that elements of the 11th Royal Fusiliers, 7th Bedford Regiment, 6th Northants Regiment and 2 machine gun teams were still holding a line approximately from J.14.a.35.20 to J.14.a.35.16, and there were also a few of the 11th Royal Fusiliers between 'A' and 'D' Companies at approximately J.14.a.30.18.

The right flank, however, was not as successful. The 55th Brigade, notably the 7th Queens had advanced from the eastern edge of Inverness Copse but had been stopped by a machine-gun post and had failed to occupy the southern edge of the copse. They retreated, being closely pursued by the enemy who re-took the copse and the 7th Queens failed to carry out any further advances losing ten officers and 272 other ranks.

Facing the 74th Brigade, and positioned to the north-west of Polygon Wood, was Musketier Bär of the 7th Company Reserve Infantry Regiment 278:

> Punctually at the appointed time we began the assault. Despite sinking at times up to our chests in water as we waded through the boggy Hanebeek, we headed in the direction of the Wupzaal up above us. There was nothing to be seen but a few destroyed houses and concrete pillboxes. We were greeted by a hail of bullets from British machine guns and took casualties as a result. However, we were soon through the swamp and close up against the buildings. Although we were reduced to a small group, the British escaped to the rear. Had we received reinforcements at that moment, we should have been able to force our way back into the Albrecht Stellung. That was certainly the view of our officers, but unfortunately, we were too weak; all we could do was to take up hasty defence and keep a sharp lookout, in order to ensure that we were not overrun by the enemy. They had taken up positions about 150–200 metres to our front. Suddenly I saw a British soldier, probably a runner, making his way to the rear carrying a large file.
>
> With one shot I brought him down. We spent a long-time bringing fire down on the enemy. The British tried repeatedly to advance, but were unsuccessful.

The 54th Brigade had far better success, occupying the German second line around Fitzclarence Farm and the eastern end of Glencourse Wood, and although German resistance was seen to be thinly held, with the forward lines offering little resistance, it was noted by the official history that it was easier to capture than to hold what had been taken.

Just after 6 a.m., the Germans fired a box-barrage designed to stop any reserves being brought up and launched localised counterattacks. All requests to bring up reserves were initially refused, and when permission was granted to move up the 53rd Brigade, they did not reach their assembly area until 7 p.m. But, by that time, it was too late, and by then, most of what had been gained was back in German hands.

At 5.30 p.m., they took over the 54th Brigade's front with the 6th Battalion Royal Berkshire Regiment. Although this relief was met with confusion the Germans did not attack and only did so at 4.30 a.m. on 11 August. At this time, the Germans attacked just as the battalion was relieving the 7th Bedfords, and the enemy captured a strongpoint and broke through, especially in the line held by 'A' and 'D' Companies:

> At about 4.15 a.m. on 11th August, the enemy commenced a light barrage on the front line held by this Battalion. At 4.30 am. this barrage became intense and under

cover of this the enemy launched an attack in strength on the strong point and the line held by the Battalion. Within a short time, the Commanding Officer the 11th Battalion Royal Fusiliers who had still remained at Battalion Headquarters until all his men were out of the front line, reported that the enemy had penetrated that portion of the strong point held by the men of his Battalion.

'B' Company was told to be ready to counterattack, but it was found that although 'A' Company had been forced back the left flank was still holding and 'C' Company was ordered to counter and take back the strongpoint. This was held by four machine guns and the CO, Col. Ferguson, decided to make a converging attack using 'C' and 'B' Companies:

> As soon as the S.O.S. Signal, which had been sent up from the front-line at 4:35 a.m., was reported to the Commanding Officer, orders were issued for B Company to hold themselves in readiness to counter attack immediately. A message then being received from a platoon Sergeant of the right platoon of A Company stating that the right flank of his company had been driven back, but the left was still holding on, the Commanding Officer ordered 'C' Company to counter attack at once and re-capture the strong point and any portion of the switch trench N.E. of the strong point that had been occupied by the enemy. On going forward and finding that the enemy who were in occupation of the strong point had brought 4 machine guns into action and appeared to be in considerable strength, the Commanding Officer decided to strike with his reserve company ('B' Company) from the right flank simultaneously with 'C' Company who were striking from the immediate front.
>
> Under covering fire of Lewis Guns and snipers, with the assistance of one platoon of the 6th Royal Berkshire Regiment, this attack was carried out by sectional rushes and the strong point recaptured and consolidated. The counter attack had been launched at 5.25 a.m. and the position was again in our hands by 6 a.m., together with 9 prisoners, our own two machine guns and elements of the garrison which had been captured by the enemy.

The attack went in with the support of Lewis Gunners and snipers and was assisted by a platoon of the 6th R. Berks and the strongpoint was recaptured. Capt. Frederic Morgan led this attack, and after the capture of the strongpoint, the enemies' fire slackened and 'B' and 'C' Company were able to support each other. In this attack, Capt. Morgan was severely wounded:

> This attack was carried out over a distance of 600 yards through very difficult country under direct observation from the strong point, and owing to the fact that the enemy was then in possession of the high ground, he was able to sweep the whole line of advance of the counter attack with machine gun and rifle fire. After our counter attack had been launched, the enemy's artillery and machine gun fire slackened

considerably on the front of the right company and this company was able to give excellent covering fire for the troops carrying out the counter attack, thus inflicting by enfilade fire, very heavy losses on the enemy who were running about in the open and endeavouring to form up between the strong point and Inverness Copse.

A German soldier, *Offizierstellvertreter* Alt, of 4th Company Reserve Infantry Regiment 271, recounted his experience of moving up to the front to face these attacks:

Finally, we were stood to during the morning of 8 or 9 August and moved forward. Bombs were being dropped from aircraft all over the area, making the whole enterprise risky. We took cover in a roadside ditch just to the east of Zonnebeke and waited for whatever we might be called upon to do. All kinds of materiel and the bodies of dead horses were strewn here and there along the shot-up road. They were giving off an appalling stench. Stray shells fell in amongst the troops with terrible results; numerous men were killed or wounded. A direct hit amongst a pile of ammunition belonging to a battery stationed right by the road blew the whole lot up. Eventually we were moved back to the rear.

A line was then reorganised and 'A' Company was put into the line to the left of the strongpoint, held by 'C' Company, and the right of the line was held by 'B' Company with 'D' Company in reserve at Surbiton Villas.

The Germans attempted to counterattack on a number of occasions, and each one was repulsed and the line held. They were relieved on 12 August 1917 and were sent back to Railway Dugouts. A German Army *communiqué* for 11th August noted:

The British attacks of yesterday morning were conducted by several divisions. On a frontage of more than eight kilometres between Frezenberg and Hollebeke the enemy advanced but, despite the deployment of strong forces, they enjoyed no success.

Initially the deeply echeloned assaulting enemy succeeded in breaking into our lines in several places, but they were thrown back once more by means of swiftly-mounted counter-attacks by our supports. In the case of Westhock (where 54th Infantry Division was deployed) this was not until after long hard fighting.

I am often contacted by people or have conversations with them on social media. Recently I spoke to Shannon Taylor, whose relative served with the 8th Battalion. John Wells came from Santon Downham and enlisted in December 1915 and went to France in December 1916.

He had contracted scabies while the battalion was in trenches around Irles in March 1917 and also received a gunshot wound four days layer on 10 March 1917 and was admitted to No. 10 Hospital in Rouen. John recovered from that so that he was present during the attack on 11 August and was killed in action during the fighting. He has no known grave and is commemorated on the Menin Gate. John was aged twenty-nine when he was killed and was the husband of Lily Emily Wells of 90 London Road in Brandon.

His death was reported in the *Brandon Times*, which stated that a sniper's bullet had killed him and he left a young daughter 'Joan' who was only ten months old when he was killed. My thanks go to Shannon for providing me with this information.

Also lost on this day was Sammy Riches who has no known grave and is commemorated on the Menin Gate.

Guidebook

At Glencorse Wood, take Wulverstraat and head towards Geluveld. You will pass a turning on the right and in the field on your left is where Fitzclarence Farm was situated; this formed the right flank of the 8th Battalion for 11 August 1917. The battalion was therefore positioned from this point and then toward Glencourse Wood. It was in this area that they fought to hold onto the strongpoint mentioned in the narrative.

What3words: soapy.decreases.streetcar.

* * * * *

During a battlefield tour in June 2017, I found three Norfolk Regiment graves in Lijssenthoek Cemetery. Not knowing much about them, I photographed them and then looked into their deaths when I got home.

They are Lt Douglas Arthur Leamon, who was the youngest son of Philip Augustus and Lucy Leamon of Headingley in Manitoba who was born in Norwich; Lt Wilfred Robert Williamson who was the son of Annie Sophia Williamson of 67 Cecile Park Crouch End London and the late William Pope Williamson; and Lt James Andrew Lewton-Brain who was the son of James and Clara Lewton Brain of The Rookery in Yaxham who was born at Swanton Morley.

All three officers died from the effects of gas when a phosgene shell penetrated the dugout they were in at Railway Dugouts near Zillebeke. A total of eleven officers and twelve other ranks were affected by the gas, seven officers being seriously affected—all of whom were evacuated.

This incident is covered in the after-action report for this time, which explains what happened:

> During the night of the 13/14th August, the enemy bombarded all tracks in the vicinity of Railway Dug-Outs and the Southern edge of Zillebeke Bund, a few shells falling in very close proximity to the Battalion billets.

At 12.30 a.m. 14th August, an enemy gas shell (5.9 Phosgene) penetrated the roof of a shelter occupied by C Company Officers of Junior Headquarters, exploding inside and completely blocking up the entrance to the shelter.

The 7 officers inside were unable to get out and could not at first put on their box respirators owing to the falling debris and general confusion. 2nd Lt Chapman, however, managed to escape through the hole in the roof caused by the shell and returning, succeeded in rescuing the remainder of the officers including 2nd Lieut A Bentley, who had also been wounded by fragments of the shell. All these officers were then suffering severely from gas poisoning.

In the meantime, the alarm had been given from Battn H.Q. situated in a shelter within a few feet of one mentioned above, and which was also filled with gas fumes, affecting to some degree the Commanding Officer, Second in Command, Adjutant, Medical Officer and Chaplin who were sleeping inside. The officers who had been seriously gassed were kept out in the open until about 3.45 a.m. when after testing the air it was found that practically all the gas had disappeared. These officers were then brought in under cover, permitted to take off their box respirators and hot drinks and ammonia capsules given to them. As soon as it was light these officers were sent down on stretchers to the A.D.S. During the period between 12.30 a.m. the enemy had sent over a large number of gas shells and H.E. of heavy calibre, most of which fell in the area between Transport Farm and the Railway arch, against which Battalion Headquarters was situated.

Our casualties in this gas bombardment amounted to 7 officers seriously affected, 4 officers and 12 O.R.s slightly affected and remaining at duty.

In total, eleven officers and twelve other ranks were affected by the gas shell. Of this total, the three officers mentioned all were evacuated and are listed as having died of gas poisoning (shell), No. 17 CCS, although Lt Leamon is recorded as having died in the ambulance before reaching the CCS.

The CO of the 8th Battalion wrote to Lt Lewton Brain's parents, noting:

I can hardly express to you what a loss he is to all of us, both officers and men of this battalion. He was a splendid stamp of officer, and a good leader, and was my Battalion Machine Gun Officer, and of great value to me. And as we are in action at the moment of writing, it is difficult for me to give you many particulars; but he died a few hours after his attack, so, please God, he did not suffer too much. He was so popular with us all, we shall miss him terribly.

His passing was also reported in the *Yarmouth Independent* on 25 August 1917:

NORFOLK OFFICER DIES OF WOUNDS
FIVE YEARS AT YARMOUTH.
Official news has just been received that Lieutenant James Andrew Lewton-Brain, Norfolk Regiment, third son of Mr, J. Lewton-Brain, of Toftwood, East Dereham,

has died of wounds and gas. Lieutenant J. A. Lewton-Brain was a native of Swanton Morley. He was educated at King Edward VII. Grammar School, King's Lynn.

After leaving School, choosing a financial career, he obtained a post in the London and Provincial Bank, and was stationed at Great Yarmouth, where he remained five years. He then received an appointment in the Bank of Montreal, and was stationed at the Vancouver branch for three years, when he was transferred to the Victoria branch as cashier, and remained there until the outbreak of the war when he immediately enlisted in the Canadian Highlanders.

He came over to England with his battalion in April, 1915, and remained here only a fortnight, when he was sent on active service to France, where he served for nine months, and in January, 1916, received his commission, and was attached to the Norfolks. He was gazetted as lieutenant at the end of April 1917. He was well-known in the Dereham and Yarmouth districts as an enthusiastic football player and cricketer. He was one of the Dereham team who won the county shield.

A brother officer also wrote: 'He was very popular amongst us all; not only the officers, but all the men who knew him well. I can assure you that your loss is shared by us all; his place will be hard to fill in our midst'. There was no let up for this loss, and on the same day, the report notes:

At about 8.30 a.m. on receiving definite information about the situation the Commanding Officer decided to re-organise the companies in the line. Accordingly, 'A' Company took over the portion of the line from the strong point (exclusive) to J.14.a.5.6, C Company (who were considerably weakened by casualties) the strong point; B Company from the strong point (exclusive) to J.13.d.9.9 (The Ypres–Menin Road exclusive): D Company were withdrawn from the line into reserve in the area around Surbiton Villas.

During the evening of the 11th and the night of the 11th/12th, the enemy made several attempts to recapture this strong point but was easily driven off on each occasion, the position having been wired and consolidated in the meantime.

The 8th Battalion moved back to a position called Crab Crawl. Conditions here were terrible:

At 4.30 p.m. on the same day an order was received from the Brigade for the whole battalion to proceed to Crab Crawl where the accommodation was to be provided by the area officer preparatory to assisting in an attack on the 16th inst. Accordingly the Battalion moved off by platoons from Railway dugouts at 8 p.m. and arrived at Crab Crawl shortly after 11 p.m. Crab Crawl is situated on the Observatory Ridge at about I.24.d.7.4 and consists of a long oval shaped tunnel with underground 'T' heads and 'recesses' for troops. The passage measurements are about 6ft by 1ft and there are about eight or nine entrances.

On arrival it was found that there were already two companies of the 6th Royal Berkshire Regiment, a Machine Gun company and various R.E. personnel and elements from a Battalion of North Staffordshire Regiment and 8th Queens Royal West Surrey Regiment. An endeavour was made to put the whole Battalion in the tunnel as well, and in fact, this move was actually carried out since there were no trenches in the vicinity to afford cover from the heavy shelling which the enemy was concentrating on Observatory Ridge. After examination of the tunnel it was found that it was absolutely impossible to keep so many men down there under such fearful conditions.

The whole of the passage ways were completely blocked with troops and owing to the 'blow-holes' at the end of the 'T' heads having been knocked in by the enemy shell fire the atmosphere in the tunnel became so bad that immediate action had to be taken. The pumps also having broken down, portions of the tunnel were flooded ankle deep and the filth and mud involved were indescribable

The matter was at once reported to Brigade by telephone and two companies were withdrawn back to Railway dug-outs under instruction from Brigade. This move slightly eased the situation and the remaining two companies were able to spread-out slightly and give themselves more freedom and space.

Some men who had been at the dead ends of the 'T' heads where there were no 'blow-holes' were slightly affected and when candles were lit in an endeavour to find the equipment of these men it was impossible to keep the candles alight in that atmosphere, a fact witnessed by the Medical Officer and one of the Company Commanders.

The advance was ordered to continue and the orders were simple and to the point, with the war diary for the 7th Battalion Bedfordshire Regiment stating: '1. The II Corps will capture and hold at an early date Inverness Copse, Glencourse Wood and the Southern end of Westhoek Ridge'.

By now, as we have already seen, the 54th Brigade straddled the Menin Road facing in the direction of Glencorse Wood and Inverness Copse and formed the left flank of the division with the 25th Division to their left and the 55th Brigade to their right. The 24th Division would support the 18th Division on the right.

This whole area, but especially Glencorse Wood and Inverness Copse, was bombarded between 8 and 9 August, with 3,000 heavy and medium shells being fired on Glencourse Wood on the 8th. There would only be a forty-six-minute pause in this bombardment for the 18th Division to attack and capture its objectives and only twenty-five minutes for the 25th Division to do the same.

The 7th Bedfords were positioned just to the east of a position known Surbiton Villas and roughly parallel to an old German trench known as Jargon Switch.

At Zero Hour, set for 4.35 a.m. on 10 August 1917, II Corps attacked. The initial advance on all fronts was successful with the left flank and the village of Westhoek being captured by the 74th Brigade of the 25th Division. The right flank, however, was not as successful. The 55th Brigade, notably the 7th Queens had advanced from the eastern edge of Inverness Copse but had been stopped by a machine-gun post and had failed to occupy the southern edge of the copse.

On 12 August, the 7th Battalion Bedfordshire regiment were ordered to join the 53rd Brigade and they also have an after-action report to describe in detail what happened to them:

> The Battalion was reorganised into four companies of two platoons each, each platoon had one rifle section one rifle grenadier section one bombing section one L/G section. Total Battalion strength about 300. Orders were received from Division to move into a field close to Div.H.Q. and rest there until the evening.
>
> After dinners the Battalion moved to the field mentioned where the Div.General (General Lee) address a few words to the men and thanked them for their gallant behaviour in the action of August 10th.
>
> He also said that he had given instructions (that) we were not to be used unless absolutely necessary. The afternoon having been spent in receiving SAA rations etc the companies moved off at 6.30 p.m. 'A' and 'D' companies to Crab Crawl 'C' and 'B' and H.Q. to Railway Dugouts.

The initial moves made by the 7th Bedfords went well and they had taken their objectives by 5.13 a.m. after clearing out around 150 Germans and destroying two machine guns in Glencourse Wood. The report notes that those Germans left alive surrendered by running forward shouting '*KAMERAD!*' Once they had reached the new line fighting patrols were sent out to the south-western end of Nonne Bosschen Wood where the barrage was still being fired. The battalion then set about consolidating the line. Throughout the day, the Germans tried to counterattack but were beaten off with rifle and machine-gun fire, but by the afternoon, this was beginning to run out and the right flank risked being overrun because of this. Artillery support was called for but could not be given even though SOS flares were sent up.

However, no artillery came, and then in the evening, the Germans were seen to be forming up at Nonne Bosschen, Inverness Copse, and the south-western part of Polygon Wood. They then advanced under the cover of smoke and gas.

By 11 p.m., the war diary states, 'The Battalion was in support to 53rd Brigade'. The reason for this is that the 53rd Brigade had been given to the 56th Division who had taken over from the 18th and were now forming the southern flank of this fresh unit. On 13 August, the battalion waited to see if it was needed in support of the 53rd Brigade. However, a thunderstorm on 14 August postponed the next attack that was now set for the 16th. This became known as the Battle of Langemarck. The 7th Bedford received orders to relieve the 10th Essex Regiment at Stirling Castle and to prepare for an attack on the 16th.

This came as a surprise to the battalion having been promised not to be used unless absolutely necessary. However, they prepared for the attack. On 15 August, 'B' Company was given orders to prepare for an attack on a German strongpoint to the south of the Menin Road and just shy of the edge of Inverness Copse.

Assistance was given to the 7th Bedfordshires by the 8th Norfolks, their after-action report stating:

> During the attack on the morning of the 16th August the Battalion was distributed as follows: 'A' and 'C' Companies finding carrying parties under orders of the Staff captain, D Company employed under the 79th Field Company R.E. with orders to assist in the consolidation of the enemy strong point at the N.W. corner of Inverness Copse when captured, and B Company in reserve at Crab Crawl ready to take the place of the Reserve Company of the 12th Middlesex Regiment should this be called upon. During the evening when it had been ascertained that the strong point at the N.W. corner of Inverness Copse had not been captured D Company was sent back to Crab Crawl.

The failure of this attack can be seen in the 7th Bedfordshire's war diary, which states:

> 'B' Company having formed up on the tapes put out by 2nd Lt. Craig during the night attacked the enemy strong point at J14 c.4.4. This attack was carried out in conjunction with a large offensive by the Division on our left; a heavy shrapnel barrage opened at Zero Hour (4.45 a.m.) and 4.5 howitzers shot on strong points. Owing to some mistake a battery of 4.5 howitzers detailed to shoot on the enemy's strong point at J.14.c.4.4 fired short and on to our B Company about to move forward to the attack, knocking 50% of their effective strength out. Captain Ferguson at once supported with a platoon of 'D' Company but owing to the heavy enemy M.G. fire little could be done and the attempt to capture the strong point was abandoned. The day was chiefly spent in artillery duels no further infantry activity taking place on our sector.

The 8th Battalion now assisted in the defence of this area and was then relieved:

> Later the Commanding Officer was ordered to send one company to the Ypres–Menin Road Tunnel in the vicinity of Clapham Junction. 'B' Company were accordingly sent to support the 7th Bedford Regiment and D Company to the Menin Road Tunnel. 'A' and 'C' Companies remained at Dormy House but were later, together with Battalion Headquarters, sent to Railway dug outs.
>
> On the evening of the 17th August, 'B' and 'D' Companies were sent down from the line and rejoined the Battalion at Railway Dugouts. On the evening of the 17th August the Battalion moved back to the new Dickebusch Camp area and remained there for the night.

This action failed in this area with only minimal gains in this sector and a few gains in the north, around the town of Langemarck. The attack that 'B' Company of the 7th Bedfords assisted in was thwarted when the Germans poured artillery fire on the leading companies and then stopped the advance by pouring fire on the survivors with machine guns sited in Inverness Copse. During the night, what was left of the 7th Bedfords were relieved by the 12th Middlesex and they saw no more offensive action at Third Ypres. The after-action report finished with eight recommendations/observations on the attack and was made by the CO of the 7th Bedfords, Lt-Col. George Pilkington Mills, DSO.

For general interest, I have listed them:

Lessons:

1. I venture to think had a fresh Battalion been close at hand when the situation on the right became obscure and pushed in, in attack formation a good deal more ground would have been taken and the Bosche routed from his position.
2. Artillery should not cease firing on protected lines until Battalion Commander is satisfied all is well. Artillery ceased on the 10th without any reference to Battalions (at least not to 7th Bedfords). I consider it of great importance that Battalion Commanders should be able to convey to Artillery, which fire other than S.O.S. is required.
3. No telephone wire to be laid beyond Brigade HQ as it is used for all kinds of things that hopelessly give away arrangements, and too many other ranks have access to it and the Commanders of the sector having no knowledge of many things happening on the wire unless he or his Adjutant sits by it. The telephone was a nuisance and not the least assistance to the Battalion on the 10th inst.
4. It took from 5 to 6 minutes before the Hun Barrage got really going on our lines; it was severe when it did do so.
5. The 54th Brigade arrangements for ordering up the reserve Coys from RITZ area and the Coys for mopping up was excellent, timing was also extremely good.
6. To avoid any Platoon going astray I placed Battalion Police posts 100–200 yds apart along the ATN track from RITZ area to MENIN road passing point.
7. Our own Artillery inflicted many casualties on our troops by firing very short what appeared to be one 8″ gun in particular.
8. The Bosche attack was guided by a line of his men at a few paces apart firing very lights, during the advance these were with the first wave.

Another reason I have brought in the 7th Bedfords into this chapter is because a man from my village died in this action serving with them. George Grimes joined the 7th Battalion Bedfordshire Regiment who had been serving in France since July 1915.

The casualty list for the 7th Bedfords records that between 10 and 17 August 1917, they lost seven officers killed, wounded, or missing and 259 other ranks went the same way. Of this total, George is listed as being wounded but did not recover and he died of his wounds on 25 October 1917.

He got as far as being moved to one of three CCS around the town of Westvleteren, which is situated to the west of the front. All three were prepared for the forthcoming offensive and were given the nicknames of Mendinghem (Mending them), Dozinghem (Dosing them), and Bandaghem (Bandaging them). He is now laid to rest in grave X. D. 9. in Dozinghem Military Cemetery.

I have visited George's grave on numerous occasions, and he now lies in a beautiful cemetery surrounded by trees and farmer's fields in a very peaceful part of Flanders Fields. I often wonder if he knew that the 8th Norfolks were close by in this action.

The casualty list for the 8th Norfolks is recorded as being sixteen officers killed or wounded with 175 other ranks killed or wounded. That can be amended to sixty-seven men killed between 10 and 17 August 1917.

Guidebook

If you remained at Railway Dugouts Cemetery, you are now in the area where the gas attack happened. The men were positioned in the railway embankment and the farm you see next to the cemetery is where Transport Farm was situated. Two men who were killed in the attack on Westhoek are also buried in the cemetery.

What3words: grin.competent.either.

A focal point of the fighting here is the area around Clapham Junction. Take the Menin Road from Ypres and after about a mile you will across two memorials. The one on the right-hand side is the 18th (Eastern) Division memorial for this sector. This includes the 8th Battalion Norfolk Regiment. This stands at Clapham Junction and was placed here due to this area being heavily fought over by the division in July and August 1917.

What3words: wasps.digger.whitish.

Across the road, you will see a small road. Take this and you will eventually come to a T-junction. Turn left and you will see Glencorse Wood in front of you. This is where the 8th Battalion ended up on 31 July 1917. There is a small road that intersects through the wood, which you can take if you would like to at this point (also see the next chapter for areas of interest in this area).

What3words: tape.flimsey.unbolted.

✻ ✻ ✻ ✻ ✻

After Oppy Wood, the 1st Battalion Norfolk Regiment had spent time around Beaumont but on 25 September 1917, it returned to Ypres, a place they had not served around since 1915. On 1 October, they went into the reserve trenches around Dickebusch Lake.

After a brief spell in reserve, they were moved up to the front and were put into the line facing the Polderhoek Chateau. They had the 1st Cheshires on their left and the 16th Warwickshires on their right.

Malcolm Ross, a war correspondent with the New Zealand Forces, described the chateau like this:

> Before the war Polderhoek Chateau was one of those pleasant Belgian country houses situated in the midst of beautiful woods and cultivated fields. But some time since the chateau and its contents went the way of all such things in the German war zone. The trees were whittled bare of branch and leaf and the fields were no longer good to look upon in all this region the Germans had made what, in the language of the soldiers, are known as 'strong points'.

By now, the weather had really set in and the ground around them was watery and described as 'obnoxious' with shell holes and craters filled with water. The conditions and difficulty with the weather are noted in their war diary:

> Moved from support trenches in the early morning for attack on Polderhoek Chateau. Coys got on their kicking off position about 4 am. Very dark night and pouring with rain. Companies had a very difficult task to get on the tape but they managed it successfully, much to the credit of their Coy commanders.

Hauptmann Wolf of Reserve Infantry Regiment 92 had moved into the chateau and occupied a bunker there on 3 October:

> I was Informed that the battalion was going to be relieved that evening. Naturally that suited me well, but things were to turnout differently. Battalion headquarters had a strange experience. Our concrete pillbox had originally been built Into Polderhoek chateau. When we first arrived some of the walls were still standing: gradually, however they disappeared, so this great white lump of light-coloured concrete stood out on the hill top, presenting a brilliant target that the British gunners just could not leave alone. Initially we and the surrounding area were engaged so heavily by medium calibre guns that not even a mouse could have escaped it.

Since we saw the initial actions by the 8th Battalion, there had been a series of battles fought around the Ypres Salient and the next action would be the start of the Battle of Poelcappelle. After gains had been made on 4 October, the next attack was planned for 9 October along a front of 13,500 yards. The intention here was to capture Passchendaele Ridge.

X Corps was to attack to hold German reserves around Becelaere and Gheluvelt. To the north, I Anzac Corps was to advance on the right flank of the main attack, with the 1st and 2nd Australian Divisions, the 4th and 5th Australian Divisions being in reserve.

Further north, II Anzac Corps with the New Zealand and 3rd Australian Divisions in reserve, was to attack two objectives, the 66th Division advancing along the main ridge, north of the Ypres–Roulers railway to just short of Passchendaele village and the 49th Division on either side of the Ravebeek stream, up Wallemolen spur to the Bellevue pillboxes.

If the first objectives were reached, the reserve brigades were to attack the second objectives in the afternoon. The second objectives were 800–1,000 yards ahead of the red line, beyond the village and the main ridge respectively. The reserve divisions were ready to move rapidly forward, by train from west of Ypres to continue the attack the next day.

On the 5th Army front, XVIII Corps with a brigade each from the 48th and 11th Divisions, was to advance 1,200 yards up to the Poelcappelle Spur and towards Westroosebeke on the main ridge. XIV Corps was to advance to the south edge of Houthoulst Forest with the 4th, 29th, and Guards Divisions, as the French First Army conformed on its left. Raids and artillery bombardments were arranged along the rest of the front, to deceive the Germans as to the objectives of the attacks.

There is an after-action report in the war diary of the 1st Norfolks so we can follow the progress of their battle on 9 October 1917. But in the main body of the war diary, there is a very brief summary, which states: 'Attacked the Chateau at 5:20 am. Attack was a failure owing to Battalion on our right apparently getting held up and losing direction. We had heavy casualties in officers and men'.

At 4 a.m., the battalion moved from support trenches to the front. 'C' Company would be on the right and 'A' Company on the left. 'B' Company would support both of the lead companies and 'D' Company was held in reserve. They moved up in complete darkness and in heavy rain.

The barrage on the German line lifted at 5.20 a.m. and the Norfolks followed the Warwickshires who were leading the advance. Sadly, both the rain and the darkness meant that the Norfolks veered off to the right and found themselves in front of the Château instead of the left of it. 'B' Company was sent up to support the two lead companies who began to falter. But enemy artillery and machine-gun fire began to take its toll, with no support from British artillery that had moved on. This led to heavy losses and no further progress could be made.

Hauptmann Wolf noted:

All my officers and men were fully occupied trying to make sure that we were not thrown out of our position and fortunately, thank heavens, they were in no position to see the counter-attack was beginning to falter and then suddenly be brought to a standstill five hundred metres behind us. But then things began to move once more. We flashed messages, fired flares into the air, then success! Our lines began to move once more.

They advanced, they pushed on beyond us. Our job was done. In front of me stood a regimental commander in his peacetime uniform, with its stand-up red collar. I think it was a regiment from Mecklenburg. He looked at his map, then asked me, 'Is that Polderhoek Chateau? Yes? Well that's a fine thing! It certainly was a fine thing.

They had reached Polderhoek Chateau and it was still being held by German troops, admittedly and unfortunately not very many of them. I shall never forget this day or the dear comrades with whom I experienced it.

The after-action report noted the following for the day:

1. Battalion formed up at zero—1:30 'A' Company on the left—'C' Coy on the right—'B' Coy in close support—'D' Coy in section reserve. 'D' Coy remained in reserve for counter attack purposes.
2. Our barrage lifting, the front line went forward but 'C' Coy and half of 'A' Coy made a right incline which brought them off their line and facing the Chateau.

Nos 1 and 2 Platoons followed the line, No 2 Platoon went slightly too much to their left and on reaching the objective found themselves isolated in front of the right of the Cheshire Regiment. They held on there till relieved on the night of the 10th–11th.

No 1 Platoon also went well forward about 400 yards. Then finding they had lost touch on the right, efforts were made to regain touch.

6 a.m. The Officer Commanding sent back a Sergeant to find out the situation. The Sergeant was wounded.

9 a.m. He then went back with a runner and was himself wounded.

9 p.m. Eventually the remnants of the Platoon re-joined the original front line by night.

5:30 a.m. Half 'A' Coy and 'C' Coy went half right and found themselves up against the Chateau

6 a.m. A retrograde movement on the part of these companies was checked by O.C. 'B' Coy who threw his company in. By this time the enemy had opened cross M.G. fire and was bombing from wing trenches near the Chateau and the barrage had gone on. No further progress was made. By night the Companies were re-organised and the old line held.

By 9 p.m. on 9th October 1917 the battalion was back where it had started and were out of the line by 11 p.m. The after-action report had this to say about the failure.

The Battalion moved to relieve the KOSB at 1 a.m. on the night of 5–6th

The Battalion had no casualties on this relief. The men had no great coats and suffered a good deal. Shelling went on all the while and losses were steady. The support companies suffered most from this shelling.

Trenches can easily be dug in but it is extremely difficult to keep them in good repair as the wet causes them to fall in.

They and all shell holes fill with water.

The men had no hot food all the time from leaving Bedford House till after relief on the night of the 10th–11th.

I think the failure was due to the worn condition of the men and the bad weather.

Acts of courage that day included Private Herbert Seago who was the only surviving company runner. He carried many messages under heavy fire and managed to lead a company to Battalion HQ when a guide had lost its way. For this, he was awarded the MM.

Private Alfred Johnson went forward into Château Wood and dressed wounded men and brought several out. The whole time it was reported that he did this under fire and showed complete disregard of the danger and saved many lives. Alfred was recommended for a DCM for this act of bravery, but in the end was awarded a MM instead.

Private Benjamin Curtis and Robert Jones brought in wounded men from different regiments who had been lying out in no-man's-land and continually searched for them. He did this even through there was a very real risk from snipers and machines guns. Both were awarded an MM. Losses on this day were high, with three officers killed and four wounded; other ranks casualties amounted to thirty-eight killed and 246 wounded or missing.

The day after the attack saw the battalion being commanded by one officer, and the wounded were left out in no-man's-land, with stragglers coming in all day. After they were relieved, the battalion was sent to Berthen, where it reorganised receiving drafts of men.

Guidebook

This is probably the most difficult site to find. On the Menin Road, having passed the theme park at Bellewaarde take the next left, Oude Kortrijkstr, this also has a CWGC signpost for the Princess Patricia's Canadian Light Infantry memorial. Continue on this road. You will pass Glencourse Wood on your left and also go by Polygon Wood. You will cross over the A19 motorway. Keep going until you reach crossroads with a restaurant on your right and at these crossroads turn right. Keep on this road until you see a turning on your right, which is marked as a dead end. Take this road and between two farm houses you will see a dirt track on your right. This is the original entrance to the Polderhoek Château. The 1st Battalion's attack came from the left if you stand facing this track and came through this area having missed their objective of the château itself.

What3words: cooked.ineptly.measure.

* * * * *

The 8th Battalion Norfolk Regiment had not been involved in any of the major offensives since they had fought in August. After this, they had been in training at Rubrouk until 23 September and then spent the first three weeks of October around Ypres on the west bank of the canal.

On 22 October 1917, the battalion moved to Cane Trench and prepared for the next assault, which would be to capture the remains of Poelcappelle. It cannot have been lost on the men left who had served on the Somme that a year previously they had fought at Regina Trench on the same date. This village had remained mostly in German hands and the frontline, running from north to south, passed through the middle of it where the British line still was positioned just part what was left of the church. Previous to this planned attack, the Germans had attempted to retake this area and some of their counterattacks had been successful:

> On the 20th October the Battalion arrived at Cane Trench and here were bivouacked for the night. The same evening 2 Lieut H.J. Chapman together with the Battalion Scouts went forward to our forming up area and laid out the preliminary guiding wires.
>
> By 12 noon on the 21st October, all battle stores had been issued and all plans completed. At 4 p.m. Lieut H.J. Chapman went forward with platoon guides and markers to lay out the forming up tapes. At about 7 p.m. all company commanders together with Battalion Headquarters went forward to reconnoitre the assembly area and meet the Battalion when it arrived. The first Company moved off towards the line at 8:15 p.m. and the remaining companies followed at intervals of fifteen minutes.
>
> At 2 a.m. a wire was sent to Brigade informing them that the Battalion was in battle position. Companies sustained remarkably few casualties during the forming up.
>
> The ground was a muddy desolation of shell holes and to make matters worse a light drizzle set in. Throughout the wait for Zero in the assembly position, the Battalion was intermittently shelled.
>
> Our right company ('C' Company) found that its forming up ground was nothing but a swamp and a few minutes before zero moved forward about 100 yards to more solid ground.

The village was now just rubble and was interlaced with German bunkers and littered with shell-holes. All previous attacks had failed, and it was decided that this time the attack would come from a different direction and a feint would occur in order to try and fool the Germans. This was in the form of using dummy figures which was called a 'Chinese Attack'.

Private Valentine Magill of the Army Cyclist Corps, who were part of the 18th (Eastern) Division, recounted how this type of operation worked:

When laid on the ground face downwards, two staples held it firm at the foot end, which was on a swivel. A thin wire would then be attached at the back and led to a trench or shell-hole in the rear. At a given time the wire would be pulled, up would come the dummy in an upright position looking from a distance as though men were going over the top. When hundreds of these things were used they were very realistic. One man in a shell-hole could operate four or five of these soldiers which would be thirty or forty yards in front of him.

The 8th Battalion report continued:

> The barrage of the Division on our left commenced 3 minutes before Zero, but punctually at 5:35 a.m. (Zero Hour), when it was still dusk and with rain still falling, our barrage opened. The half-light of dawn and the ground mist made it impossible for our men to see more than 200 yards in front of them. Our men advanced with the barrage keeping in close touch with it as it lifted.
>
> Unfortunately, the Chinese barrage on our right flank did not lift in conjunction with our own as had been pre-arranged and our right company ('C' Company) suffered severely. Capt. A.J.H. Patten, M.C. Commanding this company, realised that if the men delayed their advance their own barrage would be lost and the success of the operation endangered. Therefore, regardless of loss, he kept his men close to their own barrage and carried them through to their final objective and thus cleared the way for the 10th Bn Essex Regiment to pass through and form up under their protective barrage.
>
> Meanwhile the remainder of the Battalion were pushing on their respective objectives, the Blue Dotted Line.

The 8th Norfolks had been given the task of capturing the rest of the village assisted by the 10th Battalion Essex Regiment. The Norfolks would lead the advance and the 10th Essex would follow up later on. Aluminium discs had been placed out prior to the attack as the whole area was just a sea of mud.

Once the initial objectives had been captured, then the 10th Essex would leapfrog over the Norfolks and capture the secondary objectives. They would be supported by elements of the 34th Division on their left, which included the three Norfolk field companies that had been recruited in Norwich in 1915.

All four companies of the battalion would be involved in the assault and 'C' and 'D' Companies would lead with 'A' and 'B' following them. 'B' Company would advance and capture Requete Farm:

> At 7:29 a.m. Capt. R.E. Beckerson, M.C., commanding 'D' Company (Right Centre Company) sent a message timed 5:59 a.m. reporting that the Brewery was in our hands and that two posts had been established on the Spriet Road 100 yards ahead. This message was received at 7:20 a.m. and reported to Brigade by wire at 7:25 a.m.

At about this time an F.O.O. reported that he could see small parties of our troops moving about on the Blue Dotted Line (The final objective of the Battalion).

Our left company ('B' Company under Capt. H.V.E. Byrne) advancing well up behind its barrage met with some slight opposition at Requete Farm; this opposition however was rapidly dealt with and the company pushed on. After passing Requete Farm the company began to incline too much to the right. This was noticed by 2nd Lieut. F.G. Symonds who at once hastened to put the men on their correct alignment again. At this moment however, this gallant officer was unfortunately killed by a German shell. The company pushed on to Helles House and the concrete emplacements N.E. of it. Here 'B' Company met with considerable opposition from two light machine guns and a party of enemy bombers.

This second obstacle was soon successfully overcome by our men and yielded 1 officer and 25 men as prisoners. 11 wounded Germans were afterwards found in a concrete emplacement there. On reaching its final objective 'B' Company began to consolidate and touch was gained with 'A' Company (Left Centre Company) on its right, who had also successfully reached its final objective.

Throughout the advance a certain amount of opposition was met with from occupied pill-boxes, but so close did our men follow their barrage that they had surrounded these before many of the enemy had time to get out of them and the occupants were either killed or captured whilst still inside.

The 18-pounder barrage was good, and the lifts could easily be observed by our men, but near the Brewery there was a stationary barrage of our own 4.5 howitzers which did not lift as the 18-pounder barrage passed and our two centre companies had considerable casualties whilst following the 18-pounder barrage through this.

'Mopping-Up' was carried on expidiously under the leadership of company commanders and when the final objective was reached posts were pushed forward to clear the way for, and give every assistance to, the 10th Bn. Essex Regt which was to pass through and capture a further objective.

Along the whole of our front, companies carried on with consolidation and each company got into touch on either flank.

Following the pre-arranged plan of reorganisation, a message was sent forward from Bn. H.Q., that as soon as the 10th Essex had moved forward to the attack on the second objective 'D' Company were to take over 'C' Company's front

(Right Company) and the latter were to move to a position west of Requete Farm in support of 'B' Company (Left Coy). These movements were reported completed at about 9:30 a.m. When 'C' Company arrived at its new area it suffered heavily from enemy shell fire. It left its former position x36 but was soon reduced to 14 men.

At about 10:30 a.m. the O.C. 10th Essex Regiment requested the C.O. if possible to take over the front on the line Helles House–Nobles Farm–Spriet Road, as owing to casualties he required more men to hold his line south of Spriet Road.

(8th Norfolks had been previously ordered by Brigade to do this at dusk). The O.C. 8th Norfolk Regiment, however, ordered O.C. 'B' and 'D' Companies to do this as soon as possible. This movement was reported complete at 3 p.m. with the exception of one post on the Spriet Road which the 10th Essex continued to hold as 'D' Company had not sufficient men left to do so. From this time onwards, our front was heavily shelled by the enemy with 77 mm and 10.5 cm hows: the fire being directed by hostile aeroplanes flying at a height of about 500 feet, from which height the position of our men could easily be observed. None of our aeroplanes were in the air in the neighbourhood at the time.

This caused more casualties, but the ground they captured was kept and they were relieved by fresh troops in the evening, returning back to Cane Trench. The casualties for this action were high:

> 'A' Company moved to trenches in vicinity of Pheasant Farm, rejoining the Battalion at Cane Trench at 9 a.m.
>
> It was estimated that the Battalion captured 1 officer and 81 other ranks and 3 machine guns, but as the area behind the front line was heavily shelled it is not known how many that actually reached the Divisional P-of-W cage.

In this action, the report notes that five officers were killed or wounded and 260 other ranks were killed, wounded, or missing.

But the capture of Poelcappelle was described as 'gloriously won' in the Norfolk's history, and the 18th Division history stated: 'The triumphant Essex and Norfolks ... tramped back to hear the whole division and General Maxse singing their praise'.

I visited the area that the 8th Battalion advanced to, 100 years ago to the day. The day was bleak and windy and the fields around the area had been ploughed over for winter. This whole area was flooded 100 years ago due to the almost continuous shelling by both sides. Just walking on a ploughed field around this time of year gets your boots caked with mud. Just walking on tracks can be very difficult.

So, imagine what it must like when you have full kit, a rifle, and a tin hat with an enemy firing at you with rifles, machine guns, grenades, and artillery. It always amazes me that anyone got through that maelstrom.

What is sad about this victory is that within three months the 8th Battalion ceased to exist when it was disbanded when the Army carried out a restructure of their brigades. On 29 January 1918, the news was broken to the remains of the battalion:

> On the morning of the 29th, the Brigade Commander addressed the assembled Battalion. He told us that by order of the Army Council, our Bttn, with many others, was soon to be disbanded. He dwelt briefly on the different engagements by which the Battn. had carved for itself an imperishable name upon the Roll of Fame. As long

as England would be a nation, so long would the name of the 8th Norfolk Regt. be remembered.

　　We have all loved our Battalion, Brigade, Division as perhaps we shall never love another; yet we can carry on with that old sense of discipline and *espirit-de-corps* that has made us what we are. Let us remember always the words of St Paul—'Quit ye like men, Be Strong'.

I have a soft spot for the 8th Battalion because they were the first battalion of the Norfolk Regiment who I researched for my first book and this entry in their war diary is the epitome of the spirit of this part of the Norfolk Regiment.

Guidebook

From Ypres take the N313 road and travel through St Juliaan to Poelkapelle. There is a parking area near the church. The church is the start line for the Norfolks who then moved north-east wheeling to then advance east. You can walk this route using the road but I prefer to get in my car and then travel the road up to Poelcapelle Military Cemetery. Here using the trench map in their war diary, you can actually walk a circuitous route to look at various positions that were captured by the Norfolks on 22 October. If you do not wish to do that, then the other option is to go into Poelcappelle Cemetery and walk up the right-hand side and then look to the right. That is where the 8th Norfolk line settled.

　　What3words: flake.soggy.anonymously.

23

Shot at Dawn,
Private John Abigail (9694),
8th Battalion Norfolk Regiment

John Henry Abigail was born in 1897 to John and Maria who had eight children including John. At the time of his death, they were living at 17 Distillery Yard, Oak Street in Norwich.

John's service number is an early one in relation to the Norfolks and his service number certainly denotes August 1914. A friend of mine, Nick Stone, has looked into John's early life and has this to say about his family life:

> Records point at John's parents exhibiting what now would probably be termed a 'chaotic lifestyle' his father was a drayman dragging his demons around behind him; possibly more inclined to spend his meagre income on alcohol in the local pubs around Oak Street than to spend it on his family. Oak Street was a poor area loaded with gin and beer houses legal and otherwise. Often this would leave their children to go without food, tatty clothes and flea and lice infestations. This came to a head when the NSPCC who had been monitoring the family paid them a visit in March 1916, noted the near dereliction of the inside of the house and the state of the younger children who were basically sleeping on filthy vermin infested rags. This resulted in a Hard Labour for Mr Abigail and the workhouse for some cleaning and fresh clothes for John's siblings.

John's time in the Army was troubled. Records show that he initially served with the 1st Battalion going to France in March 1916. But other records show that he was with the 8th Battalion in July 1916. So, he would have gone over the top on 1 July 1916 on the first day of the Somme. As you will have read previously, the 8th Battalion fought at Delville Wood on 19 July 1916. A ledger known as the *Casualty Book*, held by the Norfolk Regimental Museum, notes that he was wounded on that date so this points towards the 8th Battalion.

John survived that action, but this must have had a great impact on him. By December 1916, he was back in England and went on to spend time with the 3rd (Reserve) Battalion who were stationed at Felixstowe.

He went absent twice while serving with the 3rd Battalion, the first time being on 19 December 1916; he remained as such until he was apprehended by the police on 27 December 1916. He was given a custodial sentence of 168 hours.

On 15 January 1917, he was charged with having a dirty rifle and was confined to barracks for five days. He went absent again on 22 January 1917 and remained as such until he gave himself up, records noting that he remained 'absent until surrendering himself at Britannia Barracks, Norwich at 9.40pm 27.1.17 (5 days 12 hrs 40 mins)'. For this offence he was awarded fourteen days' field punishment.

By May 1917, he was on active duty again, serving with the 8th Battalion, and went absent once more, with records noting:

In the Field 4.5.17 Rank: Pte
When on active service deserting his Majesty's Service, in that he, in the field, on 4th May 1917 having been warned that his platoon would be moving to the trenches that day, absented himself without leave and remained absent till reporting himself to Fifth Army Infantry School on 12th May 1917.

He was lucky not to have been shot for that offence and received a sentence of ten years' penal servitude. However, the sentence was suspended by the 3rd Army Commander on 22 June 1917. As we know, on 30 July 1917, the 8th Battalion moved to Zillebeke Lake to take part in the opening phase of the Third Battle of Ypres. John Abigail was not present and went absent again. He was not found until he was apprehended by a military police patrol on 2 August 1917. This time he was court-martialed.

The record of this hearing survives in parts and reads as follows:

THE CHARGE
Name of Alleged Offender (a)
   No.9504 Pte. J.H Abigail 8th Bn. Norfolk Regt.
   Offence Charged:
   Section 12 (1a) of the Army Act 1881
   When on active Service deserting his Majesty's Service in that he in the field on the 30th July 1917, absented himself from his Battalion after having been warned for the trenches and remained absent until apprehended without arms or equipment by the Military Police in a town behind the lines at about 4.30pm on 2nd August 1917.
   [Signed] H.W Higginson Brigadier
   Commanding 52nd Infantry Brigade.
   Form for Assembly and proceedings of Field General Court Martial on Active Service.

The decision as to how this should be looked at in a military court was decided very quickly:

PROCEEDINGS

On Active Service this 22nd day of August, 1917

Whereas it appears to me, the undersigned, an officer in Command of an Infantry Brigade on active service, that the persons named in the annexed Schedule, and being subject to Military Law, have committed the offences in the said schedule mentioned.

And I am of opinion that it is not practicable that such offences should be tried by an ordinary General Court Martial:

I hereby convene a Field General Court Martial to try the said persons and to consist of the Officers hereunder named.

President

Lt. Col G.V.W Hill DSO 8th Suffolk Regiment

Members

Capt. J.N Richardson MC 6th Royal Berks Regt.

2/Lt A.S Whiting 10th Essex Regiment

[Signed] H.W Higginson

53rd Inf. Brigade.

From this, his actual trial was convened and witnesses were called forward. There were four main witnesses to his absence:

THE TRIAL

PROSECUTION

1st Witness

No. 20962 Cpl W. Ellwood 8th Norfolk Regt. being duly sworn states:—

Between 3 and 4 pm on July 30th, Sgt Bains, my Platoon Sgt warned the platoon to be ready to move to the trenches in fighting order that night and stated that all packs were to be handed into the stores by 6 pm. I personally saw Pte. Abigail when Sgt. Bains warned the platoon. I heard everything Sgt. Bains said and Pte. Abigail was closer to him. About 8pm I noted that Pte. Abigail had not handed in his pack. I searched the camp but not find Pte. Abigail. He was absent when my section, to which he belongs, fell in to proceed to the trenches at about 10.50pm. I did not see Pte. Abigail again until he rejoined under arrest.

Accused declines to cross examine the witness.

2nd Witness

No. 30306 Pte. H. Jennings, 8th Norfolk Regiment, having been duly sworn states:—

Sgt. Bains, my Platoon Sgt, warned the platoon about 3.45pm on July 30th to hand on our packs to the stores by 6pm as we were going up to the line that night. I saw Pte. Abigail at the time, he was about 4 yards from me and 2 yards from Sgt.

Bains. Pte. Abigail was absent when we handed in our packs and still absent when the platoon marched off that night for a forward area. I did not see Pte. Abigail again until he rejoined the Regt. under arrest some days later.

The accused declines to cross examine the witness.

3rd Witness

No. 22854 Pte. C.E Broughton, 8th Norfolk Regt, being duly sworn states:—

About 3.30pm on July 30th Sgt. Bains, my platoon Sgt. warned the platoon to hand in packs to the stores. I saw Pte. Abigail, he was quite close to Sgt. Baines, who also warned us to collect wood for making breakfasts with the next morning after zero. I myself left for the detail camp before the platoon marched off to the forward area.

The accused declines to cross examine this witness.

4th Witness

No. 2875 Cpl. H.N. Stallworthy M.M.P sworn, states:—

About 4.30pm on August 2nd I was on duty near Staple. I met the accused walking along the road. I stopped him and asked if he was on duty and he replied 'No, I am looking for my battalion, they are billeted near here and I have been out for a walk for 2 hours and when I came back, they were gone'. He was unable to give me any further account as to the whereabouts of his battalion. I conveyed him to H.Q 2nd Army, where he was detained to await an escort. He was without any equipment whatsoever.

The accused declines to cross examine this witness.

Prosecution closed.

After the evidence was given, Private Abigail gave no mitigating circumstances as to why he had gone absent and chose not to defend himself:

DEFENCE

The accused declines to make any statement and to call any witnesses.

Court Closed.

The Certified true copy of A.F B122 is produced herewith

[signed] G.V.W Hill

Pres F.G.C.M

24.8.17

Private Abigail was found guilty of desertion and the following was read out:

SCHEDULE

August 24th 1917

Name of alleged offender: No.9504 Pte. J.H Abigail 8th Bn. Norfolk Regt

Offence Charged: Section 12 (1a) Army Act "When on active Service deserting his Majesty's Service in that he in the field on the 30th July 1917, absented himself from his Battalion after having been warned for the trenches and remained absent until apprehended without arms or equipment by the Military Police in a town behind the lines at about 4.30pm on 2nd August 1917."

Plea: Not Guilty

Finding, and if convicted, Sentence: Guilty. Death.

CONFIRMATION FROM C-in-C

Confirmed

D.Haig FM

9 Sep: 17

Looking at all of this, noting that he did not contest any of the findings or witnesses, I am of the same mind as Nick Stone, who notes:

> I think it's reasonable to suggest that he may have been suffering from shell-shock by this point, fear is a strange master and bravery odder still, it's after all not an absence of fear, but the control of it, you can't help wondering if someone in his state of mind knew what would happen if he was caught but no longer cared he just wanted out of everything.

For my second book, I had to read up on shellshock and found that those that had to contend with the symptoms suffered terrible mental breakdowns as a result of their experiences. Shellshock often took time to manifest itself and men often experienced the effects for months before they succumbed.

One sufferer described his reaction to a dawn counterattack less than forty-eight hours after he had seen 70 per cent of his battalion decimated: 'I lost control when I went into the dugout and concealed myself, and also for that week in which I could not control my tears...'

But the authorities were reluctant to admit to the mental effects of warfare. Men like John Abigail were clearly suffering from shellshock, and even though the term was mentioned in an article in *The Lancet* as early as February 1915, it was not until 1922 that a final report was published after a War Office Committee had looked into the matter.

Hundreds of men were interviewed and the committee debated and researched the condition. The report summed up its findings as follows: 'No human being, however constituted, however free from inherent weakness, however highly trained to meet the stress and strain and the wear and tear of modern warfare can resist the direct effect of the bursting of high explosive shells'.

But this did not stop the committee from concluding that proper training and recruitment would help to minimise future cases of what was also termed 'war-neurosis'. In fact, the term shellshock was discouraged from being used. Today we know this condition as PTSD, but even now the condition is only becoming fully understood.

None of the early findings on the condition helped John who was twenty years old when he was shot by firing squad on 12 September 1917 for desertion, while the 8th Battalion were out of the line at Roubrouk. This was also recorded on his soldier's effects list as 'shot for desertion'. He never receieved any campaign medals, and other than the record of his court-martial, there is very little that survives of his war service.

Guidebook

John Abigail is buried in Esquelbecq Communal Cemetery. This can be found by coming into the village on the D17 from Wormhout. Once in the village, you will pass the church on your right. Turn right onto the Rue de Bergues, the D417, and continue on this road until you see a sign on your left that says Chambre Funéraire. Turn left here and the cemetery is on your left.

What3words: nearly.fridays.excluder.

24

The 7th and 9th Battalions, The Battle of Cambrai, Ribécourt to Nine Wood: 20 November to 7 December 1917

General Hon. Sir Julian Byng, commanding 3rd Army, went to see Haig around three months before the attack, asking to be allowed to make a surprise assault on the formidable defences at Cambrai.

It required a methodical 'bite and hold' advance in four stages using six divisions. 'Bite and hold' called for an advance that would not extend beyond supporting artillery that could assist in defeating the expected enemy counterattacks.

Brigadier-General Hugh Elles, commanding the Tank Corps in France, and his chief staff officer, Lieutenant-Colonel John Fuller, made a convincing case that with growing strength in France, the corps could be used collectively to punch a hole into the enemy defences. Cambrai, being on relatively undamaged rolling chalk land, would be ideal, which effectively made it tank fighting country.

Byng's army had also developed a scheme for a surprise attack using unregistered artillery. The Tank Corps much approved of the idea, for it would avoid the devastation of ground that had caused so much difficulty for the machines at Ypres.

Cambrai had been in German hands since 1914 and had become an important railhead and garrison town. With its railways connecting Douai, Valenciennes, and Saint-Quentin and the Saint-Quentin canal, from which the front could be supplied along the River Scheldt men and material could be moved along the Western Front. If captured, it would deny the enemy a key part of his communication system. But it lay behind a formidable defensive position.

Haig approved the plan on 13 October 1917.

In 3rd Army orders—codenamed Operation GY—issued on 13 November 1917, the attack was defined as a *coup de main*, 'to take advantage of the existing favourable local situation' where 'surprise and rapidity of action are ... of the utmost importance'. It was also to be a deep attack on a 10,000-yard (5.6-mile) front that would be 'widened as soon as possible'.

Once the key German Masnières–Beaurevoir line had been breached by III Corps, the cavalry would pass through, reach around to isolate Cambrai from the rear, and cut the railways leading from it. Haig would later say that the purpose of the attack was to compel the enemy to withdraw from the salient between the Canal du Nord and the Scarpe, although the objectives must be achieved within forty-eight hours before strong enemy reserves could come into play. So, the high speed and short tactical operation had somehow become one of seizing and holding ground, and while not quite a plan for strategic breakthrough—there were never enough reserves to exploit a breakthrough—the orders had faint resemblance to the original concepts.

More than 1,000 guns and howitzers were concealed on the fronts of III and IV Corps and the opening bombardment and a total of 476 tanks, including the new Mark IV version tanks, were moved up to the front on 18 and 19 November, with aircraft flying up and down the area to mask their sound as they moved up. Their objective would be to crush wire defences and suppress fire from trenches and strongpoints.

Fascines would be dropped as makeshift bridges, enabling the crossing of a wide trench; this removed one of the known shortcomings of the current tank design. Much attention had been paid to training, particularly for co-operation between infantry and tank, with the units designated to make the initial assault being withdrawn to Wailly for this purpose. An innovation was that the infantry would follow the tanks through the gaps they made, moving in "worms" rather than the familiar lines: their training seems to have done much to improve infantry confidence in the tanks, hitherto seen as a mixed blessing. The tanks were a notable operational success. Shrouded by mist and smoke, they broke into the Hindenburg Line defences with comparative ease in many places.

Most importantly, the Germans failed to identify the imminence and nature of the British attack. Six divisions were used in the attack, and from right to left, they were the 12th (Eastern), 20th (Light), 6th, 51st (Highland), 62nd (West Riding), and 36th (Ulster). In immediate support was the 29th and ready to exploit the anticipated breakthrough and sweep round Cambrai were the 1st, 2nd, and 5th Cavalry Divisions. The Tank Corps deployed its entire strength of 476 machines and were led by Tank Corps' GOC Hugh Elles in a Mk IV tank called 'Hilda'. James Cooper saw this tank in a demonstration of the ability of this relatively new weapon on 7 November 1917:

Went and saw demonstration by tanks. 'Hilda' was twisting and turning about tearing up wire etc and finally went over the top. They have a clever idea by carrying a large bundle of wood on top and when near the trench drop it in before going over.

Lt-Col. Prior got wind of the offensive when the battalion was put into a period of training:

> There was still no rumour that a push was imminent and indeed the tank officers told us that they were to carry out manoeuvres for instructional purposes with the infantry and were then going behind the line for the winter.
>
> However, the training was out on a suspiciously thorough basis. A series of very deep trenches to the plans of the Hindenburg line with a very thick wire entanglement was set up and the troops were practised in advancing behind it in co-operation with the tanks. So far as the infantry was concerned the most important feature of this co-operation was that we were to look at the tank to flatten out a path through the wire entanglements by which the assaulting infantry could move. This was to us of the 6th Division a new and very interesting feature.
>
> Hitherto our experiences of hostile wire had been confined to one or two belts of apron wire backed up by stands of occasional concertina wire, a form of entanglement at which the enemy were very skilful. The difficulty of getting through comparatively uncut wire was only too well known to the 9th Battalion at the Quadrilateral in the Somme battle, but the reports showed that wire covering the Hindenburg line was composed of belt upon belt interlaced and joined for a thickness of upwards of 100 yards and thus forming an impassable obstacle.
>
> Now the role of the tanks was not to cut the wire but to flatten out paths through it. These paths would have to be at some considerable distance from each other since, if the tanks were too close the path flattened out by one tank was pulled taut again by its neighbour.
>
> The infantry in passing would have to get through a straight and narrow road as like as not under heavy hostile fire. Out training largely consisted in trying all kinds of alternative methods of how we could best get through the passage with the least casualties.
>
> Though we began to have more than a suspicion that something was on it was not till well into November that the commanding officers were told what the scheme was. I was pointed out to us that success or failure depended on surprise and that though we could tell our officers that there was an attack planned we were not to breathe a word even to them where it was to take place. Exceptional precautions were taken to keep the secret and though both officers and men knew something was on they did not know where. The 9th Norfolks were allotted a most important part in the projected attack. They were to form the second wave of the brigade attack, pass through the first wave (the 1st Leicesters and 9th Suffolks) whose objective was the
> Hindenburg line and assault and capture the village of Ribécourt.

The attack opened at 6.20 a.m. on 20 November 1917 with an intensive predicted-fire barrage on the Hindenburg Line and key points to the rear, which caught the Germans by surprise. Initially, this was followed by the curtain of a creeping barrage behind, which the tanks and infantry followed.

This can be evidenced in the experience of *Leutnant* J. Langfoldt, 2nd Battalion Infantry Regiment 84, who was in this sector when the battle was launched:

> During the night the British were supposed on one occasion to have brought down a concentration of heavy fire on our positions. This drew our artillery into replying with defensive fire and so depleting their already meagre stocks of ammunition. I heard none of it I was sleeping the sleep of the dead. In the morning I was rudely awakened by drum fire, which came down suddenly. I instantly looked at my watch; it was, unless my memory fails me, 7.15 am. I hurried over to the entrance of the dugout. The trench leading to it
>
>   Was under heavy high explosive and shrapnel fire and, above all, with the smoke shells which took your breath away, as soon as the fire ceased slightly, I rushed forwards along the *Stollenweg* [Dugout Way]. In the dugout were company cooks and one platoon of 6th Company. I pressed them to emerge and to occupy a section of trench which forked off a little way forward of *Stollenweg*. *Leutnant* Hlallum was very helpful to me and led the men into the section of trench where this keen, faithful officer was the first to be mortally wounded.

There was an issue with the cavalry and progress was slow when the bridge at Masnières collapsed under weight of a tank; the history of the 6th Division noted:

> The 6th Division attacked on the front Villers Plouich-Beaucamps, with the 71st Infantry Brigade (Brig.-Gen. P. W. Brown) on the left next to the 51st Division, the 16th Infantry Brigade (Brig.-Gen. H. A. Walker) on the right next to the 20th Division. These two brigades were to advance about 3,000 yards to the first objective (Ribécourt and spur to south-east of it), and another 1,000 yards to the second objective (support system). The 18th Infantry Brigade (Brig.-Gen. G. S. G. Craufurd) was ordered to advance through the 71st Infantry Brigade and secure the third objective about a mile farther on (Prerny Chapel Ridge), throwing back a defensive flank towards Flesquières for the further operations of the 51st Division on its left and securing the flank of the 29th Division on its right. The latter division passing through the right of the 6th Division and the left of the 20th Division, was charged with securing the crossings of the St. Quentin Canal at Marcoing and Masnières and seizing the high ground at Rumilly, thus facilitating exploitation to the south-east, preventing a concentration against the widely stretched defensive flanks of the III Corps and threatening Cambrai.

The 5th Cavalry Division advanced through them but were repulsed in front of Noyelles. The 51st (Highland) Division had a very hard fight for Flesquières, but its failure to capture it and keep up with the pace of the advance on either side left a dangerous salient which exposed the flanks of the neighbouring divisions.

The 9th Battalion left Longuereuil on 15 November and reached Peronne twelve hours later. They then moved to Manancourt and then to Dessart Wood. On the 17th, they took over the line to the south of Ribécourt, although thirty men of the Rifle Brigade remained in the forward trenches to mask the fact that they had been relieved by a fresh battalion. The 6th Division's history noted:

Two battalions of tanks, each of thirty-six tanks, were allotted to the Division. 'B' Battalion (Lt.-Col. E. D. Bryce, D.S.O.) operated with the 16th Infantry Brigade, and 'H' Battalion (Lt.-Col. Hon. C. Willoughby) with the 71st Infantry Brigade. The 18th Infantry Brigade advanced without tanks. The only points which caused anxiety, provided that the tanks functioned satisfactorily, were Couillet Wood on the right of the 16th Infantry Brigade front, in which tanks could not operate, and Ribécourt Village on the left of the 71st Infantry Brigade front. The former was successfully cleared by the Buffs, and the latter gallantly captured by the 9th Norfolk Regiment; the 11th Essex clearing and securing it for the advance of the 18th Infantry Brigade, while the 71st Infantry Brigade attacked the second objective.

The 71st Brigade was ordered to capture Ribécourt village and the 9th Norfolks would move off after the first wave of tanks and would leapfrog over the 1st Battalion Leicestershire Regiment. Lt-Col. Prior described the 9th Battalion's march and then their initial preparations for their assault:

Our objective Ribécourt was completely hidden by a hill and we had to go a long way north before we got to a spot from which we could see round this hill and get our first glimpse of Ribécourt village. We entrained, I think on 17th November, reached Peronne and from there had a long march up.

We took over the line at Beaucamp except the front-line posts which the regiment we relieved retained so that if a raid took place and any men were captured the advent of a new division should not be noticed. I must say that the sector seemed an extraordinary quiet and pleasant one after our strenuous time outside Lens, but how the enemy failed to spot that something abnormal was taking place I don't know. At night from our front line the roar of the motor and wheeled traffic could be plainly heard and in daylight one daring enemy aeroplane could have easily ascertained that the roads were chock a block with transport and troops.

The night before the attack the Boche put down a bombardment and raided the lines of the battalion on our immediate left and secured some prisoners. We were on tenterhooks lest these prisoners should disclose our plans but presumably they did not do so. A bombardment and hostile raid is rather disconcerting immediately before an attack and I feared might affect the morale of the troops but as a matter of fact never were troops in better heart. Indeed, the barrage after those we had experienced in the Lens sector was a very second-rate affair.

The 9th Battalion's orders were fairly simple to follow:

> I have already indicated the task allotted to the brigade. We were on the extreme
> left flank for the Division and touching on our left the 51st Division. Our plan had
> already been fully rehearsed and the distribution of the battalion was:
>
> 'A' Company on the left to proceed down the lower slope of the valley and cross
> the Hindenburg Line. They were then to push on keeping in touch with the 51st
> Highland Division, make good the trenches covering the village, take the line of
> houses on the left flank of the village and then push through and capture the railway
> station.
>
> 'B' Company in the centre, having crossed the Hindenburg Line, was to push
> straight for the centre of the village. Having made good, the bridges over the Grand
> Ravine they were to clear the village and push through to the other side prolonging
> A Company's frontage.
>
> 'D' Company had a similar task with the right flank of the village.
>
> 'C' Company was to be in close support of the centre company and thus available
> to assist anyone or more of the leading companies. On reaching the village, they
> were to seize the bridge over the Granelle Ravine and dig themselves in.

As mentioned, the objective was the village of Ribécourt, and Lt-Col. Prior
describes this in his memoirs:

> Ribécourt is more than the usual small village. It is very fair-sized market town lying
> in the hollow between the ridge on which the Hindenburg Line was sited and the
> ridge upon which stands the village of Flesquières and is practically at the foot of the
> Flesquières Hill. It will therefore be seen that the task allotted to the 9th Norfolks
> was no small one. The capture and clearance of a village of this size to say nothing of
> a very long advance over the open and the crossing of the famous Hindenburg Line
> *en-route* was quite the biggest thing that they had been called upon to do.
>
> The men, however, knew exactly what their duties were, even to the streets they had
> to clear and in war a clear understanding of what exactly is required goes a long way
> towards success. We were much annoyed with our Brigadier as he turned us out of
> our headquarters dugout to make room for the headquarters of one of the battalions
> of the 51st Division. We had to take over an old disused dug-out which was in a filthy
> state and very damp and wet. Even with the softening effect of time I can see no excuse
> for a Brigadier to turn out his own troops on the eve of a battle for the benefit of the
> headquarters of a battalion of another division attacking from a different sector. As a
> result, no one in battalion Headquarters got any rest or sleep that night.
>
> From our front-line we could see the Hindenburg Line which sites on the reverse
> slope of the Hill in front of us and at this point it was known as 'unseen trench' and
> 'unseen support' but well in front of their main line the Boche had established an
> outpost line.

I had arranged that if everything went well I would establish Battalion Headquarters in the enemy 4th line i.e. about half way between 'unseen support' and Ribécourt Village. As nothing could be seen of the advance after the Battalion had crossed the ridge in front of us I settled to go over with the Battalion accompanied by Lieutenant Dye, my Intelligence Officer, and a couple of orderlies, leaving Captain Sprott to bring on the rest of Battalion Headquarters later on.

Sometime before Zero-hour Lieutenant Dye and I went up to the front line and into No Man's Land to find the outpost company but could see nothing of them. As a matter of fact, we found afterwards that the outposts had been drawn in to the left flank to organise them in their attack formation. It was still fairly dark and we wandered well out across No Man's Land but there was no sign of either friend or foe. Everything was very peaceful and still and there was no indication of the inferno that was shortly to be let loose. We returned to the front line just about Zero and went along the companies front. The guns had opened before we got half way down the line…

The battalion advanced with 'D' Company on the right, 'B' Company in the centre, 'A' Company on the left, and 'C' Company would follow in support. The advance was quick with infantry moving quicker than the slow lumbering tanks and Lt-Col. Prior recorded the action of the battalion in an account:

> Our barrage had brought a reply from the enemy's guns and a spasmodic barrage was put down by him causing the Leicestershires and ourselves some casualties. We pushed on and successfully crossed the enemy outpost line and over the hill top.
>
> Here we found ourselves faced by the most colossal belt of barbed wire that I have ever seen. The reports of the Hindeburg Line were no exaggeration but real facts. Following a tank track we essayed the passage. We had completed about three-quarters of the journey when we came under heavy machine-gun fire. I then found myself in 'unseen trench', the front trench of the main Hindenburg Line.

The CO followed his battalion and very quickly found himself with 'C' Company who had outstripped both the tanks and the other three companies of the 9th Norfolks:

> The leading tanks, followed by the Leicesters, crossing our trenches and starting across No Man's Land—a wonderful spectacle in the half light of the early morning. Ponderous, grunting, groaning, wobbling, these engines of war crawled and lurched their way toward the enemy lines, followed by groups of men in file. Overhead our shells were pouring over. The barrage lifted from the enemy's outpost trench, where we knew that Unseen Trench was getting it hot; but the slowness of those tanks! It is at these moments that one itches for quickness and rapidity, and the slow, deliberate action of these monsters was exasperating. Neither tanks nor Leicesters were clear of our lines when we reached 'A' Company.

In the meantime, the tanks negotiated the formidable obstacle of the Hindenburg Trench and were making much more rapid progress on the downhill slope towards Ribécourt. B Company had gone through and were in the village. A Company were a little later on the left and I saw them make a beautiful attack on the line of houses on the left of the village supported by a male tank whose gun was in action. Cheery messages from A, B & C Companies reporting complete success.

The prisoners were coming in so fast and in such numbers that I had difficulty in finding escorts. One large batch of 80 to 90 I had to send back in charge of my orderly room clerk. Having despatched the reports, I went up and saw the positions occupied by the troops. The 11th Essex had come up, passed through the village and seized the trench line beyond it but the Division was not able to get much further forward on this flank owing to the failure of the 51st Division to take Flesquières Ridge.

A large force of cavalry had arrived at Ribécourt but for the most part remained there all day without moving. There seemed to be a splendid opportunity for them to work round the flank of Flesquières Village and so cut off the enemy garrison. As it was the enemy evacuated the village under the cover of darkness and got away scathless. The infantry indeed passed a number of very uncomplimentary remarks on the cavalry and at one time there was very nearly a free fight between some of the Leicesters and a troop of cavalry. The attacking strength of the Battalion was not more than 400 yet the Battalion captured over 600 prisoners.

Ribécourt was immediately in front of us. I could see parties of the enemy running through the streets. Our artillery was putting down a smoke barrage on the farther side of the village, and several houses were on fire and blazing merrily. I had to decide whether to hang on in our present position and wait for the arrival of the tanks and the three other companies, or push 'C' Company in. The enemy already showed signs of recovering from the initial surprise. We were now being shelled pretty persistently and accurately, as well as machine-gunned. I determined to take immediate action, and directed Failes to push forward at once, take the part of the village lying on this side of the ravine, and hold the bridge crossing it. 'C' Company swept on and affected this in brilliant fashion, securing a large bag of prisoners.

The account sounds as though the advance was easy. However, in parts, it was not, and 'A' and 'B' Companies met with strong opposition and became involved in hand-to-hand fighting. They came up against two machine guns, which had to be knocked out at close quarters by a party led by Lt John Hancock and CSM Bertie Neale. Another machine gun was silenced by Lewis gunners and it is estimated that the Germans lost eighty killed or wounded and another 600 wounded.

Leutnant Langfoldt noted:

Meanwhile the first reports had arrived from the front. *Leutnant* Mory arrived breathless and panicky. Almost his entire company had been captured; the British had countless tanks. I can remember to this day how the scales suddenly fell from my eyes when I heard the word tanks. It was all clear now or, rather, it was unclear, exactly what it meant to be opposed by tanks. We had a short council of war to decide what to do. The *Hauptmann* ordered us to occupy the short stretch of trench. Because it only had very short traverses, tanks driving over it would not be able to sweep it with machine gun fire. The aim was to let the tanks calmly pass us by then, leaving them for the artillery to deal with, we would attempt to close with the British infantry. If that was successful, the effect of the tanks would be neutralised.

The first step was to clear the supply dump of all available hand grenades and other ammunition and to distribute it to the infantrymen. Above all, however, we had to make contact with the regiment and inform them that we needed some ammunition. We then saw that masses of tanks were already climbing the slopes behind us towards Havrincourt, whilst on the other side they had already passed Ribécourt. It was essential to direct the artillery, which was still engaging the former defensive fire tasks, onto these targets.

However, the first of the artillery fire cut off the link to the regiment. A runner was despatched but, because of the presence behind us of a wall of flame and smoke in the valley bottom, he did not get through. I raced over to the light signalling station, where the men did their damnedest to get in contact with the regiment. I soon saw that it was impossible; a thick curtain of smoke, which even the sun's rays could not penetrate, hung there, cutting off our view of Flesquières completely. Then I spotted the tactics that the British were using. British infantry appeared at the far end of the trench, but when they saw that we were occupying it, they pulled back immediately. They obviously had orders not to get into a fight with us, but to leave it all to the tanks. I then raced back to the *Hauptmann* to inform him that it would be hopeless to try to link up with the Regiment.

By 9 a.m., the battalion had captured Ribécourt and were passed by the 11th Battalion Essex Regiment who went on to capture Kaiser Trench. The Norfolks then spent the rest of the day consolidating their gains.

The 6th Division history noted: 'The Division had a most successful day, with very light casualties (about 650), capturing 28 officers and 1,227 other ranks prisoners, 23 guns, and between 40 and 50 machine-guns and many trench-mortars, and receiving the congratulations of the Corps Commander'.

Lt-Col. Prior noted in his account:

It would be impossible to set out all the extraordinary incidents of that glorious day' how Hancock and his sergeant major rushed an enemy machine gun position and settled a bet as to who would kill most Boches. This was won by Hancock, but Sergeant-Major Neale always contends that he was unduly handicapped by having to use his bayonet, whilst Hancock had a revolver. How a runner of 'D' Company, without assistance, took over seventy prisoners, including a staff officer. How Worn, wounded in the first hundred yards of the advance, carried on with his platoon until he reached his final objective, the railway station, and consolidated his position. How Thompson of 'B' Company, who in the darkness of the night prior to the attack had fallen down and very badly sprained his ankle, deliberately refused to go sick, and, with the aid of his servant, limped over in front of his platoon, and carried on until the objective was reached. How one man of 'A' Company having very daringly and very foolishly penetrated an enemy dugout, leaving his rifle outside, knocked down the Bosche who thrust his pistol at his head, seized the pistol and harried his opponent by the vigorous application of the butt end.

The advance pushed 4 miles deep into a strong system of defence in little over four hours at a cost of just over 4,000 casualties, but 3rd Army failed to capture all of its objectives, with the cavalry being unable to push through a gap at Marcoing–Masnières and on to encircle Cambrai itself and Bourlon Ridge did not fall that day. The Tank Corps lost 179 tanks destroyed, disabled, or broken down. Cambrai would not remain a stunning victory for long.

Lt-Col. Prior finished his account by noting:

> Some of these things are written down in the records of gallantry which have earned awards; many more and equally gallant actions never will be recorded, and some are recorded only in memory of those, and, alas! their number has sadly reduced who took part in that glorious first day of the fist battle of Cambrai.

The 9th Norfolks lost seven officers and eighty-seven other ranks killed, wounded, or missing at Cambrai. The two men I have mentioned as having assaulted the machine-gun posts and the ones Lt-Col. Prior mentions having the bet were Lt John Eliot Hancock and CSM Bertie Mark Neale (7178). Both won awards for this action: Lt Hancock won a DSO and CSM Neale won a DCM. Both were listed in the *London Gazette* in 1918.

Lt Hancock's *London Gazette* entry notes on 4 February 1918:

> For conspicuous gallantry and devotion to duty. Owing to his company commander being seriously wounded, he took command of the left company in an attack. 'When they came under heavy machine-gun fire he organised a frontal attack while he, with two N.C.O.'s, rushed across the open from a flank, killed or wounded all the gun team and put the guns out of action. He himself killed six men. In the subsequent fighting he showed great initiative in clearing the houses in a village and directing the advance.

CSM Neale's *London Gazette* entry notes on 4 March 1918:

> For conspicuous gallantry and devotion to duty in volunteering with an officer and N.C.O. to put out of action some machine-guns that were holding up the advance of

his company. Under heavy fire from the two guns he succeeded in doing this, and in the hand-to-hand fighting that ensued killed four of the enemy.

Wounded in the advance on Ribécourt was Lt Terence Algernon Kilbee Cubitt, who we met on the Somme. His wounding was reported on 1 December 1917 in the *Norwich Mercury*:

> Lieut. Terence AK Cubitt M.C. of the Norfolks, son of Mr Algernon Cubitt of Norwich was severely wounded in the fighting near Cambrai on November 20th. That was the opening day of the battle when the tanks led the British advance. He now lies in a base hospital but has been able to write some cheery letters to his Norwich friends.

That was not the end of the 9th Norfolks's time in this sector, and once the line had settled, the battalion occupied Nine Wood; Lt-Col. Prior describes this area and describes the German defences around the area. He provides a fascinating observation into this mighty defensive system:

> We remained for a day or two concentrating the defences round Ribécourt and as time went on it became manifest that the enemy was not going to take his defeat lying down. Not only had he recovered from his surprise but became aggressive and the fortunes of the fighting in the front lie fluctuated. At one time we had La Fontaine and on the following day we had lost it; the whole of Bourlon Wood had been taken but a few hours later we had only half of it. Attack and counterattack of a local nature succeeded one another and each day the hostile gun fire increased in intensity. Signs were not wanting that a more serious hostile attack was pending. We were soon after detailed to take over Nine Wood which lay between Cantaing Village and Marcoing. In the centre of this wood was a shooting lodge where the Germans had put up a well built and exceedingly cleverly concealed observation station. There were a certain number of dugouts in the wood but as the place had been well behind the German old line there were none too many of these. The regiment I took over from had used a pleasant summer house for their headquarters and I continued to use it though it was clear that if the wood was heavily shelled the summer house was not the place to remain in.
>
> Most of the German defence works in this neighbourhood were incomplete but it was astonishing to see the vast scale upon which his defences were planned. The front and support line of what is generally called the Hindenburg Line was complete, very deep and substantial trenches and excellent dug-outs. The Hindenburg Line is, however, quite a misnomer. It should be called the Hindenburg system and comprised the outpost line, unseen trench and unseen support, the 4th line (in which during the fight I had established mu headquarters) almost complete and with excellent dug-outs.
>
> Behind that came the local defences of Ribécourt, trenches and houses reinforced with concrete. Behind Ribécourt two more complete lines (the Kaiser lines) on the

same system as the 'unseen' trenches. The trenches in these were dug but only a few dug-outs were completed. Incidentally these dug-outs were designed on a stupendous scale and were apparently to be huge reinforced fero-concrete structures sunk in the earth. We occupied one later on near Ribécourt and received several direct hits without damage. Behind this again running through Nine Wood another line of front line and support trench had been traced out and in part dug with here and there completed dug-outs. But between these lines in every sunken road and in every village as far back as Noyelle which was the furthest point of our advance—a charming little village in happier times, the summer residence of the Bishop of Cambrai—deep and substantial dig-outs had been prepared. As can be imagined these dug-outs were most useful and it was only unfortunate that there were not enough of them to go quite around.

In the sunken roads, the enemy method of concealing the entrance to his dug-outs were very cleverly done by making verandas of overhead wire coved with grass and earth. From the air nothing could be seen of the dug-outs entrance nor in the air photographs.

Even close to the difference between the end of the road bank and the beginning of the veranda or wire screen was difficult to spot and I came a tremendous purler into one sunken road by inadvertently walking on to the screen. Interesting as these things were where we soon had more important things to consider.

The shelling increased in intensity and Nine Wood from a comparatively pleasant spot became very much the reverse. There were two battalion headquarters in the wood, one at the shooting box, another in a small sandpit, with the summer house close by and a third in a fair sized dug-out in a sand pit between Nine Wood and Marcoing. The 9th Suffolks relived us at the summer and the wood having become a most unpleasant spot the C.O. decided most wisely to go into the dug-out. His second in command, however, insisted on sleeping in the summer house and was killed there that night.

The Suffolk Regiment officer described in Lt-Col. Prior's memoirs can be identified as Maj. Wilfred Robert Whitson, who had served in the Highland Light Infantry; at the time of his death, he was attached to the 9th Battalion Suffolk Regiment. He was aged thirty and the son of Alexander and Isabella Whitson of 5 Prince's Terrace Dowanhill in Glasgow. He now lies in Grave II. C. 18. in Fins New British Cemetery at Sorel-Le-Grand.

Lt-Col. Prior continued with his memoirs, noting that the situation was getting worse and worse:

The Leicesters headquarters were shelled out of the shooting box in the cellar of which they lived. There was those two-battalion headquarters in a miserably small dugout and when our turn came to take over we had to share this place with the 2nd Sherwood Foresters. From the increased shelling it was quite clear that the enemy were going to make an effort to clear us out but the exact point of his attack was cleverly concealed. In a very short time the enemy appeared to obtain complete observation of our line. The casualties to the men were serious, never a day passing without several being killed or wounded. It was extremely cold at night and for the most part there was no shelter and the strain and exposure began to tell its tale. One of the front-line companies was holding the village of Noyelles and another prolonging the line to the left in front of the village of Cantaing. These two companies were really outpost companies with the main lines of resistance.

Although the situation here was not looking good, Lt-Col. Prior also found a good point to write about:

After trench warfare it was a very pleasant change to have an open warfare formation and to be able to visit your posts without having to crawl through trenches to them. Towards the end of the month we were relieved from the outpost line and took over the headquarters on the Marcoing Road. In the next 24 hours no one was safer anywhere in the battle area.

James Cooper was also able to record his experiences of this battle in his diary:

Tuesday 20th November

Artillery Barrage started at 6 o'clock a.m. and it was splendid. We moved off with the tanks and gradually walked our way into Fritz's trenches and everything worked like clock-work. It was a sight I would not have missed. The way the artillery barrage was worked we soon had some prisoners. They came running towards us with their hands up and looked a miserable lot.

A party of 8 came along and one was shot about a yard from me, mortally wounded. Then we worked our way into the village of Ribécourt which was our objective and I soon found some souvenirs and we left in a great hurry bearing plenty of bread, sausages, cheese and butter. I was hungry and soon had some. Found some good wine and took a bottle to the boys. I think our casualties are about 100. We have lost senior officers Capt Blackwell and Lt Jones killed, besides others wounded. Poor old George Veal of the band was hit in the leg. I expect he will lose it. Jon Thatcher was killed by tank gun. Darky Page wounded, Bill Hardyman wounded … feel done up now and I hope I can have a few hours rest. We carried in 4 stakes, each man, and they weighed 60 lbs, besides rifle, ammunition and pack. Every man got them, those out of our squad. It's a red-letter day for me and I thank god I am through alright without a scratch.

James was quite thankful that he had come through this without a scratch and reflected on his own personal losses over the next few days:

Wednesday 21st November

Prisoners coming in by the 100s looking very forlorn, tired and dirty but pleased to be prisoners and would give you anything they have got. We are still advancing but we are waiting in reserve.

Thursday 22nd November

Capt Cross died of wounds. Dye (of Norwich a school teacher) died. Poor old Bush who just recently went home and got married was also killed. Up early this morning and on guard. None too pleasant in trenches which only 24 hours ago were in Fritz's hands. Went over and had a look at three tanks out of action. One was set on fire by Fritz. I could see some of the charred limbs of the operators inside. Must have been an awful death. Aeroplane just come down, busted out by machine gun. The pilot unhurt. Shall be glad to get some grub up, I'm really hungry. No rations yet. Fall back for Fritz's bread and lay down.

One man who was not so lucky was Lewis Thaxter who was killed in action during the advance on Ribécourt. He is now buried in Grave II.H.14 in Fifteen Ravine British Cemetery at Villers Plouich. In the research for this book, I met his grandson and other family members and was allowed to see a number of personal artefacts that Lewis either owned or sent to his family. It is known that his wife, Florence, moved to Sheringham and never remarried. She wore a brooch with his picture in every day and rarely spoke about him.

Based on that, I visited him in January 2020 to pay my respects to someone who is still greatly loved and remembered by his family.

Guidebook

At Ribécourt-la-Tour head to Ribécourt British Cemetery; there are ten Norfolks buried in this cemetery, should you wish to visit them. The road you are on is the D89, which goes to Villers-Plouich. Opposite the cemetery entrance is a track. Take this track and drive up to the top of the ridge and park up by the wind turbine you will come to on the left.

Once there, you will be in the position to see where Unseen Trench and Unseen Support Trench were positioned. If you walk 100 metres back the way you came, you will see the road bends slightly. At this point in the field to your left heading towards the D29 is where Unseen Trench was positioned. Another 50 metres from this position, again heading back, is where Unseen Support Trench was situated running in the same direction in the field on your left. If you carried on walking back the way you came up, you will see a concrete electricity pylon on your right. Mole Trench ran across this road from left to right.

If you walk back to your car, with the wind turbine on your left, you will also see the small hamlet of Beaucamps in the distance. This is the direction that the Norfolks advanced from.

What3words: trilogy.reproduced.choral.

Return to where you parked up and then take the D29 heading towards Marcoing. As you come out of the village you will see a track on your left. Park up here. This is where the 9th Battalion got to and you are stood on the site of Kaiser Trench, which ran from left to right across the road.

To get to Nine Wood, you need to head towards Marcoing on the D29. Once in the town, keep on the D29 and head towards Noyelles-sur-Escaut. Once you come to this village, you will see pedestrian lights on your right and a turning on the left. Turn here and take this track. You will see a no entry sign with the words '*Sauf Riverains*' below it. This means 'Except Residents', so you can take this road. Go up the rise and you will come to the edge of Nine Wood. You will see this is a crossroads and, on your right, there is a public footpath. Park here and on the left you will see a track. If you take this track you can walk around the edge of the wood. As you walk along here, you will come to a German bunker on the edge of the wood and will be able to see the remains of trenches and shell holes inside the wood.

What3words: persuasive.reimpose.navigate.

* * * * *

As the British took Bourlon and Bourlon Wood on 23 November 1917, the Germans began reinforcing the area. As early as the 23rd, the German command felt that a British breakthrough would not occur and began to consider a counteroffensive. Twenty divisions were arrayed in the Cambrai area.

The Germans intended to retake the Bourlon salient and also to attack around Havrincourt while diversionary attacks would hold IV Corps; it was hoped to at least reach the old positions on the Hindenburg Line. The Germans intended to employ the new tactics of a short, intense period of shelling followed by a rapid assault, leading elements attacking in groups rather than waves and bypassing strong opposition. For the initial assault at Bourlon, three divisions of *Gruppe* Arras under Otto von Moser were assigned.

On the eastern flank of the British salient, *Gruppe* Caudry attacked from Bantouzelle to Rumilly and aimed for Marcoing. *Gruppe* Busogny advanced from Banteux. These two corps groups had seven infantry divisions. Lt-Gen. Thomas D'Oyly Snow, commander of the British VII Corps to the south of the threatened area, warned III Corps of German preparations.

The German attack began at 7 a.m. on 30 November; almost immediately, the majority of III Corps divisions were heavily engaged. The German infantry's advance was unexpectedly swift. The commanders of 29th and 12th divisions were almost captured, with Brig.-Gen. Vincent having to fight his way out of his headquarters and then grab men from retreating units to try to halt the Germans.

In the south, the German advance spread across 8 miles and came within a few miles of the vital village of Metz and its link to Bourlon. At Bourlon, the men under Moser met with stiffer resistance. The British had assigned eight divisions' worth of fire support to the ridge and the Germans suffered heavy casualties. Despite this, the Germans closed and there was fierce fighting. British units displayed reckless determination; one group of eight British machine guns fired over 70,000 rounds in their efforts to stem the German advance.

The ferocity of the German counterattack can be seen in Ernst Junger's book *Storm of Steel* in the chapter entitled 'The Double Battle of Cambrai'. Junger was initially positioned in the grounds of Baralle Castle:

> At nine o'clock in the morning our artillery began a powerful pounding, which from quarter to twelve to ten to twelve achieved the intensity of drumfire. The woods of Bourlon, which were not even under direct attack as they were too heavily defended, simply vanished in a chartreuse fog of gas. At ten to twelve we observed through our binoculars lines of riflemen emerging on to the empty crater landscape, while the rear batteries were harnessed up and rushed forward to new positions.

The 9th Battalion were still positioned at Nine Wood and Lt-Col. Prior takes up the story of their experience during the counterattack:

> We all awoke very early sneezing violently and with our eyes streaming from the effects of gas shells and it was barely light before the enemy started shelling in grim earnest. He evidently knew of our headquarters for he bombarded our gravel pit unceasingly.
>
> I received a warning message from Brigade that we were to be especially careful of our left flank as the Bosche counter attack was expected towards Cantaing. I warned C Coy (my reserve company) accordingly but there was already every indication that the attack had already been launched and was developing on my right flank and not on my left.
>
> I had all the Battalion Headquarters out and got them into the best defensive position I could find round the sand pit and overlooking Marcoing. Marcoing lies in a valley and on the slopes on the other side we could see line after line of troops advancing. The 2nd Sherwood Foresters were on my right front and I went to them to learn what they knew of the situation. I found they had a very fair defensive position and learnt where their various companies were located
>
> They had no knowledge however, whether Marcoing was in our hands or the enemy's' and I directed the company commander to send out a good N.C.O. to find out. As I came back I met the M.O. of the Leicesters (an American doctor) who with his stretcher bearers and one or two orderlies had just left Marcoing.
>
> From him I learnt that Marcoing was still held by us. No advance had been reported on my left and I came to the conclusion that at any rate the right was the

most urgent affair and that I could get 'C' Company up to prolong the left of the Sherwood Foresters and cover the exits from Marcoing in case that town fell into the enemy's hands.

All this time not only were we being unmercifully shelled but the air was alive with the enemy's aircraft who were swooping down using their machine guns as well as directing their artillery fire.

'C' Company deployed and advanced in extended order to the line I had indicated. They had barely got to their position, which was quite in the open and unprotected when an enemy plane came over, dropped some lights and the enemy dropped shell after shell on or near their line. These guns enfiladed their line and it would have been useless sacrifice for the troops to have remained in this exposed and enfiladed position until they were actually needed to repel the advance by rifle fire. I accordingly prepared to tell them to withdraw to the nearest cover when I saw that they were retiring by platoons.

They got under cover of sorts and had then to consider the position of Battalion Headquarters. the enemy attack developing on our right instead of on our left put Battalion Headquarters on the extreme right of the Battalion front, moreover the shelling on the sandpit was so intense that it was almost impossible for runners to get safely in or out. By degrees I got headquarters out of the sand pits into a small open trench near Nine Wood. This was conveniently situated for all companies and here we remained all day until nightfall when I took over a dug-out nearby which Major Moon, commanding the Brigade M.G. Coy found for me.

It was a day of constant alarms, constant shelling and terrific air fighting but the enemy never got Marcoing and could not therefore deliver an infantry attack against us. That night our transport officer (Sinclair) arrived with blood curding tales of what had occurred in our right rear.

How the Bosche had got quite into Gouzeacourt where our transport lay and how our last transport wagons had just got out of one end of the lines as the enemy had come in on the other. For the next two days our position was most uncomfortable. We were a pronounced salient and were shelled from every angle. We had again take over the outpost line but I had managed to found another headquarters, by no means a comfortable of palatial one but a good deal better than sharing the miserable hole in Nine Wood with the Sherwood Foresters.

James Cooper's diary entry is more succinct:

Friday 30th
Had to leave our position. Fritz advancing. I stayed until the last. Got here (Fins) about 4 o'clock a.m. Lost all my kit. It's a day I shall not forget.

The 7th Battalion had been in reserve for the opening of Cambrai on 20 November and only 'C' Company had been involved in the 12th (Eastern) Division that day. They had then spent a relative period of quiet after the battle and went back into the line on 29 November facing Banteux situated on the western side of the Canal St Quentin.

At 6.30 a.m., the Germans began to bombard Villers-Guislain, hitting the entire divisional front and the divisions either side. The war diary for this period was destroyed in the fighting so what is written in it was retrospective of the fighting on 30 November 1917. The entry is brief and states:

> About 7 a.m. a very heavy Hun Barrage commenced and at 7.40 a.m. he attacked in mass in enormous numbers from Gonnelieu which he had just previously taken about 7.35 a.m. and also from Banteaux. The Bosche attacked the battalion from the right flank and the front. Our Lewis guns did splendid work, mowing down the enemy in large numbers, but by weight of numbers, he forced the Battalion to fall back on to Battalion Headquarters in Bleak Trench and a strong point on our left front.
>
> The Hun succeeded in surrounding many of our men, who were thereby forced to surrender. We made a splendid fight and accounted for enormous numbers of the enemy. About 10 a.m. 2nd Lieut G MADDISON was only officer left, and he, with the remaining men of the battalion, attached himself to the 9th Fusiliers Regt.

At that point in time, it was not certain who had been killed or who had been captured. This included the CO Lt-Col. Henry Lex Francis Gielgud who was reported missing.

Further German attacks forced the battalion back to the south of the Cambrai road where they ended up around Fusilier Reserve and Fusilier Trench at La Vacquerie. On 3 December 1917, a much-depleted battalion marched to Heudicourt. Because there is very little information on the fate of the 7th Battalion, I think it is important to try and gather as much as we can on that terrible action. Therefore, we can look at the German perspective for this. *Hauptmann* Schede, commander of 2nd Battalion Grenadier Regiment 110, noted:

> It was late on the morning of 30 November. The German counter-attack against the break in by the British west and southwest of Cambrai during the tank battle was making victorious progress. The 28th Division which had proved itself in heavy fighting Verdun during 1917, was deployed on the flank of the southern pincer movement. Headquarters Second Army had designated the build-up area of Gouzeacourt as the first objective of the southern wing, but standing in the way were the British positions at Gonnelieu.
>
> With exemplary dash the Baden *Leibgrenadier* Regiment 109, commanded by *Oberstlentnant Freiherr* von Forstner already thrust forward into the German *Siegriedstellung* on the bank of the *Schelde* [Escaut], which had been in enemy hands since the British attempt at breakthrough.
>
> In order to break the bitter British resistance, it had been necessary to send all battalions into action. Weakened by heavy losses, especially amongst leaders, its sub-

units mixed up following the trench fighting the *Leibgrenadiers* Came up against additional British pockets of resistance to the east of Gonnelieu. It was impossible for them to clear these from their own resources; fresh forces had to intervene.

The 2nd Battalion of the Baden *Kaisergrenadier* Regiment 110 from Heidelberg was quickly on the scene having, in accordance with orders, followed up a tactical bound behind the *Leibgrenadier* Regiment 109. After the battalion had moved under artillery and machine gun fire, first along the narrow track through the marshy margins of the Schelde then across the Schelde canal by means of half-destroyed crossing points—fortunately with only slight casualties—it kept close up behind its sister regiment as it drove forward, in order to be able to support it whenever and wherever it was required

With the *Leibgrenadiers* stalled in front of Gonnelieu, the moment had arrived.

Hauptmann Schede, commanding officer of the 2nd Battalion, went forward to join the commander of *Leibregiment* in the front line who was conducting a reconnaissance. One heavily defended strongpoint located along the Banteux–Gonnelieu road had so far beaten off with bloody losses every attempt to capture it. The light machine gun sections of *Unteroffiziers* Alexander and Seuffert, which were amongst the leading elements of 5th Company. Thrusting forward under its daring commander Reserve *Leutnant* Kempf, were already engaging this enemy nest of resistance. Swift action was needed. It was essential that the British were not allowed to reorganise their resistance within and to the west of Gonnelieu.

The commanding officer ordered Reserve *Leutnant* Kempf to capture the strongpoint with his company. Alter brief preparation in the available trenches and shell holes, the company launched an attack on a broad front with exemplary daring. Heavy fire brought down by the British, some of whom were firing from the cover knocked out tanks, forced the company into cover after the initial dashes forward. However, the example shown by their platoon commanders, *Landwehr Leutnant* Geiges and *Vizefeldwebels* Heinzler and Hermann, together with other courageaous men, kept the platoons moving forward unstoppably. It proved possible to force a way into the densely manned position at two different points.

The British defended desperately and the trenches had to be wrested from bit by bit using grenades. Quickly the cry went up, 'Grenades forward' and every single available grenade was taken forward to 5th Company along communication trenches by carrying parties from the other companies. It was effectively impossible to attempt to cross open ground around the maze or trenches because of the machine gun fire which swept it.

Right at the front stood the platoon commanders, providing their grenade teams with a superb example of coolness under fire However it was not long before *Leutnant* Geiges was mortally wounded during this determined advance.

He was swiftly followed by both *Vizefeldwebels* Heinzler and Hermann, who were both killed by enemy grenades. The very youthful *Fahnrich* Heinzler, who had been with the regiment since Verdun, rushed up to replace them. He pressed forward but also met a hero's death. Others stepped into the breach and took the lead. There was no hanging back. Above all it was thanks to the energetic and exemplary forcefulness of the daring *Unteroffizier* Gersbach that the enemy was forced back more and more.

After two hours of bitter trench fighting, which cost the lives of many brave grenadiers, the enemy resistance collapsed. The remnants of the garrison of the strongpoint attempted to escape across the open ground to Gonnelieu, but machine gun here cut down the would-be escapers. A surprise attempt at a counter-attack withered away in the fire of a light machine gun which the watchful *Unteroffizier* Gersbach had brought into action. The way to Gonnelieu was open. The attack gathered momentum once more and, by the afternoon, the trenches to the west of Gonnelieu were in German hands.

The battle for the strong point had courageous 5th Company sixteen killed, including two commanders and a further sixteen wounded, most of the company had shown what iron-willed Baden grenadiers will achieve. The exemplary daring and death-defying courage involved in the capture of this strongpoint means that it will ever remain one of the laurel leaves in the wreath of fame of the Baden *Kaisergrenadier* Regiment.

Sadly, Lt-Col. Gielgud had been killed in action, along with a total of eighteen officers and 333 other ranks killed, wounded, or missing. His obituary in his old school magazine, *The Aldenhamian*, noted:

Henry Lex Francis Adam Gielgud (S.H. 1892–1900) was the only son of the late Henry Gielgud. In Sept., 1898, he became Head of the School and Editor of the *Aldenhamian*. He was elected a scholar of Pembroke College, Cambridge, in Dec., 1899, and in 1903 he was placed in Class I., Div. 2, of the Classical Tripos. In 191)3 he rowed in the University Trial Eights. He became a Chartered Accountant, and in 1910–1911 was in S. America as a member of the Commission formed to look into the affairs of Peruvian Amazon Company.

In 1912 he went to Messrs. Erlanger & Co., as Secretary to Leach's Argentine Estates, Ltd., and the Argentine Iron & Steel Co., Ltd. In December, 1914, he was gazetted to the Norfolks, and received his second star in Jan., 1915. In May, 1915, he went to France with his Battalion, was promoted Captain in October after the heavy fighting near the quarries, and later was in some of the heaviest fighting on the Somme.

He was awarded the M.C. in August, 1916, and became Major and second in command the following month. He was severely wounded in May, 1917, but was able to return to the front in November, when he took command of his old Battalion. On Nov. 30th the last sight of him was 'completely surrounded by Germans and fighting desperately, although already wounded in several places'. A brother officer wrote: 'I can only say that the Colonel gave his life in a cause that I know was dearest to him, and died like a brave man in the face of fearful odds.

He was the finest type of an Englishman'. His late C.O. described him as an extraordinarily brave man, a very fine soldier, and the loyalist 2nd in command any man ever had.

Pretty much all that had been taken in the previous offensive was now back in the hands of the Germans, and it was only counterattacks by the Guards Division, the arrival of British tanks, and the fall of night that allowed the line to be held.

By the following day, the impetus of the German advance was lost but pressure on 3 December led to the German capture of La Vacquerie and a British withdrawal east of the St Quentin canal. The Germans had reached a line looping from the ridge at St Quentin to near Marcoing.

On the same day, Haig ordered a retreat from the salient, especially the aspects of the British line, which still held, and around the Marcoing front. Lt-Col. Prior received orders to withdraw after holding the outpost line for another two days:

> Here after two nights we received orders to evacuate our line and retire to a prepared position at Ribécourt. We had rather anticipated that something of this sort would have to be done but it is a hateful thing to have to give up hard won ground. I got my orders which were for the gradual withdrawal of the outpost line through the support companies holding Nine Wood and then for the withdrawal of the support companies.
>
> The withdrawal was carried out excellently with only a few casualties. Indeed, I don't think the enemy was aware of the evacuation until long after it had been effected. We found ourselves once more in Ribécourt. We now began to have hopes of getting relieved.
>
> For over a fortnight we had lived and slept in our clothes without as much as removing our boots. Moreover, the German is a dirty beast and we had lived in his dugouts. However, our spell was not yet at an end. We were allotted the sector in the valley through which ran the Grande Ravine and which eventually found its way into Marcoing. It was though quite likely that there would be a further enemy offensive and as the position was still most sketchily prepared we had a heap of work before us both digging and wiring especially the latter.
>
> The men were pretty fairly done up but nevertheless worked very well and the shelling was not much above the average of trench warfare. The enemy did not really know where we were and I remember one afternoon seeing him shell steadily a small group of houses about half way between our front line and Marcoing under the impression that we were holding them.
>
> Equally we did not know the exact position of the enemy. Presumably he was re-occupy Marcoing and he certainly had patrols out in front of that town but on one occasion Sergeant Grand took out a patrol which made a daring reconnaissance quite into Marcoing returning via the isolated houses without seeing a Bosche.
>
> Our front-line across the valley was nothing less than a running stream all efforts to drain which had failed. The troops in this line and to a lesser degree in the support line had a miserable time as there was practically no shelter. Christmas was rapidly approaching when the glad news of our relief arrived. We all breathed a sigh of relief when we got clear of Ribécourt through which we had to march on our way back.

Both day and night the enemy kept this village under almost constant shell fire, but I believe all the companies got through without casualties.

We had a very long trek out for the weary men but it was a cold frosty night and they got along very well. A dirtier looking crowd than the 9th Norfolk Regiment were on the night they came out of the line would have been hard to find.

Just four weeks without a change, living and sleeping anywhere and anyhow, fighting, marching and digging without respite. The battalion came to rest in the Arras sector in a village not far behind the old front-line.

By 7 December, the British gains were abandoned except for a portion of the Hindenburg line around Havrincourt, Ribécourt, and Flesquières. The Germans had exchanged this territorial loss for land to the south of Welsh ridge. Casualties were around 45,000 for each side, with 11,000 Germans and 9,000 British taken prisoner. In terms of territory, the Germans recovered most of their early losses and gained a little elsewhere, albeit with a net loss of ground. The battle showed the British that even the strongest trench defences could be overcome by a surprise artillery-infantry attack using the newly available methods and equipment, with a mass tank attack as a bonus; it also showed the Germans the effectiveness of their similar new tactics so recently used against the Russians.

These lessons were later successfully implemented by both sides. The German revival after the shock of the British attack improved morale, but the potential for more attacks like this meant that the Germans had to divert resources to anti-tank defences and weapons, a diversion of resources the Germans could ill afford.

In total, ninety-four men from the 7th Battalion Norfolk Regiment were killed in action or died of wounds between 30 November and 3 December 1917. Most have no known graves and are commemorated on the Cambrai Memorial at Louverval.

The 9th Battalion got off relatively lightly during their time in and around Nine Wood during the German counterattack, and the Commonwealth War Graves Commission records their loss as twenty men killed between 21 November and 7 December 1917.

Guidebook

For the 7th Battalion, from Gonnelieu, take the D96 towards Banteux. On your left, you will come to a very small fenced off area with an electricity transformer inside. In the field beyond that fenced off area is where Bleak Trench once stood.

What3words: eats.facemask.selfish.

25

The 7th and 9th Battalions, The Kaiser's Battle, Lagnicourt to Bouzincourt Ridge: 21 March to 5 April 1918

After Cambrai, the 9th Battalion had spent a spell in training and had then gone back into the line around the Bapaume–Cambrai railway and also in the reserve lines around Frémicourt. At the beginning of February, fifteen officers and 300 other ranks from the recently disbanded 8th Norfolks joined the battalion. By mid-February, they had moved to the area around Queant and Pronville. By 17 March, very much like the fictitious battalion from R. C. Sheriff's book *Journey's End*, the battalion found itself in the trenches on the right sub-sector at Lagnicourt. In that book, a battalion is in the line waiting for a German attack, which they know is coming.

The same can be said for the 9th Battalion, and for this chapter, we can again fall back on the memoirs of Lt-Col. Bernard Henry Leathes Prior for this period of the war. Since Cambrai, he had had a period of leave where he had recovered from the effects of the gas that had landed in Nine Wood. Lt-Col. Prior described his new position:

> The front held by the division was generally on a forward slope opposite the villages of Queant and Pronville. 'No Man's-Land' averaged three-quarters of a mile in width. The whole area was downhill and very suitable for the action with tanks. The position lay astride a succession of well-defined broad spurs and narrow valleys (like the fingers of a partially opened hand), merging into the broad transverse valley which separated the British line from the two villages above mentioned.

By now, the British had taken over ground to the south of Saint Quentin that had been in the control of the French, and by the end of January 1918, this area was in a woeful state and could not be considered a line that could easily be defended. The British 5th Army was sent to the new battle zone and took up positions along the whole front from the River Oise to the River Sensee.

Other areas were not in a good state of repair either, with Lt-Col. Prior noting:

> The ground was a portion of that area wrested from the enemy in the Cambrai offensive of November–December 1917, but had only improvised trenches. A month's hard frost in January had militated against digging, and, though there were a complete front trench and reserve trench, the support trenches hardly existed, and dug-outs were noticeable by their absence.

By then, the German High Command were looking at making a decisive attack on the BEF. This was to be a final gamble before the Americans, who had declared war on Germany on 6 April 1917, could be brought into the fray on the Western Front. Once that happened, it would be all but impossible to win against the might of America and her vast resources of men and materials.

With Russia now defeated, the empire there had collapsed by 1 January 1918 and had become Soviet Russia; Germany could now rely on further divisions that had now come back from the Eastern Front after they had signed a treaty with the Russians at Brest-Litovsk on 3 March 1918.

Germany's plan was to punch a hole through the old Somme battlefield and then turn to the north-west in order to cut the British supply lines and then surround the remaining British defences around Flanders, which would bring the collapse and surrender of the BEF.

The German strategy was further bolstered by the belief that the British had burnt themselves out in the heavy fighting 1917, and it can be stated that part of this was quite true because the British were now suffering from a manpower crisis, and many of the battalions that had fought bravely and with honour in the battles of 1916 and 1917 now ceased to be as the BEF was reorganised to make up for its losses. The overall offensive became known as '*Kaiserschlacht*' (Kaiser's Battle).

Their tactics relied heavily on speed and surprise and the use of storm troops who, along with the use of artillery that specifically targeted the enemy's rear lines, found and infiltrated the British weak points and thus bypass and isolate heavily-defended positions in the front line. Heavy Infantry would then attack the isolated strong points with reinforcements exploiting the breaches forcing the enemy to retire. It was believed that the Germans would strike and that 5th Army would take the brunt of the attack:

> General Gough first drew the attention of GHQ to the fact that the presence of General von Hutier, who, as is now definitely known, was accompanied by his Chief of Staff, General von Sauberzweig, had been ascertained on the Fifth Army front; he also emphasised the various signs of the mounting attack. The probability was, he thought, in view of the state of the ground further north and the natural desire of the Germans to obtain an early decision that the blow would fall against the Fifth Army.

Gough's predictions would be correct that the brunt of the attack would fall on 5th Army, but the initial attack, which began on 21 March 1918, known as Operation Michael, also fell on the 3rd Army front, who held the line between Arras and Cambrai, and the 9th Battalion would find themselves in the thick of it.

The line held by the three brigades of the 6th Division was 4,500 yards long and had the 18th Brigade on the right, the 71st in the centre, and the 16th on the left. The depth of the front outpost zone to the battle-zone, effectively the reserve line, was about 2,000 yards. All three of the brigades were committed to the defence of this area, having to assign one battalion each to defend the outpost zone and two battalions each on the battle-zone. The defence was hampered by the undulating nature of the ground, which did not provide good fields of fire. On 21 March 1918, the 9th Battalion had 'B' and 'D' Companies in the frontline and 'C' and 'A' Companies in support. To the left of the 9th Battalion were the 2nd Battalion Sherwood Foresters, with the 1st Battalion Leicestershire Regiment in reserve.

Lt-Col. Prior provided a detailed account of this initial thoughts on the coming of this battle. He was so sure the attack was imminent that after checking his battalion, he went out into no-man's-land:

> In the Bosche lines there was a stillness which, at the same time, was not a complete silence, just as if a large number of men were already in position, waiting in intense excitement, and speaking to each other in whispers. So much so that, on my return to battalion headquarters, I told Lieutenant Tyce, the officer on duty, that I felt convinced that the attack would be made, and that I therefore should not turn in until daylight.

Lt-Col. Prior's fears were correct, and at 5.10 a.m. on 21 March 1918, Gen. Sir Hubert Gough, commanding the British 5th Army, was awakened by the roar of a bombardment:

> … so sustained and steady that it at once gave me the impression of some crushing, smashing power. I jumped out of bed and walked across the passage to the telephone in my office and called up the General Staff. On what part of our front was the bombardment falling? The answer came back immediately: All four corps report heavy bombardment along their front.

This is borne out from the 9th Battalion war diary:

> At 5 a.m. the enemy heavily bombarded our system with gas and heavy calibre shells and an attack was evidently imminent. The bombardment continued intensely all day, obliterating our front and close support lines, also strong-points. Owing to the heroic resistance of our men the enemy had only penetrated our front and close support lines up to 12 p.m. This was due to the overwhelming numbers of the enemy, and the obliteration of our system of defence.

James Cooper also recorded the opening of this offensive in his diary:

Thursday 21st March

Artillery duel all night. A fierce artillery fire started at 5 o clock and is still proceeding, time 10.30. I have been informed our casualties are light; Fritz found our air balloons found mark by the German airmen. Later on, our airmen bring down a Fritz plane.

This attack was aided by the fact that thick fog lay around the ground the Germans were to assault. The artillery bombardment also had gas shells within it, and the 9th Battalion men had to don their gas-masks as well. Initial reports noted that although the bombardment on 'C' Company was intense, there was no sign of the enemy.

'B' Company was suffering from casualties and had lost Lt Cecil Arthur Williams, late of the 1/5th Battalion Norfolk Regiment, killed and Capt. Bernard Cutbill gravely wounded and this company was now in the command of Lt R. L. Percival.

The German attacks came through the three valleys at Noreuil to the left, Lagnicourt in the centre, and Morchies on the right. By 11 a.m., the 59th Division had been driven back, this division was on the left of the 6th Division, and the 16th Brigade had to retire back to Noreuil.

German officer Ernst Junger was positioned with his company from the 73rd Fusilier Regiment. Junger's regiment had the task of punching through the villages of Écoust-St-Mein and Noreuil. His route would take him just to the north-west of where the 9th Battalion were positioned as his company pushed toward Vraucourt. He described his observations of the battle as it opened:

It had become light. At our rear, the massive roaring and surging was still waxing, even though any intensification of the noise had seemed impossible. In front of us an impenetrable wall of smoke, dust and gas had formed. Men ran past, shouting cheerily in our ears. Infantrymen and artillerymen, pioneers and telephonists, Prussians and Bavarians, officers and men, all were overwhelmed by the elemental force of the fire storm, and all were impatient to go over the top at nine-forty. At twenty-five past eight our heavy mortars, which were being massed behind our frontlines, entered the fray. We watched the daunting two-hundredweight bombs look high up into the air, and come crashing down with the force of volcanic eruptions on the enemy lines. Their impacts were like a row of spurting craters.

The *Official History of the Great War* notes that the 71st brigade put up a strong defence of their sector:

The 71st Brigade, astride the narrow spur opposite Queant also made a good defence in the Battle Zone. Up to about 11.15 a.m. its front remained intact, several successful local counter attacks having been made. But he although he failed on the right, which held out all day, the enemy, coming in great force, succeeded in breaking through Lagnicourt and, circling round the north side, soon gained possession of it. Having done so he could enfilade the rest of the brigade line; a strong point outside the south east corner of the village, was twice penetrated, but on each occasion was retaken by counter attack in hand to hand fighting during the morning.

The 9th Norfolk's positions were overrun by the enemy and Lt-Col. Prior ordered Capt. John Hancock, of 'A' Company, to counterattack. Capt. Hancock lost three of his junior officers wounded while being briefed by Lt-Col. Prior and he watched Hancock move across what Prior described as 'shell-swept ground'. Wounded men from the Norfolks reported to their CO that casualties were very high, but he also learnt from a wounded man that Capt. Hancock had been successful in reaching the Sherwood Forester's headquarters. Capt. Gerald Failes of 'C' Company reported that he had completely routed the enemy and could hold his trenches against a frontal attack.

This good news was quickly hampered by the fact that Prior then saw the enemy on the brow of a hill not 40 yards away from him:

> I got a machine gun on to this party at once and they fled back. The position was, however, most alarming. It was obvious that the enemy had broken quite through the defences on our left flank, the promised reinforcements had not arrived, and I had only about sixty men left with me.

Lt-Col. Prior got what was left of his men together, reported his predicament to Brigade HQ, and told them he would hang on at all costs. The Leicestershires then came up and took up positions in a sunken road, but Prior was told by Brigade HQ that the Germans had captured positions and that they were to withdraw to the Vaulx-Morchies line:

> It is difficult to explain on paper the extraordinary position we were in. 'C' Company, with few remnants of 'B' and 'D', were holding the original battle position, with the remains of the Sherwood Foresters on their left. The remains of 'A' Company, after a most desperate fight, had dropped back and formed the first stage of a protective flank. With a large interval between them, this was carried on by the two Leicester companies, and on their left flank, as I moved to the Morchies-Vaudricourt line, I dropped out small flanking parties from Battalion HQ and such stragglers from 'D' Company and the Sherwood Foresters as I could pick up.

Lt-Col. Prior now held a front of less than 500 yards and a protective flank of 2 miles. He was lucky to get out of this area intact as the enemy were now holding a sunken lane called the Report Centre, which he had to pass within a hundred yards of. Having reached his new line, he found a company of Leicesters and another company of Leicester Pioneers. Lt-Col. Prior became worried over the withdrawal of the rest of his troops and learnt from the brigade on his right, the 18th, that their Battle Zone had now been evacuated. Prior went forward to see for himself and luckily met Capt. Failes coming out of that area:

> All day long had they fought the oncoming enemy hordes, and each attack had withered and broken down before their fire. Failes himself estimated that his company alone had accounted for upwards of 2,000 of the enemy. They had fought until their rifles were too hot to hold and their Lewis guns had to be cooled down before they could fire another magazine. Finally, when ordered to withdraw, they had come out bringing all their casualties.

What was later noted by Prior was that 'C' Company had had to deal with a frontal attack and a breakthrough from the enemy into the Sherwood Foresters's lines. This in turn had threatened 'C' Company. It was only through repeated bombing attacks that this had failed. Captain Failes had been in the thick of the fighting and with the support of his company had stopped the advance of the enemy.

What was left of the Sherwood Foresters also managed to get back and the Morchies line was then held by what was left of all three battalions of the 71st Brigade. The *Official History* noted:

> From this pivot the Sherwood Foresters, reinforced by a company of the 9/Norfolk and two companies of the 1/Leicestershire formed a new line facing north along the crest, and later one of the Leicester companies made a left defensive flank by manning a wired communication trench known as the Lagnicourt Switch, which extended from the western side of Lagnicourt to Morchies along the spur.
>
> Although surrounded on three sides this position continued to be held during the afternoon, and thus all the enemy's attempts to break out of Lagnicourt were defeated, though he succeeded, about 2 p.m., in capturing two strong points on its outskirts.

The *Official History* noted that at the end of this day the combined strength of the Norfolks and the Sherwood Foresters was 130 and the Leicesters had 338 from all ranks left.

The Norfolk history notes that in total they lost ten officers killed and five wounded. The total casualty toll for other ranks was 347. The total deaths for the battalion between 21 and 23 March 1918 can be amended to eighty-three men. From that total, from the officers Lt-Col. Prior mentioned in his reports, it is known that Capt. Hancock was killed in action during the counterattack he led. Lt-Col. Prior later heard from survivors from the Sherwood Foresters that Capt. Hancock's counterattack had come in at a crucial time, bringing the enemy advance to a standstill, and they had accounted for at least six of the enemy for every one of their casualties. Capt. Cutbill did not recover from his wounds and died in captivity the next day. Lt-Col. Prior was himself gravely wounded on 22 March 1918 when the battalion was retiring towards Beugny. He records this in his memoirs:

> I accordingly started forward to give the necessary orders when I was brought down by a bullet. Bassingthwaite bound me up and I thought at first, I could carry on. I felt, however, weak and I was losing a lot of blood and the enemy were so close. I thought I had better try and get back whilst I could still walk. I therefore sent a message to Failes that I had been wounded and that he was to take command of the battalion. I took a runner with me to report the Brigade and as I was feeling very groggy got my servant and the H.Q, cook to bring along a stretcher in case I could not walk the whole distance.

James Cooper noted this loss and the high officer casualty rate in his diary:

> Friday 22nd
> Just heard all company commanders killed. C.O. alright and only about 30 of the Batt left who were in the line, Tubby Hills adamant. Had to first bury the dead this morning at Frémicourt cemetery awful lot of them and they still come. Heavy shelling all round us I think we are falling back on Bapaume.

James Cooper was quite correct in this. The 9th Norfolks, the 2nd Sherwood Foresters, and the 1st Leicesters continued to hold the line on high ground to the north of Beugny until they were relieved by the 123rd Brigade during the night of 22–23 March.

Once the 9th Norfolks had moved out of the line, they retired via the Frémicourt–Bapaume Road ending up at Bihucourt, situated to the north-west of Bapaume, at 6 p.m. On 26 March 1918, after entraining at Puisieux-au-Mont, they arrived at 'H' Camp at St Sixte, at 2 a.m. and then moved on to Winnezeele on 27 March where they tried to sort out their kit, although the war diary noted that most of the men were without the greater part of that.

Another officer lost that day was Capt. Maurice William Campbell Sprott, MC, who had served as the adjutant for the 9th Battalion. Lt-Col. Prior wrote of him:

> Probably no one knows as well as I do the loss he is to the regiment and to the country. As my Adjutant, he carried out his work with the utmost capability. His exceptional brain power was backed by earnest hard work and his sense of duty was of the highest. Indeed, it was that grim sense of duty which led him taking command of the front-line trench, and he met his death like the brave soldier he was, in the front-line trench waiting for the German advance. Some 40 minutes before the attack I went round the outpost with him, and he was then more cheery than I had seen him for some time. He has earned the respect of every officer and man in the battalion.

For his part in the defence of Lagnicourt, Lt-Col. Prior was awarded the DSO, his citation stating:

> Lt.-Col. Bernard Henry Leathes Prior, D.S.O., Norf. R.
>
> For conspicuous gallantry and devotion to duty. Throughout two days of an enemy advance, and until wounded, he set a splendid example of coolness and courage under most trying conditions, personally supervising the readjustments which had to be made to meet the enemy attacks, and the gallant resistance offered by his battalion was largely due to his magnificent example of fearless determination.

Lt-Col. Prior did not return back to the battalion until July, and when he did, he found his wounds were still giving him trouble and eventually he had to inform his divisional commander and was sent to a medical board who sent him home: 'It was with the deepest regret that I left the battalion. I had had unpleasant experiences and uncomfortable times whilst serving with them but from first to last I had receieved the most splendid and wholehearted support from all ranks'. We will catch up with Lt-Col. Prior in the postscript.

Guidebook

At the edge of Lagnicourt, on the D5 heading towards Doignies, park up. Walk on this road where you will see the road becomes a sunken lane. The Norfolks were situated in the field to the left as you walk along this road. They made their fighting withdrawal from here, crossing over this road, and then heading back through the fields on your right, which intersects between Lagnicourt and Morchies.

What3words: majorly.donations.hosting.

* * * * *

The 7th Battalion had been at Merville since its terrible experience during the German counterattack at Cambrai. On 6 February 1918, it received a draft of five officers and eighty-four men from the disbanded 8th Norfolks. They had also received a new CO, with Lt-Col. Evan Thomas Rees joining them in December 1917.

In February, the battalion moved in and out of the line around Sailly and Fleurbaix, and while there, they managed to repel a German trench raid and also took part in a training exercise. At the beginning of March, a small trench raid under the command of Capt. Charles Nash was successful in getting into the German lines and capturing a prisoner. For this action, Capt. Nash was awarded a bar to his MC. They also had to contend with active German artillery all through the month and also had to contend with another two German trench raids.

When the Germans launched their offensive on 21 March 1918, the battalion was moved quickly to Albert along with the rest of the 35th Brigade. Here they set up a defensive line between Albert and Aveluy.

At this time, the Germans were pushing five divisions towards the River Ancre in an effort to create a bridgehead across the river. The war diary for this period was lost in the fighting so what was written about this time is retrospective.

The Norfolks were positioned with outposts on the River Ancre with their main line on the Arras railway. On 26 March 1918, as the Germans pushed onward, the battalion was ordered back; as a result, the 7th Battalion Suffolk Regiment created a gap as they moved back from Albert. At dusk, the Germans attacked the 7th Norfolks's positions and were only beaten off when they were reinforced by a company of the 9th Essex Regiment and one company of the 5th Northamptonshire Regiment.

Once the attack had been stopped, 'A' and 'C' Companies positioned themselves in a brick factory, and on the morning of 27 March, they took heavy artillery and machine-gun fire and their right flank had to retire but no attack materialised. With no right flank and with no news on the 7th Suffolks, who had been pushed out of Albert, Lt-Col. Rees had to establish a line with forty men, which came under fire from a low-flying aircraft around the high ground off the Bouzincourt–Aveluy road known as Bouzincourt Ridge. Posts sent out to the right were harassed by artillery, but one was eventually established by Capt. Richard Weaver and RSM William Golder.

They were facing the 3rd Marine and the 79th Regiments. These two regiments were pushing towards Aveluy and were putting both flanks of the battalion at risk. Lt-Col. Rees ordered a retirement of his line back to a sunken road off the ridge under heavy artillery and machine-gun fire. The retrospective war diary notes:

> The position became precarious during the afternoon as the enemy established machine guns enfilading the road and were also working round our left flank. Captain Tapply therefore went back to Bde HQ for instructions. Brigade said that the post was to be held if possible and sent up three Vickers guns to assist. These never arrived however. At dusk the enemy had entirely surrounded the post and eventually rushed it.
>
> Lt Col Rees was by this time wounded and was taken prisoner together with Captain Soames who remained with him. Most of the garrison however were able to withdraw. Captain Tapply had this time reached the line held by the Northants in rear of the post and hearing that it was hard pressed had taken up two platoons of reinforce. He met the garrison withdrawing and put them in position on the right flank of the Northants which was in the air.

On the morning of 28 March, the remnants of the battalion were relieved and sent to Hennencourt. The battalion was put under the temporary command of Maj. West of the Suffolk Regiment and 200 men answered the roll call.

Losses here amounted to nineteen officers killed, wounded, or captured and 282 other ranks killed, wounded, or missing. This can be amended to thirty-three dead, most of whom have no known grave and are commemorated on the Pozières Memorial.

One of the officers lost that day was Capt. Charles Frederic Wybrow Nash, MC & Bar, of 'C' Company. Capt. Nash is recorded as being buried where he fell, and his CO wrote: 'He was a splendid officer, always cheerful and ready for anything'. The adjutant of the battalion noted: 'I have never had an officer who was loved as well as he was. He was exceptionally brave, always cheery and took such good care of his men. His loss will be felt in the battalion most keenly'. Another officer noted: 'He was a hero and a man in every sense of the word. He was without doubt the best a bravest boy I have ever served with'.

Capt. Nash was aged twenty when he died and was the son of the Rev. Charles Barnett Nash and Ethel Phoebe Nash of The Vicarage of Watton. He has no known grave and is commemorated on the Pozières Memorial.

During the fighting around Bouzincourt Ridge, a VC was posthumously awarded to the CO of the 4th Battalion Bedfordshire Regiment: Lt-Col. John Stanhope Collings-Wells, DSO. His battalion had been ordered to counterattack Bouzincourt Ridge on 27 March; he rallied and he led the exhausted battalion in the attack himself where he was wounded in both arms in the attack. Despite these wounds, he led the remnants of his battered battalion, who took the position despite appalling enemy fire and drove the enemy back. Witnesses saw Lt-Col. Collings-Wells being physically dragged back to a bunker to have his wounds dressed as he was extremely reluctant to leave his men. Moments later, the bunker received a direct hit from a mortar shell and thirty-seven-year-old Collings-Wells, his second in command Maj. Nunnelly, and two other officers, including the medic, were killed outright.

His VC citation was listed in the *London Gazette* citation dated 24 April 1918:

His Majesty the KING has been graciously pleased to approve of the award of the Victoria Cross to the undermentioned Officers: Capt. (A./Lt.-Col.) John Stanhope Collings-Wells, D.S.O., late Bedf. Rg. For most conspicuous bravery, skilful leading and handling of his battalion in very critical situations during a withdrawal. When the rearguard was almost surrounded and in great danger of being captured, Lieutenant-Colonel Collings-Wells, realising the situation, called for volunteers to remain behind and hold up the enemy whilst the remainder of the rear-guard withdrew, and with his small body of volunteers held them up for one and a-half hours until they had expended every round of ammunition. During this time, he moved freely amongst his men guiding and encouraging them, and by his great courage undoubtedly saved the situation.

On a subsequent occasion, when his battalion was ordered to carry out a counterattack, he showed the greatest bravery. Knowing that his men were extremely tired after six days' fighting, he placed himself in front and led the attack, and even when twice wounded refused to leave them but continued to lead and encourage his men until he was killed at the moment of gaining their objective. The successful results of the operation were, without doubt, due to the undaunted courage exhibited by this officer.

Lt-Col. Collings-Wells is now buried in Bouzincourt Ridge Military Cemetery.

On 2 April 1918, the 12th Division went back to Bouzincourt Ridge placing the 35th Brigade on the right and the 36th Brigade on the left with the 37th Brigade in reserve. The area received heavy bombardments on 3 and 4 April, and the Germans launched an attack on the battalions in the front, the main thrust landing on the 7th Battalion Suffolk Regiment who were situated to the west of Albert. Here they again faced the 3rd Marine and the 79th Regiments. To the right of the Suffolks was the 12th Australian Division, who also bore the brunt of the German attacks, the attacks primarily falling on the 48th Battalion AIF. The Norfolks had to assist both battalions and 'B' Company relieved the Suffolk battalion and 'C' Company provided a defensive flank for the Australians. The main defensive line here fell on the Albert–Millencourt road.

Elements of the Suffolks retired through the Norfolk defensive line and the line here stabilised. Although the German attacks on 5 April had managed to capture part of Aveluy Wood, the Germans could not advance any further in this area.

The 7th Battalion were eventually relieved on 10 April and spent time in and out of the line around the old Somme battlefields of 1916. They would not go back into any major offensive action until August 1918.

The opening phase of Operation Michael had been a stunning success for the Germans and the British lost 177,739 men killed, wounded, and missing. Of this total, 90,000 were captured and 15,000 killed, but the Germans lost a higher number, the total being given as around 348,300 with the French losing just 92,000 men. However, this initial attack did slow down and the line was eventually drawn to the east of Amiens when determined German attacks were stopped by fresh Australian and British units and the attack was called off on 5 April 1918.

Guidebook

From Aveluy, take the D20 towards Bouzincourt. On your left you will see a CWGC sign for Bouzincourt Ridge Cemetery. Take this track and park up at the cemetery. Once there, walk down the track with Aveluy on your left. The sunken lane seen here is the focal point of where the Norfolks made their stand on 27 March 1918.

What3words: inroads.colonies.fitted.

26

The 9th Battalion,
The Battle of the Lys,
Neuve-Église to Château Segard:
1–29 April 1918

On 1 April 1918, the 9th Battalion moved to the Ypres Salient and went into the line at Polybecke, with Battalion HQ situated at Polygon Wood. This placed the main body of the battalion to the south of the Menin Road.

By now, the Germans had turned their attention to this area in their second phase of *Kaiserschlacht*, known as Operation Georgette. This is more commonly known as the Battle of the Lys, which opened on 9 April 1918 on a narrow front between Armentières and Béthune and targeted the Channel ports of Calais, Boulogne, and Dunkirk. German success here could choke the British into defeat and the Germans chose a weak point in the Allied lines attacking the Portuguese, who were rapidly overrun, but the British defenders on the southern flank held firm. The next day, the Germans widened their attack to the north, forcing the defenders of Armentières to withdraw before they were surrounded, and they managed to recapture most of the Messines Ridge. By the end of the day, the few British divisions in reserve were hard-pressed to hold a line along the River Lys. The German advance put them in a favourable position and it seemed as if the Allies could not stem the German onslaught. On 11 April 1918, Haig issued his famous order of the day that stated:

> Three weeks ago, today the enemy began his terrific attacks against us on a fifty-mile front. His objects are to separate us from the French, to take the Channel Ports and destroy the British Army. In spite of throwing already 106 Divisions into the battle and enduring the most reckless sacrifice of human life, he has as yet made little progress towards his goals. We owe this to the determined fighting and self-sacrifice of our troops. Words fail me to express the admiration which I feel for the splendid resistance offered by all ranks of our Army under the most trying circumstances.

Many amongst us now are tired. To those I would say that Victory will belong to the side which holds out the longest. The French Army is moving rapidly and in great force to our support. There is no other course open to us but to fight it out. Every position must be held to the last man: there must be no retirement. With our backs to the wall and believing in the justice of our cause each one of us must fight on to the end. The safety of our homes and the Freedom of mankind alike depend upon the conduct of each one of us at this critical moment.

Between 12 and 15 April, the Germans launched further attacks towards the critical logistics centre of Hazebrouck but were slowed by the defending British troops, before being stopped by the Australian 1st Division.

On the day that Haig put out this order, the 9th Battalion were in the line in anticipation that the Germans might attack; this did not happen. They moved out of the line, but were back on 15 April, at a position known as Crucifix Corner, when the Germans did launch another attack. Crucifix Corner can be identified as a position to the west of Neuve-Église. This position was noted by Capt. Cyril Bassingthwaite in his memoirs which are held by the Royal Norfolk Regiment Museum: 'A crucifix standing some 16 feet high, on a ridge, in the centre of this area, made a good artillery ranging object for both sides'.

Here they assisted in a local counterattack, involving 'B' Company, who assisted in driving out the enemy and they now held the line. Within the *Official History of the Great War*, the 9th Norfolks's counterattack is mentioned. In their narrative, they call Crucifix Hill 'Crucifix Corner':

It was not until midday that a very intensive bombardment was opened against the trenches on the higher ground where Crucifix Corner was situated. This bombardment spread at 2 p.m. to the right and left until it covered the whole front of the 177th Bde and part of those of the 176th and 71st on either side. The infantry attack followed at 2.45 p.m. Although the 176th and 177th Bdes were holding a 6,000 yards front taken over in the dusk and were composed mainly of young soldiers under fire for the first time, only Crucifix Corner was entry into the position affected. The enemy was speedily ejected by a counter attack, and, though he twice fought his way back to high ground, it was only to be driven off each time with heavy loss by the 4/Lincolnshire and 9/Norfolk. At 3.45 p.m., after an hour's struggle, the British line was still intact.

However, due to heavy fire from machine guns and the overwhelming numbers of enemy, as well as seeing other units retreating, 'B' Company had to retire. A new line was formed between the railway and Clapham Junction. Clapham Junction in this instance was where four roads converged to the south-east of Dranoutre.

Between 13 and 18 April, the Germans attacked and then eventually captured the town of Bailleul, despite staunch defence from the British.

On 16 April, the battalion moved into divisional reserve behind Mount Kemmel. The importance of the situation here cannot be underestimated. If Kemmel fell then there would not be much left for the Germans to go through in order for them to reach the Channel ports. Reserves were being brought up and the importance of holding the line here was stressed in a communique from the 71st Brigade commander, which is present in the battalion's war diary:

> Line now held must on no account be given up. French Cavalry and infantry divisions are behind our front and other reserves are coming up. The enemy will probably try to turn Kemmel by attacking fronts of 34th and 49th Divs. All valleys and sunken roads must be carefully watched and covered by machine guns placed in bottom of valleys.
>
> Plunging fire into valleys is useful. Ref B.M. 745 of today it may be necessary to employ the 2nd Sherwood Foresters as well as 1st Leicestershire Regt to counter attack to restore situation on lower slopes of Kemmel. No 7 Motor machine Gun Battery will remain in their present position tonight and will be prepared to fill in the same role tomorrow as that detailed today.

Between 17 and 18 April, the Germans tried to capture Mount Kemmel, which would provide them the high ground around Ypres and put them in a position to move towards the Channel Ports; however, Kemmel did not fall and German attacks on the defending British forces around the town of Béthune were repulsed.

Frank Enticott, who had initially served in the Army Service Corps since May 1915, was now with the 9th Battalion, and in April 1918, he went from Béthune to Ypres and then found himself at Neuve-Église:

> Dug in night, Sunday night counter attacked. Monday afternoon retired and dug in front of railway. Monday night sent out on outpost. No food, lost my pack, six of us left in front line tried to crawl 2 kilos to Batt 9. No one there, but food which thank God we were pleased to get. Two wounded and one poor boy we had to leave as we could not carry him. We were crawling and a German aeroplane came over us not a hundred yards in the air and we thought out last moment had come but it was brought down and we crawled on through to BHQ where after having a meal we were eventually captured 9.30 16.4.1918.

In this action, the 9th Battalion were positioned to the east of Locre and north-east of the road from Kemmel. Their actual positions for this period were 'C' and 'D' Company on the Bruilooze (now spelt Bruiloos) to Kemmel road facing north. 'A' and 'B' Company were positioned in a field off of the road from Locre facing south. They remained here until 17 April 1918, when they moved into dug-outs after coming under heavy artillery fire. On 18 April, they provided close support to the 1st Battalion Leicestershire Regiment. As directed in the 12th

Division *communiqué*, French reserves came up and the battalion was relieved by the 11th Company of the 83rd French Infantry Regiment on the night of 19–20 April 1918. Capt. Cyril Bassingthwaite was witness to this and noted:

> No battalion of the line could have made a more glorious stand in their defence than the 9th Battalion of the Norfolk Regiment.
>
> There is a winding road, running south west from Ypres, to the small village of Neuve-Église, passing Dickebusch, Locre and Dranoutre, three more smaller villages in comparison, and mid-way standing like a giant overreaching, and overseeing all, the towering heights of Mount Kemmel.
>
> Leaving the Lagnicourt Battle Zone, the Battalion arrived at the outskirts of Ypres, on a cold and misty morning in numerous omnibuses, that had at one time carried the peace-loving business man to his daily work in London, and to march down a road, to the unknown perhaps to death but for the glory of the Regiment and for England.

They reached a derelict camp and rested there under fire: 'The line has been broken' was the message received and soon all ranks stood ready to march forward to the attack'. The battalion's band played 'Rule Britannia' when they marched out to the front. This can be confirmed by James Cooper's diary, which noted:

> Sunday 14th
> Left Cafe Belge up at 4.30 went by motors to Locre played the boys into the line heavy shelling all the time went back to transport lines.

Capt. Bassingthwaite continued his account of the fighting:

> Many fell, in the battle around Kemmel, in so much, the help of our French Allies, was necessary, and the commander of the 60th Regiment whose men, as were our own, solely depleted, received a message which read, '*Le 60th Regiment d'Infte sera releve, cette nuit pat le 13th Batt de Chasseurs, qui soit contre attaquer, retablir, la ligne. L'Heure de la contre attaque n'est par encore fixee.*' [Translated: 'The 60th Regiment of Infantry will be relieved this night by the 13th Battalion Chassuers, which is against attacking, restoring, the line. Counter attack time is not fixed yet.']
>
> This welcome news, meant our relief also after many hours of holding on to a line broken, shattered and containing remnants of platoons, companies and men with the enemy but a few yards away remained at their posts waiting, watching and struggling against natures demand of sleep, but still heroically holding on. Such was the position of many of the men from Norfolk and later when news seemed to fly by magic down the sorely depleted lines, we know the enemy had at last spent his strength and the sacrifices of those who had given their all had not been in vain.

Further south on 25 April 1918, on the old Somme Front, the Germans tried to take the strategically important town of Villers-Bretonneux but failed through staunch Australian defence and counterattacks. This defence was a testament to the Australians who repelled the enemy on the third anniversary of Anzac Day, which commemorated their landing at Gallipoli.

However, between 25 and 26 April 1918, Mount Kemmel did fall after the French were routed from the top by three German divisions, which included their elite mountain troops. The 9th Battalion was put at readiness for this and were sent to an assembly point near to Belgian Château and dug in around Moat Farm. They were not used in any counteroffensive and returned to Dranoutre on 26 April: 'Officers and men from many units just hopelessly lost during a momentary struggle against overwhelming odds and after a temporary formation again and again to enter the theatre of war in an apparently never-ending struggle'.

On 29 April 1918, German forces were able to capture the hill to the north-west of Mount Kemmel, known as the *Scherpenberg*. But further advances were stopped when the French reinforced the area and the attacks in front of Hazebrouck ground to a halt. By this time, the battalion was positioned in strongpoints near Goldfish Château west of Ypres.

The war diary records the loss of eleven officers killed or wounded and 424 other ranks killed, wounded, or missing. By the time that the battalion had finished with their counteroffensive on 15 April, they could only muster six officers and 150 other ranks. Notably one of the officers killed on 15 April was Capt. Failes who had been instrumental in the defence around Lagnicourt during the fighting in March. He was awarded a posthumous DSO for his actions on 15 April and this appeared in the *London Gazette* on 18 September 1918:

> For conspicuous gallantry and devotion to duty. He showed good initiative in promptly moving all his Lewis guns to meet the direction of an enemy attack, breaking their attack up. He also led a bombing squad successfully, rallied and reorganised stragglers, and by his fine example greatly conduced to the splendid resistance made by his men.

Gerald Failes was the son of Watson and Mary Failes, a farmer and landowner of Tilney Hall. He had attended the Paston Grammar School in North Walsham and then in 1909 went as a boarder to Wellingborough Grammar School in Northamptonshire where he played cricket and football and joined the Officers' Training Corps, excelling in rifle shooting. When war broke out he initially enlisted as a trooper in the Hussars in February 1915 but then received his commission as a second-lieutenant in the 9th Battalion.

He landed in France on 4 October 1915 and was wounded in action during the assault on Mild Trench on 18 October 1916. He returned to France in 1917 and was promoted to captain and saw action at the Battle of Cambrai. His obituary in the *Eastern Daily Press* stated:

Capt G.W. Failes M.C.

Mr and Mrs Watson Failes, of Tilney St Lawrence have been officially informed that their son, Capt. Gerald Watson Failes MC of the Norfolk Regiment, has been killed in France during the recent offensive.

He commenced his education at King Edward VII Grammar School, Lynn, and from there proceeded to Wellingborough Grammar School. There he entered keenly into all kinds of sport, and during his last year there he won the school cup of shooting. He also shot at Bisley on several occasions. On leaving school, he took a post in the valuation office in Leicester. He was one of the first to answer his country's call, joining the Hussars as a trooper. His training in the O.T.C., of which he was a member whilst at school, stood him in good stead, and he had little difficulty in obtaining a commission in the Norfolks early in 1915. Having been gazetted as a lieutenant, he proceeded to France.

At the battle of Ypres, in the autumn of 1916, he was wounded and sent to England for three months to recuperate, and on returning to the front in due course was promoted to the rank of temporary captain, and subsequently was given command of a company. At the battle of Cambrai, he greatly distinguished himself, and for the gallant and dashing way in which he led his men he was awarded the Military Cross.

In the present battle, although not officially announced, not mentioned in his letters—which were very brief—it is generally known that his company very greatly distinguished themselves with him as their leader, and he met his death fearlessly carry out his duty with characteristic disregard of his own safety.

The 9th Battalion stayed in the Ypres sector and were involved in the sporadic fighting here and did have to become a flank defence for the 6th Division when the French were driven back in an attack that happened on 28 and 29 April 1918. Here they moved to strongpoints 1 kilometre south-west of Goldfish Château, but they were not used in any counteroffensive.

From May to July, the battalion remained around Ypres, going back to trench warfare. One thing of note is that Lt-Col. Prior returned to the battalion in July, but his wounds and the effects of gas had taken its toll and he had to leave the battalion through medical grounds:

It was cold wet weather and I soon found out that all was not right with my shoulder. Not only did I have constant pain but it travelled down by arm into the old wound in my forearm. This kept me from sleeping properly but my worst trouble was that a fall or a jar of any sort caused sharp pain. The result was that after one or two spills in one or two shell holes and over barbed wire I began to funk going out in the dark. The position of a commanding officer who cannot get round his lines at night is impossible. I accordingly saw my Divisional Commander and explained matters to him with the result that I was medically boarded and sent to the base as unfit for the trenches. It is with deepest regret that I left the battalion.

Lt-Col. Francis Reginald Day took over command and Lt-Col. Prior would not return back to active service.

Capt. Bassingthwaite certainly felt this action was worthy of note:

The 9th Battalion lost over 75% of its men in the defence of the Kemmel Heights and the survivors straggled out, one would ask, 'What had it accomplished?'

What had other units, whose suffering were similar to ours accomplished?

Those on the spot knew. The loss of life and the loss of a few yards of territory. What had been gained by the enemy? A few yards of land that probably bore some resemblance to Dante's Inferno, but the cost probably double the loss of life.

Jack Paul, who we met earlier in the book, was now serving with the 9th Battalion after the 8th Battalion had been disbanded. He wrote to his sister Nellie on 2 May 1918:

L/C J Paul 13090
5 Platoon B Coy
9th Norfolk Regt

May 2nd 1918
My Dear Nellie,

Many thanks for your letter of the 25th. Was pleased to hear you were still keeping in the running. Am glad to say I am alright, although as you can guess we have had some rough adventures just recently we are still close to the line, but things are fairly quiet at present. We do not get much time to ourselves however and it's quite a job now to get your correspondence up to time.

No, I have not heard from George, I don't expect he has much time to write either. By his address he's a bit disorganised as there cannot be No 1 Platoon in C Coy in normal times as they number from one to sixteen throughout the Battn.

Yes, I had a letter from home and Lizzie touched on the grand doings at Thetford for the following week. I guess Olive and herself were amongst the doings even if you weren't.

I am sorry to hear about George's brother Bob being missing since 4th March, I am afraid there are several besides, Eva Steward's brother who was with me, has been missing since 21st March and I am afraid there is very little hope for him.

Yes, I am glad to say Winnie is well. I had a line from her the other day, she has gone to live with her sister again now so her address has altered again. I daresay she will be as comfortable there as anywhere if her sister can manage as she has several kiddies of her own to look after.

Well I do not think I have much more news. I had a pack of cigarettes from Aunt L the other day.

Must conclude now with fondest love.

Your loving Brother.

Jack

At this point in time, the 9th Battalion were in the reserve lines a kilometre south-west of Goldfish Château. Jack wrote another letter on 11 May 1918:

May 11th 1918

Dear Nellie,

Many thanks for your letter of the 5th which I received on the 9th. I was pleased to hear you were still keeping well. I hope you have; since writing to me, received my last letter, which I doubt you have.

I was pleased to hear George is still alright and no doubt he is more or less settled now he has been posted to the 7th Battalion. I was sorry to hear of his brothers capture but we must think that it is better than to be killed or missing as so many are in this fierce battle which is in progress on the Western Front.

I am glad to say I am keeping alright, although I must admit we are having a busy time, being close to the line at present. It seems a long time since we were able to have a good night's sleep and to be able to take off our boots or clothes, as it is now over a month since we were able to do so. I am afraid I shall not be able to write to George at present, so please remember me to him when you write. Must conclude now with fondest love etc,

From your loving brother,

Jack

It would be the last letter Jack wrote as he was killed in action on 15 May 1918 when his company were in a forward position near Château Segard situated to the south of Ypres. He is now buried in Grave XIV. A. 8 in Voormezeele Enclosure No.3.

The German offensives carried on and Operation Blücher-Yorck started on the morning of 27 May 1918 when the Germans attacked the French and British along the Chemin des Dames. Here they destroyed the frontlines with artillery and gas shells and attacked with seventeen divisions led by the Kaiser's son Crown Prince Wilhem. The defenders were routed and the Germans managed to advance through a 25-mile gap in the line reaching the River Aisne in less than six hours having pushed the Allies back to the River Vesle. By 6 June 1918, the Germans were within 34 miles of Paris but met various problems with supply and reserves as well as the fact that the German Army was also close to exhaustion.

It was here that the Americans first saw their major actions as they attacked the Germans at the Battles of Château-Thierry and Belleau Wood along with

French counterattacks, which stopped the German advance. On 9 June 1918 the Germans launched Operation Gneisenau, which tried to exploit the gains made on the Chemin des Dames. They attacked with twenty-one divisions along a 23-mile front and managed to advance 6 miles capturing 8,000 prisoners.

However, on 11 June 1918, a French counterattack, led by General Mangin, with four divisions, 144 tanks, and with the support of low-flying aircraft was stopped the advance and captured well over 1,000 German prisoners.

The Germans tried one last attack at the Second Battle of the Marne, which opened on 15 July 1918 when they attacked to the east of Rheims. The German troops managed to cross the River Marne but the French launched a major counterattack which, although stopped by the Germans, effectively stopped any further advance and *Kaiserschlacht* came to an end.

Guidebook

There are two main sites to visit here.

First of all is Neuve-Église, now pronounced Nieukerke. In Nieukerke at the junction of the N331 and N332, take the road called Heirweg, this has signposts for Armentières and Ballieul directing you to turn left. Keep on this road and eventually you will come to a T-Junction for Kauwakkerstraat. Turn left here. Continue on this road until you come to another T-junction on your right and a crucifix, which will be on your left. This is the high ground where the Norfolks carried out their counterattacks on 15 April 1918. They attacked from the direction you are facing.

What3words: politics.unruly.gutless.

Locre is now pronounced Loker. Once at this village you need to head towards Kemmel, taking Kemmelsbergweg. You pass through a small hamlet called Bruiloze, this road also veers to the right. On a clear day, you will see Kemmel in the distance, and on your right, you will come across a small red bricked Calvary and on your right, you will also see a First World War Demarcation Stone. Between 1921 and 1927, on the initiative of the French Touring Club and its Belgian counterpart, 118 monuments were erected (ninety-six in France, twenty-two in Belgium) to mark the important sites of the Great War. In France, they were to mark the limit of the German advances during the great offensive of 18 July 1918. The monuments stand at 1.25 metres high, are made from pink granite, and were designed by the Parisian sculptor Paul Moreau-Vauthier.

'C' and 'D' Companies were positioned in the field you see to your left. Turn right onto Koenraadstraat. On 16 April 1918, the Battalion HQ was in the field on your right as the road bears round to the left.

What3words: innately.drench.trombone.

Continue on and you will come to crossroads, with Kemmel seen in the distance; the field facing you on your left was where 'A' and 'B' Companies were positioned. Continue on and as you drive on this road look to the right because this is the field where the Battalion HQ was positioned on 18 April 1918.

What3words: rouses.league.untouched.

Should you wish, you could also visit Château Segard. To do this, come out of Ypres and take the Lille Road, N336. Just prior to the railway crossing turn right onto the N331, keep on this road and eventually you will see a large barn of the left and two concrete posts either side of a track to a farm on the right. This is the original entrance to Château Segard, which was completely destroyed in the war.

What3words: prefers.cheaply.unhinge.

27

The 12th (Norfolk Yeomanry) Battalion, Nieppe Forest: 25 June to 27 July 1918

This battalion was formed in Egypt on 11 February 1917 from the dismounted 1/1st Norfolk Yeomanry and was initially attached to the 230th Brigade in the 74th Division. Prior to moving to France, this battalion had seen active service at Gallipoli in 1915 and had gone on to see action in Palestine, Gaza, Beersheba, Sheria, and Jerusalem. On 1 May 1918, they embarked at Alexandria for Marseilles, landing there on 7 May. By 21 June 1918, they came under the orders of 94th Brigade in the 31st Division. Of all of the battalions of the Norfolks who served in the First World War, I feel this unit is the forgotten battalion.

After a period of training in May and June, the battalion first went into the line on 25 June 1918 relieving the 10th Battalion East Yorkshire Regiment in the reserve trenches situated to the west of the German lines at Outtersteene. Here they would go in and out of the line until the end of September. This was not a quiet time for the battalion and it is important to note their war in this sector of the Western Front.

On 25 June 1918, they moved into the line in the Forest of Nieppe facing Armentières. An attack happened here whereby the 5th and 31st Division attacked positions in the forest and the Becque, which is a stream that runs through this area. Here two companies acted as reserve. After this, they had a sustained period of executing raids on the German lines to deny them access to bridges across the Becque.

The first raid was launched on 8 July when one platoon from each of 'A' and 'D' Companies went out to destroy two bridges across the stream. The war diary for these raids are quite brief the first report notes: 'On the night of July 8th/9th one platoon of A Coy and one platoon of D Coy carried out a small enterprise assisted by a detachment of 211 Field Coy R.E. with the object of blowing up two bridges over the Becque'.

These bridges still exist today and can be found La Vierhouck situated to the south of Vieux-Berquin. Second Lieutenant F. W. Wagner was successful and blew one of the bridges. But the second bridge remained intact when 2Lt J. C. Know with the 'A' Coy platoon came up against heavy MG fire from a farm and a post held by the enemy. This meant he could not get near the bridge. The next night, another attempt was made to blow this bridge; the war diary stated:

> On the following night 2nd Lieutenant Know went out again with his platoon with the object of occupying the farm at K.12.a.2.7 and possible blowing up bridge at K.12.a.3.4. he succeeded in occupying the farm and establishing a post of 1 NCO and 6 men there. He reconnoitred forward himself but on approaching the bridge found it swept by enemy MG fire from the front and both flanks. He decided that without artillery bombardment it was not practicable to blow up the bridge.

The battalion then came out of the line and did not go back in until 16 July 1917. Another raid was launched on 26 July, with the war diary noting:

> On the night 26th/27th July two platoons of 'A' Coy under Major Birbank carried out a raid on enemy posts on the east side of the Becque. The left group artillery and the 31st Machine Gun Battalion co-operated in this raid. The raiding party when the artillery barrage lifted rushed the enemy posts but were only in time to see the enemy numbering about 20, running away.

In this raid, the battalion lost five wounded and two missing. The rest of the 12th Battalion's war will be covered in a later chapter.

Guidebook

This can be a difficult one to find. From Vieux-Berquin, on the D947 heading towards Estaires, take the Rue de Merville, marked as the D23 on an IGN map. There is a CWGC signpost on your left for Aval Wood Cemetery as a marker. This road will now take a sharp left and you should continue on this road. You will eventually come to a bridge over the Becque, which has a small hamlet sign on the right for La Vierhouck. This is one of the bridges that the Norfolks attacked during these trench raids. The second one can be found by turning left onto the Rue des Cerisiers, which comes after you have driven over the bridge. This takes you up to a farm track on your left. You will see a farm house and barn and a small bridge, which takes you over the Becque. This is the other bridge the Norfolks attacked in their trench raids during this period.

What3words: 1st Bridge—boggled.assured.bakes; 2nd Bridge—unapproved. launching.advert

28

The 7th Battalion,
The Battle of Amiens, Morlancourt:
8–9 August 1918

I have covered the Western Front timeline up to July 1918. The next major battle fought was at Amiens, and it is generally considered the turning point for the Allies on the Western Front and was fought between 8 and 11 August 1918. It was designed to counteract the German advances that had been made after their massive offensive that had almost pushed the BEF right to the outskirts of Amiens. This city was of strategic importance to the Allies because of its railway network. Had the Germans been able to capture this supply route, it would have seriously hampered the Allies ability to wage war.

A counterattack was planned that would involve American, Australian, British, Canadian, and French divisions under the overall command of Haig who directed Henry Rawlinson to plan and prepare the offensive. It would also involve a ten-division attack on a 10-mile front from Morlancourt in the north to Hargicourt in the south. Surprise was essential as the majority of the fighting would be carried out by the Australians and the Canadians who were respected by both friend and foe alike for their determined ferocity in battle. Had the Germans got wind that these two elements were being concentrated in this area, then it could have gone very differently on the day.

There was an even bigger gamble for this offensive as Rawlinson was given virtually all of the Allied armour totalling to around 600 British and French tanks. This included seventy-two Whippet and 342 Mark V and V* tanks, all of which were the newer variants of the tanks used in 1916 and 1917. Rawlinson also had 2,070 artillery pieces and 800 aircraft. The German sector chosen was defended by 20,000 soldiers and they were outnumbered six to one by the attacking troops. The plan relied on the infantry and tanks acting in co-operation and there would be no preliminary bombardment with Rawlinson relying on a creeping barrage as the troops advanced.

The battle was a major success for the hard-pressed Allies, and by the end of the first day, they had advanced 9 miles into the German lines, capturing well over 13,000 men and around 200 artillery pieces. It prompted Ludendorff to write of the battle that it 'was the black day of the German Army in this war.... The 8th of August put the decline of that [German] fighting power beyond all doubt.... The war must be ended'.

Under the command of III Corps and on the left flank of this corps front along the River Ancre, the division generally played only a holding role on 8 August 1918 when Fourth Army made its great attack. However, the German withdrawal from the Ancre and from Dernancourt being observed before the attack took place, the 35th Brigade, on the division's right, became involved.

The 7th Battalion had been out of the line since their stand at Bouzincourt Ridge and had a new CO namely Lt-Col. Henry Ashley Scarlett. After a period of rest and training, they went into the line around Forceville and Senlis. Here the battalion suffered casualties not from war but from the influenza epidemic that was ravaging the world. In July, they took part in two trench raids and then moved to Treux where they held the line on the River Ancre.

On the night of 5–6 August 1918, the 7th Norfolks relieved the 132nd American Infantry, facing Morlancourt, and assisted in repelling an enemy trench raid on the division to their right on 6 August.

On 8 August 1918, the 12th (Eastern) Division took part in the Battle of Amiens and they would act as a subsidiary to the main attack, which was going in to the south. The *Official History of the Great War* notes:

The subsidiary attack north of it, carried out by the 35th Brigade of the 12th Division, although Br-General was nearly blinded by gas and had to be invalided next day, achieved all that was required, an advance of nearly a thousand yards being made. The attack was launched at 6.20 a.m., two hours after zero, with half the 1/1st Cambridgeshire, the 7/Norfolk and the 9/Essex in line and the rest of the Cambridgeshires in reserve. To deal with a possible counter-attack the 6/Queens of the reserve brigade, the 37th, was attached. Under a barrage fired by 48 field guns he centre and left battalions, in spite of difficulties of mist and the wearing of gas masks, reached their objective, capturing 3 officers and 316 men.

In this attack, the 7th Battalion would put 'A' Company in support of 'B' and 'D' Companies in the front, supported by 'A' and 'D' Company. Retaliatory enemy fire saw 'B' Company take heavy casualties prior to zero hour. The war diary for the battalion is brief for this day, but notes:

8 a.m. from forward HQ in old front line. Wounded man from 'A' Coy states Coy has gained trench (1st objective) and pushing forward toward second objective. O.C.' C' Coy has sent for another platoon of 'D' Coy to help man the old support

line. A Sergeant of 'A' Coy says that there is a gap on 'A' Coy's left, the Essex having apparently lost direction slightly.

'C' Company, assisted the 9th Essex in plugging a gap in the line with a platoon, and by 9 a.m., all objectives had been captured, with the capture of two light machine guns. 'B' Company took more fire for enemy mortars and had to retire to a rear shallow trench, and although the battalion was in an exposed position, all that could be seen was enemy retreating.

An attack now went in on the right with the 1/1st Cambridgeshires. Their history stated:

> Once again, the guns took up the chorus, and 'C' and 'D' moved up, changing direction half right, and lay down waiting for the barrage to lift at 12.28 p.m. The time arrived and the leading wave charged through and completed the capture of the support line. The surprise was complete; about 30 of the enemy were killed, but the rest of the garrison surrendered causing embarrassment; there were only 140 Cambridgeshires, while the wounded and unwounded Wutembergers numbered 316.

The *Official History of the Great War* notes that the enemy units captured were from the 123rd Regiment of the 27th Division who were caught by this attack and the fact that their rear was attacked by four tanks. One of these tanks was Tank J22 nicknamed 'Ju-Ju', a Mark V Male tank was part of 'B' Coy, 10th Tank Battalion, commanded by an American officer named James Alexander McGuire. This is what he witnessed of the 1/1st Cambridgeshires attack:

> The Cambridgeshires were in battle order when I came along and all ready to go. I stood next to their officer, who clasped a whistle between his teeth and eyed his wrist-watch closely. A shrill blast! Up and Over! The wild scramble up the parapet left me in the ruck. Once out of the trench, I ran to a little knoll to give the double-time signal to the oncoming Ju-Ju. Down the slope he came like a charging rhinoceros, his exhaust belching sparks and smoke. Already those Cambridgeshires were high-tailing it over 'No Man's Land'. What if a machine gun started tapping off the death notes? I never saw gallantry surpassing theirs during a long stay on the Western Front. It is one of those cherished pictures on cannot find in the art galleries.

Morlancourt fell the next day and the 7th Norfolks remained in this sector. The 37th Brigade took up this attack later on 9 August and succeeded in further captures. By the evening of 10 August, the old Amiens defence line had been recaptured. In all, the division had by now advanced almost 2 miles.

On 10 August 1918, the French 3rd Army attacked and recaptured Montdidier, which gave the Allies the freedom to use the Paris–Amiens railway unmolested.

On 12 August, as the advance stopped, the first phase of this offensive ended.

On 21 August, they again went into action in what became known as the Battle of Albert. This would also involve the 1st Battalion.

Guidebook

On the D1 from Fouilly, head towards Bray-sur-Somme, or from Bray-sur-Somme on the same road head toward Fouilly. You will come to crossroads signposted Morlancourt on the D42. If coming from Bray, you will pass Beacon Cemetery on your left. Or, if heading towards Bray and you pass Beacon Cemetery on your right, you have gone too far. Coming from Bray you will turn right, heading towards Bray you will turn left. Keep on this road and the field on the right is where the Norfolk's Battalion HQ started out on 8 August 1918.

What3words: grained.banners.sympathetic.

You can then have the option to go into Morlancourt and visit Morlancourt No. 2 Cemetery where eleven men from the 7th Battalion now lie. To get here go into Morlancourt and at the road signposted Ville sur Ancre turn left. At the next crossroads you will see a CWGC sign for Morlancourt Cemeteries Nos 1 and 2. Turn left here and No. 2 cemetery will be found on the left in a little while.

What3words: unglued.flush.untimed.

29

The 12th (Norfolk Yeomanry) Battalion, The Advance into Flanders, Vieux, Berquin, and Bailleul: 18–31 August 1918

On 18 August 1918, the 2nd and 5th Armies begin operations in the Lys valley, in an effort to capture the ground lost in April 1918.

The 12th Battalion had continued with their trench raids, but by 18 August, they were in the line facing Labis Farm, a German strongpoint, with another strongpoint farm, known as Lynde Farm to the north-east, finally another farm, Lesage, was situated to the east of Lynde Farm. Both these farms exist today and are situated to the north-east of Vieux Berquin.

On the first day, the 12th Battalion stood ready, but the battalion to their left, with 'C' Company of the 2nd Battalion Royal Fusiliers. However, battalions of the 87th Brigade did not succeed in capturing all of their objectives completely on the 12th Norfolks' left. Therefore, the next day, the 12th Battalion went into action with the same company of 2/R. Fusiliers on their left. Zero Hour was set for 5 p.m.:

Punctually at 5 p.m. the barrage opened on the line, moved forward, keeping by the barrage causing many casualties among our other ranks and N.C.O.s. This caused the right flank to he held up also the left was held by machine guns and snipers. The two left platoons (A Coy) had closed in too much to the left, thus leaving some of the enemy strong point at E.18.d.05.70 untouched.

OC 'D' Coy seeing this immediately pushed forward his right-hand platoon and engaged the enemy. He then brought up the remainder of D Coy and joined a line with A Co's right and pushed forward, taking the enemy strong-points at E.18.a.9.8. and strong points in trenches at E.18.a 1.1. The enemy fell back fighting all the way, to shell holes. A small party of B Coy then pushed forward to within a short distance of the final objective overcoming on the way considerable resistance on the part of the enemy bombers and snipers concealed in shell holes.

This party seeing that the flanks were held up sent back for reinforcements. These came up causing the enemy to retire and thus leaving the flanks to move forward to final objectives, overcoming on the way considerable resistance from numerous bombers and snipers concealed in the location. The whole line was in touch took the final objectives, causing many casualties to the retiring enemy.

The strongpoints mentioned in the battalion's war diary were in the field opposite Labis Farm and the line eventually passed the farm and ended up to the east of it. The war diary notes that they captured sixty men and twelve machine guns, with casualties to their ranks of eight officers and thirty-eight other ranks killed and wounded, one officer and 100 other ranks wounded, and the war diary notes that 100 of the enemy were killed.

Charles Milligan also advanced with the 12th Battalion:

In August we moved up on the night of the 18th, lay in a ditch on the edge of a field of growing corn, so different to the muddy waterlogged trenches of a previous winter. At 5 p.m. in the afternoon of the 19th we went forward through the waving corn and found our adversaries in slit trenches of offering resistance. A number surrendered and those who did not were eliminated. We sustained casualties and our company was left with one officer and a few other ranks. The next morning, we were relieved and retired to Battalion HQ in the rear, where we cleaned up and received a further draft of reinforcements.

After Labis Farm was captured, the battalion pushed out patrols to try and locate the enemy and was then relieved early in the morning of 20 August. They spent time in and out of the line mounting patrols. One of these came into contact with the enemy of 28 August: 'Bn still in the line. Line was patrolled nightly. On the night of the 29th one of our patrols encountered an enemy post. Our casualties were 1 officer wounded or missing, 1 OR killed, 2 OR missing'. The men killed in this action were 2Lt Frederick Watts and Pte Alfred Steel from Deptford. In the Norfolk's history, 2Lt Watts is officially recorded in that he 'was never heard of again...'

On 30 August, it was rumoured that Bailleul had been evacuated by the Germans:

During the morning the enemy was reported to have evacuated his positions. Patrols were immediately pushed out towards Bailleul and reported that the enemy had retired to a ridge 800 to 1000 yards beyond Bailleul. The Brigades on our flanks then pushed forward thereby shortening our line, this compelling our Brigade to withdraw from the line.

The battalion then withdrew to the rear. On 31 August, the battalion received this message from General Plumer reference their actions on 19 August 1918:

Please express to all ranks the Divisional Commander's appreciation of the most excellent work done by the officers, NCOs and men during the minor operation yesterday. Success was largely due to the skilful planning of the operation and the excellent cooperation between artillery and infantry. Plans, however good, do not succeed unless the men display the fine fighting spirit which enabled the 12 (Yeomanry) Battalion Norfolk Regiment to overcome strong opposition.

Guidebook

From Vieux-Berquin take the D23 towards Outtersteene. Labis Farm is the first set of buildings you will come to on your right. The strongpoints dealt with by the 12th Battalion were in the field on your left.

What3words: global.draped.denture.

30

The 1st and 7th Battalions, The Battle of Albert and Bapaume: 21 August to 3 September 1918

At the end of 1917, the 5th Division had been warned and then moved to the Italian front. They had ended up on the plains of the River Piave. Here they had held the line around Montello Hill on the right bank of the river. This aspect of their war was quite uneventful, attacks were planned and cancelled, and by 17 February 1918, the division found itself back on the move to France.

During the March offensive, the division was on the move and did not arrive in France until April. Eventually, they found themselves around St Venant, situated to the south of the Forest of Nieppe.

The 5th Division were ordered to capture Merville, this did not happen and the 1st Norfolks found themselves in support of the 95th Brigade during an attack by the enemy. By 15 April, the enemy advance here had been stopped at Hazebrouck and the line here stabilised. Like the 12th Battalion, the 1st Norfolks now got involved in trench raids in this sector. Here they remained until the 5th Division moved to Aire and then to the east of Doullens where the division came under the command of the 4th Corps.

On 28 June 1918, as with their 12th Battalion cousins, the 1st Battalion supported an advance over the River Bourre, during what was known as La Becque, the war diary stating:

Left Coy of left Btn (1st Cheshire Regt) in conjunction wide Bdes on our left pushed forward on right band of River Bourre and succeeded in gaining and holding objectives. Our front line Coys B, C and A were harassed by enemy shelling during the day and 'D' Coy had several casualties. 2/Lt West wounded slightly by piece of shrapnel. Various patrols under Capt A.C. Wood and 2/Lt E.W. Shaw left our trenches and obtain information and blow up enemy shelters. They were successful in gaining information and identification and destroyed 5 shells with bombs.

One of the men lost in this action was Alfred Johnson who had won a MM at Polderhoek Château for bringing in wounded men. He was aged thirty-seven and was the son of William and Mary Johnson of Redenhall near Harleston; he is buried in Plot 3. Row D. Grave 2 in Tannay British Cemetery.

Also lost that day was Sidney Durrant. He had been in a forward post when the advance occurred and as he was moving forward a shell exploded behind him. He went to assist a wounded comrade and another shell fell, killing him instantly. He is also buried in Tannay Cemetery, next to Alfred in Grave 2.

On 21 August, the British attacked even further north and the French 10th and 3rd Armies resumed their attacks. A further advance by the British 1st Army also put pressure on Ludendorff and he ordered a general withdrawal along a 55-mile front. He came under further pressure as the Anzacs advanced across the Somme capturing Péronne and Mont St Quentin.

On 21 August, the 5th Division were given the task of capturing the heights east of Buquoy. The 1st Battalion war diary states: 'The 5th Division will attack the enemy defences between Buquoy and Achiet Le Petit with the 15th Brigade on left, 95th on right and 13th in support'. They would advance with the 63rd (Naval) Division and would pass through the left brigade of the 37th Division and also assist the 3rd New Zealand Division, both of whom were in the frontline. Zero Hour was set for 4.55 a.m., and when the advance happened, the 1st Norfolks took up the rear behind the 1st Cheshires and the 16th Warwickshires, the battalion advanced with 'D' Coy on the right and 'C' on the left with 'A' on the right and 'B' on the left in support. The 1st Cheshires were very nearly cut off and the 1st Norfolks were sent to their aid filling in a gap in the line between the Cheshires and the 63rd Division. Sadly, due to fog, the Norfolks did not find the Cheshires and ended up in positions near Achiet le Petit.

Overnight, the battalion suffered German shelling and during this time the CO, Lt-Col. Cecil Frederick George Humphries, and his adjutant, Capt. Tyler, were seriously wounded and died soon afterwards. The war diary also records that the losses of other ranks in this barrage was heavy.

Lt-Col. Humphries was an exceptional man. He had been born in Mataura in New Zealand on 27 October 1886. When war broke out he was on holiday in England with his mother, Ada. He initially enlisted with the Army Service Corps and was quickly promoted and insisted that he be posted to the infantry where he went to the 1st Battalion Manchester Regiment.

In December 1914, he was awarded the DCM, with his citation reading: 'For conspicuous gallantry and coolness at Givenchy in the attack of Dec 20 & 21 and for endeavouring to bring into cover the body of his company commander, who had been killed'. His interpretation of this action was noted in a letter written on 9 January 1915:

We had a bit of a 'bust up' on deck on the 20th and 21st last. I got hit several times, but was lucky and got through without a scratch. I have sent my shirt to the Mater as a souvenir. It has eight holes in the tail (please don't think I was running away), but I happened to be leaning over a poor chap who had 'stopped one', when they turned the machine gun on to me, and God knows how I am here with a whole skin. But it's the way of the world, so there you are.

On 12 March 1915, he was wounded at Neuve Chapelle, and while recovering from his wounds, he was given a commission and was gazetted second lieutenant in the 12th Battalion Highland Light Infantry. By September 1915, he had been promoted to captain, had been injured again, and while recovering from these wounds, he spent some time with the Labour Corps when he was awarded the MC for bravery on 6 June 1917. The action for which he was awarded the MC was reported in the *Taranaki Daily News*, 29 December 1917:

Captain Cecil Humphries of Christchurch was awarded the Military Cross for an act of bravery on June 6 1917. Further information contained in a private letter shows that the circumstances under which the decoration was won were as follows (the quotation being an extract from his commanding officer's despatch) 'An ammunition train was being bombed by aeroplanes, and Captain Humphries commanding SSO. 10 Labour Company, arrived on the scene and took charge of the party. Under this officer's guidance and help eight trucks were salvaged. The, eighth was uncoupled by Captain Humphries and Sgt.-Major Harland, while the ninth truck was burning fiercely, and its load of shells was exploding freely. This remarkably gallant piece of work was carried out under' a hail of shell and fragments, anyone of which could have exploded the [SS1] contents of the trucks which were being moved. I consider, from my observation of the explosion, that Captain Humphries and the other members of the party are deserving of the highest praise, and have the honour to bring to your notice their gallant and valuable work.' Captain Humphries who is also the holder of the D.C.M. is one of the 'Old Contemptibles,' as those who went to France prior to November, 1914, are known.

Cecil then went on to serve with the 1st Battalion Duke of Cornwall's Light Infantry and was awarded a Bar to the MC for leadership of his company.

In April 1918, as the commander of his battalion, he was gassed in the Forest of Nieppe while personally reconnoitring the company's position under heavy fire but returned to duty leading his battalion forward, despite a fierce counterattack by the enemy, and he was awarded the DSO for 'fine leadership'. He personally led his men and inspired confidence with his courage.

In May 1918, he was posted to the 1st Norfolks. He was aged thirty-one when he died and was very close to his mother as he wrote in his diary: 'If the fates are against me I hope I will die an honourable death with my heart full of love for my darling Mother'. Lt-Col. Humphries is buried in Grave III. B. 8. at Foncquevillers Military Cemetery.

Also killed that day was Terence Algernon Kilbee Cubitt who was now serving with the 1st Battalion after recovering from his wounds receieved at Cambrai. His loss was reported in the *Norwich Mercury* on 31 August 1818:

> The sad intelligence has been received by Mr. Algernon Cubitt of Thorpe Road Norwich that his eldest son Capt. Terence A.K. Cubitt, M.C. was killed in action on the 22nd inst. Born at Sloley Old Hall 22 years ago and educated at Norwich Grammar School and Paston Grammar School he took up a clerkship in Barclay's Norwich Bank. Thence he enlisted in September 1914, in the Norfolks. 14 months later he was gazetted to a commission. Sent out to France at the end of September 1916, in less than three weeks he had been wounded and received his Military Cross. In November 1917 he was so severely wounded on the Cambrai front as to cause an invaliding of five months. He went abroad again in April of this year, and attained his captaincy. A fellow officer writing in Norwich says—'Terence Cubitt has been the life and soul of the battalion with his songs and poems. He was our greatest moral heightener and an excellent leader.'

Capt. Cubitt is now buried in Grave III. B. 6. in Foncquevillers Military Cemetery.

Maj. de Grey took over the command of the battalion and the fighting continued. On 23 August, the advance fell upon the Arras–Albert railway where enemy machine guns wreaked havoc on the advancing battalions and they had to negotiate three lines of barbed wire and the advance was held up until tanks could be brought up.

During this phase, the 1st Battalion supported the 1st Bedfordshires who had suffered losses in the advance, and by the next day, they had been withdrawn back to Achiet le Petit before being moved to trenches near Achiet le Grand on 25 August. Maj. de Grey was wounded on this day and Maj. H. S. Walker from the 1st Cheshires had to assume command on the battalion.

The advance carried on, and on 30 August 1918, the battalion was fighting on the Sapignies–Bapaume road supporting an attack being made by the 95th Brigade north of Bapaume. This attack carried the objective and what was described as the 'Old Army Line' west of Beugny with the 15th Brigade facing the village, here under high explosive and gas shells, they moved out of the line and moved to the east of the Sapignies–Bapaume road. It was a slight reprieve as they were back in the line on 1 September 1918.

Here they took part in the attack on Beugny where they advanced with the 1st Cheshires on their left. They took most of their objectives and captured 250 prisoners and assisted in repulsing an enemy counterattack. Another counterattack saw them having to withdraw slightly to hold the ground to the south of Beugny and the line held with the New Zealanders on their right. By nightfall, with further advances made by the 1st Bedfordshires, the line stabilised.

On 3 September 1918, the 1st Battalion advanced in support of the main advance helping to consolidate the line around Delsaux Farm, situated to the south of Beugny and got to the western edges of Le Brucquerie where they were rejoined by Maj. de Grey. It was here that they came out of the line and went to billets in the Biefvillers-lès-Bapaume area.

It is noted in the Norfolk's history that the divisional commander wanted to make special mention of the extraordinary good work that the 1st Battalion had made during the fighting, noting:

> During the operations near Beugny village of September 2nd the 1st Battalion the Norfolk Regiment was the only battalion, out of three divisions, that reached the final objective in its entirety, and it was only due to the fact that the battalion held on throughout the night to the high ground south of the village that the village became untenable to the enemy, and he was forced to retire.... The fruits of the victory were made clear to all ranks by the advance that was made, almost without opposition, on the following morning.

This particular action had been heavy on the senior commanders of the battalion and the battalion had lost eleven officers and sixty other ranks killed or wounded in this fighting along with the three officers mentioned in this chapter.

Guidebook

Come out of Buquoy on the D8 heading towards Achiet Le Petit. The road naturally takes a slight S-Bend. If you stop here then the main area of advance for the 1st Battalion for 21 August 1918 can be seen in the field on the right.

What3words: strengthened.password.sailing.

On the D930, head to Beugny, and as you pass through the village, turn right onto the D20. You will also see a signpost for Delsaux Farm CWGC here. The farm still exists today and can be found on the left just before the CWGC cemetery. At Delsaux Farm Cemetery, turn left and take the road to the edge of Le Brucquerie. This forms the farthest point to where the 1st Battalion advanced on 3 September 1918.

What3words: elated.dockside.contencious.

* * * * *

On 21 August 1918, the 7th Norfolks moved out of Ville sur Ancre and relieved the 9th Essex in their frontline trenches and prepared for a fresh advance. In this attack, the 35th Brigade would lead and 36th Brigade would be on their left with the 47th Division on the right. The 7th Norfolks were given the task of taking the first objective with the 1/1st Cambridgeshires. The 9th Essex and the 5th Buffs were then to pass through and take the second objective, with the two leading battalions following on later. The Norfolks took their objective, but other battalions were not successful and the tanks who were there to support the infantry were late.

On 22 August 1918, the Germans counterattacked, specifically targeting the 47th Division. The 141st Brigade had initially led the advance for the 47th Division, whose objective was the capture of Happy Valley, a position situated to the south-east of Méaulte.

The war diary for the 7th Battalion is very scant for this action but the *Official History* records the chaos in this action:

In mist and smoke, it had to cross a valley and a spur before it could reach Happy Valley, its objective. Owing to bad staff work and the insufficient training of the young troops in movements in darkness, smoke, and mist, the two leading battalions, 1/20th and 1/19th London, lost count of distance and though the Germans surrendered freely, the battalions halted considerably short of the intermediate objective, as much as half a mile short on the right.

The 142nd Brigade, which had followed a mile behind the 141st, now took up the attack with the 1/22nd, 1/23rd and 1/24th London in line. It at once met with strong opposition, and, having started too far back at the appointed time, from the mistaken line of the 141st, lost the barrage. When visibility improved and the 141st discovered its error and moved forward to the intermediate line, the enemy shelling had had become so heavy that it was impossible to consolidate there.

Meantime, soon after 8 a.m., the extreme right of the 1/22nd London had reached its objective, the Chalk Pit at the southern end of Happy Valley, and established touch with the 33rd Australian Battalion; but the rest of the brigade could not get within three hundred yards of the objective.

The German artillery men on the front were now firing over open sights, whilst oblique fire came from Ceylon Wood to the south east and particularly fierce machine-gun fire from Hill 105, part of the objective; thus, all further movement became impossible. To make matters worse, a gap arose between the 142nd.

Brigade and the 35th Brigade (12th Division) which left the enemy free to enfilade the troops of both. Of the ten tanks allotted to the 47th Division, the four with the 141st Brigade, carrying entrenching tools, reached the intermediate objective; but of the six with the 142nd, only one. This tank entered the Happy Valley and rounded up a number of Germans, but owing to engine trouble and casualties among the crew had then to be withdrawn.

By 12 noon, therefore, although in the centre the 142nd and 35th Brigades were a few hundred yards short of the final objective, excellent progress had been made; but the day was hot, the men exhausted and short of water, and a great deal of ammunition had been expended. The Germans, now the mist had lifted, had good observation over the field from the higher ground which it been hoped the cavalry would secure, and from observation balloons, it was impossible to get up supplies, or for the field artillery to move forward from its original positions, now out of range, to support the infantry, although the heavy guns, farther back were brought forward. Signs of German movement had been reported during the morning and shortly after 1 p.m. observers with the 33rd Australian Battalion, the left wing of the 9th Australian Brigade, saw German infantry emerge from Caftet Wood, near Carnoy, in artillery formation, preceded by a line of skirmishers, moving in the direction of the left flank of the 47th

Division north of the Happy Valley. This information was immediately sent back, but did not reach the 47th Division headquarters until 2.20 p.m. Meantime Major-General Gorringe had received reports from other sources that bodies of Germans were crossing the Bray-Fricourt road making for the junction of the 47th and 12th Divisions, and at 2 p.m. a German barrage to cover the movement had begun. It was obvious a counter attack was being launched. The line of the 142nd was very thin, about six hundred men spread over about two miles. Br.- General McDouall sent up two officers and 80 men with eight

Lewis guns, part of an improvised brigade reserve, and called for a barrage from supporting artillery, which could not be complied with owing to shortage of information at the gun positions. The enemy was able to filter through the line, and the 1/23rd and 1/24th London and 3rd Australian Division.

Against the latter no progress whatever was made; the 1/22nd London formed a defensive flank, which was eventually extended by two battalions of the 11th Australian Brigade and a battalion of the 14th Brigade sent up by Br.-General Kennedy. The resistance was sufficient to stop the Germans, who lost heavily, fell into complete confusion and at night withdrew from their advanced and salient position.

The war diary entry for this time confirms there was some confusion as to who had taken what, with the Norfolks moving on from their initial objective; the confusion in this advance can be seen in the war diary:

Battalion HQ then moved forward to K6a. Lt Peyton has been killed and 2 Lts King, Cuthbertson, Palmer, Fowell and Pratley wounded. CSM Jackson has been badly wounded and about 100 OR casualties.

REs and a company of Northants Pioneers have moved up to assist in consolidation and REs are also attached for testing safety of dug-outs. We are in touch with units on our left, but apparently the 47th Division were not entirely successful and our right flank is rather uncertain. The enemy has counter attacked the Division to our right and two battalions' officers have fallen back. It has therefore been necessary to form a defensive flank.

This has been done by the Buffs holding the Brigade front facing north and the Essex and ourselves forming a line on our right and partly restored the situation. We have advanced our line facing east.

On 22 August, a man whom I have come to know was lost. This was Harry Betts, whom I wrote about in the chapter detailing the actions at St Eloi in March 1915. Harry had risen to becoming one of the youngest CSMs in the British Army. He had won the MC and DSM and Bar for actions against pillboxes in the fighting, having first been awarded a DCM for outflanking one around the Tower Hamlets area during Third Ypres; his DCM was awarded on 26 September 1917.

His next award, the Bar to his DCM, came when the battalion was involved in heavy fighting on 27 March; here they were facing Rainecourt to the south of the road. By now, the 39th Division, along with many of the divisions, were fighting a desperate rearguard action during *Kaiserschlacht* and were severely depleted of men, becoming fewer and fewer; the original brigades had become two smaller composite battalions made up from what was left of the survivors.

By 28 March, it became apparent that the 39th Division was in danger of being cut off and that they were ordered to move back. However, it was also ascertained that the enemy was occupying high ground to the south, which was hampering the withdrawal and a composite group of Cambs and Black Watch were ordered to mount a counterattack on the Marcelcave–Wiencourt railway. This was undertaken but the attackers came under fire from a German position known as Hill 90; the history of the 1/1st Cambridgeshires describe what happened:

> We were in the open lying flat, sweating profusely and vainly trying to shovel up soil in front of us. I quite expected we should be annihilated when suddenly a miracle took place. C.S.M. Betts rose to his feet with a blood curdling yell and ran forward straight towards the machine gun, which ceased as if by magic. We all followed, but Betts arrived first and chased about thirty of the enemy towards a dug out.
>
> He laid out six with his bayonet before we arrived, and would have gone for the rest of them if Mr driver had not arrived and ordered them to surrender. Betts had to comply with this order, and about twenty were made prisoners, Betts relieving the officers and N.C.O.'s of their field-glasses, which he festooned over his equipment.

His citation, gazetted on 3 September, states:

> 325753 C.S.M. H. Betts, D.C.M., Camb. B. (Nr. March, Cambs.).
>
> For conspicuous gallantry and devotion to duty. During ten days' very hard fighting this warrant officer, who had taken over the duties of regimental serjeant-major early in the operations, showed an impressive example of courage and coolness under heavy fire on all occasions. On one occasion the battalion, which had been very much reduced in numbers, both of officers and men, delivered a successful counter-attack, driving back the enemy a, considerable distance, and capturing men and machine guns. Company Serjeant-Major Betts was conspicuous for the fearless manner in which he attacked the machine- gun positions, and his behaviour had a marked effect on the men.
>
> (D.C.M. gazetted 26th November, 1917.)

As the advance on Morlancourt started on 9 August, the 1/1st Cambridgeshires came under fire from artillery and MG fire from enfilade positions to the south of the village. This would have held up 'C' and 'D' Companies and inflicted heavy casualties had it not been for Harry:

> Without hesitation Betts, who was C.S.M. of 'D' Company on the right, dashed off alone. Taking advantage of a hedge running across the front, he worked his way resolutely forward until 'D' Company lost sight of him. When he reappeared, he was in the rear of the enemy position which was causing all the trouble. There were about thirty of the enemy all engaged in firing at 'C' and 'D' Companies. Superior numbers had no terrors for Betts, practically single handed he had re-captured a position in March, 1918. With a blood curdling yell, he dashed in with his bayonet at the nearest machine-gun crew. This unexpected attack from the rear was the last straw, those who had survived Betts' frenzied onslaught meekly surrendered, and were handed over by him to some men of the buffs who happened to arrive before the astonished enemy had regained their wits.... The success of the whole operation was mainly due to the gallantry and initiative displayed by Betts. A typical Fenman, hailing from near Wisbech, he had served in the Battalion from the commencement of the war. At the age of twenty-one he was C.S.M. and held the D.C.M. and Bar, and for his services in this action he was recommended for the V.C.'

His gazette citation, listed on 1 February 1919, states:

> No. 325753 C.S.M. Harry Betts, D.C.M., 1/1st Bn., Cambs. Regt., T.F.
>
> During the attack on Morlancourt on 9th August, 1918, the right flank was held up by a nest of machine guns. This warrant officer immediately went forward alone, and, with great gallantry and disregard of danger, killed three and captured 30 of the enemy and four machine guns, thereby clearing the way for his company and disposing of an obstruction which might have upset the whole operation. He did magnificent work.

He did not live to receive these awards.

Much like the 7th Norfolks, the Cambridgeshires had had a brief rest prior to the attack on 22 August. It was here that Harry was killed in action trying to outflank another MG post. The regimental history also makes mention of his death:

> I found out why C.S.M. Betts had not reported to H.Q. with the other C.S.M.'s. Just as the attack was starting, an enemy machine-gun opened up only a short distance in front. Impulsive as ever, he could not resist the challenge and sprang over the parapet, doubtless intending to work round and take the machine-gun from a flank. He had only gone a few yards when he fell, and with him Cambridgeshire lost one of its bravest sons and the Battalion a devoted and fearless warrant-officer.

Harry is now laid to rest in Beacon Cemetery at Sailly-Laurette. This cemetery overlooks the battlefield that he advanced over on 22 August 1918. He, like so many others, left all that was dear to them, endured hardness, faced danger, and finally passed out of the sight of man. He is gone, but he is not forgotten, and is still proudly remembered by his family—some of whom I have helped with research into Harry and I have stood over his grave a fair few times.

Further advances on 24, 25, and 26 August saw the battalion advancing with the Cambridgeshires, with a machine-gun post in Pommiers Redoubt being stormed by a party led by Capt. Weaver, Lt Plant, Company Sgt-Maj. Fuller, and Sgt Everitt, which led to the killing and capture of a number of the enemy and two machine guns. On 27 August, they were up to Trones Wood, the scene of intense fighting in 1916, and formed a defensive flank facing north-east.

On 28 August 1918, Maltz Horn Ridge was captured by the 9th Essex and the 1/1st Cambridgeshires and 100 prisoners were captured. What is missed in the Norfolks's history is that the 7th Battalion HQ was very nearly caught in heavy shellfire where the Battalion HQ for the 1/1st Cambridgeshires was hit and both Norfolk and Cambridgeshire men became casualties. The war diary for the 7th Battalion noted:

> The battalion were under orders to move forward at short notice. This evening we relieved the 1/1 Cambs in the outpost and front-line. Just before HQ arrived at the HQ of the 1/1 Cambs the area was very heavily shelled and 2nd Lt Maddison was killed.
>
> Together with the Signalling Officer of the Cambs, Lt Col Saint Commanding the Cambs was very badly wounded and Adjutant slightly so.

The Cambridgeshires's history noted:

> I had only time for a glance at the wrecked HQ. Saint, Driver, the Norfolk SO and Walker had been sitting round the table working out the relief. Cooper and Churchman, assisted by some of the runners, were packing up ready for moving. Clinton and Padre had just gone across to the aid-post.
>
> The shelling, which had lasted all day, had been quieting down, and only one gun was still firing, but at increasing intervals. The very last shell to be fired that day crashed through the roof and table and exploded in the ground.

The signals officer mentioned in the narratives was Geoffrey Maddison who had been commissioned on 28 September 1917 from the ranks having served in both the Machine-Gun Corps and the Essex Regiment prior to joining the 7th Battalion as an officer.

His probate notes he resided at 224 Sadler Street in Durham and had studied at Marlborough College. Another casualty that day was Edgar Gray from Great

Yarmouth who was a signaller for the 7th Battalion. He had been with the battalion since they had landed in France in May 1915.

By 3 September, he was in Blighty, and it is said that he won a MM for carrying wounded officers back to their lines but got drunk that night and was nearly court-martialled for laying a wreath on someone's bed. He was rightly awarded the MM on 11 February 1919. Known as 'Jack the Lad', he died in an accident in 1948.

Sadly, Lt-Col. Edward Twelftree Saint, DSO, of the 1/1st Cambridgeshires, died of his wounds. Having studied this battalion as well, I know that his loss was a terrible blow to the Cambridgeshires. He had served with them from 1909 and on active service when they had first gone to France in February 1915 and had a remarkable career with them. He had won a DSO in the March 1918 fighting for leadership and skill his citation reading:

> For gallantry throughout ten days operations, during the first seven of which he showed marked initiative in organising lines of defence, especially in front of a town, where he held up the enemy advance, enabling the guns to be withdrawn. When the officer commanding another battalion became a casualty, he assumed command of both battalions. Later, when the officer commanding brigade became a casualty, he took command of the brigade, organised a counter attack at a critical time, reoccupying the line. He kept the men splendidly together when nearly all the officers and non-commissioned officers had become casualties.

The Cambridgeshires's website says it all when it notes in his biography:

> News of Saint's death was a shock to all, as one of the few remaining pre-war officers he had come through so much unscathed already. At the time of his death he was only 33, leaving behind his widow and two young children, aged seven and five. With the rank of Lt Colonel, he is the highest-ranked officer killed during the Regiment's service in WW1 and is remembered on numerous war memorials, including the Old Perseans Memorial at the Perse School.
>
> He is buried, close to the site of the CCS where he died, at what is now known as Daours Communal Cemetery. The epitaph on his grave, reflecting the dedicated service to both regiment and country that dominated so much of his life, reads *DULCE ET DECORUM EST PRO PATRIA MORI.*

Over the next few days, Maurepas and Falfemont Farm, so gallantly stormed by the 1st Battalion in September 1916, was recaptured. After a brief rest, the 12th Division eventually pushed right across the wilderness of the old Somme battlefield, capturing Méaulte, Mametz, Carnoy, Hardecourt, and Favières Wood, which was reached after a week's continuous fighting.

On 30 August 1918, after advancing 11 miles, capturing thirteen machine guns, three trench mortars, and sixty prisoners, the battalion came out of the line and moved to Favières Wood and then to Montauban where it spent the first three days of September reorganising.

In total, it is estimated that the battalion lost twelve officers and 313 other ranks killed, wounded, or gassed. However, with that said, the death toll here was light. The Commonwealth War Graves Commission records the loss of twenty-six men in the fighting for this period.

On 2 September, near Quéant, the Canadian Corps forced the Germans to retreat even further. By 3 September, the Germans were back where they had started in March, and by 10 September, the Allies had closed up the Amiens Salient and it was here that Ludendorff realised that it was the end and that Germany would have to sue for peace.

Guidebook

This is a difficult one to exactly pinpoint. But you could start by taking the D42 out of Méaulte and you will see a track leading off to the left. If you take this track and go up to the high ground this is where 'A' Company initially advanced and occupied the German trench on 22 August 1918. The 12th Division swept north east all the way over a large part of the old 1916 battlefield of the Somme to Maltz Horn Farm and then onto Falfemont Farm. Falfemont Farm is covered in my chapter on the 1st Battalion who fought there on 4 September 1916.

What3words: tacklers.wrenches.primers.

To get to Maltz Horn Farm, head towards Guillemont on the D64. You will pass Bernafay and Trones Wood on your left, if you pass Guillemont Road Cemetery you have gone too far; next to Trones Wood, there is a turning on the right signposted Hardecourt Aux Bois. Take this turning and you will come to a calvary on the left. This a memorial and is the site of Maltz Horn Farm.

What3words: believable.brightening.experimental.

31

The 1st Battalion, Norfolk Pioneers: 2 December 1916 to 30 August 1918

During my research for my second book, I came across a snippet of a newspaper report from the *Weekly Press*, dated 2 December 1916. The caption read: 'Norfolk Pioneers'. A picture showed nine men from the Norfolk Regiment with their dog. A description of the photograph read:

> Pioneers—Battalion Norfolks, with their trench-worn dog Pedro, who is suffering from wounds caused by contact with barbed wire entanglements.
>
> Standing:—E. Denham (Norwich), H. Francis (Shotesham), Lance Corporal Williams (Yarmouth), W. Russell (Norwich). H.A. Dunnett (Downham), Sergeant Gilham (Dereham), C. Russell (Lynn), A.B. Dunnett (Cambridge), Pedro, J. Ringer Gissing).

I wanted to know more about these men and have left this story until now because between the date of the piece and August 1918 is the time where all of the men can be located and their story told. From the order of the men mentioned, they can be identified as the following men from the 1st Battalion.

Private Ernest Denham (17234) had been with the battalion since 25 May 1915, having been a draft. Aged thirty-nine, he was killed in action on 28 October 1917 and was the son of the late Mr and Mrs W. Denham, of 65, Patteson Road in Norwich and was the husband of Martha Sarah Ann Denham of 14 Cross Street in Norwich. The war diary noted for this period that there was shelling that caused a few casualties. Ernest has no known grave and is commemorated on the Tyne Cot Memorial.

Private Herbert William Francis (16723) had been with the battalion since 18 May 1915. Herbert survived the war, although he had been wounded in August 1918, and was discharged from the Army on 20 April 1919.

Lance Corporal Gordon Williams (43415) originally came from Ditchingham and died of wounds on 30 August 1918. He had previously served as a private (923) in the 1/6th Battalion and would have been a draft for the 1st Battalion when they received reinforcements from the 1/6th Battalion in July 1916. He is now buried in Grave II. F. 16. Terlincthun British Cemetery. See my chapter on the Battle of Albert and Bapaume to see what was happening to the 1st Battalion during August 1918.

Private William Russell (8834) landed in France with the 1st Battalion on 16 August 1914. William survived the war.

Private Arthur Henry Dunnett (8254) was born at Denver Sluice and enlisted in Cambridge. He landed with the 1st Battalion on 16 August 1914, so the same day as William Russell. Arthur survived the war and died on 5 September 1978. Sadly, his brother was not so lucky.

Private Alfred Banham Dunnett (9094), also from Denver Sluice, landed in France on 2 February 1915 as a draft for the 1st Battalion. Aged twenty-nine, he was killed in action on 28 October 1917 and has no known grave and is commemorated on the Tyne Cot memorial. Alfred and Arthur were the sons of Alfred and Rosanna Dunnett. Alfred would have been killed in the same artillery barrage that Ernest Denham was killed in.

Sergeant Robert William Gilham (4237) also landed in France on 16 August 1914 and came from North Tuddenham. He was killed in action on 30 May 1918. The war diary noted that, on 29 May 1917, 'About 10 a.m. a direct hit with 5.9″ was obtained on our Bn HQ seriously wounding Capt Musters the Adjutant & Capt Mann, acting 2 in Command. Artillery active about noon on C Coy HQ and machine guns active. Direct hit on D Coy caused 4 killed and 3 wounded casualties'. Aged forty-nine, he was the son of Robert and Sarah Gilham and the husband of Florence R. Gilham of 59 Englefield Road in London. He is buried in Grave III.A.2. in Bagneux British Cemetery at Gezaincourt.

Private Claude Charles Russell (18091) landed in France on 12 May 1915; he was medically discharged on 3 July 1918 after being considered no longer physically fit to serve.

Private Auriel Jack Ringer (8309) landed in France on 16 August 1914 and originally came from Gissing. In the 1911 Census, he is listed as serving in the Norfolk Regiment. He survived the war but died at the age of fifty-five in 1947. His brother, Benjamin Ringer, died serving with the 9th Battalion on 15 April 1918 while they were fighting around Crucifix Hill to the west of Neuve-Église. See my chapter on this action for more information.

So, four of these men died and five survived the war. From that, one was medically discharged and the rest left the Army through the normal route.

32

The 7th and 9th Battalions, The Battles of the Hindenburg Line, Nurlu to the St Quentin Canal: 18–30 September 1918

After the fighting in August, the 7th Battalion spent the first part of September refitting around Montauban. But by 5 September 1918, the 12th Division was back in the line at Ville Wood relieving the 18th (Eastern Division). Ville Wood is situated south-east of the Canal du Nord and just south-west of Nurlu.

They were given the objective of capturing Nurlu where they were set to advance at 6.45 a.m. The 7th Battalion advanced through the wood having to deal with pockets of the enemy and gas. But it reached its objective to the west of Nurlu. The next day saw the battalion in support of the 1st Cambridgeshires and the 9th Essex who were advancing north of Nurlu, and by evening, they were out of the line and in divisional reserve and carried out a period of training before going back to the line at Ville Wood on 17 September. This was positioned half a mile south of Nurlu. At 5.20 a.m., the battalion formed up and advanced:

… the battalion commenced the attack in 4 waves C Coy forming the 1st wave under 2nd Lt Warren. A Coy the 2nd wave under Lt Foster and the 3rd and 4th waves were made up by D Coy on the right under Lt Plant and B Coy on the left under Captain Dillon. The battalion attacked in a north easterly direction with Room Trench the final objective an advance of about 1700 yards in all, just north east of Épehy. The leading wave gained their objective with no difficulty except that it was very dark and raining hard. The second wave went through the first and owing to the darkness went too much to the right. Machine gun fire was very heavy also considerable hostile shelling especially on the railway embankment due south of Épehy.

Due to this hostile fire, the battalion became disorganised at the railway embankment but three parties of about forty men under the command of three officers managed to get to about 200 yards short of Princes Reserve trench, where they held on for the rest of the day coming under intermittent shelling and machine-gun fire. The war diary notes that the battalion killed large numbers of the enemy and captured fifty prisoners and several machine guns.

The 12th Division had to cope with strong wire defences and German counterattacks but Nurlu was captured with Germans retreating in disarray for several miles, pursued by the division, which regained contact with them between Sorel Wood and Lieramont cemetery.

Losses here for the battalion are listed as 120; included in this number was Lt George Bede Hornby Plant who had joined the 7th Battalion on 31 March 1918 from the Norfolk Yeomanry. Prior to the war, he had St Cuthbert's College Sparken Hill in Worksop. His passing was recorded in his old school magazine, *The Cuthbertian*, in January 1920:

> Plant (the son of the Rev. Thos. Plant, Theddingworth Vicarage, Rugby) joined the Inns of Court O.T.C. shortly after the war broke out, and before he was 17 years of age. He was described by his colonel as 'very energetic, very keen, and very brave.' The following extract is taken from the *London Gazette*, 30th July, 1919, and refers to the posthumous award of the Military Cross. 'For conspicuous gallantry on Aug. 25th, 1918, north east of Mametz. On nearing the objective, the advance was held up by machine gun fire from a strong point. He at once organised and led an attack on the strong point, which was beaten off by the enemy. Undismayed he rallied his men, and again attacked and captured the position, killing many of the enemy. His fine courage and determined leadership enabled the advance to be continued, and the objective gained.'

George was twenty years old and is now buried in Grave I I 1 in Épehy Wood Farm Cemetery. I was able to visit George's grave in January 2020 and stood by his grave at sunset. Others have been there because there was a photo of him propped up against his headstone. He is very much the epitome of the young officers who led their men from the front and who paid the ultimate sacrifice in trying set an example to others.

After a rest in the area of Manancourt, the 12th Division was ordered to renew the attack this time on Épehy situated to the east of Nurlu. This initially took place on 18 September with the enemy staunchly defending Malassise Farm and Fishers Keep causing heavy casualties.

The advance for the Norfolks continued on 19 September with the 1/1st Cambridgeshires and two companies of the 5th Northamptonshires advancing through the battalion's positions towards Ockenden and Room trenches situated to the east of Épehy. This advance did not get very far initially, but by the end of the day, these were captured and the battalion moved up to the south-eastern part of Épehy and then moved into Room Trench relieving the 5th Royal Berkshires.

Épehy, along with Havrincourt for the British and St Mihiel for the Americans before it, confirmed the Germans were weakening and this spurred the Allies on to keep the pressure up.

Guidebook

From Aizecourt-le-Haut take the D917 towards Nurlu. Ville Wood, which was the start line for the battalion on 5 September 1918, can be seen on the left prior entering the village. Head into Nurlu and take the first turning on the right after the large house with the double roof. This is the Rue Hocquet. Keep on this road and you will come to the centre of the village.

At the fork in the road, keep right and then you will turn slightly left and then take the next right, which is La Petite Rue. You will then come to a five-way crossing, stop here. Most of the roads here are farm tracks. One runs to the right, two can be seen in front and then the road you are on veers round to the left and takes you back up to the D917. In the field on the right is where the trench system was situated.

What3words: diviner.throughput.snail.

* * * * *

Pressure was continued with heavy attacks on the Hindenburg Line involving the British 3rd and 4th Armies. By September, the 6th Division had been placed under the command of IX Corps and would also fight at Épehy. After a period of rest and reorganisation, they were put into the line facing the area around Holnon situated to the west of St Quentin. Here they would participate in attacks on St Quentin and The Quadrilateral. This position was not the same one that the battalion had faced in 1916 and was situated to the north-east of Holnon.

On the night of 17 September 1918, the 9th Battalion moved into position to the south of Holnon into a quarry situated on the eastern edge of the wood. As they were forming up, the enemy was pouring artillery into the area and this hampered their advance and only three companies reached the quarry. This meant they were late for Zero Hour at 5.30 a.m. and their advance did not start until 6 a.m. with three companies:

> Owing to the hostile barrage being very intensive the Battalion, having to march parallel to the front from the Quarry to the forming up position, the heavy mist, rain and casualties, these companies became scattered and lost direction.
>
> Only one Company and five platoons of two other Companies reached the cross roads at M.32 where they formed up. As the Quadrilateral had not been taken these went forward at 9 a.m. but owing to the heavy machine gun fire from the Quadrilateral they swung to the right and remained in action in S.3 and during the remainder of the day.

The remaining Companies were assembled in the sunken road S.2 and during the afternoon by 3 p.m. The Bn was reorganised into three companies one engaged against the Quadrilateral and two others in reserve in the sunken lane at S.2 and those two companies were detailed to the attack to the 2nd Bn. Sherwood Foresters for an attack which was cancelled.

Here they remained until early morning on 19 September when orders were received to renew the attack. By this time, two companies of the 9th Battalion had wheeled around to the north-east of Holnon and were holding onto positions between Douai Trench and North Alley, which were situated to the north of the Quadrilateral. But these men had to retire back to Douai Trench where they remained in action all day with 'A' Company and two platoons withdrawn back to the sunken road at S.2. On 20 September, the battalion reorganised their front around Douai Trench: 'The Bn took over the Bde front from junction of American Alley and Douai Trench. The Bn was disposed as follows. Three platoons in Douai Trench his platoons dug in in front of North Alley facing east. Three platoons in Valley Trench facing north. One platoon in reserve in Quarry'.

On 22 September, the battalion was relieved by the 1st Battalion Buffs and took up positions at New and Valley Trenches before going back to Keepers Lodge to the west of Holnon Wood and then further back once more to Fresnoy where they occupied trenches around that position until they were relieved on 29 September by the French 11th Regiment of Chasseurs. They then marched back to positions to the east of Vermand.

Casualties were high, and 191 officers and men were killed, wounded, or missing after this engagement. This can be amended to thirty-one men killed. One of the officers to die in this fighting was Lt Albert Arthur Walsha, who was killed when he was being carried off the field wounded after he was hit by machine-gun fire and buried in the wood. His CO said of him: 'He led his men forward splendidly. We all liked him so much and his loss will be felt by the whole battalion, he was such a good soldier'.

Guidebook

In order to get to the Quadrilateral, you have to use a one-way system. At Fayet, coming from St Quentin on the D57, you will see the sign for Holnon on the left. Take this road and you will cross over the A26 and then take a bend to the left. Eventually, on your right, you will pass a copse of trees and then a track will appear just before a one-way and 30-kilometre sign. Park here and then walk up the track. You will come to a T-junction on this track. You are now stood on the Quadrilateral.

What3words: blurred.typhoon.pulled.

* * * * *

As with the orders of the 6th Division, the 12th (Eastern) Division had also been ordered to put pressure onto the defenders of the Hindenburg Line.

The 12th Division was ordered to push past Épehy and secure the vantage points up to the St Quentin Canal. They were also to protect the left flank of the 27th Division of the United States Army, which was attacking under orders of 4th Army. At this point in time, it should be noted that the Americans were now being placed into the line alongside their allies to get essential battle experience.

So, as noted by the battalion's war diary, on the night of 24–25 September, the 27th American Division relieved the British 18th (Eastern) and 74th Divisions opposite the Hindenburg Line, west of Bony. They were given the task to secure the designated line of departure for the general attack against the Hindenburg Line and ordered to make the necessary advance on 27 September 1918. At 5:30 a.m., the 106th Infantry attacked the general line from the Bois de Malakoff to the Knoll. From the 7th Battalion war diary:

> The 27th American Division, at 5.30 a.m. launched an attack on the enemy. They captured the Knoll but later fell back and finally formed up with our right flank. C Coy maintained patrols in Bird Lane with the objective of occupying Lark Post, in the event of the enemy withdrawing, the enemy did not withdraw.

The Americans were relying on British artillery for support and an error saw this barrage give no support so the Americans had to advance without it. The 27th Division came under severe resistance and took heavy machine-gun fire from the rear and flanks, and strong counterattacks from the valleys leading to the Hindenburg Line made it impossible to consolidate the ground gained. From the American Battle Monuments Commission history:

> The failure of the preliminary operation had a grave effect upon subsequent general attack because British, whose artillery was supporting 27th Division, made error starting barrage in front line which been set as objective instead actual jump-off line. Consequently, when attack was made, British artillery fire in the intervening zone, which was about 1,100 yards in depth, was entirely lacking, thus placing upon the assault troops of the 27th Division the impossible task of capturing a strong position with-out the aid of close-in artillery support. This attack illustrates the serious situations which would have resulted from any permanent amalgamation of American troops with the Allied Armies. The reason given for this decision, which proved so extremely costly in American lives, was the probable presence of wounded and isolated groups of Americans stranded in the intervening zone.

Parts of the attacking line were forced back and others withdrew, although small parties, whose numbers were unknown and which remained isolated in shell holes on the ground, advanced over. At the end of the day, there were no gains except on each flank, where the frontline was advanced a few hundred yards.

The casualties in this regiment were unusually heavy, all company officers except two being killed or wounded. Localised actions took place at first before the main attack on 29 September, in which the division fought up through the formidable mass of enemy trenches in front of Ossus Wood before reaching the western outskirts of Vendhuile.

The battalion had spent time cleaning up before moving into positions east and south-east of Épehy, these were called Mule Trench and Yak and Zebra Posts. On the trench map, Yak and Zebra posts can be seen as forward posts, which would be used to listen in on the enemy. From the 7th Battalion war diary:

> At about 10 a.m. the enemy put down a heavy barrage on our front and support lines. Lieut Spencer was killed, also about 9 men wounded the barrage lasted about half an hour, during which time the enemy made a local frontal attack on the troops on our left, but with no success. At about midnight the battalion front was taken over by part of the 27th American Division.
>
> The battalion moved into support of the Essex (to the left). Relief was complete by about 4 a.m. At about 5 a.m. the enemy put down a barrage on the 9th Essex and attempted a small counter attack. He again met with no success and left several dead and two machine guns behind.

The attack was continued on 29 September, with the Australian Corps and the American 27th and 30th Divisions advanced on Gillemont and Quennemont Farms and the Knoll. The Americans led this attack, and the 7th Battalion again witnessed this advance: 'The Battalion is still in the same line. The 37th Bde launched an attack through us, at 5 o'clock in conjunction with 27th American Division on our right and 33rd British Division on our left. Heavy shelling all day'. The 27th Division, with tanks in the lead, left its trenches on time and started across the wide expanse of level ground in the German outpost zone. The British barrage again failed and came down beyond the powerful German positions at The Knoll, Guillemont Farm, and Quennemont Farm, and the Germans were able to open heavy machine-gun fire that swept the entire front of the 27th Division. From the American history:

> Meanwhile, in preparation for the main attack, the British heavy artillery had been hammering away for two days at the strong points and other defences of the Hindenburg Line in this vicinity. This was the situation at 5: 30 a. m. on September 29 when the 27th and 30th Divisions, on a battlefield enveloped by autumn mists and low-hanging clouds, jumped off for the main offensive. Behind a heavy rolling

barrage, the 30th Division, accompanied by tanks, moved forward with great rapidity across the main German trench system. In spite of the fog the leading waves pushed on beyond the Hindenburg Line and the tunnel to near Nauroy, leaving in their wake many unseen and uncaptured strong points. The southern mouth of the tunnel was quickly blocked and Bellicourt was captured, but the enemy, who were able to reach their positions above ground by means of underground passages of which the Americans were unaware, desperately remanned machine-gun nests previously overrun by the 30th Division. From these and the strong points passed by in the fog the Germans opened fire on the American reserve units, wire details, runners and other groups which were following up the assaulting waves. This caused much confusion and many isolated corn bats continued throughout the morning over a large part of the zone of action. The dash of the American troops, how-ever, finally prevailed and in the end all the German soldiers who had been found in rear of the American front lines after the initial assault were killed or captured.

The supporting tanks were put out of action and the American reserves also encountered fire from machine-gun nests that the troops preceding them had passed by in the fog. In many ways, the Americans were making the mistakes we made in 1916. Casualties here for the 27th Division, especially round Guillemont Farm and The Knoll were high. From the American history:

> The 27th Division, with tanks in the lead, left its trenches on schedule time and started across the wide expanse of level ground in the German outpost zone. The British artillery fire supporting the American attack came down beyond the powerful German positions at The Knoll, Guillemont Farm and Quennemont Farm, and their garrisons, unhampered by any Allied artillery bombardment, at once opened a withering machine-gun fire that swept the entire front of the 27th Division. The tanks were soon put out of action, throwing an additional burden on the infantry, which gallantly struggled forward in shattered waves. As the reserves moved for-ward they encountered the fire of machine-gun nests that the troops preceding them had passed by in the fog. Most of the divisional zone between the jump-off line and the tunnel thus became one vast maelstrom of violence. Around Guillemont Farm and The Knoll, the 107th Infantry Regiment of the 27th Division had 337 men killed and 658 wounded on September 29. No other American regiment suffered such a heavy loss in a single day during the war. In spite of all this, however, the troops attacked boldly and incessantly. By noon, Quennemont Farm, part of the elaborate trench system south of Bony, the ground now occupied by the American cemetery and The Knoll were in the bands of the 27th Division.

The advance was eventually carried by British, Australian, and American troops, and in total, since 8 August 1918, the 12th Division alone had advanced 26 miles.

By nightfall, Nauroy had fallen and from there a line that ran generally north-westward to a point about half a mile south-west of Vendhuile.

The division was withdrawn for rest, and on 30 September 1918, the 7th Battalion withdrew to positions 500 yards from Guyencourt. On 1 October 1918, they moved by bus to Proyart. The war diary notes that during the month of September, they had lost fifteen officers and 270 other ranks. This can be amended to seventy-nine men dying in this month who now lie in British cemeteries in France.

Guidebook

From Lempire, take the D28 (Rue de Lempire), heading towards Vendhuile. Pass under the A26 and on your right you will pass a farm called Le Tombois. Past this farm, you will come to staggered crossroads. Keep going and as you come into Vendhuile you will see a turning on the left. Take this turn, which is a track that takes you up the area where Bird Lane was situated and where the Norfolks secured the right of the American advance and pushed out patrols. The track comes around into a slight bend with trees on the right. The track you see there, leading up to high ground on the right is where Bird Lane was situated.

What3words: case.rezoning.acquits.

As an extra, you could visit the American cemetery at Bony, which also puts you on the line of advance for the Americans for this timeline. To get there, head to Bony and then take the D57 towards Hargicourt. The cemetery will be on your right.

What3words: pick.orchestral.homebound.

33

The 1st Battalion, Battle of the Canal du Nord, Gouzeaucourt to Gonnelieu: 28–30 September 1918

The Battle of Canal du Nord was fought between 27 September and 1 October 1918, and in September 1918, the Canal du Nord was still under construction. In the north between the Sensée River and *écluse* No. 3 at Sains-lès-Marquion, the canal had been finished and it was filled with water. However, below that, the canal was still under construction as far as the Havrincourt Tunnel.

The canal itself was between 25 and 35 metres wide, with an average depth of 10 metres. By now a big part of this obstacle had been captured and crossed leaving the Canadians in front of Marquion with the task of crossing it as well as capturing the part of the Hindenburg Line that also lay in front.

Gen. Sir Julian Byng's plan foresaw that 1st Army (under the command of Gen. Sir Henry Horne) on his left, with the Canadian Corps facing the Canal du Nord and 3rd Army would support the Canadians to the south.

Part of the southern flank of the 3rd Army's advance here would involve the 42nd (East Lancashire) Division and the 5th Division. Both would have separate Zero Hours. The 42nd Division would go over at 8.20 a.m. and the 5th Division at 7.52 a.m. The reason for this was to allow the 5th Division to capture high ground to the south before the 42nd Division began their assault. The 42nd Division's 127th Brigade initially made good progress, but the 125th Brigade was stopped to the left of Beaucamp by heavy machine-gun fire on its own front and from Beaucamp which the 5th Division had failed to take.

Within this advance, the 1st Battalion Norfolk Regiment formed up to the east of Metz en Couture on 26 September. Here they witnessed the New Zealand Division go over the top on their left at 5.20 a.m. on 27 September. Their Zero Hour was at 7.52 a.m. in time with the rest of the 5th Division, and they advanced through part of Havrincourt Wood to reach a position to the south-west of Beaucamp and remained in a sunken road.

Their war diary records a constant movement with casualties being taken while they assisted a supply tank. This was hit and exploded, killing three and wounding one other, with one missing. On 28 September, the battalion again advanced, keeping to the south of Beaucamp:

6.30 a.m. 'A' and 'B' Coys moved forward to Lincoln Reserve E of Battery Post in support of 95th Brigade.

10 a.m. Battalion moved forward to Lincoln Reserve, halting for a short period on the line of Snap Reserve. Batt HQ on the Trescault, Dunraven, Gouzeaucourt road at its junction with Lincoln Reserve. 2/Lt Rickwood wounded.

5.30 p.m. Battalion moved in advance guard forward towards railway in R 25. 'C' and 'D' Coys leading followed by 'A' and 'B', 'C' and 'D' Coys arrived on the railway and consolidated. 'B' Company consolidated in Pope Alley. 'A' Company was then pushed through and reoccupied the line of Flag Ravine.

At 4.30 a.m. on the 29th September 1918 the battalion carried on with their advance.

Battalion moved forward again part of attack reach Fusilier Ridge right flank completely in the air and eventually compelled to withdraw to a line Flag Ravine, Gouzeaucourt, Lateau Wood. Battalion consolidated on the line 2 Coys in support in sunken road immediately west of railway. Very heavy shelling with gas and H.E. at daylight on 29th.

Battalion remained in above mentioned position during the day many M.G.s, snipers and trench mortars very active against Flag Ravine, but two T.M.s placed in ravine during the afternoon silenced the snipers.

This advance saw the battalion advance to the south of Beaucamp and then pushing through to the south of Villers Plouich and the north of Gouzeaucourt. Their eventual position at Flag Ravine was situated to the north-east of Gouzeaucourt and to the west of Gonnelieu.

There was no let up here, and on 30 September, the battalion advanced with the 1st Battalion Cheshire Regiment. Here they pushed forward to the north-east of Gonnelieu and captured positions that had been held by the 7th Battalion on 30 November 1917, namely Bleak Trench and Bleak Support. This line was held and patrols were sent out towards Banteux, but these had to withdraw due to artillery.

In this action, the war diary records that they had captured 200 prisoners and Lt Boast was killed. The battalion also had to withstand artillery and gas shells before being relieved by elements of the 37th Division.

Lt Thomas Townsend Boast had initially served in the 9th Battalion as another rank but had been commissioned on 1 August 1917. He joined the battalion that

September. He was killed in action when he was shot by a sniper, having captured a position and a number of prisoners. His CO wrote to his wife, stating:

> Your husband was one of my best officers, always cheerful under any circumstances, thoroughly efficient in all his work, and one of the nicest fellows I've ever met. All the men had the very highest opinion of him and would follow him anywhere; frequently I have overheard them talking about him and all the splendid thigs he had done with the regiment. It is a sad loss to us all and his death is a bitter grief to us.

One of his men also noted in a letter: 'He was always one of the best of our officers and always did his best to look after the welfare of his boys'.

He was aged twenty-eight when he died and was the son of George John and M. A. Boast of Taxal Edge in Whaley Bridge in Cheshire and a native of Holt.

During September 1918, the battalion lost 230 men killed, wounded, or missing. That can be amended to seventy-three killed in the fighting, many of whom have no known grave and are commemorated on the Vis-en-Artois memorial.

Guidebook

On the D56 out of Gouzeaucourt, heading towards Villers-Plouich, finding the first track you see on your right, stop and park here and walk along this track, then walk over the railway line. This is Flag Ravine.

What3words: paid.coarser.retool.

34

The 1st and 9th Battalion Norfolk Regiment, Cambrai and the Pursuit to the Selle, Brancourt to Bazuel: 8–25 October 1918

The 9th Battalion had spent time after their action at the Quadrilateral around Tetry where they received a draft of 150 men, allowing it to have four companies again. But, on 4 October 1918, it moved by bus to Magny la Fosse and then to the front where it relieved the 1st Battalion Buffs.

On 8 October 1918, it again went into action in the 1918 battle of Cambrai. St Quentin had fallen and now the town of Cambrai was to be captured. The 1st, 3rd, and 4th Armies were chosen for this, and the battle would start on 8 October and would use tanks again, much like it had in the November 1917 battle.

Facing the British were three German lines, spanning some 7,000 yards defended by the 20th *Landwehr* and the 54th Reserve divisions, supported by no more than 150 guns. They would be wholly unmatched against a heavy bombardment supported by 324 tanks, infantry, and aircraft.

The 9th Battalion would advance with the 2nd Battalion Sherwood Foresters on their right and the American 118th Infantry Regiment on their left. The advance would be supported by a battalion of Whippet Tanks.

At 5.10 a.m., the battalion advanced and reached a line around Brancourt Station, situated to the south of Brancourt. They then moved into a sunken road that went to Fresnoy. Here they managed to keep in touch with the Americans and the 2nd Sherwood Foresters:

'A' Coy of the 1st Battalion Leicestershire Regiment was sent to the Bn as a reserve. Orders were received that in the event of the AIR taking Brancourt a counter attack by the enemy might develop and the battalion were to keep close watch for this and assist by Lewis Gun fire and rifle fire if the counter attack developed. At 1500 hours orders were received that the 118 AIR were moving forward to exploit their success and the Bn would have to move forward to Rip Trench. Orders were at once issued to try a push forward to exploitation line keeping touch with AIR on the left.

At 18.20 hours orders were received to re-organise companies, platoons and sections, consequently at 20.30 hours orders were received that it was probable the 71 I.B. would attack the high ground in square H 19 to I 5 on morning of the 9th. With this operation in view the following reorganisation will take place.

The 1st Battalion Leicestershire Regt will relieve the 2nd Bn Sherwood Foresters and part of the 9th Bn Norfolk Regt in C 28 d to I 5 a. The Bn to establish a line of posts from C 29 central to I 5 c 3 4. A liaison post with 118 AIR to be established at Brancourt Farm.

This advance took them in a line between Brancourt and Fresnoy to the east of the sunken lane previously mentioned in the war diary. Their advance continued at 2.30 a.m. on 9 October:

> ... the Bn orders were received that the offensive would be continued in morning of the 9th and the Bn would take part in attacking and capturing high ground in squares D 19 and 25. The 9th Norfolk Regt will relieve the 118 AIR as far north as the Farm on the railway in C 24.... In this Bn Boundary being east and west grid line through C 29 central and C 36 central. Bn HQ at once moved forward to Brancourt Station where a conference was called and the situation explained to those concerned. Coys were then formed up on railway line touch being maintained with the 118 AIR. Bn commenced the attack with barrage fire minutes up to zero and fought their way forward to high ground on squares D19 and 25 as ordered by 07.20 hours.

The battalion had effectively moved east and was now positioned in front of Bohain. Here they sent out patrols and Battalion HQ moved into a sunken road to the north-east on Brancourt and outposts were put out to the east of Bohain. Their advance was also noted in the *Official History of the Great War*:

> 9/Norfolk, on the left, assisted by three whippets, whose action neutralized Brancourt though all were hit by armour- piercing bullets, advanced without meeting much resistance, and eventually managed to establish connection with the Americans at Brancourt station....
>
> A patrol of the 9/Norfolk, of the 71st Brigade on the left, then found Bohain clear, and about 2 p.m. the 1/Leicestershire and the 9/Norfolk advanced again, and by 6 p.m. had established a line east of the village. Four thousand five hundred French inhabitants of the district, concentrated in Bohain by the Germans, were found and liberated.

They were congratulated for their work by their brigade commander and recorded that they captured fifteen prisoners, one trench mortar, one 4.2-inch

Howitzer, and three wagons. At 10 a.m. on 10 October 1918, they were relieved by the 2nd Sherwood Foresters and went back to Brancourt Station.

Guidebook

From Bohain-en-Vermandois, on the D28 heading towards Brancourt-le-Grand, you will come to a farm called Haute Cour on your right. To the left is a track, which takes you to Brancourt Farm. Walk up this track and then face eastward. This is where the 7th Battalion relieved 118 AIR on 8 October 1918. It passed through your position and headed towards the high ground to the east of Bohain. Should you wish, you can go into Brancourt and then take the D70 heading towards Fresnoy-le-Grand.

What3words: monthly.fibbing.finer.

Quite soon on the left, you will see the cemetery and then another small copse. This is where Brancourt Station used to be and where the Battalion HQ was set up. Opposite the town cemetery, you take a track off the Rue de l'Église et Cimetière, you can also visit Brancourt le Grand Cemetery which has five Norfolk Regiment graves within it.

What3words: Brancourt Station—obeys.native.reputable; Brancourt le Grand Cemetery—orchid.unnerves.drips.

* * * * *

After the 1918 Battle of Cambrai was complete, the Germans retreated and they were pursued. This pursuit continued to the River Selle. The action for this took place between 9 and 12 October 1918, with the Germans falling back to prepared positions and resisted heavily. They fell back on a defensive line known as 'Hermann' and they used the River Selle as a natural barrier in order to hold off the Allied advance. There was not let up for the 9th Norfolks who assisted with this advance.

The main thrust was going to be by the 2nd Sherwood Foresters and the 1st Leicestershires. The 9th Norfolks were held in reserve at Bohain and the initial advance was held up due to the failure of the 46th Division being checked. The advance continued on 11 October and the 9th Battalion were brought up with the advance with the task of participating in the advance to capture the high ground to the east of Bellevue Ridge.

Here they took up position centrally between the Leicestershires who were on the right and the Sherwood Foresters on the left. Battalion HQ moved up to Guyot Farm and the advance started at 5.30 a.m. By 6.40 a.m., the Norfolk's advance had stalled due to heavy machine-gun fire coming in on their flanks. Artillery fire was brought down on the machine-gun positions and the advance continued:

At 12.50hrs orders were issued to Coys to endeavour to move forward in conjunction with the Bn on the left as they were going to attack the Ridge from N.W. It was arranged for artillery to support their advance. At about 13.00hrs two tanks reported to Bn HQ for duty. These were at once sent forward to destroy the gun nests and assist in the advance. Orders were issued to Coys to move forward and attack in conjunction with the tanks, this was done and the Copse in D.7.a. occupied, but owing to our artillery fire falling short Coys were obliged to fall back to their original line and consolidate.

In this advance the battalion lost 276 officers and other ranks but captured an anti-tank gun and 390 prisoners.

On 11 October, the 9th Battalion were brought up to be on the right flank of the 1st Battalion Leicestershire Regiment who would be central in the advance with the 2nd Battalion Sherwood Foresters on the left flank of the Leicestershires. Their advance was to capture ground east of Bellevue Ridge. At 5.35 a.m., the Battalion HQ moved to Guyot Farm situated to the east of Bohain:

> Coys fought their way forward to a line E 1.d. and E.7.6 by 0645 ours. Owing to heavy machine gun fire and the flanks being held up Coys were unable to advance but touch with flanks was maintained. Artillery fire was brought to bear on the machine gun nests some of which were in a copse in D.7.d.
>
> At 1250 hours orders were issued to Coys to endeavour to move forward in conjunction with the Bn on their left as they were going to attack the ridge from N.W. It was arranged for artillery to support their advance. At about 1300 hours two tanks reported to the Bn HQ for duty. These were at once sent forward to destroy M Gun nests and assist in the advance.
>
> Orders were issued to Coys to move forward and attack in conjunction with the tanks this was done and the copse in D.7.a. occupied, but owing to artillery fire being short Coys were obliged to fall back to their original line and consolidate.

The advance here placed the battalion to the north-west of Regnicourt and here they remained until they were relieved by elements of the 2nd Durham Light Infantry and the 11th Battalion Essex Regiment, which occurred over the night of 11–12 October 1918. Once complete the battalion moved back to billets in Bohain.

Guidebook

On the other side of Bohain, on the D28 heading towards Regnicourt you will pass by Riqueval Wood on your right. Prior to the wood ending on your left you will see a small piece of hard standing. Park here and use the tree line on your left looks towards Goyet Farm. Midway, between the road and the farm look to your right, the copse of trees you see in the distance is where the Norfolks consolidated the positions captured on the day.

What3words: concort.wrestlers.singular.

* * * * *

On 13 October 1918, the French Army took the village of Laon and the British 4th Army had reached the River Selle and now prepared to cross this natural defence. They would have to cross the river, a railway embankment and a ridge on the other side. Because this attack would be fraught with risk the decision was made to cross the river at night. The river was not very wide therefore planks could be used to move the infantry across and pontoons would be used to ferry artillery over. The attack would involve XIII and IX Corps and would be fought on a 10-mile front and the British would be facing three German divisions.

The attack was planned to start on 17 October 1918 and when the battle started the British advanced into thick fog and became embroiled in a scrap where the advancing divisions from both the XIII and XI Corps got mixed up together. XI Corps also adopted deception techniques, which worked.

On this day, Len Durrant died in a prisoner of war camp at Lamsdorf. He had been wounded on 6 October while serving with the 7th Battalion Leicestershire Regiment. It is possible he was sent to them after his bought of trench foot in October 1917. On 5 October, the 7th Leicestershires had advanced and occupied a part of the Hindenburg Line after the Germans had withdrawn from it and had been in action the next day when they remained in positions as another battalion passed through them. He is now buried in Grave XVIII.A.9 in Berlin South Western Cemetery. This, along with the loss of Sydney in June, deeply affected their family, especially their mother, Amelia, who it is said was blighted with grief and sorrow for her lost boys.

The 5th Division initially remained in reserve for the attack on the River Selle, but they were back in the line on 22 October 1918. Here they occupied trenches along the Selle with the 15th Brigade in support of the 13th Brigade who occupied trenches from Neuvilly to Biastre. As the 1st Battalion moved into support trenches they came under artillery fire and lost their chaplin, Reverend Richard William Dugdale, MC. The war diary noted: 'Battalion moved into support at Map Ref 57 B N.E E21.B where they dug in shelling slight. Rev R W Dugdale M.C. C.F. killed 22/23 October 18'. This placed them in positions to the south-east of Solesmes. The Rev. Dugdale had been with the battalion for four months and the CO of the 1st Norfolks, Lt-Col. George de Grey, noted in a letter to his parents:

He was killed instantly by a shell which exploded in the Regimental Aid Post where he was sitting. By the death of this young officer, the Church, the State and the Army have lost a valuable promising life. He was certainly far and away the best Chaplain I have ever met, and one of the best fellows. The men just loved him, and no wonder. He was indefatigable in his efforts to increase their comfort, and the greatest help to me in this respect. His conduct in action—and he never missed a show—was always most gallant, and by his efforts the sufferings of our wounded were greatly reduced. In every fight he worked unceasingly, helping the Regimental Medical Officer in his Aid Post, and the stretcher bearers getting wounded men in. He will be sadly missed in the Regiment. We all feel we have lost not only our Padre, but a personal friend.

A friend noted of Richard in a letter written after the end of the war:

Most loveable, most gentle, and most strong, he was the ideal type of Christian priest. The loss to the Church and to those who would have come under his spell is even greater than the loss to his friends and to those who have known him and treasure his memory. His enthusiasm for reform, his humanity, and his strength of purpose assured him a future rich in honour and full of benefit to his country. Cut short on the eve of victory, his life is an inspiration and example, and his death an earnest of the truth by which he lived

He was twenty-eight years old and the war diary noted that he was buried in Caudry Military Cemetery, now known as Caudry British Cemetery.

On 23 October, the battalion moved in artillery formation to positions north-east of Beurain, putting them between the village and a position known as Hirson Mill. Here they were relieved by elements of the 112th Brigade of the 37th Division and moved back to Caudry.

The Battle of the Selle saw an advance of 6 miles in two days, and the Hindenburg Line was now 20 miles behind with the Germans retreating with the new line positioned between Valenciennes and the Sambre.

Guidebook

On the D43 out of Solesmes, you will see a track on your right. This will be found just prior to a farm house called Marou. Drive up this track to the next crossroads. At these crossroads look left. You are now in the area where the Norfolks dug in on the night that the Rev. Dugdale was killed.

What3words: fillings.stunning.exaggerated.

Hirson Mill can be difficult to find but can be reached by taking the D43a into Beaurain. You then need to go through the village and then towards a small hamlet called Vertigneul. You cross over the River Harpies and then come to crossroads. Turn right here. Keep on this road, you will pass a farmhouse on the right, and keep going until you see a track on the right where you can park up.

Take this track, which then has a right turn and take that turn. Walk up this track and you will eventually come to the remains of the mill on your left.

What3words: entwined.tight.ruffles.

* * * * *

Also participating in the Battle of the Selle was the 9th Battalion who had been in training at Bohain before being bussed to St Souplet where they relived the 108th American Infantry on 20 October 1918.

The 71st Brigade began preparations to continue with the attack on German positions between Catillon and Le Cateau. They would advance towards Bois-l'Évêque with the 9th Battalion on the left, the 1st Leicestershires on the right, and the 2nd Sherwood Foresters in reserve. The attack went in at 1.20 a.m. on 23 October 1918.

The 9th Battalion's line of advance came from the south of Basuel, now spelt Bazuel, situated to the north-west of Catillon. Their advance would push north heading towards a light railway situated on the other side of the town: 'At 0120hrs Bn attacked and fought their way forward to R9.c.60.90 a force of about 50 reaching R3.d.50.20'. This placed the battalion in a line across the railway facing to the east. They came up against wire, wired hedges, and fences, and were not able to get any further than 400 yards from their start line. This placed the battalion in Bois-l'Évêque, but their advance was checked and they could not anything more than some scattered parties into the wood:

> The 71st Brigade, with l'Evêque Wood, three-quarters of a mile in front of it, was soon in difficulties, and about 7 a.m. was still held up four hundred yards from the starting line. Not until 11 a.m. was the left, the 1/Leicestershire, on the first objective, just inside the wood, with the 9/Norfolk not yet abreast.

A renewal of this attack was then ordered and the two tanks ordered up to support the Norfolks:

> Towards 1 p.m. the resistance weakened perceptibly, and about that hour the 2/Sherwood Foresters was sent up to continue the attack of the Norfolk, whilst the latter battalion was reorganized and sent through the 25th Division area to the Bazuel–Malgarni road to work south-eastwards through l'Evêque Wood.
>
> Before this operation could be completed darkness came on, so that the position of the 6th Division for the night lay between the first and second objectives. The casualties, including the gassed, amounted to a little over three hundred, but 4 enemy officers and 96 other ranks had been captured, with two field guns and 40 machine guns.

This allowed the advance to push halfway into the wood before darkness stopped any further advance and the Norfolks were then ordered to withdraw:

> Owing to the barrage having moved far forward and the enemy MG fire the Bn dug in and awaited assistance from the tanks 2 tanks. At 16.30hrs orders were received that the Bn would push out a line of pickets from L34.b.0.8 to L23.d.9.8. The BHQ moved forward to R9.a.2.2. At 18.00hrs orders were issued from Bde that the Bn were to withdraw to La Quennelet Grange. At 20.30hrs the Bn withdrew from positions to proceed to La Quennelet Grange as ordered. On arrival there the Bn were accommodate in a few sheds and out buildings of the farm. Bn arrived at about 23.00hrs.

The action on 23 October 1918 allowed the 16th Brigade to push on and capture the rest of the Bois-l'Évêque on 24 October 1918. Losses for the battalion were fifteen killed, sixty-one wounded, and sixty missing. This can be amended to eighteen men dying between 22 and 25 October 1918.

The battalion spent time in and out of the line up to 31 October 1918, but then went back to Fresnoy le Grand and then spent the rest of the war around Le Souplet and Bohain.

Guidebook

Head for Bazuel and from this town take the D643 towards Catillon-sur-Sambre. The road gently bears round to the left, on the right is a small red-bricked calvary, and on the left is a farm. Turn your car round and park up next to the entrance to the farm. Looking between the two large barns in the distance is the right flank of the Norfolks who were in a line on the old light railway, which went back north-west of here.

What3words: indent.ever.lagers.

Now head back into Bazuel, and at the turn off for the D160a, signposted Ors, turn right. Keep on this road until you come to a single house on the left; just prior to the house is a turning, take this. Go as far as the railway crossing. This is where fifty men from the battalion got to on 23 October 1918.

What3words: dabbled.camper.goggled.

The 12th Battalion,
The Final Advance into Flanders,
St Yves to Audenarde:
11 September to 31 October 1918

On 4 September 1918, the 12th Battalion moved forward to Bailleul assisting in the relief of the 86th and 88th Brigades of the 29th Division. The battalion went into the support line, but this was only temporary, and on the night of 8 September 1918, they were in the Ploegsteert Sector where they took up positions around Hyde Park Corner.

The war diary for this period is quite lacking in detail and does not really provide much information. For instance, the entry for the period between 8 and 13 September 1918 just states: 'From the 8th to the 13th the Battalion held this position on the front. Patrols were pushed out in daylight and each night and much useful information about the enemy was obtained'.

The Divisional war diary does provide a little bit more information for that period, noting on 11 September 1918:

A platoon of the left Bde (12th Norfolks) proceeded down the southern end of Ploegsteert village at 2 p.m. to 4 p.m. and occupy it. On reaching the last house the platoon came under heavy machine gun fire from their front and from both flanks, and were unable to send in a report of their situation. The Sergt in charge of the platoon was badly wounded and was met by his Coy Cmdr on return. Two subsequent attempts were made during the night to locate the platoon but nothing could be heard or seen of it. Their fate is not yet known.

This was quite frustrating until I was given access to a letter written by Robert Williamson who was serving with them at that time. On 11 September 1918, he was one of a number of men who took part in one of the patrols mentioned in the war diary:

On Sept 11th our Platoon was sent out about 900 yds to occupy a farm house in no man's land. Well we hadn't gone far before we found there were Germans about as we saw some run back. We'll we advanced to within 300 yds of our objective when a German machine Gun fired at us from our right flank. We got within 50 yds of this machine gun when I got my Lewis Gun into action and fired on the German machine gun.

I was out in the open and the German gun was in an in trenched position and he was cutting the ground up just inches in front of me and it's a wonder I didn't get hit. Meanwhile the rest of the Platoon had got into a ditch with a thick fence in front of it and plenty of Germans were in front as well. But the Germans fired at us with about 6 machine guns from the farm we were supposed to take and we couldn't advance on account of the ditch. We'll we kept the Germans back for 3 hrs we used a good but our ammunition up and also most of our bombs.

The Germans advanced to take us prisoners under a heavy machine Gun barrage behind grave stones got within bombing range of us and stated sending broom stick bombs over at us at the same time a trench mortar battery was firing at us and making things extremely uncomfortable. One of our lads was killed by machine gun fire and two more were killed trying to get back after being wounded and one just before we were taken prisoners was hit on the back by a bomb and blown to pieces. Several were wounded and at last the Germans were on us and we were forced to give in but if there had been a chance to have got back we should soon have taken it.

Well we were taken back by a German officer and men to their battalion headquarters and we were given some water to drink and treated fairly well. One or two of our lads were pumped for information but the Germans didn't get much out of them.

And this can be evidenced in the entry that was made in the war diary in October 1918 where the following appeared in the Army, Corps, Divisional, and Brigade Routine Orders:

The following extract from a captured German Regtl. Orders shows the excellent behaviour after capture of a patrol from the Norfolk Regt. who were captured by the enemy on the 11th September 1918 near Ploegsteert. The enemy appreciates their soldierly bearing and holds them up to his own men as an example.

Method of Capture

The prisoners belong to a big patrol ordered to make good the occupation of a farm (apparently Hof Osternelle near Ploegsteert) and to put out of action the machine guns conjectured to be there. The 21 prisoners among whom were 4 NCOs had all taken off their badges and could not and would not give a satisfactory reason for having done so.

The majority of the prisoners belong to the workman class. They make good military impression but in their statements are so extraordinary reticent that one must assume that their superior officers have instructed them clearly and warned them how to behave when taken prisoners.

The GOC feels sure that officers will spare no pains to instruct their men accordingly.

The GOC congratulates the OC and all ranks on the fine spirit shewn by these NCOs and men of the 12th (Yeo) Bn Norfolk Regiment.

This patrol which was captured, was one found by C Coy whilst the Battalion was in the line in the Ploegsteert Sector.

Along with the twenty-five men captured in this patrol, the battalion lost eleven men killed who are now buried in two specific cemeteries nearby, namely Strand Military and Trois Arbres Cemeteries. Two men have no known grave and are commemorated on the Ploegsteert Memorial.

On 28 September 1918, the Allied Army Group of Flanders attacked and broke through the German Front to the north, east and south of the city of Ypres. By now that famous town was very much distanced from what once had been a daily grind of a battle that ran just to the north and east of its walls.

The plan involved both the British 2nd and the Belgian Army under the command of King Albert I of Belgium, as well as French and American troops, launch a combined effort combine to finally break out of the Ypres Salient.

Into this battle, the 12th Battalion would find themselves assisting in the advance to the south of Messines. Just prior to this the 12th Battalion received a new CO, with Charles Milligan noting:

Early September saw us with a new C.O., an experienced officer with seven wound stripes on his sleeve and chestful of ribbons including the V.C., D.S.O. and M.C. He gathered us together and told us we were going into the line again we could write home and tell Mum we were having tea the following afternoon with Jerry.

The new CO was Lt-Col. John Sherwood Kelly who had won a VC at Cambrai. John Sherwood Kelly was born in the Eastern Cape Province in South Africa on 13 January 1880. By November 1917, he was CO of the 1st Battalion, The Royal Inniskilling Fusiliers. His *London Gazette* citation for the VC stated:

Maj. (A./Lt.-Col.) John Sherwood-Kelly, C.M.G., D.S.O., Norf. R., comd. a Bn., R. Innis. Fus.

For most conspicuous bravery and fearless leading when a party of men of another unit detailed to cover the passage of the canal by his battalion were held up on the near side of the canal by heavy rifle fire directed on the bridge. Lt.-Col. Sherwood-Kelly at once ordered covering fire, personally led the leading company of his battalion across the canal and, after crossing, reconnoitred under heavy rifle and machine gun fire the high ground held by the enemy. The left flank of his battalion advancing to the assault of this objective was held up by a thick belt of wire, whereupon he crossed to that flank, and with a Lewis gun team, forced his way under heavy fire through obstacles, got the gun into position on the far side, and covered the advance of his battalion through the wire, thereby enabling them to capture the position.

Later, he personally led a charge against some pits from which a heavy fire was being directed on his men, captured the pits, together with five machine guns and forty-six prisoners, and killed a large number of the enemy.

The great gallantry displayed by this officer throughout the day inspired the greatest confidence in his men, and it was mainly due to his example and devotion to duty that his battalion was enabled to capture and hold their objective.

On 28 September 1918, the 12th Battalion moved from Hazebrouck to Bailleul to be brigade support, and by 10.45 p.m. had occupied a camp vacated by the 15th Battalion West Yorks. At 1 a.m. on 29 September, they were ordered to advance on Neuve-Église and then eastward to Bakery Post situated to the north of Ploegsteert Wood.

They arrived here at dawn and moved forward in Artillery Formation supporting the 93rd brigade still heading east. The companies worked along the road from Bakery Post to Ash Crater meeting up with the 93rd Brigade coming to a halt in a line between St Yves and Avenue Farm positioned to the south-east of Messines.

The battalion then moved onto St Yves trench, which were old British trenches from 1917. 'B' and 'A' Coys then moved eastward to old German trenches known as Ultimo Avenue and 'C' and 'D' Coys remained at St Yves trench.

The advance then continued on 30 September, with the battalion again moving east towards and then wheeling south so that their line then stretched either side of La Bassée-Ville just shy of the River Lys.

Their second objective was to then push slightly east and also south in order that their line rested on the Ploegsteert–Warneton road. Charles Milligan noted that with regards to the enemy: 'Fortunately for us he had decided to retire and met no resistance'. This objective was achieved and the battalion consolidated their ground and then withdraw, their orders stating:

At 5 p.m. orders were received to withdraw the two rear Coys. (A and B), leaving C and D under Capt Ruggles Brise to be withdrawn when he was satisfied the 92nd and 93rd Brigades were in touch and were covering his front. On completion of withdrawal, Coys marched back independently to old bivouac area at A9.a.5.3. The last Coy marching in at 2.30 a.m.'

This placed them at Douve Farm and to the south of the Douve River. Casualties were light for the advance, with five killed and fifteen wounded. The battalion remained at Douve farm until 6 October when they went into trenches to the south of Ploegsteert Wood facing Pont Rouge.

They put out patrols along the River Lys and then prepared to take part in a feint attack by continuing with these patrols with the hope that the enemy might think that the attack would take place here. Their war diary noted:

> On the morning of the 11th two feint attacks were carried out with the idea of the enemy thinking an attack was to take place. These feints took the form of an artillery creeping barrage opening for 10 minutes on the enemy front-line trenches and lifting every four minutes for about four lifts and continuing as a box barrage for a further 10 minutes to give the enemy the impression that an attempt was about to be made to cross the Lys.

This feint fell from Warneton, towards Deulemont and onto Pont Rouge along the River Lys. Heavy artillery also fell on Freilinghein.

From their positions, 'A' Coy sent out a patrol to try and cross a bridge across the Lys, but they were stopped by machine-gun fire. Looking at the battalion positions for his period that bridge is more than likely the one at Pont Rouge. Charles Milligan noted:

> We had seen no civilians during this period but later came into contact with some as we passed through areas which had been occupied by the enemy. A remarkable thing was the absence of any vehicles, not even bicycles had been left behind, factories in Roubaix and Turcoing were stripped of machinery. There was little damage to buildings by shellfire.

On 12 October 1918, the battalion was relieved by the 15th West Yorks and they marched back to Bailleul. During this initial stage of the offensive, there was a significant advance where Kemmelberg and several miles of territory lost to the German advance in April earlier that year was recaptured. More ground was gained in a day that in the entire Third Ypres offensive of 1917.

Guidebook

At the roundabout in the centre of Ploegsteert, take the N365, Rue d'Armentières, this is the area where the battalion sent a platoon to capture the last house in the southern area of the village. Now head towards Messines. As you drive on the N365, you will see signs for a number of CWGC cemeteries, one of them being Prowse Point Cemetery. Turn right here and you will come to Prowse Point Cemetery on the right. Park here and you will see the UEFA Christmas Truce memorial, which is based on myth. If you would like to read the true story, then I advise you look at my chapter on the 1st Battalion and the Christmas Truce. From here you can look towards Messines. The 12th Battalion came from that direction in a long right wheel and took up positions from St Yves, across the sunken road and up to what became known as the Ultimo Crater, situated on what was Ultimo Avenue Trench.

What3words: posed.sizzled.warbler.

Now return to your car and head towards Gheer. If you can try and have Ploegsteert Wood on your right you will come to a junction on the N515. Turn left here and just before the bridge under the N58 you will see a turning on the left. Take this turn and the first farm you see on your left farm is Trois Tilles farm.

What3words: analogy.surreal.physical.

Now retrace your steps and turn left onto the N515 and go under the bridge and take the next right, Route de la Grande Haie. At the T-Junction turn right onto Chaussée du Pont Rouge. Keep on this road and this comes to a dead end. In front of you, you will see a footbridge over the Lys, although not the original railway bridge, this is the same area where the 12th Battalion attempted to cross the river.

What3words: remind.snore.army.

* * * * *

Once at Bailleul, they then spent time in and out of trenches around Ploegsteert. They had then advanced across the Lys at Warneton on 18 October 1918. A further period of training at Lannoy then saw them advance again via Mouscron and Staceghem where they went into the current line on 29 October 1918.

On 31 October 1918, they participated in the Action of Tieghem, which saw an advance that was designed to clear the way forward for a full advance to secure the Schelde and was also designed to provide a springboard for the advance of French 6th Army who were advancing towards the Scheldt between Waregem and Kruishoutem.

Each of the divisions had the support of three or four brigades of field artillery. All the corps' artillery plus the guns of resting brigades and the heavy artillery of X Corps were to be utilised in support of the attack. The key objective here was the neutralisation of enemy batteries and machine-gun positions, plus the masking of enemy-held high ground by smoke, on the east bank of the Schelde. Zero Hour was set for 5.25 a.m., with the infantry moving forward under a creeping barrage of artillery and machine guns, moving at a rate of 100 yards in three minutes.

The 12th Battalion saw itself taking part in the advance north of the Scheldt towards Audenarde, now pronounced Oudenaarde, as a support battalion. Here resistance from the enemy slackened and the 12th Battalion did not take part in any fighting but moved forward as the advancing battalions moved.

For this advance, they supported the 24th (Denbigh Yeomanry) Battalion, Royal Welsh Fusiliers. The Battalion War Diary for the Royal Welsh Fusiliers records what occurred on 30 October:

Battalion went in the line at Ingoyghem. Fairly heavy 5.9, 7.2 and gas shelling. Few casualties.

31 October 1918

Battalion advanced the line to S of Caster, capturing 10 Field Guns and about 250 prisoners. Time did not permit other material being counted.

Fortunately for this part of the timeline, we have Charles Milligan who noted this in his memoirs:

Toward the end of October and in a forward position I took down a message to look out for a white flag party of Germans and give them safe conduct through our lines. Sure enough a few days later, while passing through Courtai in column of route we parted our ranks to allow some cars bearing white flags and containing German staff officers knew the end was in sight and speculation as to the actual day was rife. For some time, past we had been demoralising the enemy with barrages of gun fire and 15 rounds rapid on our rifles with the sights up. Hit those in the canteen what a joke!

On 31st October we were on the field of Oudenarde with 18 pounders just to the rear of us. At dawn the sky was illuminated with flashes of light right back to the heavies. We went forward in text book extended order, a sight I shall never forget, to left and right one long line of men spaced apart and advancing at walking pace. No returning fire from Jerry as without resistance we went forward. That was our last action and November 10th found us on the banks of the River Scheldt at Avelghem, practically undamaged and only recently evacuated by the civilians.

By 3 November 1918, the battalion had moved back to Courtai where their war ended. The 12th Battalion had only spent a very small part of its war on the Western Front, but it had distinguished itself enormously in that time.

Guidebook

Ingoyghem is now pronounced Ingooigem. From Ingooigem, take the N36. You are literally taking the same direction to 94th Brigade took on 31 October 1918, the only difference being they advanced in the fields to your left. Keep going and at Kaster, at the crossroads, turn right and continue on the N36. Keep going until you come to a turning on your left, Kouterlindweg, park up here and in the fields, you are looking at is where the 12th Battalion ended up before being withdrawn back to Courtai.

What3words: lately.scrapping.sinewy.

36

The 1st Battalion,
The Battle of the Sambre,
The Forest of Mormal:
5–8 November 1918

The last battalion to see offensive action was also the battalion that first saw action in 1914. On 3 November 1918, the 1st Battalion moved up to positions to assist in the attack on the Forest of Morval. They had skirted this forest during the retreat from Mons.

On the morning of 4 November 1918, the last major British offensive of the Great War began. Seventeen British divisions attacked on a 40-mile front with an objective to break the German Army and force an end to the war. It became the last large-scale set-piece battle of the Great War. The German Army was determined to hold a defensive line incorporating the Forest of Mormal Forest and the Sambre-Oise canal, hoping to buy time for a strategic withdrawal to the Meuse and thereby negotiate a compromise peace.

This battle fought between 4 and 11 November 1918 became the hardest-fought of the final offensive actions. It involved the 1st, 3rd, and 4th Armies who had pushed across the Rivers Selle and Sambre, recapturing Valenciennes and finally liberated Mons, where the 1st Battalion had first started its fight in the Great War.

At 5.30a.m., the 1st Battalion led the attack with the 1st Battalion Bedfordshire Regiment in support at Jolimetz. The attack was carried out, pushing eastwards through the forest, in heavy rain, and the first objectives were gained by 7.30 a.m. At this point, the 1st Bedfordshire passed through the 1st Battalion who reformed at the Crossroads at Le Godelot, ready to give assistance; however, this was not required.

On 6 November, the 1st Battalion went on to La Haute Rue, near the eastern edge of the forest. This is what the battalion's war diary reported for the final aspects of their war:

6th November 1918

17.30 1/Norfolk Reg moved to Quatre Area, where an assembly position had been selected for an attack, which was to cross the river Sambre, via bridge. This bridge had been reported safe. Disposition for attack, 'D' and 'B' Companies in front line. 'C' and 'A' in immediate support. At 20.00 his two platoons of B Coy were to rush the bridge being closely supported by two of D Coy.

19.30 Two leading companies in assembly position. Advance report upfront centre reports bridge had been blown up. Operations were then temporarily suspended.

19.45 The commanding officer decided to send a platoon to reconnoitre a foot bridge, which was said to be still over locks just south of bridges.

20.45 Patrol reported bridge useless, owing to locks having been mined, explosion of some had shaken foundations and rendered bridge useless. The patrol met with no hostile fire.

23.30 The battalion formed a working party, which started reconstruction work on bridge and lock. Bn moved to Pont Sur Sambre.

7th November 1918

06.00 Work on bridge was forced to be abandoned owing to hostile machine gun fire.

07.30 Batt attacked over Sambre River. Objective railway running N and S.

13.00 'B' Coy reported on objective. Machine Gun fire from E of La Pannetarie. This was successfully dealt with by a platoon.

14.35 Advance upfront centre report the Devonshire Regiment passing through Pantigny and continuing advance.

16.30 Batt HQ moved to Pantigny.

17.30 1/Devon wounded coming back report advance held up casualties heavy.

At 05.30hrs on the 8th November 1/Devons attacked near Avesnes-Maubeuge Road pushing through when Cavalry patrols noted that the area was clear. At 09.30hrs the   Norfolks were ordered to withdraw and ended up Puissance Farm and then back to Jolimetz.

Their offensive war had ended.

Guidebook

At the crossroads signposted for Berlaimont Aulnoye Ay, turn right on the D951. The 1st Battalion pushed east through the forest to La Haute Rue. To get there take the road at the crossroads, which has the brown signpost 'Route Forestière du Chemin Planté'. This takes you to the D961 and when you get there, at the crossroads to Hargnies turn right. Keep on this road and La Haute Rue is found when you turn right onto the D32.

What3words: passage.submissions.brightening.

Now turn around, turn right onto the D961 and head into Pont-sur-Sambre. Once in the town you will come to crossroads, turn left here onto the Rue de Bel Air, also listed as the D117, and head towards Pantegnies. Keep on this road and you will come to the bridge and lock that the battalion started reconstruction work on 6 and 7 November 1918. The lock is accessed by parking up just past the bridge on the left and then walking back to the bridge. You will see the lock on the right.

What3words: division.reworked.frescos.

After passing over this bridge, you will pass through Pantegnies and eventually you will come to the railway line, which was the final objective for the battalion. You can, if you so wish, also take the track on the left, prior to reaching the railway, to reach La Panneterie.

What3words: jammer.rhino.soundtracks.

37

Armistice

The line of the Scheldt was crossed on 8 November 1918, with Ghent and Mons being captured. The French–American offensive further south had ultimately made more dramatic progress, but it was the combined impact of these two thrusts that finally brought the war to an end.

It was not as well-known on the ground that the German Government had approached the Americans for terms for peace based on President Woodrow Wilson's Fourteen Points plan as early as January 1918, but by October that year, any chance of an American deal had faded with American troops heavily committed in the fighting. It was the overall commander of the Allies, Ferdinand Foch, who held the cards who negotiated the terms for peace. With unrest growing in Germany itself, Kaiser Wilhelm abdicated on 9 November, and on 11 November 1918, hostilities finally ceased at the eleventh hour and the war on the Western Front came to an end.

The 1st Battalion was situated at Jolimetz, their war diary noting: 'Reorganisation and general cleaning of billets and surroundings. Notice received of suspension of hostilities'. The 7th Battalion were at Haute Rive: 'At 8 a.m. news comes through that the Armistice has been signed coming into operation at 11 o'clock this morning'. The 9th Battalion was at Bohain:

The Brigadier General Commanding inspected the Bn as follows:
    'C' Coy and the band in marching order at 10.00 hours
    'D' Coy in fighting order and 10.30 hours
    'A' Coy in Drill Order at 11.00
    'B' Coy Musketry Order at 11.30 hours
    Billets were inspected after the company inspections. The Regt transport at 12.00hrs.
    At 10.30hrs the order for cessation of hostilities at 11.00hrs were received.

The 12th Battalion was at Avelghem: 'News was received that the Armistice was signed and a general advance ordered. The Battalion marched to Renaix going into billets about 15.00'.

Charles Milligan noted:

> We were now informed that we would be crossing over on a pontoon bridge in the morning and that hostilities would cease at 11.00 a.m. on the 11th. We wondered if we should be strafed on our way but all was quiet and we reformed and marched along the road. At 11.00 a.m. we halted for 10 minutes as we the hourly custom but there were no official celebrations and we continued on our way until late afternoon and we were billeted in a deserted factory. After a meal served from our company field cookers we wandered around the town, there were civilians about and we heard music coming from one cafe. We did not know what there was to be had and in any case most of us were broke!

The last men to die through enemy action came a few days before the Armistice and it was the 1st Battalion who suffered those losses on 8 November 1918. The war diary reported: 'Battalion billeted at La Puissance Farm. Enemy shelling neighbourhood, one man killed and three wounded'. The man who was killed in action was Private Reginal Thomas Beaufoy (45073), aged twenty, who was born at Great Heath and was the son of Mr and Mrs Thomas Beaufoy of 'St Keyne', Queen Mary's Road in Coventry. He is one of four men buried in in the south corner of Bachant Communal Cemetery.

One man also died of his wounds; this was Private Thomas Charles Hayfield (45011), aged twenty, who was the son of Charles and Elizabeth Hayfield of Hill Farm, Nether Whitacre in Coleshill near Birmingham. He is buried in Grave I. A. 9. in Caudry British Cemetery.

This makes them the battalion who were the first and last to take casualties in the First World War.

38

Boy Soldiers

A total of sixteen boys are recorded as having served in the Norfolk Regiment, aged between sixteen and seventeen years old. Of this total, the Commonwealth War Graves Commission records that three of them were serving in other theatres, such as Gallipoli. Another six died in the United Kingdom. Of that total, one can be linked to having been wounded serving with the 1st Battalion in France and Flanders. That leaves seven who died serving in France and Flanders who are now buried there. These are their stories by date of death.

Private Henry Thomas Harford (16644) had landed in France on 12 May 1915 and became a draft for the 1st Battalion. He was killed in action in trenches around Hill 60 near Ypres and had only been in France for fourteen days. He was aged seventeen and was the son of Thomas Fred and Rosina Martha Harford of 37 Goldyke in Wrydecroft near Peterborough. He has no known grave and is commemorated on the Menin Gate in Ypres.

Private Isaac Albert Laud (13983) was aged sixteen when he was killed in action on 9 August 1916 while serving in 'A' Company in the 1st Battalion. The battalion had relieved the French 119th Regiment on 2 August 1915 and then spent twenty days in trenches facing Fricourt. Isaac was one of six killed while the battalion were in this area. A large number of casualties around this time were from snipers. He was the son of Isaac and Ada Elizabeth Laud of Myrtle Villa New Road Sutton Bridge near Wisbech and he is now buried in Grave I.A.11 in Norfolk Cemetery near Becordel-Becourt.

Private John 'Jack' Machin (12637) landed in France with the 7th Battalion when they went to war on 30 May 1915. This battalion initially spent time around Ploegsteert Wood and Jack was killed by shellfire. He was aged seventeen and the son of John and Nelly A. Machin of 43 Windsor Road in Willesden

Green. He is buried in Grave II.A.2 in Rifle House Cemetery in Ploegsteert Wood.

Private Albert Edward Gayford (16181) died of wounds on 28 October 1915 after artillery hit 9th Battalion trenches near Ypres. Aged seventeen, he was the son of Arthur William Gayford of 33 Church Lane in Eaton. He is buried in Grave IV.C.1A in Lijssenthoek Military Cemetery.

Private Clement John Hailstone originally served in the 1/5th Battalion and was a draft for the 8th Battalion, arriving in France on 29 December 1915. He was aged seventeen when he was killed in action on the first day of the Somme when the 8th Battalion assisted in the capture of Montauban. Clement was the son of Morris Charles and Rebecca Wheatley Hailstone of 11 St Mary's Road in Thetford and has no known grave and is commemorated on the Thiepval Memorial.

Private Harry James Hood (3/8104) landed in France on 2 November 1915 and became a draft for the 8th Battalion. Aged seventeen, he was killed in action at Delville Wood on 19 July 1916. Harry was the son of George F. E. and Emily Hood of Gressenhall. Harry is now buried in Grave VIII.V.D in Delville Wood Cemetery at Longueval.

Private Robert Charles Cooper (9473) arrived in France in 1916. He died of wounds on 7 November 1916 aged sixteen. Robert was able to be evacuated to Endell Street Military Hospital in Covent Garden, so it is possible that he was wounded in the assault on Regina Trench in October of that year, but that cannot be confirmed. Robert was the son of Mr and Mrs Robert Cooper of 13 Row 127 King Street in Great Yarmouth and is now buried in Kensal Green (All Souls') Cemetery.

Private George Bailey (9516) did not go to France, at the earliest, until 1916. Aged seventeen, he died at the Battle of Poelcappelle. He has no known grave and is commemorated on the Tyne Cot Memorial and was the son of Mrs C. O'Neill (formerly Bailey) of High Street Whissonsett and the late Timothy Bailey.

Postscript

You will hopefully have noticed that at the end of each chapter in this book, I have listed reported casualties and then listed how many men actually died between certain dates. Here is an example of that for the period of 4 August to 23 November 1914.

The 1st Battalion started the war with thirty officers and 1,000 men, confirmed as their war establishment on 10 August 1914. Having gone to war, you will have read their main actions were Élouges, Le Cateau, and Missy sur Aisne. You will have also read how they then moved to the south of Ypres and fought a number of defensive actions around Festubert and La Bassée.

There a number of distinct actions where casualties are recorded; they are the following:

The Retreat from Mons to Le Cateau: 258
Missy sur Aisne: 125
Festubert/La Bassée: 73

If you are not careful, you might think these records show how many men died. This is not the case. Total dead for each action is as follows:

The Retreat from Mons to Le Cateau: 54
Missy sur Aisne: 51
Festubert/La Bassée: 43

I hope you will note that this is a huge difference between what is perceived and what is fact. In fact, in total, for the timeframe of August to December 1914, the battalion lost 189 men killed or died of wounds. And yet, for that timeframe, 1,712 medals known as the 1914 Stars were issued.

The 1914 Star, also known as the Mons Star, was authorised in April 1917 and was awarded to those who served in France or Belgium on the strength of a unit, or service in either of those countries between 5 August and midnight on 22–23 November 1914. This covers the declaration of war to the end of the First Battle of Ypres.

For each of those actions, we can state that the following can also be clarified when we look at those who were either wounded or became prisoners of war:

The Retreat from Mons to Le Cateau: 204
Missy sur Aisne: 74
Festubert/La Bassée: 30

That is a massive difference in numbers. Let us jump ahead to the first day of the Somme. The 8th Battalion lost 335 officers and men on 1 July 1916. How many men actually died? In total, between 1 and 3 July 1916, it was 109. Let us jump ahead to *Kaiserschlacht* and the 7th Battalion defence of Bouzincourt Ridge between 26 and 28 March 1918. Losses here are recorded as 301 officers and men. The reality is thirty-six men were killed. What I am trying to get at here is that there are many myths with the Great War and one of them is how many men died. The total works out as follows:

Dead: 11 per cent
Returned with wounds: 29 per cent
Returned unscathed: 60 per cent

It works out as one in ten dying, meaning nine men for every fatality returned home. In total, 34,750 men served in the Norfolk Regiment, a further 1,199 are listed as Norfolk Yeomanry, although some of those are listed as then moving onto the Norfolk Regiment. Of that total, but also mentioning that not all of those men served on the Western Front, 741 now lie in Belgium and 3,462 are in cemeteries in France—a total of 4,203 men. It would be wrong of me to not list the other dead in other theatres of war.

Egypt: 104
Germany: 22
Greece: 23
India: 68
Iraq: 545
Palestine: 579
Syria: 4
Turkey: 252
United Kingdom: 444

A further 116 men from the Norfolk Yeomanry or the 12th Battalion, also lie in France and Flanders. So, from a total of 34,750 men who joined the Norfolk Regiment or the Norfolk Yeomanry, 6,335 died serving with both the Norfolk Regiment and Yeomanry in the Great War.

This, to me, debunks the myth of senseless slaughter where hundreds of thousands men were supposedly lost in one fell swoop. The figures do not add up. But please do not just take my word for it, look at what others have written about this over the centenary and beyond that.

One of the subjects that annoy me the most is the throwaway comment that the war was pointless and did not have to happen. That it was a waste of life and it was for nothing. Germany in 1914 and prior to that war was certainly not Nazi Germany, but it was Imperial Germany and it had an agenda that involved what they perceived to be their enemies and had desires to widen their territories. This subject was brushed over and forgotten when the Second World War came. But after that war ended, and Germany had to atone for their crimes in that conflict, it did return in the 1960s and came from the research carried out by Professor Fritz Fischer of Hamburg University.

Fischer found documents in the 1950s that pointed the blame for starting the First World War, something which Germany had denied for decades, in archives at Potsdam. Here he used the new evidence to push back the argument that all of the powers involved in the Great War were more or less equally guilty of pushing Europe over the brink. He argued that Germany bore the main share of responsibility for the outbreak of the war. He moved forward the new argument that the Kaiser, as head of Imperial Germany, had deliberately unleashed the war in pursuit of aggressive foreign policy aims, which in many ways mirrored those pursued by Hitler in 1939. One of the arguments used prior to this was that Germany was only fighting a defensive war; Fischer's new evidence showed that Germany's policy was one of aggression and conquest.

These ideas became widely accepted, although there was hostility for this in Germany itself. Although some this was challenged and revised later on, much of Fischer's evidence stands today. Ultimately, it is widely accepted that had Germany not been stopped, then the world itself would have been a very different place and this was known by the countries that fought against them, which included Great Britain.

What about the term 'Lions Led by Donkeys'? In 1961, historian Alan Clark wrote a book entitled *The Donkeys*; Clark based this title was on the memoirs of General Erich von Falkenhayn, the chief of the German General Staff of the German Army between 1914 and 1916; he is supposed to have had a conversation with another German general, Max Hoffmann.

Ludendorff was supposed to have said, 'The English soldiers fight like lions.' Hoffmann's reply was supposed to have been, 'True. But don't we know that they are lions led by donkeys'. This was challenged at the time and Ludendorff's memoirs remain untraced. Although Alan Clark continued to counter argue that he had seen this evidence, it is suggested that he admitted to a friend that he had made the whole thing up. Modern-day historians are scathing of Alan Clark, and the late Professor Richard Holmes wrote of *The Donkeys*: '…it contained a streak of casual dishonesty. Its title is based on the "Lions led by Donkeys" conversation between Hindenburg and Ludendorff. There is no evidence whatever for this: none. Not a jot or scintilla. Liddell Hart, who had vetted Clark's manuscript, ought to have known it'. This term has continued to plague the reality of the generals, their strategy, their tactics, and the perception of what they thought of the men they commanded. If that is the case, why is it that we won the war?

If that is the case, then why is it that Haig was open to adapt and learn from his mistakes and with that he was more than happy to adopt new strategies? I have used examples of this in the book. So, if you have missed any of that, then I recommend you go back and reread chapters such as the 1st Battalion at Oppy Wood on 28 June 1917.

Secondly, it is a myth that no general ever saw the frontline; this from Lt-Col. Prior writing about his brigade commander:

> General Feetham had joined the Brigade at the same time I took over the battalion. He was a very stern strict disciplinarian and was held in awe by his brigade. When one knew him better one recognised that his bark was much worse than his bit. Few Brigadiers, certainly none of his years, could have undertaken the daily complete round of his Brigade front that he invariably carried out and he won the respect of everyone serving under him for his complete disregard of danger. His luncheon always consisted of a few gingerbreads and he would generally consume these standing on the fire step of a front-line trench accentuating his remarks by waving a partly consumed gingerbread.

There are numerous accounts like that in regimental histories, and seventy-eight senior officers were killed or died of wounds serving at the front. All that term does is disrespect those that fought in the BEF in the First World War in whatever capacity they served. It also misses the fact that those that returned found that those at home wanted to forget about the war and as a result many just kept their experiences to themselves, less those that wrote about the war, often with bitter tones, which did not help to fuel the myth that everyone felt the same about Haig and his generals when the opposite is actually the truth. Believe it or not, many men cite the war as the best time of their lives, but felt betrayed by the politicians that sent them to war when they returned home to unemployment and poverty.

I believe the bitterness, and certainly the myths and fake news of the First World War, came afterwards because the primary evidence for what the battalions felt and how they perceived themselves can be found in their war diaries.

Lt-Col. Prior said this of his battalion:

I once heard the battalion described as a 'happy family'. At any rate I am sure it was a happy battalion. The discipline was excellent, there was practically no crime and a splendid feeling of cordiality and respect, respect on both sides, between officers and men. My one deep regret is that I could not be with the battalion in the final move against the enemy, in which, I am told, magnificent work was done.

The one thing that I found often came out of the war diaries for all of the battalions who served on the Western Front is their *esprit de corps*. This can be evidenced in the war diary of the 8th Battalion when they learnt that they were to be disbanded in January 1918. The final entry for that month noted this when their brigade commander visited them to give them the news of their disbandment:

> He dwelt briefly on the different engagements by which the Bttn had carved for itself an imperishable name upon the Roll of Fame. As long as England would be a nation, so long would the name of the 8th Norfolk Regt be remembered. We have loved our battalion, Brigade, Division as perhaps we shall never love another, yet we can carry on with the old sense of discipline and *esprit de corps* that has made us what we are. Let us remember always the words of St Paul—'Quit ye like men. Be Strong'.

I do not believe that the average Tommy had no idea what he was fighting for; this comes from a speech made by the mayor of Grand Leez in Belgium when the 1st Battalion marched into that village on 22 December 1918:

> We thank you from the bottom of our hearts for the sacrifices your noble country and its children have made to rescue poor Belgium. We thank you all you brave defenders of right and justice. The glory of immortality shines round your heads and posterity will tell again and again of your great deeds.

Capt. Bassingthwaite of the 9th Norfolks also reflected on this in his memoirs:

> Who remembers their pals; who came not back, we think they know, we will not forget…. Let those who contemplate war sit down and count the cost, we who have seen something of the cost will not forget neither will our memory fade of who those gallant sons from Norfolk, who made the supreme sacrifice.
>
> Forty-six years have passed since the battalion; a fine body of men were in that sector. One remembers the unselfish devotion to duty of old comrades who have passed on. Those who remain remember the bonds of comradeship that existed, and will continue to exist throughout the years.

Old soldier reunions and the inception of the British Legion all helped to allow men to still meet up with their comrades. Others did their best to help those that were not as fit as others. An example would be Cecil Upcher, mentioned by Steve Snelling in his foreword for this book. Upcher had served in the 9th Battalion and was wounded at Loos. He suffered from shellshock and depression after being badly shaken by a shell burst in 1916 and then went on to serve in the Machine Gun Corps.

An architect by trade, he designed the first set of Memorial Cottages on Oaktree Drive off Mousehold Lane. They were designed to house men who suffered from ill health or poor. They were there to remember the fallen and funds were raised locally to build them. Having obtained land to build on, they were started in July 1920 and completed in November 1921; later on others were built so that in total twelve were built. The initial inscription, because others were built after the Second World War, read:

IN MEMORY OF 6000 OFFICERS AND MEN OF THE NORFOLK REGT. WHO FELL IN THE GREAT WAR, 1914–1919. THESE COTTAGES WERE ERECTED FOR DISABLED SOLDIERS OF THE REGIMENT, 1920.

I want to finish with Herbert Reeve and what he to say about his time in the trenches. Herbert, at times, was damning of the High Command. But this reminiscence of his time as he concluded his memories for his old solider mate, George, resonates with me:

So, I have quoted many memories as a Soldier. As time passes, many others come to mind, but always with me is the thought that I have been so fortunate to escape with my life. I recall the two occasions when my mules were killed as I delivered ammo to the troops in the firing line during the retreat of 1914, the day in Festubert in October 1914 when 8 of us were enfiladed by the Germans as we lined a ditch and I was the only one who escaped; the occasion on the Somme front when I went to relieve a Section in a dugout, we arrived half an hour late and during this half hour a shell had hit the dugout and all were buried alive; the occasion during the Somme offensive when we were making slit trenches with our entrenching tools—I had made a trench about waist high when a shell exploded in the loose earth—I was just bowled over and said a prayer. These things remind me of the person who once asked another person what struck him most during the war and he replied that what struck him the most was the number of bullets and shells that did not hit him.

Many people have asked me what my thoughts were as I went over the top. I will honestly say that as I fixed Bayonets to go over the top I did so with the prayers of my Mother on my lips and the prayers of the Sunday School teachers I knew in my youth.

As we sit and think of it all today, we wonder if it was all worthwhile, for Nations today are all heading for War. Nations have forgotten 'Love Ye One Another' and 'If Ye Love Me Keep My Commandments'.

So perhaps I have written you a rambling letter of my memories. The Old Soldiers of 1914 have mostly passed away, so we cherish the friendship of those that are left, and the friendship of those we respect and admire today.

So, I imagine that the reading of this letter will bring back many memories to you, memories that are tragic and humorous, and bitter memories of the suicidal battles we fought through the inefficiency of the High Command and the Staff Officers under whom we served.

So, cheerio, keep your chin up, from one Old Soldier to another.

That is what we must now do. We must keep their memories alive, we must try to understand their experiences and grousing, and we must understand why many chose not to talk about it. We must not dwell on the duff history of the Great War, we must look to the great deeds these men who survived did in a war that sadly led to their being forgotten when they came back.

We must, of course, remember those that did not come back, many of whom were lost from sight and sound who are now just names on a wall.

And that is why I have written this book for you to follow and remember their great deeds.

Commanding Officers for the Five Battalions

1st Battalion

Lt-Col. Colin Robert Ballard, 4 August 1914 to 23 November 1914, posted on promotion.

Lt-Col. Herbert Richard Done, 23 November 1914 to 24 February 1915, posted on promotion.

Lt-Col. Lloyd Newton Jones-Bateman, 24 February 1915 to 23 April 1915, replaced by Lt-Col. Herbert Richard Done, 23 April 1915 to 14 December 1915, posted on promotion.

Capt. Percy Frederick Wall, 14 December 1915 to 3 January 1916, replaced by, Lt-Col. Percy Vere Powys Stone, 3 January 1916 to 17 January 1917, posted on promotion.

Maj. Robert Wace Patteson, 17 January 1917 to 10 February 1917, replaced by, Lt-Col. John William Vincent Carroll, 10 January 1917 to 5 October 1917. Wounded in the foot while the battalion was in trenches at Tor Top. The war diary noting that it suffered three hours from an enemy barrage.

Maj. Eustace William Montgomerie, 5 October 1917 to 1 December 1917, replaced by Lt-Col. Thomas Henry Clayton Nunn, 1 December 1917 to 9 January 1918, replaced by Lt-Col. Eustace William Montgomerie, 9 January 1918 to 15 February 1918. Wounded while the battalion was serving on the Italian Front.

Maj. Robert Duncan Marshall, 15 February 1918 to 1 March 1918, replaced by Lt-Col. Eustace William Montgomerie, 1 March 1918 to 1 June 1918, replaced by Lt-Col. Cecil Frederick George Humphries, 1 June 1918 to 22 August 1918, killed in action on 22 August 1917, see my chapter on the Battle of Albert and Bapaume.

Maj. George de Grey, 22 August 1918 to 25 August 1918. Wounded when the battalion moved forward to Achiet le Grand. The Battalion HQ was positioned in a railway cutting and was shelled.

Maj. Henry Stewart Walker, 25 August 1918 to 3 September 1918, replaced by Lt-Col. George de Grey, 3 September 1918 to 11 November 1918, remained as CO.

7th (Service) Battalion

Lt-Col. John William Vincent Carroll, 19 August 1914 to 25 September 1915, posted on promotion.

Maj. John Clayton Atkinson, 25 September 1915 to 3 October 1915, replaced by Lt-Col. Francis Edward Walter, 4 October 1915 to 9 October 1917. Invalided after being admitted into hospital and was replaced by Lt-Col. Ronald Gethen, 9 October 1917 to 27 November 1917, took temporary absence and was replaced by Lt-Col. Henry Lex Francis Adam Gielgud, 28 November 1917 to 1 December 1917, killed in action on 30 November 1917, see chapter the Battle of Cambrai.

Lt-Col. Evan Thomas Rees, 1 December 1917 to 27 March 1918. Wounded on 27 March 1918 and became a POW, see the chapter on Bouzincourt Ridge.

Maj. George West, 15 March 1918 to 10 April 1918, replaced by Lt-Col. Frank Sandiford Cooper, 10 April 1918 to 20 April 1918, replaced by Maj. George West, 20 April 1918 to 29 April 1918, replaced by Lt-Col. Ronald Gethen, 30 April 1918 to 20 May 1918, replaced by Lt-Col. Henry Ashley Scarlett, 21 May 1918 to 11 November 1918, remained as CO.

8th (Service) Battalion

Col. Frederick Clinton Briggs, 6 September 1914 to 14 October 1915, transferred to another active service battalion.

Lt-Col. Henry Gaspard de Lavalette Ferguson, 14 October 1915 to 10 January 1917. Invalided due to sickness, replaced by Lt-Col. Francis Reginald Day, 10 January 1917 to 22 February 1917, replaced by Lt-Col. Henry Gaspard de Lavalette Ferguson, 22 February 1917 to 8 October 1917, replaced by Lt-Col. Ernest Neville Snepp, 8 October 1917 to 5 November 1917. Seriously wounded when Coldstream Camp was shelled while the battalion was employed on duties to protect the camp from hostile aircraft.

Maj. Charles Frederick Ashdown, 5 November 1917 to 23 November 1917, replaced by Lt-Col. John Dumford Crosthwaite, 23 November 1917 to 20 February 1918, remained as CO until the battalion was disbanded.

9th (Service) Battalion

Col. Mansel Travers Shewen, 1 October 1914 to 21 September 1915, posted on promotion.

Lt-Col. Ernest Henry Denne Stracey, 21 September 1915 to 12 August 1916, took temporary absence and was replaced by Lt-Col. Frederick Ewart Bradshaw, 13 August 1916 to 15 September 1916, replaced by Lt-Col. Francis Latham, 19 September 1916 to 29 September 1916, transferred to another active service battalion.

Lt-Col. Bernard Henry Leathes Prior, 1 October 1916 to 10 December 1916, replaced by Lt-Col. Richard Stewart Dyer-Bennet, 16 December 1916 to 14 January 1917, took temporary absence and was replaced by Lt-Col. John Breteton Owst Trimble, 27 January 1917 to 26 February 1917, transferred to another active service battalion.

Lt-Col. Richard Stewart Dyer-Bennet, 27 February 1917 to 9 March 1917, replaced by Lt-Col. Ernest Henry Denne Stracey, 10 March 1917 to 23 March 1917, replaced by Lt-Col. Bernard Henry Leathes Prior, 24 March 1917 to 30 January 1918, took temporary absence and was replaced by Lt-Col. William James Spurrell, 31 January 1918 to 13 March 1918, replaced by Lt-Col. Bernard Henry Leathes Prior, 14 March 1918 to 21 March 1918, took temporary absence and was replaced by Lt-Col. Francis Reginald Day, 1 April 1918 to 28 July 1918, took temporary absence and was replaced by Lt-Col. Bernard Henry Leathes Prior, 29 July 1918 to 22 August 1918, replaced by Lt-Col. Francis Reginald Day, 23 August 1918 to 11 November 1918, remained as CO.

12th (Norfolk Yeomanry) Battalion

Lt-Col. Arthur Francis Morse, 11 February 1917 to 1 September 1917, took temporary absence and was replaced by Maj. Maurice Edward Barclay, 1 September 1917 to 15 September 1917, replaced by Lt-Col. Joseph Francis Barclay, 15 September 1917 to 9 May 1918, replaced by Lt-Col. Arthur Francis Morse, 9 May 1918 to 5 July 1918. Wounded while the battalion was in trenches between Le Cornet Perdu and Gars Brugghe.

Lt-Col. Joseph Francis Barclay, 5 July 1918 to 18 August 1918, replaced by Maj. Maurice Edward Barclay, 18 August 1918 to 23 September 1918, replaced by Lt-Col. John Sherwood-Kelly, 23 September 1918 to 6 October 1918, replaced by Maj. Henry Anthony Birkbeck, 6 October 1918 to 19 October 1918, replaced by Lt-Col. John Sherwood-Kelly, 19 October 1918 to 11 November 1918, remained as CO.

Bibliography

American Battle Monuments Commission, *A Guide to the American Battle Fields in Europe: A History, Guide and Reference Book* (United State Government Printing Office, 1938)

Arthur, M., *Forgotten Voices of the Great War* (Edbury Press, 2006)

Ashworth, T., *Trench Warfare 1914–1918: The Live and Let Live System* (Pan, 2004)

Bairnsfather, B., *Bullets and Billets* (Grant Richards, 1916)

Barton, P., *Passchendaele Hardcover* (Constable, 2007)

Bassingthwaighte, C. P., Personal Diary Captain Cyril P. Bassingthwaighte, Royal Norfolk Regiment Archives Ref. No. 156.1

Beales, H., Letters & Ephemera, Beales Family Archive

Bean, C. E. W., *The Australian Imperial Force in France 1916 Volume 3* (Australian War Memorial 12th edition, 1941)

Betts, H., Personal Diary, Harry Betts, 1915–16

Braken P., *Irish Cricket and the Great War* (Pat Braken, 2018)

Brown, M., and Seaton, S., *Christmas Truce: The Western Front December 1914* (Pan, 2001)

Burgoyne, A., Correspondence with Annette Burgoyne, Facebook, 2016

Cameron, H. S., Letters from the Western Front, Royal Norfolk Regiment Archives Ref. No. 5096.1

Chenery, B., *War Memories 1914–1918 I Was There* (Bertie Chenery PDF, 2016)

Commonwealth War Graves Commission, www.cwgc.org/

Cooper, J., Personal Diary, James Cooper, 1917–1918

Douglas, D., Personal Diary, Dennis Douglas, 1916

Drewey, W., Letters & Ephemera, Drewey Family Archive

Dugdale, R. W., thegreatwar.whitchurch-shropshire.co.uk/rev-richard-dugdale/

Eastern Daily Press Archives, *Eastern Daily Press* (1914–1915)

Edmonds, E., *A Subaltern's War* (Anthony Mott Ltd, 1984)

Edmunds, J. E., *The Official History of the Great War 1914 Volume 1* (Imperial War Museum, 1938); *The Official History of the Great War 1914 Volume 2* (Imperial War Museum, 1925); *The Official History of the Great War 1915 Volume 1* (Imperial War Museum, 1927); *The Official History of the Great War 1915 Volume*

2 (Imperial War Museum, 1928); *The Official History of the Great War 1916 Volume 2* (Imperial War Museum, 1932); *The Official History of the Great War 1916 Volume 2* (Imperial War Museum, 1938); *The Official History of the Great War 1918 Volume 1* (Imperial War Museum, 1935); *The Official History of the Great War 1918 Volume 2* (Imperial War Museum, 1925); *The Official History of the Great War 1918 Volume 3* (Imperial War Museum, 1939); *The Official History of the Great War 1918 Volume 4* (Imperial War Museum, 1947); *The Official History of the Great War 1918 Volume 5* (Imperial War Museum, 1925); *The Official History of the Great War 1917 Volume 2* (Imperial War Museum, 1948)

Enticott, F., The diary of Frank Enticott, Royal Norfolk Regiment Archives

Falls, C., *The Official History of the Great War 1917 Volume 1* (Imperial War Museum, 1925)

Fox, A., greatwar.nibchg.org.uk/ (Alfred Fox Letter, 1916)

Gent, J. H. G., Remembrances of my First Time in Action, John Henry Gent 1915

Gielgud, H. L. F. A., *The Aldenhamian*, Aldenham School Archives 2014

Gleichen, E., *The Doings of the Fifteenth Infantry Brigade, August 1914 to March 1915* (William Blackwood & Sons Edinburgh and London, 1917)

Great Ryburgh, www.standrewsgreatryburgh.org.uk/world-war-1-commemorations/not-on-the-roll-of-honour/arthur-william-allison.php

Haig, D., General Haig's 'backs to the wall' message to all ranks of the British Army in France and Flanders, 11 April 1918, National Library of Scotland reference: Acc.3155/125, f.80

Hammond, J., Letters and Documents, Royal Norfolk Regiment Archives Ref. No. 6292.1

Head, H., Herbert Head Letters & Postcards, Family Archive of Herbert Head, 1915–16

Humphries, C., 'Military Cross Winners,' *Otago Daily Times*, Issue 17058, p. 6, 1917

Inst. in the Great War, online: www.instgreatwar.com/page20.htm (2018)

Jack, P., Personal Letters, Family Archive of Jack Paul, 1915–1918

Junger, E., *Storm of Steel* (Penguin, 2004)

London Gazette Archives

McCrae, J., *In Flanders Fields and Other Poems* (G. P. Putnam's Sons, 1919)

Middlebrook, M., *The First Day on the Somme: 1 July 1916* (Penguin, 1984)

Miles, W., *The Official History of the Great War 1917 Volume 3* (Imperial War Museum, 1948)

Milligan, C., C. R. Milligan on Trench Warfare, Norfolk Regiment Archives

National Archives, 1 Battalion Norfolk Regiment—Reference: WO 95/1573/1 to WO 95/1573/2 Date: Oct. 1914 to Apr. 1919

National Archives, 12 Battalion Norfolk Regiment—Reference: WO 95/2366/2 Date: May 1918–May 1919

National Archives, 7 Battalion Bedfordshire Regiment—Reference: WO 95/2043/5 Date: 1917 1st July to 30 Sept. 1917

National Archives, 7 Battalion Norfolk Regiment—Reference: WO 95/1853/1 Date: June 1915–May 1919

National Archives, 8 Battalion Norfolk Regiment—Reference: WO 95/2040/1 Date: July 1915–Feb. 1918

National Archives, 9 Battalion Norfolk Regiment—Reference: WO 95/1623/1 to WO 95/1623/5 Date: Aug. 1915–Apr. 1919

National Archives, WO 213/11, Field General Courts Martial, Volume Number: 11. Date: 21 Sept. 1916–14 Sept. 1917

Niemann, J., *The History of the Saxon IR 133: Das 9. Koeniglich Saechsische Infanterie-Regiment Nr. 133 im Weltkrieg 1914–18* (Johannes Niemann, 1969)

Norfolk Records Office, *Eastern Daily Press* Reports, 1914–1915

Petre, F. L., *History of the Norfolk Regiment 4th August 1914 to 31st December 1918* (Naval & Military Press, 2003)

Pidgeon, T., *Tanks on the Somme: from Morval to Beaumont Hamel* (Pen & Sword, 2010)

Plant, G. B. H., *The Cuthbertian*, Issue No. 1, 1920

Powell, A., *The Fierce Light: The Battle of the Somme July-November 1916: Prose* (The History Press, 2006)

Reeve, H., A Letter from 'One Old Soldier to Another', Herbert Reeve, 1976

Richards, A., *Report of the War Office Committee of Enquiry into 'Shell-shock' by HMSO* (Imperial War Museum, 1922)

Riddell, E., and Clayton, M. C., *Cambridgeshires 1914 to 1919* (Naval & Military Press Ltd; New edition, May 2005)

Ross, M., historygeek.co.nz/2013/11/13/ww1-polderhoek-chateau-this-is-where-i-was-wounded/ (Lemeul 2013)

Saint, E. T., www.cambridgeshireregiment1914-18.co.uk/saint.html

Sheldon, J., *The German Army on the Western Front 1915* (Pen & Sword, 2012); *The German Army on the Somme 1914–1916* (Pen & Sword, 2005); *German Army at Passchendaele* (Pen & Sword, 2007); *The German Army at Cambrai* (Pen & Sword, 2009)

Sheldrake, R., Collection, Royal Norfolk Regiment Archives Ref No 6401.1

Smith, S., Letter from Sidney Smith, Norfolk Police Archives; Letters, Royal Norfolk Regiment Archives Ref. No. 5254; *And They Loved Not Their Lives Unto Death: The History of Worstead and Westwick's War Memorial and War Dead* (Menin House, 2012); *Great War Britain Norfolk: Remembering 1914–18* (History Press, 2014); greatwarreflections.co.uk/2020/12/18/festive-guest-feature/

Snettisham Remembers, www.snettisham-remembers.co.uk/the-45/james-auker- (Brown Archives)

Stone, N., Shot at Dawn, Nick Stone, 2014

Taranaki Daily News, 29 December 1917

Williamson, H., *A Fox Under My Cloak* (Panther, 1963)

Williamson, R., Letter Robert Williamson, Robert Williamson 1918

Index